Racing & Football Outlook

FOOTBALL

GUIDE 2008–2009

Edited by Paul Charlton and Daniel Sait

GW00724524

Contributors: Alan Bone, Paul Charlton (Premier League), Steve Cook, Alex Deacon, Andy Dietz (League 2), Sean Gollogly, Derek Guldberg, Dylan Hill (League 1), Glenn Jeffreys, Chris Mann, Daniel Sait (Championship), Andy Scutts, Andy Smith, James Smith, Nigel Speight, Dominic Sutton (Scotland)

Published in 2008 by Outlook Press
Raceform, Compton, Newbury, Berkshire RG20 6NL
Outlook Press is an imprint of Raceform Ltd.

Copyright © Raceform Ltd 2008

A catalogue record for this book is available from the British Library.

ISBN 978-1-905153-76-3

Printed in the UK by CPI William Clowes Beccles NR34 7TL

Cover photo: John Terry and Fernando Torres battle for the ball in the first leg of their Champions League semi-final at Anfield

Contents

Sponsored by Stan James

Editors' introduction

KEVIN KEEGAN might have been a bit bored by it all, but 2007/08 offered plenty of entertainment.

The big four dominated the Premier League and the promoted sides struggled, but the title race was a thriller and went to the final game.

In the FA Cup, Portsmouth were the only Premier League side standing by the semi-finals and, although they went on to win it, it was their first major trophy since they last won the cup in 1939.

Tottenham caused another upset to beat Chelsea in the League Cup final.

The Championship was spectacular for its level of competitiveness – any team was able to beat any other on their day and, to emphasise the point, Leicester had the second-best defensive record in the division, despite being relegated.

Hull provided the fairy tale story with local lads Nick Barmby and Dean Windass scoring the Play-Off final goals that sent the Tigers into the top flight for the first time in their history.

English sides dominated the Champions League, providing three of the semi-finalists and, for once, justifying the 'best league in the world' tag.

Scotland did themselves justice in Europe too, with Celtic getting to the knockout rounds of the Champions League, Rangers reaching the Uefa Cup final and both sides being underrated by the bookies at every turn. The Scottish title race wasn't bad either!

But it wasn't all good news and plenty of sides continued to struggle. Leeds, Luton, Bournemouth and Rotherham all incurred points deductions as a result of their financial problems and there are more points deductions set for 2008/09.

In Scotland, Gretna collapsed entirely after Brooks Mileson was forced to withdraw his financial clout from the side – the prospect of a club folding with the exit of a wealthy sugar daddy will send a chill down the spines of Chelsea fans.

It wasn't just club sides that suffered either – with none of the home nations qualifying for Euro 2008, shirt sellers, flag

makers and pint pullers alike must all have joined the FA in cursing Steve McClaren for failing to get England to Austria/Switzerland.

Nevertheless, it turned out to be a superb tournament and betting turnover was high – nearly £23m was matched on the 90-minute market alone in Croatia v Germany – proving that, while the BBC's build-up to the finals took the 'who will you support' line, punters need no such excuse to get involved.

Part of the reason why it was so good – better than the World Cup, at least in the group stage – was surely that, with just 16 nations at the finals, the teams were nearly all quite evenly matched.

It's a shame then, that Euro 2016 looks certain to have 24 teams involved, especially as so many of Michel Platini's actions as Uefa president have been so encouraging – no to Game 39, the demise of the G-14, talk of capping permitted debt levels for Champions League clubs, opening up the game to some of Europe's less fashionable outposts, satisfyingly retro trophy presentations in the stands, etc.

Of course, it's television money that pays for it all but let's hope the tournament isn't compromised too badly.

As we go to press, the fallout from the tournament is still to be felt fully in terms of the transfer market, but the *Racing & Football Outlook* will be there throughout the season to help you make the most of your betting bank.

The *Outlook Index* is a unique ratings system that allows you to compare teams objectively and find the value bets without being distracted by back-page hype – you'll find the ratings on pages 90-97.

Figaro (pages 12-13 and 98-100) provides his own unique analyses and form figures, while our team of tipsters find the best bets for readers every week.

Out every Tuesday, the *Outlook* covers the whole week's football – and racing – for just £1.60. We'll be celebrating our centenary in 2009, so we must be doing something right!

JULY

15-16	Champions League first qualifying round, first legs
17	Uefa Cup first qualifying round, first legs
19	Intertoto Cup third (final) round, first legs
22-23	Champions League first qualifying round, second legs
26	Scottish Challenge Cup first round
27	Intertoto Cup third (final) round, second legs
29-30	Champions League second qualifying round, first legs
31	Uefa Cup first qualifying round, second legs

AUGUST

1	Champions League third qualifying round draw
	Uefa Cup second qualifying round draw
2	Start of the Scottish Football League
5-6	Champions League second qualifying round, second legs
5-6	CIS Cup first round
8	Start of the Blue Square Premier
9	Start of the Football League
	Start of the Scottish Premier League
	Start of the French Ligue 1
	FA Community Shield
	Manchester United v Portsmouth
11	Carling Cup first round (exact dates to be confirmed)
12-13	Champions League third qualifying round, first legs
	Scottish Challenge Cup second round
14	Uefa Cup second qualifying round, first legs
15	Start of the German Bundesliga
16	Start of the Premier League
	FA Cup extra preliminary round
25	Carling Cup second round (exact dates tbc)
26-27	Champions League third qualifying round, second legs
	CIS Cup second round
28	Champions League group stage draw
28	Uefa Cup second qualifying round, second legs
29	Uefa Super Cup
	Manchester United v Zenit St Petersburg
	Uefa Cup first round draw
30	FA Cup preliminary round
30	Start of Spanish Primera Liga (subject to confirmation)
31	Start of Italian Serie A (subject to confirmation)

SEPTEMBER

1	Johnstone's Paint Trophy first round (exact dates tbc)
6	World Cup 2010 qualifiers
	Andorra v England
	Georgia v Rep Ireland
	Macedonia v Scotland
	Slovakia v N Ireland
	Wales v Azerbaijan
	FA Vase first preliminary round

7	Scottish Challenge Cup third round
10	World Cup 2010 qualifiers
	England v Croatia
	Iceland v Scotland
	Montenegro v Rep Ireland
	N Ireland v Czech Republic
	Russia v Wales
13	FA Cup first qualifying round
16-17	Champions League group stage, matchday one
18	Uefa Cup first round, first legs
20	FA Vase second preliminary round
22	Carling Cup third round (exact dates tbc)
23-24	CIS Cup third round
27	FA Cup second qualifying round
	Scottish Cup first round
30	Champions League group stage, matchday two

OCTOBER

1	Champions League group stage, matchday two
2	Uefa Cup first round, second legs
4	FA Trophy preliminary round
	FA Vase first round
6	Johnstone's Paint Trophy second round (exact dates tbc)
7	Uefa Cup group stage draw
11	World Cup 2010 qualifiers
	England v Kazakhstan
	Scotland v Norway
	Slovenia v N Ireland
	Wales v Liechtenstein
	FA Cup third qualifying round
12	Scottish Challenge Cup sem-final
15	World Cup 2010 qualifiers
	Belarus v England
	Germany v Wales
	N Ireland v San Marino
	Rep Ireland v Cyprus
18	FA Trophy first qualifying round
22-23	Champions League group stage, matchday three
23	Uefa Cup group stage, matchday one
25	FA Cup fourth qualifying round
	Scottish Cup second round
28-29	CIS Cup fourth round

NOVEMBER

1	FA Trophy second qualifying round
3	Johnstone's Paint Trophy area quarter-finals (exact dates tbc)
4-5	Champions League group stage, matchday four
6	Uefa Cup group stage, matchday two
8	FA Cup first round
10	Carling Cup fourth round (exact dates tbc)

15	FA Vase second round
16	Scottish Challenge Cup final
22	FA Trophy third qualifying round
25-26	Champions League group stage, matchday five
27	Uefa Cup Group stage, matchday three
29	FA Cup second round
	Scottish Cup third round

DECEMBER

3-4	Uefa Cup group stage, matchday four
5	Carling Cup fifth round (exact dates tbc)
6	FA Vase third round
9-10	Champions League group stage, matchday six
13	FA Trophy first round
15	Johnstone's Paint Trophy area semi-finals (exact dates tbc)
17-18	Uefa Cup group stage, matchday five
19	Champions League Last 16 draw
19	Uefa Cup Last 32/Last16 draw

JANUARY

3	FA Cup third round
5	Carling Cup semi-final, first legs (exact dates tbc)
10	FA Trophy second round
	Scottish Cup fourth round
17	FA Vase fourth round
19	Carling Cup semi-final, second legs (exact dates tbc)
	Johnstone's Paint Trophy area finals, first legs (exact dates tbc)
24	FA Cup fourth round
27-28	CIS Cup semi-final
31	FA Trophy third round

FEBRUARY

7	FA Vase fifth round
	Scottish Cup fifth round
11	World Cup 2010 qualifiers
	Rep Ireland v Georgia
	San Marino v N Ireland
14	FA Cup fifth round
16	Johnstone's Paint Trophy area finals, second legs (exact dates tbc)
18-19	Uefa Cup Last 32, first legs
21	FA Trophy fourth round
24-25	Champions League last 16, first legs
26	Uefa Cup Last 32, second legs
28	FA Vase sixth round

MARCH

1	Carling Cup final
7	FA Cup sixth round
	Scottish Cup sixth round
10-11	Champions League last 16, second legs

Sponsored by Stan James

12	Uefa Cup Last 16, first legs
14	FA Trophy semi-final, first legs
15	CIS Cup final
18-19	Uefa Cup Last 16, second legs
20	Champions League quarter-final/semi-final draw
20	Uefa Cup quarter-final/semi-final draw
21	FA Trophy semi-final, second legs
28	World Cup 2010 qualifiers

Holland v Scotland
N Ireland v Poland
Rep Ireland v Bulgaria
Wales v Finland

FA Vase semi-final, first legs

APRIL

| 1 | World Cup 2010 qualifiers |

England v Ukraine
Italy v Rep Ireland
N Ireland v Slovenia
Scotland v Iceland
Wales v Germany

4	FA Vase semi-final, second legs
5	Johnstone's Paint Trophy final
7-8	Champions League quarter-final, first legs
9	Uefa Cup quarter-final, first legs
14-15	Champions League quarter-final, second legs
16	Uefa Cup quarter-final, second legs
18-19	FA Cup semi-final
25-26	Scottish Cup semi-finals
28-29	Champions League semi-final, first leg
30	Uefa Cup semi-final, first legs

MAY

5-6	Champions League semi-final, second legs
7	Uefa Cup semi-final, second legs
9	FA Trophy final
10	FA Vase final
20	Uefa Cup final, Istanbul
23	Scottish Cup final

(May be moved to May 30 to accommodate Champions League/Uefa Cup finals)

| 27 | Champions League final, Rome |
| 30 | FA Cup final |

JUNE

| 6 | World Cup 2010 qualifiers |

Bulgaria v Rep Ireland
Kazakhstan v England
Azerbaijan v Wales

| 10 | World Cup 2010 qualifiers |

England v Andorra

SCHEDULED LIVE MATCHES

Date	Game	Time	Channel	Competition
August				
8	Barrow v Oxford	7.45pm	SS	Conference
9	Birmingham v Sheffield Utd	12.45pm	Sky	FLC
9	Falkirk v Rangers	12.30pm	SS	SPL
10	Nottingham Forest v Reading	1.15pm	Sky	FLC
10	Celtic v St Mirren	12.30pm	SS	SPL
11	Hamilton v Dundee Utd	7.45pm	SS	SPL
14	York v Wrexham	7.45pm	SS	Conference
16	Arsenal v West Brom	12.45pm	Sky	PL
16	Bristol City v Derby County	5.20pm	Sky	FLC
16	Sunderland v Liverpool	5:30pm	SS	PL
17	Chelsea v Portsmouth	1.30pm	Sky	PL
17	Dundee Utd v Celtic	2pm	SS	SPL
17	Man United v Newcastle	4pm	Sky	PL
18	Torquay v Ebbsfleet	7.45pm	SS	Conference
19	Norway v Scotland	8pm	SS	International
20	England v Czech Republic	8pm	SS	International
20	Scotland v N Ireland	8pm	Sky	International
20	Wales v Georgia	8.05pm	Sky	International
21	Wrexham v Oxford	7.45pm	SS	Conference
23	Aberdeen v Rangers	12.30pm	SS	SPL
23	Fulham v Arsenal	5:30pm	SS	PL
24	Wigan v Chelsea	1:30pm	SS	PL
24	Man City v West Ham	4pm	Sky	PL
25	Cambridge v Kettering	4.15pm	SS	Conference
25	Portsmouth v Man United	8pm	Sky	PL
28	Torquay v York	7.45pm	SS	Conference
30	Watford v Ipswich Town	5.20pm	Sky	FLC
30	Arsenal v Newcastle	5:30pm	SS	PL
31	Chelsea v Tottenham	1.30pm	Sky	PL
31	Aston Villa v Liverpool	4pm	Sky	PL
September				
5	Poland v N Ireland	8pm	SS	International
5	Cyprus v Rep of Ireland	8pm	SS	International
6	Wales v Azerbaijan	TBC	Sky	International
6	Slovakia v N Ireland	8pm	SS	International
6	Andorra v England	7pm	SS	International
6	Georgia v Rep of Ireland	5.30pm	SS	International
6	Macedonia v Scotland	4.30pm	SS	International
10	Croatia v England	8pm	SS	International
10	Iceland v Scotland	7.30pm	SS	International
10	Montenegro v Rep of Ireland	6pm	SS	International
10	N Ireland v Czech Rep	TBC	Sky	International
10	Russia v Wales	4pm	SS	International
13	Liverpool v Man United	12.45pm	Sky	PL
13	Derby County v Sheffield Utd	5.20pm	Sky	FLC
13	Man City v Chelsea	5:30pm	SS	PL
14	Stoke v Everton	1.30pm	Sky	PL
15	Tottenham v Aston Villa	8:00pm	SS	PL
20	Bolton v Arsenal	5:30pm	SS	PL
21	West Brom v Aston Villa	12noon	Sky	PL
21	Chelsea v Man United	2pm	Sky	PL
27	Everton v Liverpool	12.45pm	Sky	PL
27	Ipswich v Crystal Palace	5.20pm	Sky	FLC
27	Arsenal v Hull	5:30pm	SS	PL
28	Portsmouth v Tottenham	1.30pm	Sky	PL
28	Wigan v Man City	4pm	Sky	PL
October				
4	Coventry City v Southampton	5.20pm	Sky	FLC
4	Blackburn v Man United	5:30pm	SS	PL
5	West Ham v Bolton	1.30pm	Sky	PL
5	Everton v Newcastle	4pm	Sky	PL
10	Finland v Wales	8pm	SS	International

11	Scotland v Norway	TBC	Sky	International
11	Slovenia v N Ireland	8pm	SS	International
11	Wales v Lichtenstein	TBC	Sky	International
14	Czech Rep v N Ireland	8pm	SS	International
15	Belarus v England	8pm	SS	International
15	Rep of Ireland v Cyprus	TBC	Sky	International
15	N Ireland v San Marino	TBC	Sky	International
18	Middlesbrough v Chelsea	12.45pm	Sky	PL
18	Crystal Palace v Barnsley	5.20pm	Sky	FLC
18	Man United v West Brom	5:30pm	SS	PL
20	Newcastle v Man City	8:00pm	SS	PL
19	Sheffield Wed v Sheffield Utd	1.15pm	Sky	FLC
19	Stoke v Tottenham	4pm	Sky	PL
25	Sunderland v Newcastle	12.45pm	Sky	PL
25	Reading v QPR	5.20pm	Sky	FLC
25	Blackburn v Middlesborough	5:30pm	SS	PL
26	Chelsea v Liverpool	1.30pm	Sky	PL
26	West Ham v Arsenal	4pm	Sky	PL
28	Stoke v Sunderland	8pm	Sky	PL
29	Arsenal v Tottenham	8pm	Sky	PL

November

1	Everton v Fulham	12.45pm	Sky	PL
1	Tottenham v Liverpool	5:30pm	SS	PL
2	Derby County v Nottm Forest	1.15pm	Sky	FLC
2	Bolton v Man City	4pm	Sky	PL
3	Newcastle v Aston Villa	8:00pm	SS	PL
8	Arsenal v Man United	12.45pm	Sky	PL
8	Southampton v Bristol City	5.20pm	Sky	FLC
8	Liverpool v West Brom	5:30pm	SS	PL
9	Blackburn v Chelsea	1.30pm	Sky	PL
9	Fulham v Newcastle	4pm	Sky	PL
15	Bolton v Liverpool	12.45pm	Sky	PL
15	Doncaster v Ipswich Town	5.20pm	Sky	FLC
16	Everton v Middlesbrough	1.30pm	Sky	PL
16	Hull v Man City	4pm	Sky	PL
19	Denmark v Wales	TBA	Sky	International
22	Nottm Forest v Norwich City	5.20pm	Sky	FLC
22	Aston Villa v Man United	5:30pm	SS	PL
23	Tottenham v Blackburn	1.30pm	Sky	PL
23	Sunderland v West Ham	4pm	Sky	PL
24	Barnsley v Burnley	7.45pm	Sky	FLC
24	Wigan v Everton	8:00pm	SS	PL
30	Swansea City v Cardiff City	11.30am	Sky	FLC
30	Man City v Man United	1.30pm	Sky	PL
30	Chelsea v Arsenal	4pm	Sky	PL

December

1	Liverpool v West Ham	8:00pm	SS	PL

February

11	Rep of Ireland v Georgia	TBC	Sky	International

March

28	Holland v Scotland	3pm	SS	International
28	N Ireland v Poland	TBC	Sky	International
28	Rep of Ireland v Bulgaria	TBC	Sky	International
28	Wales v Finland	TBC	Sky	International

April

1	N Ireland v Slovenia	TBC	Sky	International
1	Scotland v Iceland	TBC	Sky	International
1	Wales v Germany	TBC	Sky	International

June

6 Jun	Azerbaijan v Wales	8pm	SS	International
6 Jun	Bulgaria v Rep of Ireland	8pm	SS	International
6 Jun	Kazakhstan v England	3pm	SS	International

Sky – Live on Sky Sports, SS – Live on Setanta Sports

Old Firm's biggest wins come against their closest rivals

HEARTS: third in the SPL betting last term but 5-0 losers at Parkhead last August

CELTIC and Rangers have always been a law unto themselves, or, in the case of some Rangers fans in Manchester, a lawlessness unto themselves.

They dominate the SPL and our TV screens so much that sassenach outsiders like myself are often left wondering how best to punt them.

"Straight into touch" would be the response of some Scottish fans allergic to the history and passion of the rivalry.

They might believe that the pair of them make up a more genuine Scottish monster than Nessie, but even they must admit that the intensity of Old Firm games is mesmerising and feel that the pair have flown the flag for Scottish football in the Champions League and Uefa Cup in recent times with some distinction.

Betting on the Glasgow duo in domestic football is tricky though, even for their own supporters.

One Celtic fan of my acquaintance won a tipping competition in 2006/07 by doing little except backing the opponents of his 'enemy' at anything between 2-1 and 13-2. He, and I'm sure countless others, sent Ibrox 'end of season's greetings' at Christmas!

Unfortunately, he tried the same tactic last year and came nowhere in the same competition. On a regular basis he tips his own side to win by 5-0, 6-0 or more, and usually ends up being mocked for being a Loopy Hoopy.

Because both Rangers and Celtic are so often long odds-on even in away games the temptation to back them to beat handicaps of +2 or more, or to land big correct-score victories, is more or less permanent.

This applies especially to their own fans who I am sure flock to the betting exchanges in search of the best deal they can find for the unquoted score – on Betfair, that's any result where one or both teams score four or more.

So it's time for a reality check. Just

Celtic's record (H&A) 87/88-07/08

Final score	Opponents were 1-3 league places below	Opponents were 4-6 league places below	Opponents were 7-9 league places below	Opponents were 10+ league places below	All games
1-0	42 (14.14%)	28 (11.81%)	21 (15.91%)	7 (15.56%)	98 (13.78%)
2-0	24 (8.08%)	29 (12.24%)	16 (12.12%)	6 (13.33%)	75 (10.55%)
3-0	10 (3.37%)	16 (6.75%)	10 (7.58%)	3 (6.67%)	39 (5.49%)
4-0	11 (3.7%)	4 (1.69%)	12 (9.09%)	6 (13.33%)	33 (4.64%)
5-0	9 (3.03%)	7 (2.95%)	5 (3.79%)	2 (4.44%)	23 (3.23%)
6-0	1 (0.34%)	1 (0.42%)	4 (3.03%)	0 (0%)	6 (0.84%)
2-1	30 (10.1%)	31 (13.08%)	12 (9.09%)	7 (15.56%)	80 (11.25%)
3-1	12 (4.04%)	13 (5.49%)	5 (3.79%)	3 (6.67%)	33 (4.64%)
4-1	10 (3.37%)	11 (4.64%)	3 (2.27%)	2 (4.44%)	26 (3.66%)
5-1	4 (1.35%)	8 (3.38%)	3 (2.27%)	1 (2.22%)	16 (2.25%)
6-1	1 (0.34%)	1 (0.42%)	0 (0%)	0 (0%)	2 (0.28%)
3-2	10 (3.37%)	6 (2.53%)	1 (0.76%)	2 (4.44%)	19 (2.67%)
4-2	3 (1.01%)	4 (1.69%)	6 (4.55%)	0 (0%)	13 (1.83%)
5-2	1 (0.34%)	0 (0%)	0 (0%)	0 (0%)	1 (0.14%)
6-2	0 (0%)	2 (0.84%)	0 (0%)	0 (0%)	2 (0.28%)

Excluding Old Firm games

Rangers' record (H&A) 87/88-07/08

Final score	Opponents were 1-3 league places below	Opponents were 4-6 league places below	Opponents were 7-9 league places below	Opponents were 10+ league places below	All games
1-0	38 (14.02%)	24 (11.06%)	22 (12.09%)	4 (10.53%)	88 (12.43%)
2-0	36 (13.28%)	27 (12.44%)	20 (10.99%)	5 (13.16%)	88 (12.43%)
3-0	17 (6.27%)	22 (10.14%)	21 (11.54%)	3 (7.89%)	63 (8.9%)
4-0	14 (5.17%)	14 (6.45%)	11 (6.04%)	4 (10.53%)	43 (6.07%)
5-0	2 (0.74%)	2 (0.92%)	7 (3.85%)	2 (5.26%)	13 (1.84%)
6-0	2 (0.74%)	0 (0%)	1 (0.55%)	0 (0%)	3 (0.42%)
2-1	30 (11.07%)	19 (8.76%)	17 (9.34%)	5 (13.16%)	71 (10.03%)
3-1	17 (6.27%)	13 (5.99%)	12 (6.59%)	4 (10.53%)	46 (6.5%)
4-1	10 (3.69%)	8 (3.69%)	4 (2.2%)	1 (2.63%)	23 (3.25%)
5-1	2 (0.74%)	3 (1.38%)	3 (1.65%)	0 (0%)	8 (1.13%)
6-1	0 (0%)	3 (1.38%)	1 (0.55%)	0 (0%)	4 (0.56%)
3-2	9 (3.32%)	8 (3.69%)	6 (3.3%)	0 (0%)	23 (3.25%)
4-2	2 (0.74%)	4 (1.84%)	3 (1.65%)	1 (2.63%)	10 (1.41%)
5-2	2 (0.74%)	2 (0.92%)	0 (0%)	0 (0%)	4 (0.56%)
6-2	1 (0.37%)	0 (0%)	0 (0%)	0 (0%)	1 (0.14%)

Excluding Old Firm games

what are the typical winning margins when the two titans beat up those forming the rather substantial rump of the SPL? Our tables give you the answers.

What we have done is compile the league wins for the Old Firm sides since the 1987/88 season, ignoring their clashes with each other and classifing their opponents by the number of league places they were below them when the game was played.

There is space here only for combined home and away results, but we'll be displaying and discussing the separate home and separate away records as well as related Old Firm issues in the *Outlook* during the autumn.

The basic lessons are clear enough, however. Note that in Celtic's record the incidence of 1-0 wins actually increases as their opponents get weaker. The really big wins (5-0, 6-0, 5-1 and 6-1) have come pretty much just as often against teams 1-6 places below them as they have against the duffers lower down.

And Gretna are only the last of a perennial series of SPL duffers – plenty of SPL minnows have done dufferdom rather well down the years.

The Rangers table tells a similar story. They have not had one 5-1, 6-1 or 6-0 hit against a bottom-of-the-table team in the whole period.

There's a simple footballing explanation for this. The no-hopers concentrate on damage-limitation from the start, work hard at delaying the first goal and after that at delaying all further goals. Their sole aim is to keep the score respectable, whereas the better sides will be more ambitious but then concede more when chasing the game.

ARSENAL

Nickname: The Gunners
Colours: Red and white
Ground: Emirates Stadium
Capacity: 60,432
Tel: 020 7704 4000
www.arsenal.com

ARSENAL'S season was again one of un-fulfilled promise. They played beautiful football at times and, by mid-February, led the table by five points.

However, looking like they had started to believe their own hype, the Gunners put in a shocker in a 4-0 loss to Man United in the FA Cup, a result that was followed by four successive draws in the league.

The first of those, against Birmingham, saw Eduardo's season ended with a broken and dislocated ankle, and William Gallas in meltdown at the final whistle.

After losing to Chelsea on Easter Sunday, Arsenal were six points off the pace.

Eduardo's injury exposed a lack of depth in the squad, and Arsene Wenger's refusal to play the game as his peers do is in danger of looking anachronistic – according to Deloitte, they are the fifth-richest club in the world but Wenger rarely pays big money for the finished article.

The financial landscape has changed since Wenger took charge in 1996. It's four years since Arsenal won the league and three since they won any silverware.

With the likes of Flamini and Diarra gone, and, as we go to press, Hleb having his head turned, and Adebayor targeted by Barcelona, Wenger faces a battle to keep his team together.

Even so, Samir Nasri is a class act, Aaron Ramsey will be worth looking out for in the League Cup, and Theo Walcott is starting to live up to his reputation. As always at Arsenal, the future looks bright but another season of transition lies in store.

Longest run without loss: 17
Longest run without win: 6
High – low league position: 1-9
High – low Outlook form figure: 68-44
Final Outlook Index figure: 934

Key Stat: *No team gained more points (21) after falling behind than Arsenal.*

2007/08 Premier League Stats

	Apps	Gls	YC	RC
M Adebayor	32 (4)	24	3	0
M Almunia	29	0	0	0
N Bendtner	7 (20)	5	2	1
G Clichy	37 (1)	0	5	0
Denilson	4 (9)	0	0	0
V Diaby	9 (6)	1	0	1
L Diarra	4 (3)	0	1	0
J Djourou	1 (1)	0	0	0
E Eboue	20 (3)	0	5	0
Eduardo	13 (4)	4	3	0
L Fabianski	3	0	0	0
F Fabregas	32	7	9	0
M Flamini	30	3	5	0
W Gallas	31	5	6	0
A Hleb	29 (2)	2	3	0
J Hoyte	2 (3)	0	1	0
J Lehmann	6 (1)	0	1	0
M Randall	0 (1)	0	0	0
T Rosicky	15 (3)	6	1	0
B Sagna	29	1	3	0
P Senderos	14 (3)	3	0	1
G Silva	12 (11)	1	1	0
A Song Billong	5 (4)	0	0	0
K Toure	29 (1)	2	3	0
A Traore	1 (2)	0	0	0
R Van Persie	13 (2)	7	2	0
T Walcott	11 (14)	4	0	0

League and Cup Stats
Clean sheets: 27 (15 league)
Yellow cards: 83 Red cards: 5
Players used: 27
Leading scorer: Emmanuel Adebayor 30 (24 league)

Outlook forecast: 4th
Your forecast:

ASTON VILLA

Nickname: The Villans
Colours: Claret and blue
Ground: Villa Park
Capacity: 42,640
Tel: 0121 327 2299
www.avfc.co.uk

ASTON VILLA'S summer has been dominated by the Gareth Barry transfer saga but transfer target Steve Sidwell would be an able replacement and Villa might miss Juventus-bound Olof Mellberg even more.

However, it is testament to the quality in Martin O'Neill's side that Fabio Capello included four Villans in his first England squad.

Barry looked the part as expected, but Ashley Young also won three caps last term and, with 17 Premier League assists – a figure surpassed only by Arsenal's Cesc Fabregas – he can consider 2007/08a success.

Off the pitch, things have been going well too. Randy Lerner's 2006 takeover is a model for potential foreign owners of Premier League clubs, with none of the protests that greeted his counterparts at Man United and Liverpool. The owner is to get more hands-on this season.

Villa have not been saddled with debt and the redevelopment of the historic Holte Hotel, which had stood derelict for 28 years, shows that those in charge are doing more than pay lip service to the club's heritage.

Lerner's right-hand man, General Charles C Krulak, is a regular on Villa message-boards, and the club's decision to forgo a shirt sponsorship deal to support the Acorns Children's Hospice is a classy touch.

They missed out on the Uefa Cup after finishing sixth in May, so Villa's season starts in the last ever Intertoto Cup in July.

Expect them to hit the ground running this term – back Villa to overachieve in the early exchanges of the season and look for potential to trade their points.

Longest run without loss: 5
Longest run without win: 5
High – low league position: 6-14
High – low Outlook form figure: 70-38
Final Outlook Index figure: 880
Key Stat: *41 Villa goals were scored by Englishmen – the most in the top flight.*

2007/08 English Premier Stats

	Apps	Gls	YC	RC
G Agbonlahor	37	11	4	0
G Barry	37	9	5	0
P Berger	0 (8)	0	1	0
W Bouma	38	1	5	0
G Cahill	1 (1)	0	0	0
J Carew	32	13	5	0
S Carson	35	0	1	1
C Davies	9 (3)	1	1	0
C Gardner	15 (8)	4	4	0
M Harewood	1 (22)	5	2	0
Z Knight	26 (2)	1	1	1
M Laursen	38	7	1	0
S Maloney	11 (11)	4	0	0
O Mellberg	33 (1)	2	4	1
L Moore	8 (7)	1	1	0
I Osbourne	1 (7)	0	1	0
S Petrov	22 (6)	1	3	0
N Reo-Coker	36	1	10	1
W Routledge	0 (1)	0	0	0
M Salifou	0 (4)	0	0	0
S Taylor	3 (1)	0	0	0
A Young	37	9	6	0

League and Cup Stats
Clean sheets: 10 (all league)
Yellow cards: 54 Red cards: 4
Players used: 22
Leading scorer: John Carew 13 (all league)

Outlook forecast: 9th
Your forecast:

BLACKBURN ROVERS

Nickname: Rovers
Colours: Blue and white
Ground: Ewood Park
Capacity: 31,367
Tel: 0871 702 1875
www.rovers.co.uk

LOSING Mark Hughes is a massive blow, although Rovers can be pleased to have had him for 2007/08 as he was apparently at the top of Mike Ashley's wishlist when purchasing Newcastle last summer.

Hughes made the most of a tight budget, with three domestic cup semi-finals, three successive top-ten finishes, and regular European football, albeit via the Intertoto Cup last year.

It did them no harm last season, even if their European adventure ended in the first round of the Uefa Cup – early competitive football saw Rovers make a blistering start, losing just one of their first 11 league games. That run saw them draw with Arsenal, Chelsea and Liverpool prior to defeat at Old Trafford in their twelfth match.

That meant Blackburn were never out of the top ten last term even if they never quite recaptured that early form.

If anyone can pick up the baton, it's Paul Ince. In his two seasons in management, he has been successful in what looked a hopeless relegation battle with Macclesfield and then a title push with MK Dons.

He can keep Rovers in the hunt for European football next term but it won't be easy. The club are looking for new investors and the trust set up by the late Jack Walker has stopped funding the club, at least for the moment.

And he faces a big challenge over the summer to keep hold of David Bentley, who stepped up from U-21 to full international, and Roque Santa Cruz, the top scorer outside the big four. Both want to go.

Longest run without loss: 7
Longest run without win: 5
High – low league position: 5-12
High – low Outlook form figure: 66-37
Final Outlook Index figure: 885

Key Stat: *Rovers had only two wins against other top-half teams.*

2007/08 Premier League Stats

	Apps	Gls	YC	RC
D Bentley	37	6	8	0
B Berner	2	0	1	0
M Derbyshire	4 (19)	3	1	0
D Dunn	25 (6)	1	7	1
B Emerton	31 (2)	1	3	1
B Friedel	38	0	0	0
Z Khizanishvili	10 (3)	0	2	0
B McCarthy	21 (10)	8	1	0
A Mokoena	8 (10)	0	2	0
R Nelsen	22	1	4	2
M Olsson	0 (2)	0	0	0
A Ooijer	23 (4)	0	2	0
M Pedersen	32 (5)	4	5	0
S Reid	20 (4)	0	6	0
M Rigters	0 (2)	0	0	0
J Roberts	11 (15)	3	2	0
C Samba	33	2	10	1
R Santa Cruz	36 (1)	19	3	0
R Savage	11 (2)	0	4	0
Tugay	12 (8)	2	5	1
J Vogel	6	0	0	0
S Warnock	37	1	8	0

League and Cup Stats
Clean sheets: 11 (8 league)
Yellow cards: 83 Red cards: 6
Players used: 22
Leading scorer: Roque Santa Cruz 23 (19 league)

Outlook forecast: 10th
Your forecast:

BOLTON WANDERERS

Nickname: The Trotters
Colours: White and blue
Ground: Reebok Stadium
Capacity: 27,879
Tel: 01204 673673
www.bwfc.co.uk

AFTER five points from Bolton's first nine games, Sammy Lee was shown the door.

Gary Megson was an unpopular choice to succeed him but he walked out on Leicester after just six weeks to inherit a side that was bottom of the table and staring a relegation battle squarely in the face.

The Trotters started to improve and pull away from the drop zone, eventually reaching a high point of 13th, but following the January sale of Nicolas Anelka – the only Bolton player to score double figures in the league – goals were hard to come by.

They blanked in seven of their remaining 17 league games, scoring just 13 more.

Is Johan Elmander the answer? Not on the basis of his Euro 2008 form, but he did score 11 goals for a struggling Toulouse side in Ligue 1 last season.

The Uefa Cup was an unwelcome distraction and Megson treated the competition with contempt – it backfired after he left out seven first-team regulars for the trip to Sporting Lisbon to keep his powder dry for a relegation six-pointer against Wigan. Naturally, they lost both.

Bolton did pick up towards the end of the season though, and their top-flight status was virtually assured before their final game, which they drew at Stamford Bridge.

Andy O'Brien and Gary Cahill looked solid together at the back. The latter has earned rave reviews since his January transfer from Aston Villa and looks likely to get a chance with England in the future.

Fabrice Muamba should add energy to the midfield but a nervous season awaits.

Longest run without loss: 5
Longest run without win: 8
High – low league position: 14-20
High – low Outlook form figure: 62-34
Final Outlook Index figure: 852

Key Stat: *They conceded two or more in eight of their aways at the top nine.*

2007/08 Premier League Sta

	Apps	Gls	YC	RC
A Al Habsi	10	0	0	0
M Alonso	4 (3)	0	0	0
N Anelka	18	10	1	0
D Braaten	0 (6)	1	0	0
G Cahill	13	0	0	0
I Campo	25 (2)	1	8	0
G Cid	6 (1)	1	0	0
T Cohen	3 (7)	1	1	0
K Davies	31 (1)	3	10	0
E Diouf	30 (4)	4	11	0
A Faye	1	0	0	0
R Gardner	25 (1)	0	2	0
S Giannakopoulos	1 (14)	2	0	0
D Guthrie	21 (4)	0	4	0
H Helguson	3 (3)	2	1	0
N Hunt	12 (2)	0	6	0
J Jaaskelainen	28	1	1	0
G McCann	21 (10)	1	4	0
A Meite	21	0	1	0
L Michalik	5 (2)	1	4	0
K Nolan	33	5	10	0
A O'Brien	31 (1)	0	5	0
J O'Brien	15 (4)	0	2	0
G Rasiak	2 (5)	0	1	0
J Samuel	14 (6)	1	1	0
G Speed	11 (3)	1	2	0
G Steinsson	16	0	2	0
M Taylor	17	4	1	0
A Teymourian	1 (2)	0	0	0
R Vaz Te	1	0	0	0
C Wilhelmsson	0 (8)	0	0	0

League and Cup Stats
Clean sheets: 12 (all league)
Yellow cards: 107 Red cards: 0
Players used: 31
Leading scorer: Nicolas Anelka 10 (all league)

Outlook forecast: 16th

Your forecast:

CHELSEA

Nickname: The Blues
Colours: Blue
Ground: Stamford Bridge
Capacity: 42,055
Tel: 0871 984 1955
www.chelseafc.com

2007/08 was ultimately disappointing for Chelsea. After a 1-1 draw at home to Rosenborg in the Champions League, Jose Mourinho was shown the door in September with the Blues trailing in the league.

Under Avram Grant, they rallied to take the title race to the final day but defeats in the League Cup and Champions League finals, and unrest in the dressing room – Didier Drogba claimed Chelsea were "broken" – sealed Grant's fate.

Luiz Felipe Scolari is likely to be more popular among the players and, like Mourinho, is a larger-than-life personality. It remains to be seen whether he can deliver the swashbuckling style of football Roman Abramovich wants at Chelsea though.

He was not universally popular as Brazil coach, and received criticism for a pragmatic brand of football. That died down after adding the World Cup to a trophy haul that includes Copa Libertadores titles – South America's equivalent of the Champions League – he earned with two different clubs.

Chelsea must defend set-pieces better than Portugal did at Euro 2008 if they are going to win anything this term, though.

Jose Bosingwa is an exciting signing, although he has something to prove defensively after Euro 2008, and Deco is pure class. It will be interesting to see what his arrival means for Frank Lampard – as we go to press he's still a Chelsea player.

In the long term, Scolari's real value might be in importing Brazilian and Portuguese talent to Chelsea. In the short term, more pragmatism will see them push United hard.

Longest run without loss: 15
Longest run without win: 3
High – low league position: 2-9
High – low Outlook form figure: 68-48
Final Outlook Index figure: 969
Key Stat: *85 points last term was the highest ever by a team finishing second.*

2007/08 Premier League Stats

	Apps	Gls	YC	RC
Alex	22 (6)	2	4	0
N Anelka	11 (4)	1	0	0
M Ballack	16 (2)	7	5	0
J Belletti	20 (3)	2	5	0
T Ben-Haim	10 (3)	0	2	0
W Bridge	9 (2)	0	0	0
R Carvalho	21	1	6	1
P Cech	26	0	0	0
A Cole	27	1	5	1
J Cole	28 (5)	7	4	0
C Cudicini	10	0	0	0
L Diarra	1	0	0	0
D Drogba	17 (2)	8	6	1
M Essien	23 (4)	6	5	1
P Ferreira	15 (3)	0	1	0
Hilario	2 (1)	0	0	0
G Johnson	2 (1)	0	0	0
S Kalou	24 (6)	7	1	0
F Lampard	23 (1)	10	4	1
C Makelele	15 (3)	0	1	0
F Malouda	16 (5)	2	2	0
J Obi Mickel	21 (8)	0	5	1
C Pizarro	4 (17)	2	1	0
A Shevchenko	8 (9)	5	0	0
S Sidwell	7 (8)	0	1	0
S Sinclair	0 (1)	0	0	0
J Terry	23	1	6	0
S Wright-Phillips	20 (7)	2	1	0

League and Cup Stats
Clean sheets: 32 (21 league)
Yellow cards: 92 Red cards: 8
Players used: 27
Leading scorer: Frank Lampard 20 (10 league)

Outlook forecast: Runners-up
Your forecast:

EVERTON

Nickname: The Toffees
Colours: Blue and white
Ground: Goodison Park
Capacity: 40,170
Tel: 0870 442 1878
www.evertonfc.com

CHANGE is afoot at Everton, with plans for a new stadium at Kirkby approved by the council, but there's no change in the dugout, with David Moyes now in his seventh year as Everton boss.

He made a couple of decent buys last year, notably spending a club record fee to land Yakubu Ayegbeni, who scored 11 minutes into his debut and finished the campaign as the first Evertonian to reach 20 goals in a season (15 in the league) since Peter Beardsley in 1992.

But it was a good season all round. The Toffees put up a decent fight for fourth place for most of the season, reached the last 16 of the Uefa Cup and the semi-finals of the League Cup, and finished fifth to guarantee European football again this term.

Results against the big four – one point from eight matches – showed that they are still short of breaking into the elite, but in only one of those games were they truly outclassed, losing 4-1 at home to Arsenal.

Joleon Lescott – an England debutant last term and scorer of eight league goals from defence – and Victor Anichebe are both promising talents but, if Everton are to challenge for a Champions League place again, Moyes must strengthen the squad.

They missed Tim Cahill, who spent much of the season on the treatment table, and Mikel Arteta had to play for most of the second half of the season with a stomach injury that required surgery in the summer.

And Cahill, along with Tony Hibbert and possibly Joseph Yobo, looks set to miss the first few weeks of this season.

Longest run without loss: 9
Longest run without win: 4
High – low league position: 3-11
High – low Outlook form figure: 67-44
Final Outlook Index figure: 895

Key Stat: Everton did not win against any of the other sides in the top seven.

2007/08 Premier League Stats

	Apps	Gls	YC	RC
V Anichebe	10 (17)	1	1	0
M Arteta	27 (1)	1	2	1
L Baines	13 (9)	0	1	0
T Cahill	18	7	4	0
L Carsley	33 (1)	1	6	0
M Fernandes	9 (3)	0	0	0
T Gravesen	1 (7)	0	1	0
T Hibbert	22 (2)	0	3	1
T Howard	36	0	1	0
P Jagielka	27 (7)	2	2	0
A Johnson	20 (9)	6	1	0
J Lescott	37 (1)	8	3	0
J McFadden	6 (7)	2	2	0
P Neville	37	2	4	1
Nuno Valente	8 (1)	0	1	0
L Osman	26 (2)	4	0	0
S Pienaar	25 (3)	2	6	0
J Rodwell	0 (2)	0	0	0
A Stubbs	7 (1)	1	0	0
J Vaughan	0 (8)	1	0	0
S Wessels	2	0	0	0
Yakubu	26 (3)	15	2	0
J Yobo	29 (1)	1	0	0

League and Cup Stats

Clean sheets: 20 (14 league)
Yellow cards: 69 Red cards: 3
Players used: 23
Leading scorer: Yakubu 21 (15 league)

Outlook forecast: 6th
Your forecast:

FULHAM

Nickname: The Cottagers
Colours: White and black
Ground: Craven Cottage
Capacity: 24,600
Tel: 0870 442 1222
www.fulhamfc.com

FULHAM'S season was one of two halves. Lawrie Sanchez, who had kept them up the season before, took the job full-time and spent heavily over the summer.

However, he took just 13 of the 51 points on offer from the Cottagers' first 17 matches and was given his P45 before Christmas.

Roy Hodgson came in less than a week later with the club third from bottom and looking doomed. With limited time to operate in the January transfer window, he nevertheless brought in a few new faces.

Norwegian defender Brede Hangeland looked a good buy from the off and Eddie Johnson could be a useful player given time to settle in – the USA international striker has an excellent scoring record in the MLS and for his country.

It was the return of Jimmy Bullard after 16 months out injured that revitalised Fulham and he is coveted by a number of clubs.

As usual, the Cottagers were poor on the road, but once they got their first away win of the season at Reading on April 12, they couldn't stop winning, taking three points away at Man City and Portsmouth as they won four of their last five to finish out of the relegation zone on goal difference.

However, results at Craven Cottage got them into trouble – only Derby took fewer points than Fulham's paltry 20 at home.

It was a great achievement to stay up and did much to restore Hodgson's reputation after a mixed spell at Blackburn. He has had a summer clearout and one thing is certain – his new-look side can hardly make a worse start than Sanchez's did last year.

Longest run without loss: 4
Longest run without win: 14
High – low league position: 13-19
High – low Outlook form figure: 61-35
Final Outlook Index figure: 846
Key Stat: *They only lost once against other sides in the bottom seven.*

2007/08 Premier League Stats

	Apps	Gls	YC	RC
L Andreasen	9 (4)	0	3	1
N Ashton	1	0	0	0
C Baird	17 (1)	0	2	1
C Bocanegra	18 (4)	1	5	0
H Bouazza	15 (5)	1	2	1
J Bullard	15 (2)	2	0	0
P Christanval	0 (1)	0	0	0
S Davies	36 (1)	6	6	0
S Davis	22	0	2	0
C Dempsey	29 (7)	6	4	0
P Diop	1 (2)	0	1	0
B Hangeland	15	0	1	0
D Healy	15 (15)	4	2	0
A Hughes	29 (1)	1	0	0
C John	0 (2)	0	0	0
E Johnson	4 (2)	0	0	0
D Kamara	17 (11)	5	6	0
K Keller	13	0	0	0
S Ki-Hyeon	4 (8)	0	0	0
Z Knight	4	0	0	1
P Konchesky	33	0	5	1
S Kuqi	3 (7)	0	0	0
B McBride	14 (3)	4	2	0
D Murphy	28 (5)	5	4	0
E Nevland	2 (6)	2	1	0
A Niemi	22	0	0	0
E Omozusi	8	0	2	1
I Pearce	0 (1)	0	0	0
A Smertin	11 (4)	0	2	0
P Stalteri	13	0	3	0
D Stefanovic	13	0	4	0
M Volz	5 (4)	0	2	1
T Warner	3	0	1	0

League and Cup Stats
Clean sheets: 9 (7 league)
Yellow cards: 61 Red cards: 7
Players used: 33
Leading scorers: all 6 – Dempsey (all league), Kamara, Murphy (5 league), Healy (4 league)

Outlook forecast: 14th
Your forecast:

HULL CITY

Nickname: The Tigers
Colours: Amber and black
Ground: Kingston Communications Stadium
Capacity: 25,404
Tel: 0870 8370003
www.hullcityafc.net

NOT ONLY will this be Hull's first season in the top flight, but the Play-Off final was also the club's first trip to Wembley in their 104-year history.

These are heady days for the East Riding outfit, but promotion to the Premier League has been a chastening experience for Play-Off champions in recent seasons – of the last five Play-Off winners, Wolves, Palace, Watford and Derby have all gone straight back down again. Only Palace avoided finishing bottom and only 2005 winners West Ham have stayed up.

It looks as though Phil Brown has his work cut out for him but six years as assistant to Sam Allardyce at Bolton might come in handy, not least because the Trotters are still plying their trade in the top flight after going up via the Play-Offs in 2001.

While Brown has money to spend, he will struggle to attract the players he needs. A Bolton-like approach – recruiting players coming to the ends of their careers or in need of rehabilitation – may be what's required and looks likely, given that 39-year-old Dean Windass was such an important player for them last season.

The impact of Fraizer Campbell, who scored 15 goals on loan from Man United last season, suggests a few fringe players from bigger sides might be getting a taste of first-team action in a Hull shirt this term.

But however shrewdly Brown plays things, he faces an almighty struggle to defend the Tigers' place in the Premier League – the 6-4 about Hull finishing bottom looks pretty tempting.

Longest run without loss: 6
Longest run without win: 4
High – low league position: 2-20
High – low Outlook form figure: 67-40
Final Outlook Index figure: 820
Key Stat: *Only champions West Brom have beaten Hull at home since October.*

2007/08 Championship Stats

	Apps	Gls	YC	RC
I Ashbee	42	3	4	1
N Barmby	5 (10)	1	2	0
M Bridges	1 (6)	0	0	0
W Brown	41	1	4	0
F Campbell	32 (2)	15	3	0
N Clement	4 (1)	0	0	0
D Coles	1	0	0	0
A Dawson	24 (5)	1	4	0
D Delaney	21 (2)	0	5	0
N Doyle	0 (1)	0	0	0
M Duke	3	0	0	0
S Elliott	3 (4)	0	1	0
C Fagan	4 (4)	0	0	0
N Featherstone	0 (6)	0	0	0
C Folan	18 (11)	8	4	1
R France	3 (10)	0	0	0
R Garcia	35 (3)	5	5	0
B Hughes	26 (9)	1	1	0
D Livermore	9 (11)	1	5	0
D Marney	35 (6)	6	8	0
S McPhee	7 (12)	2	1	0
B Myhill	43	0	3	0
J Okocha	10 (8)	0	0	1
H Pedersen	18 (3)	4	0	0
S Ricketts	44	0	8	1
M Turner	44	5	6	0
S Walton	5 (5)	0	2	0
D Windass	29 (8)	11	6	0

League and Cup Stats
Clean sheets: 19 (15 league)
Yellow cards: 80 Red cards: 4
Players used: 28
Leading scorer: Dean Windass (11 league), Fraizer Campbell 15 (all league)

Outlook forecast: 20th
Your forecast:

LIVERPOOL

Nickname: The Reds
Colours: Red
Ground: Anfield
Capacity: 45,362
Tel: 0151 263 2361
www.liverpoolfc.tv

FEUDING in the boardroom cast a long shadow over Liverpool's season. George Gillett and Tom Hicks first fell out first with Rafa Benitez after the news broke that they had spoken to Jurgen Klinsmann about the manger's job, and then with each other, as their working relationship increasingly came to resemble an episode of Dallas.

There was plenty of speculation about the ownership of the club too, with an attempted buyout by Dubai International Capital foundering, and Liverpool supporters launching a venture to get fans to invest in a Barcelona-style shared ownership scheme.

Apparently Hicks and Gillett are speaking again and Benitez's job is safe, but he doesn't have the money to spend that his title rivals do. The manager must sell to raise funds and that won't help him to close the gap on Man United, Chelsea and Arsenal.

Benitez's transfer dealings have been hit and miss over the years, but he did well last year and struck absolute gold with Fernando Torres – the Spaniard scored 33 goals in all competitions and 24 in the league.

Martin Skrtel looks a good buy too, despite a nightmare start against Havant & Waterlooville. Dirk Kuyt has found his feet and Ryan Babel has bags of potential.

However, once again, it took an impressive Champions League campaign to cover a multitude of sins domestically.

The Reds went close in Europe, going out to Chelsea in extra-time of the semi-final, but they never looked any better than fourth-best in the top flight and failed to beat any of the top three in the league.

Longest run without loss: 16
Longest run without win: 4
High – low league position: 1-7
High – low Outlook form figure: 66-47
Final Outlook Index figure: 937

Key Stat: *They scored 20 goals in the last five minutes last season.*

2007/08 Premier League Stats

	Apps	Gls	YC	RC
D Agger	4 (1)	0	0	0
X Alonso	16 (3)	2	3	0
A Arbeloa	26 (2)	0	4	0
F Aurelio	13 (3)	2	1	0
R Babel	15 (15)	4	1	0
Y Benayoun	15 (15)	4	0	0
J Carragher	34 (1)	0	4	0
P Crouch	9 (12)	5	0	0
S Finnan	21 (3)	0	2	0
S Gerrard	32 (2)	11	3	0
J Hobbs	1 (1)	0	0	0
S Hyypia	24 (3)	2	1	0
E Insua	2 (1)	0	1	0
H Kewell	8 (2)	0	0	0
D Kuyt	24 (8)	3	2	0
Lucas	12 (6)	0	0	0
J Mascherano	25	1	6	1
J Pennant	14 (4)	2	3	0
D Plessis	2	0	0	0
J Reina	38	0	2	0
J Riise	22 (7)	0	3	0
M Sissoko	6 (3)	1	2	0
M Skrtel	13 (1)	0	1	0
F Torres	29 (4)	24	5	0
A Voronin	13 (6)	5	2	0

League and Cup Stats
Clean sheets: 25 (18 league)
Yellow cards: 72 Red cards: 3
Players used: 25
Leading scorer: Fernando Torres 33 (24 league)

Outlook forecast: 3rd
Your forecast:

MANCHESTER CITY

Nickname: The Citizens
Colours: Blue and white
Ground: City of Manchester Stadium
Capacity: 47,726
Tel: 0870 062 1894
www.mcfc.co.uk

A TOP-TEN finish, qualification for Europe – albeit via a sixth-place finish in the Fair Play league – and completing a double over Man United means that 2007/08 was a very decent season in the eyes of most City fans.

But it wasn't enough for Thaksin Shinawatra, who showed his ruthless side by sacking Sven-Goran Eriksson.

Sven started well – despite having just days to spend Shinawatra's money after his appointment late last summer, they won their first nine games at Eastlands, in stark contrast to the season before when they won just five at home and scored ten goals.

Not all of Eriksson's transfers worked out – Rolando Bianchi went back to Italy in the January transfer window – but Elano and Martin Petrov were notable successes.

Now, after the Citizens faded over the second half of the season, Mark Hughes is in charge. While he has done well with both Wales and Blackburn, shopping with a big budget is a different challenge altogether, but he's started by handing CSKA Moscow £19m for Brazilian striker Jo.

His first job will be to win over the supporters – he enjoyed two successful spells as a Man United player – and the players, who downed tools in an 8-1 defeat by Boro on the final day of the season, once it had become clear that Eriksson was going.

Hughes is said to be keen to ensure that certain players curtail the late nights out – how that might sit with Shinawatra target Ronaldinho is anyone's guess.

The owner wants Champions League football next season. It's a big ask.

Longest run without loss: 6
Longest run without win: 4
High – low league position: 1-9
High – low Outlook form figure: 62-41
Final Outlook Index figure: 860
Key Stat: *Flat track bullies? They were 8-1-1 at home against bottom-half teams.*

2007/08 Premier League Stats

	Apps	Gls	YC	RC
M Ball	19 (9)	0	2	0
Benjani	14	3	0	0
R Bianchi	7 (12)	4	0	0
V Bojinov	1 (2)	0	0	0
F Caicedo	0 (10)	0	1	0
N Castillo	2 (5)	0	0	0
V Corluka	34 (1)	0	4	0
R Dunne	36	1	3	2
Elano	29 (5)	8	3	0
K Etuhu	2 (4)	1	1	0
J Garrido	21 (6)	0	4	0
Gelson	21 (5)	2	5	0
Geovanni	2 (17)	3	3	0
D Hamann	26 (3)	0	8	0
J Hart	26	0	0	0
S Ireland	32 (1)	4	1	1
A Isaksson	5	0	0	0
S Jihai	7 (7)	1	2	0
M Johnson	23	2	4	0
E Mpenza	8 (7)	2	0	0
N Onuoha	13 (3)	1	0	0
M Petrov	34	5	2	1
M Richards	25	0	4	0
G Samaras	2 (3)	0	0	0
K Schmeichel	7	0	0	0
D Sturridge	2 (1)	1	0	0
D Vassell	21 (6)	6	2	0
S Williamson	0 (1)	0	1	0

League and Cup Stats

Clean sheets: 15 (11 league)
Yellow cards: 59 Red cards: 4
Players used: 28
Leading scorer: Elano 10 (8 league)

Outlook forecast: 7th
Your forecast:

MANCHESTER UNITED

Nickname: The Red Devils
Colours: Red and white
Ground: Old Trafford
Capacity: 76,212
Tel: 0870 442 1994
www.manutd.com

2007/08 was a vintage season at Old Trafford as they retained the title and won the Champions League, but the Ronaldo saga was an unwelcome postscript.

The Portuguese was a vital part of United's success and, while the undignified tug of love between United and Real Madrid wasn't exactly *Kramer vs. Kramer*, there was just as much angst.

Ferguson's statement that he intends to retire in two or three years does not bode well either – the uncertainty did United no favours the last time he announced his intention to stand down.

They will miss Carlos Queiroz too, if Ferguson's assistant, widely credited with organising the United defence and believed to have a big influence on tactics, succeeds Luiz Felipe Scolari as Portugal boss.

But United take plenty of positives into the new season – with or without Ronaldo, still a United player as we went to press.

Nemanja Vidic and Rio Ferdinand were the heart of the strongest defence in the division, and Wes Brown impressed at right-back, becoming a regular in the league and a mainstay of the European XI.

Michael Carrick and Owen Hargreaves showed class in midfield, Anderson looked excellent when he wasn't shooting and fellow new boy Nani has star potential – think back to his superb goal against Boro.

Up front, Carlos Tevez and Wayne Rooney have dovetailed nicely – against many pundits' expectations – and United are hoping to get a work permit for Angolan striker Manucho for this term.

Longest run without loss: 7
Longest run without win: 4
High – low league position: 1-19
High – low Outlook form figure: 70-49
Final Outlook Index figure: 950
Key Stat: *Surprise, surprise – United won the most penalties (8).*

2007/08 Premier League Stats

	Apps	Gls	YC	RC
Anderson	16 (8)	0	2	0
W Brown	34 (2)	1	8	0
F Campbell	0 (1)	0	0	0
M Carrick	24 (7)	2	2	0
C Eagles	1 (3)	0	0	0
P Evra	33	0	4	0
R Ferdinand	35	2	4	0
D Fletcher	5 (11)	0	1	0
B Foster	1	0	0	0
R Giggs	26 (5)	3	1	0
O Hargreaves	16 (7)	2	2	0
T Kuszczak	8 (1)	0	0	0
Nani	16 (10)	3	2	1
J O'Shea	10 (18)	0	1	0
J-S Park	8 (4)	1	0	0
G Pique	5 (4)	0	0	0
C Ronaldo	31 (3)	31	5	1
W Rooney	25 (2)	12	8	0
L Saha	6 (11)	5	0	0
P Scholes	22 (2)	1	3	0
M Silvestre	3	0	0	0
D Simpson	1 (2)	0	0	0
C Tevez	31 (3)	14	1	0
E Van der Sar	29	0	2	0
N Vidic	32	1	5	0

League and Cup Stats

Clean sheets: 31 (21 league)
Yellow cards: 74 Red cards: 3
Players used: 25
Leading scorer: Cristiano Ronaldo 42 (31 league)

Outlook forecast: Champions
Your forecast:

MIDDLESBROUGH

Nickname: Boro
Colours: Red and white
Ground: The Riverside Stadium
Capacity: 35,100
Tel: 0844 499 6789
www.mfc.co.uk

MIDDLESBROUGH proved just as frustrating for punters as ever last season.

They avoided defeat in half of their games against the big four but won just a third of their matches against teams from the bottom half of the table and, while Gareth Southgate's side looked superb at times, they never climbed higher than tenth.

After losing Yakubu and Mark Viduka, Boro initially looked toothless and Stewart Downing was top scorer, finishing with ten goals in all competitions.

However, Tuncay Sanli grew in stature as the season went on and Afonso Alves, who looked overweight and overpriced on his arrival in the January transfer window despite his 34 goals for Heerenveen in the Dutch Eredivisie in 2006/07, started to show what he can do towards the end of term.

Alves hit the post in a 1-0 defeat to Chelsea, got his first two goals in a 2-2 draw with Man United and bagged a hat-trick in the farcical final-day thrashing of Man City. He looks likely to go well in his second season and might be a lively each-way shout for the Golden Boot or one to trade early.

At the back they lost Jonathan Woodgate, but David Wheater had a breakthrough season and earned a call-up into one of Fabio Capello's provisional England squads.

Mark Schwarzer has left and it won't be easy to find a replacement, but the main challenge facing Southgate is producing more consistency from his side.

He is lucky in that chairman Steve Gibson is both patient and prepared to back his managers financially.

Longest run without loss: 8
Longest run without win: 11
High – low league position: 12-18
High – low Outlook form figure: 60-35
Final Outlook Index figure: 860
Key Stat: *Boro's second-half record (5-16-17) was second-worst in the Prem.*

2007/08 Premier League Stats

	Apps	Gls	YC	RC
J Aliadiere	26 (3)	5	3	1
Afonso Alves	7 (4)	6	0	0
J Arca	23 (1)	2	6	0
G Boateng	29 (4)	1	9	0
L Cattermole	10 (14)	1	4	0
T Craddock	1 (2)	0	0	0
A Davies	3 (1)	0	0	0
S Downing	38	9	3	0
J Grounds	5	1	1	0
S Hines	0 (1)	0	0	0
B Hutchinson	0 (8)	1	0	0
R Huth	9 (4)	1	3	0
A Johnson	3 (16)	1	2	0
B Jones	1	0	0	0
Lee Dong-gook	5 (9)	0	1	0
T McMahon	0 (1)	0	0	0
Mido	8 (4)	2	4	1
G O'Neil	25 (1)	0	8	0
E Pogatetz	23 (1)	1	3	0
C Riggott	9 (1)	2	0	0
F Rochemback	21 (5)	1	7	0
T Sanli	27 (7)	8	5	0
M Schwarzer	34	0	2	0
M Shawky	3 (2)	0	1	0
A Taylor	18 (1)	0	1	0
R Turnbull	3	0	0	0
D Wheater	34	3	8	0
J Woodgate	17	0	4	0
Yakubu	4	0	0	0
L Young	35	2	8	0

League and Cup Stats

Clean sheets: 12 (8 league)
Yellow cards: 100 Red cards: 2
Players used: 30
Leading scorer: Stuart Downing 10 (9 league)

Outlook forecast: 12th
Your forecast:

NEWCASTLE

Nickname: The Magpies
Colours: Black and white
Ground: St James' Park
Capacity: 52,387
Tel: 0191 201 8400
www.nufc.co.uk

NEWCASTLE had problems from the off last term as new owner Mike Ashley was rumoured to be keen to replace new gaffer Sam Allardyce even before the big kick-off.

Allardyce had spent heavily during the summer but with mixed results, and Joey Barton proved beyond even his knack for rehabilitating football's misfits.

Even so, the Mags enjoyed their best start to the season in a decade – five wins from their first nine – before hitting a rocky patch.

Rumours of unrest in the dressing room and open rebellion in the stands in the face of Allardyce's unlovable brand of football meant his days were numbered.

It was one of the stories of the season when Kevin Keegan returned – Alan Shearer was the early favourite, and no less outlandish – but the second coming started with eight games without a win.

In the end, the Magpies did enough to secure a mid-table finish, with Michael Owen reinventing himself playing 'in the hole'.

And Keegan was as entertaining as ever, speaking his mind and happy to wash Newcastle's dirty linen in public as it emerged that his relationship with Ashley might not be all he had been hoping for.

No matter how much money Ashley spends, a title challenge is beyond them and probably the top six too – in his last spell in the top flight, in charge of Man City, Keegan didn't prove the wisest shopper.

However, if he was to target the cups, both Tottenham and Portsmouth proved last term that the second tier of clubs within the top flight can grab some silverware.

Longest run without loss: 7
Longest run without win: 9
High – low league position: 5-15
High – low Outlook form figure: 66-32
Final Outlook Index figure: 856
Key Stat: *One point away to the top nine, conceding two or more in eight of those.*

2007/08 Premier League Stats

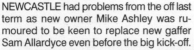

	Apps	Gls	YC	RC
S Ameobi	2 (4)	0	0	0
J Barton	20 (3)	1	4	0
H Beye	27 (2)	1	5	0
N Butt	35	3	12	0
C Cacapa	16 (3)	1	1	0
S Carr	8 (2)	0	0	0
A Carroll	1 (3)	0	0	0
L Diatta	0 (2)	0	0	0
D Duff	12 (4)	0	3	0
D Edgar	2 (3)	0	0	0
Emre Belozoglu	6 (8)	1	1	0
A Faye	21 (2)	1	4	0
Geremi	24 (3)	2	3	0
S Given	19	1	2	0
S Harper	19 (2)	0	0	0
Jose Enrique	18 (5)	0	1	0
K LuaLua	0 (2)	0	0	0
O Martins	23 (8)	9	1	0
J Milner	25 (4)	2	3	0
C N'Zogbia	27 (5)	3	5	0
M Owen	24 (5)	11	2	0
P Ramage	0 (3)	0	0	0
D Rozehnal	16 (5)	0	0	0
A Smith	26 (7)	0	9	1
N Solano	0 (2)	0	0	0
S Taylor	29 (2)	1	3	0
M Viduka	19 (7)	7	0	0

League and Cup Stats
Clean sheets: 10 (8 league)
Yellow cards: 62 Red cards: 2
Players used: 27
Leading scorer: Michael Owen 13 (11 league)

Outlook forecast: 11th
Your forecast:

PORTSMOUTH

Nickname: Pompey
Colours: Blue and white
Ground: Fratton Park
Capacity: 20,224
Tel: 023 9273 1204
www.pompeyfc.co.uk

POMPEY were a force on the road last season, with no side outside the top three winning more aways, but their home record was affected by a weird barren spell during which they failed to score in six league games at Fratton Park.

Eighth was a decent finish but last term was all about the FA Cup. Pompey only played one Premier League side in their cup run, but you can't complain about a win at Old Trafford en route to Wembley.

Jermain Defoe, who arrived in the January transfer window, was unlucky to miss out on two cup finals. He missed the League Cup final with Tottenham and then, cup-tied, the FA Cup final with Pompey.

However, he looked sharp in the league with eight goals from 12 starts and got his reward with two England goals against Trinidad & Tobago. He teams up with England colleague Peter Crouch this term.

David James had a big season too – Pompey kept 16 league clean sheets, a figure behind only Chelsea, Man United and Liverpool.

Of the new arrivals, Sulley Muntari worked out well, as did Lassana Diarra, who has promised to stay for another season despite interest from other clubs. Niko Kranjcar is on the radars of bigger clubs too after a good season and a decent Euro 2008.

The key man though, and the key to replacing those players should they move on, is Harry Redknapp – maybe the biggest moment of Pompey's season was in January when he turned down the chance to manage Newcastle.

Longest run without loss: 7
Longest run without win: 5
High – low league position: 5-16
High – low Outlook form figure: 68-39
Final Outlook Index figure: 871
Key Stat: *They didn't concede in five away ties en route to winning the FA Cup.*

2007/08 Premier League Stats

	Apps	Gls	YC	RC
J Ashdown	3	0	0	0
L Aubey	1 (2)	0	0	0
M Baros	8 (4)	0	0	0
Benjani	22 (2)	13	1	0
S Campbell	31	3	2	0
M Cranie	1 (1)	0	0	0
S Davis	18 (4)	0	8	0
J Defoe	12 (1)	8	2	0
L Diarra	11 (1)	1	2	0
P Diop	25	0	6	0
S Distin	36	1	4	0
H Hreidarsson	30 (2)	3	3	1
R Hughes	8 (5)	0	2	0
D James	35	0	2	0
G Johnson	29	1	3	0
N Kanu	13 (12)	4	1	0
N Kranjcar	31 (3)	4	2	0
Lauren	11 (4)	0	4	0
S Muntari	27 (2)	4	6	2
A Mvuemba	3 (5)	0	0	0
D Nugent	5 (10)	0	0	0
G O'Neil	3	0	0	0
N Pamarot	14 (4)	1	3	0
Pedro Mendes	14 (4)	0	3	0
F Songo'o	0 (1)	0	0	0
M Taylor	4 (10)	1	1	0
D Traore	1 (2)	0	0	0
J Utaka	25 (4)	5	1	0

League and Cup Stats
Clean sheets: 23 (16 league)
Yellow cards: 68 Red cards: 3
Players used: 28
Leading scorer: Benjani Mwaruwari 12 (all league)

Outlook forecast: 8th
Your forecast:

STOKE CITY

Nickname: The Potters
Colours: Red and white
Ground: Britannia Stadium
Capacity: 28,000
Tel: 0871 663 2008
www.stokecityfc.com

TONY PULIS is in his second spell at The Potteries, and in his two years back at the club, he has taken Stoke from a mid-table outfit to three points off the Play-Offs in 2006/07, and runners-up and promotion to the Premier League last season.

He has never been relegated as a manager but his first spell in charge of the Potters started with a relegation battle in 2002/03 following their promotion to the Championship, and that's what he can look forward to this term.

He is the pragmatist's pragmatist, and their opening game away to Bolton is unlikely to attract too many neutrals.

However, despite a reputation for dour football, Stoke were the second-highest scorers in the Championship last season.

Ricardo Fuller was a vital part of that, with 15 league goals, but the club are currently sweating over his fitness after the striker damaged knee ligaments on international duty with Jamaica.

Ryan Shawcross also earned good notices in the centre of defence and, at 20, looks a player for the future.

There is no doubt that the Potters need reinforcements though, and they have made a slow start to the summer sales – by the end of June, the Potters had made no new signings since winning promotion.

However, Pulis does his homework before spending money and, having made good use of the loan market in recent seasons, he is likely to do so again.

No matter who arrives though, it's going to be a struggle for survival.

Longest run without loss: 12
Longest run without win: 6
High – low league position: 1-10
High – low Outlook form figure: 63-43
Final Outlook Index figure: 824

Key Stat: *Stoke lost only once away to other sides in the Championship top ten.*

2007/08 Championship Stats

	Apps	Gls	YC	RC
S Ameobi	3 (3)	0	2	0
J Bothroyd	1 (3)	0	0	0
L Buxton	0 (4)	0	1	0
L Cort	34	8	0	0
J Craddock	4	0	0	0
R Cresswell	42 (1)	11	9	0
R Delap	44	2	5	0
S Diao	8 (3)	0	1	0
C Dickinson	19 (8)	0	2	0
J Eustace	21 (6)	0	3	1
R Fuller	39 (3)	15	11	0
P Gallagher	2 (5)	0	0	0
A Griffin	15	0	1	1
D Higginbotham	1	0	0	0
C Hill	5 (1)	0	1	0
R Hoult	1	0	0	1
L Lawrence	40 (1)	14	12	0
D Matteo	14	0	1	0
C Nash	10	0	0	0
J Parkin	4 (25)	2	1	0
S Pearson	3 (1)	0	0	0
V Pericard	2 (3)	0	0	0
D Phillips	0 (2)	0	0	0
D Pugh	27 (3)	0	5	0
A Pulis	0 (1)	0	1	0
C Riggott	9	0	0	0
R Shawcross	39 (2)	7	9	0
M Sidibe	33 (2)	4	1	0
S Simonsen	35 (1)	0	0	0
P Sweeney	0 (5)	0	2	0
G Whelan	14 (1)	1	2	0
A Wilkinson	16 (7)	0	3	0
S Wright	14 (2)	0	3	0
G Zakuani	11 (8)	0	1	0

League and Cup Stats

Clean sheets: 12 (11 league)
Yellow cards: 81 Red cards: 2
Players used: 34
Ricardo Fuller 15 (all league), Liam Lawrence 15 (14 league)

Outlook forecast: 18th

Your forecast:

Sponsored by Stan James

SUNDERLAND

Nickname: Mackems / Black Cats
Colours: Red and white
Ground: Stadium Of Light
Capacity: 49,000
Tel: 0191 551 5000
www.safc.com

ROY KEANE showed the scale of the task facing newcomers to the top flight last term when, despite spending a fortune in the summer, his Sunderland side endured a nervous season and finished just three points clear of the relegation places.

It was a massive improvement on their last foray into the Premier League, but Keane has shown his ruthless streak, releasing Andy Cole, Stanislav Varga and Stephen Wright over the summer.

Not all of his buys worked out but Kenwyne Jones was a success with seven league goals and, perhaps just as importantly, a knack for unsettling defences, but he may be out until Christmas after injuring knee ligaments on international duty.

Rangers' Daniel Cousin is targeted as cover while Celtic's excellent winger Aiden McGeady, who would probably require a club-record bid, is also on Keane's radar.

At the back, Jonny Evans put controversy at Man United behind him to impress in his second loan spell at Sunderland and Craig Gordon showed that a decent keeper is a worthwhile investment after his £9m move from Hearts.

The Mackems' big problem was their away form. With a 2-3-14 record on the road, only Derby did worse away from home last season and it was only one point better than their pathetic showing in their record-breaking relegation season of 2005/06.

The Stadium Of Light was a tricky place to visit where, crucially, they beat four of the five sides that finished below them, but a difficult second season lies ahead.

Longest run without loss: 3
Longest run without win: 8
High – low league position: 11-19
High – low Outlook form figure: 54-37
Final Outlook Index figure: 842
Key Stat: *Desperate defending? They conceded the most pens (9).*

2007/08 Premier League Stats

	Apps	Gls	YC	RC
R Anderson	0 (1)	0	0	0
P Bardsley	11	0	3	0
M Chopra	21 (12)	6	7	0
A Cole	3 (4)	0	0	0
D Collins	32 (4)	1	6	0
D Connolly	1 (2)	0	0	0
C Edwards	11 (2)	0	0	0
D Etuhu	18 (2)	1	4	0
J Evans	15	0	0	0
M Fulop	1	0	0	0
C Gordon	34	1	1	0
G Halford	8	0	2	1
I Harte	3 (5)	0	0	0
D Higginbotham	21	3	1	0
S John	0 (1)	1	0	1
K Jones	33	7	2	0
G Leadbitter	17 (14)	2	5	0
P McShane	20 (1)	1	3	1
L Miller	16 (8)	1	3	1
D Murphy	20 (8)	4	2	0
N Nosworthy	29	0	3	0
R O'Donovan	4 (13)	0	2	0
R Prica	0 (6)	1	1	0
A Reid	11 (2)	1	2	0
K Richardson	15 (2)	3	3	0
A Stokes	8 (12)	1	1	0
M Waghorn	1 (2)	0	0	0
R Wallace	18 (3)	2	3	0
D Ward	3	0	0	0
D Whitehead	27	1	7	0
D Yorke	17 (3)	1	5	1

League and Cup Stats
Clean sheets: 7 (all league)
Yellow cards: 67 Red cards: 4
Players used: 31
Leading scorer: Kenwyne Jones 7 (all league)

Outlook forecast: 17th
Your forecast:

TOTTENHAM HOTSPUR

Nickname: Spurs
Colours: White and navy blue
Ground: White Hart Lane
Capacity: 36,240
Tel: 0870 420 5000
www.tottenhamhotspur.com

DOGGED by uncertainty over Martin Jol's future at the club, Spurs made their worst start to the season since the war.

The manager was being undermined from within and, after it emerged that Spurs had approached Juande Ramos and chairman Daniel Levy had offered Jol his "100% support", the writing was on the wall.

The first thing Ramos did was get the players in for a double training session – Spurs had dropped points to late goals against Sunderland (0-1), Fulham (3-3), Liverpool (2-2) and Blackburn (1-2) in the weeks prior to his arrival and Ramos' disciplined approach paid dividends as he set about restoring Spurs' reputation as a cup team.

They went out of the Uefa Cup on penalties, and won the League Cup to end a nine-year drought of silverware (unless you count their 2005 triumph in the Moonie-organised Peace Cup, of course).

Alan Hutton and Jonathan Woodgate arrived in January to shore up a defence that had kept just one league clean sheet (against Derby) before Ramos turned up and the Spurs boss has addressed his biggest defensive concern by signing outstanding keeper Heurelho Gomes from PSV.

Dimitar Berbatov and Robbie Keane stole the show at the other end with 15 league goals apiece.

Their futures are still up in the air, but Luka Modric can provide the creative spark and Giovani Dos Santos, a summer signing from Barcelona, is an exciting player brimming with potential.

Longest run without loss: 5
Longest run without win: 5
High – low league position: 11-18
High – low Outlook form figure: 54-44
Final Outlook Index figure: 873

Key Stat: *Spurs lost a record-equalling 33 points from a winning position.*

2007/08 Premier League Stats

	Apps	Gls	YC	RC
B Assou-Ekotto	1	0	1	0
G Bale	8	2	1	0
D Bent	11 (16)	6	0	0
D Berbatov	33 (3)	15	3	0
K Boateng	7 (6)	0	2	0
R-Cerny	13	0	1	0
P Chimbonda	31 (1)	2	5	0
M Dawson	26 (1)	1	3	0
J Defoe	3 (16)	4	3	0
A Gardner	4	1	1	0
Gilberto	3 (3)	1	0	0
C Gunter	1 (1)	0	0	0
T Huddlestone	18 (10)	3	5	0
A Hutton	14	0	1	0
J Jenas	28 (1)	4	3	0
Y Kaboul	19 (2)	3	1	0
R Keane	32 (4)	15	2	1
L King	4	0	0	0
Y-P Lee	17 (1)	0	2	0
A Lennon	25 (4)	2	1	0
S Malbranque	35 (2)	4	4	0
J O'Hara	9 (8)	1	3	0
P Robinson	25	0	0	0
R Rocha	4 (1)	1	1	0
W Routledge	1 (1)	0	0	0
P Stalteri	3	0	0	0
A Taarabt	0 (6)	0	0	0
T Tainio	6 (10)	0	1	0
J Woodgate	12	1	2	0
D Zokora	25 (3)	0	6	0

League and Cup Stats
Clean sheets: 15 (9 league)
Yellow cards: 88 Red cards: 4
Players used: 30
Leading scorer: Robbie Keane, Dimitar Berbatov both 23 (15 league)

Outlook forecast: 5th

Your forecast:

WEST BROMWICH ALBION

Nickname: The Baggies / Throstles
Colours: Navy blue and white
Ground: The Hawthorns
Capacity: 25,396
Tel: 0871 271 1100
www.wba.co.uk

WEST BROM'S promotion as champions last term was the third time in seven seasons that the Baggies had yo-yoed between the Championship and Premier League, although they did it in a very different way than they did under Gary Megson.

Far from being the 1-0 merchants of Megson's day, Tony Mowbray's Baggies were the most attractive footballing side in the Championship last term, and the division's top scorers by 19 goals.

However, their aptitude going forward covered a mulitiude of sins defensively, especially at set-pieces. Relegated Leicester conceded fewer goals than the Throstles last season and the question is whether they can get away with it in the top flight.

Kevin Phillips was top scorer with 22 league goals but, at the time of writing, looks unlikely to stay for another season.

However, his most recent spells in the top flight, with Southampton and Aston Villa, could hardly be described as prolific.

Roman Bednar has signed following his successful loan spell, but Zoltan Gera's exit to Fulham will be keenly felt.

The manner of their 1-0 FA Cup semi-final defeat suggests that they will at least put up a decent fight against relegation this season, but unless they bring in a few quality signings the odds-against about them going back down again will start to look tempting.

As we go to press, the club are seeking new investment – the chairman is willing to sell for the right price – and it could take lots of cash to keep the Baggies up.

Longest run without loss: 8
Longest run without win: 3
High – low league position: 1-18
High – low Outlook form figure: 68-43
Final Outlook Index figure: 827

Key Stat: *Won only two homes against the eight sides immediately below them.*

2007/08 Championship Stats

	Apps	Gls	YC	RC
M Albrechtsen	28 (4)	2	0	0
L Barnett	30 (2)	3	4	0
C Beattie	6 (15)	3	0	0
R Bednar	18 (11)	13	2	0
C Brunt	22 (12)	4	1	0
B Cesar	19 (1)	1	6	0
R Chaplow	2 (4)	0	0	0
N Clement	8 (1)	0	3	0
N Ellington	0 (5)	0	0	0
Z Gera	33 (10)	8	4	0
J Greening	46	1	8	0
J Hodgkiss	3 (1)	0	0	0
C Hoefkens	42	0	4	0
D Kiely	44	0	1	0
Kim Do-Heon	1 (3)	1	1	0
R Koren	38 (2)	9	2	0
S MacDonald	0 (10)	0	0	0
S Martis	2	0	1	0
I Miller	24 (10)	9	4	0
L Moore	3 (7)	0	1	1
J Morrison	25 (10)	4	1	0
Pele	13 (8)	0	0	0
K Phillips	29 (6)	22	2	0
P Robinson	43	1	7	2
B Slusarski	0 (1)	0	0	0
L Steele	2	0	0	0
Filipe Teixeira	24 (6)	5	1	0
Tininho	1	0	0	0

League and Cup Stats
Clean sheets: 18 (14 league)
Yellow cards: 56 Red cards: 3
Players used: 28
Leading scorer: Kevin Phillips 24 (22 league)

Outlook forecast: 19th
Your forecast:

WEST HAM

Nickname: Hammers / Irons
Colours: Claret and blue
Ground: Boleyn Ground
Capacity: 35,647
Tel: 020 8548 2748
www.whufc.com

AFTER spending a fortune in the close season, 2007/08 was something of an anti-climax as the Hammers took up residence in mid-table early on and stayed there.

Dean Ashton returned following a lengthy lay-off with an ankle injury to top score for West Ham in 2007/08, and also signed up to a new five-year deal. But that highlight was rivalled by the emergence of 18-year-old Freddie Sears.

An academy product, Sears came on to score the winner against Blackburn on his debut, ending a successive run of 4-0 defeats to Chelsea, Liverpool and Spurs.

Those defeats were part of a typical Alan Curbishley season, as the Hammers tailed off towards the end, winning just five of their final 19 games.

Lots of the new signings spent plenty of time on the treatment table – that can hardly have surprised Curbs where Craig Bellamy and Kieron Dyer were concerned, but it was bad luck with Scott Parker and Julien Faubert, with the latter making just four starts after signing from Bordeaux.

This term, Jonathan Spector may be out until Christmas with a hip injury.

Curbishley has been forced to cut the wage bill this time around, after Icelandic billionaire Bjorgolfur Gudmundsson took over the chairman's role last December – Nolberto Solano was the first casualty of this new austerity.

Improvement in the league looks unlikely but the Irons can definitely do better in the cups – they went out of both to the first Premier League sides they faced.

Longest run without loss: 6
Longest run without win: 4
High – low league position: 6-14
High – low Outlook form figure: 67-38
Final Outlook Index figure: 862

Key Stat: *They were ninth or tenth for the whole of the second half of the season.*

2007/08 Premier League Stats

	Apps	Gls	YC	RC
D Ashton	20 (11)	10	0	0
C Bellamy	7 (1)	2	2	0
L Boa Morte	18 (9)	0	3	1
L Bowyer	12 (3)	4	6	1
H Camara	3 (7)	0	1	0
C Cole	21 (10)	4	9	0
J Collins	2 (1)	0	0	0
J Collison	1 (1)	0	0	0
K Dyer	2	0	0	0
M Etherington	15 (3)	3	2	0
J Faubert	4 (3)	0	1	0
A Ferdinand	22 (3)	2	1	0
D Gabbidon	8 (2)	0	1	0
R Green	38	0	2	0
F Ljungberg	22 (3)	2	3	0
G McCartney	38	1	4	0
H Mullins	32 (2)	0	3	0
L Neill	34	0	5	0
M Noble	25 (6)	3	6	0
J Pantsil	4 (10)	0	5	0
S Parker	17 (1)	1	3	0
K Reid	0 (1)	0	0	0
F Sears	1 (6)	1	0	0
N Solano	14 (9)	4	3	0
J Spector	13 (13)	1	1	0
J Tomkins	5 (1)	0	0	0
M Upson	29	1	2	0
B Zamora	11 (2)	1	1	0

League and Cup Stats
Clean sheets: 10 (8 league)
Yellow cards: 71 Red cards: 2
Players used: 28
Leading scorer: Dean Ashton 11 (10 league)

Outlook forecast: 13th

Your forecast:

WIGAN ATHLETIC

Nickname: The Latics
Colours: Blue and white
Ground: JJB Stadium
Capacity: 25,138
Tel: 01942 774 000
www.wiganlatics.co.uk

FEW WERE surprised when the Latics made a terrible start to the season under Chris Hutchings, who stepped up from the assistant's job after Paul Jewell left at the end of 2006/07.

However, Wigan finished well enough to know that they would be playing Premier League football in 2008/09 whatever happened in their final game at home to Man United.

Wigan have Steve Bruce to thank for their survival. His long, drawn-out appointment may have descended into farce as a row with Birmingham meant an empty chair greeted the cameras at the press conference where his appointment was to be announced, but he turned the club around once he got there.

He made important signings, restored confidence and had Wigan playing some decent football over the second half of the season. They drew with Liverpool, Arsenal and Chelsea in the league in 2008 and expectations are high among the supporters.

He got the best out of underachieving Antonio Valencia, while Wilson Palacios, who arrived during the January transfer window, was an inspired buy.

Bruce has been clocking up the airmiles over the summer watching World Cup qualifiers with a view to picking up a few more players of a similar quality.

They could really use a striker – only Derby scored fewer and, although they picked up over the second half of the season, Marcus Bent, on loan from Charlton, was top scorer with just seven goals.

Longest run without loss: 5
Longest run without win: 14
High – low league position: 3-19
High – low Outlook form figure: 59-34
Final Outlook Index figure: 852
Key Stat: *All six of their home defeats came against the top eight sides.*

2007/08 Premier League Stats

	Apps	Gls	YC	RC
J Aghahowa	2 (12)	0	2	0
M Bent	25 (6)	7	1	0
E Boyce	24 (1)	0	1	0
T Bramble	26	2	5	0
M Brown	27 (4)	0	11	0
D Cotterill	2	0	0	0
E Edman	5	0	0	0
M Figueroa	1 (1)	0	0	0
C Folan	1 (1)	0	0	0
A Granqvist	13 (1)	0	1	0
E Hagen	1	0	0	0
F Hall	0 (1)	0	0	0
E Heskey	27 (1)	4	5	0
K Kilbane	33 (2)	1	3	1
M King	8 (7)	1	1	0
C Kirkland	37	0	0	0
J Koumas	21 (9)	1	1	1
D Landzaat	19	3	2	0
M Melchiot	31	0	2	1
S Olembe	2 (6)	0	0	0
W Palacios	17	0	5	1
M Pollitt	1	0	0	0
P Scharner	37	5	6	0
A Sibierski	10 (20)	4	1	0
J Skoko	7 (5)	0	4	0
R Taylor	12 (5)	3	4	0
L Valencia	30 (1)	3	5	0

League and Cup Stats
Clean sheets: 13 (12 league)
Yellow cards: 63 Red cards: 4
Players used: 27
Leading scorer: Marcus Bent 7 (all league)

Outlook forecast: 15th

Your forecast:

BARNSLEY

Nickname: Tykes
Colours: Red and white

Ground: Oakwell
Capacity: 23,009

Tel: 01226 211211

www.barnsleyfc.co.uk

AFTER sailing close to the wind in the past two seasons, Barnsley are second favourites for the drop.

The Yorkshire side are restricted by a tight budget but Simon Davey has done well in his first managerial role, after taking the reins at Oakwell in November 2006.

He kept them up in 2006/07 and last season he conjured up stunning wins over both Chelsea and Liverpool en route to the semi-final of the FA Cup.

There are two big concerns, the biggest of which is Davey's future, as he is being touted as a possible replacement for Carlos Queiroz at Man United.

Captain Brian Howard's next step is also important – the captain starred in their cup run.

However, Davey has done well in securing Anderson De Silva, Jon Macken and Luke Steele in 2008 and – if he stays – he can build on his growing reputation by keeping the Tykes up.

Longest run without loss: 7
Longest run without win: 6
High – low league position: 4-22
High – low Outlook form figure: 61-42
Key Stat: *Only won once after falling behind, only lost twice after taking the lead.*

Outlook forecast: 19th

Final Outlook Index figure: 772
Clean sheets: 14 (12 league)
Yellow cards: 79 Red cards: 6
Players used: 32
Leading scorer: Brian Howard 14 (13 league)

Your forecast:

BIRMINGHAM CITY

Nickname: Blues
Colours: Blue

Ground: St Andrews
Capacity: 30,009

Tel: 0844 557 1875

www.bcfc.com

HISTORY suggests that Birmingham's best chance of bouncing back to the top tier is as champions.

Six sides relegated from the Premier League have returned as champions in 15 years (40%), but just 12 have taken up the combined 46 automatic and Play-Off slots available in that time, a 26% chance. If you're going to back Blues, back them to do it in style.

After Alex McLeish arrived at St Andrews

last November, Blues averaged a point per game – that would have been enough to keep them up had he been in charge all season and only Chelsea beat them at home after his appointment.

McLeish has work to do though – Lee Carsley is a good signing but Mikael Forssell's loss is a blow, James McFadden is unsettled and Olivier Kapo and Franck Queudrue missed the first day of pre-seaon.

Longest run without loss: 4
Longest run without win: 9
High – low league position: 12-19
High – low Outlook form figure: 52-38
Key Stat: *They have kept no clean sheets since Boxing Day – that's 20 games!*

Outlook forecast: Winners

Final Outlook Index figure: 832
Clean sheets: 3 (all league)
Yellow cards: 73 Red cards: 3
Players used: 28
Leading scorer: Mikael Forssell 9 (all league)

Your forecast:

BLACKPOOL

Nickname: The Seasiders / the Tangerines
Colours: Tangerine and white

Ground: Bloomfield Road
Capacity: 9,788

Tel: 0870 443 1953

www.blackpoolfc.co.uk

WITH relegated Colchester and Scunthorpe being replaced by a couple of big boys from League 1, Blackpool are now the smallest club in the Championship – even League 1 Play-Off winners Doncaster have a third more seats.

Chairman Karl Oyston risked incurring the wrath of the fans by hiking up ticket prices to present Simon Grayson with a bigger war chest, but it's telling that Blackpool still had to release 11 players – including captain Michael Jackson – to keep things ticking over.

With so little to spend the club are having to take risks on the likes of Marlon Broomes, who hasn't played competitively in two years following injury.

Grayson is a promising young manager but, with the loss of key defender Kaspars Gorkss looking inevitable, a second season of survival is a massive ask.

Longest run without loss: 7
Longest run without win: 8
High – low league position: 6-22
High – low Outlook form figure: 60-39
Key Stat: *In no league game did they come from behind to win.*

Final Outlook Index figure: 784
Clean sheets: 12 (11 league)
Yellow cards: 45 Red cards: 4
Players used: 28
Leading scorer: Ben Burgess 10 (9 league)

Outlook forecast: 24th

Your forecast:

BRISTOL CITY

Nickname: The Robins
Colours: Red and white

Ground: Ashton Gate
Capacity: 21,497

Tel: 0871 222 6666

www.bcfc.co.uk

BRISTOL CITY were the golden boys last season, storming into the top six of the Championship at the start of the season and never leaving it.

They got to within touching distance of the Premier League, narrowly losing to Hull in the Play-Off final, but they may have to settle for a more mundane 2008/09.

Gary Johnson can take a lot of credit for bringing a small club so far, but without the momentum that his team carried into 2007/08 following promotion, they could be in for a long, hard slog.

They are not among the favourites for promotion and that's about right – now that the Robins have lost the element of surprise, they could find their second season that much tougher.

The big concern is goals. Bit-part player Darren Byfield was their top league marksman with eight goals last term and he was released this summer.

Longest run without loss: 8
Longest run without win: 5
High – low league position: 1-7
High – low Outlook form figure: 63-36
Key Stat: *They won 18 of the 20 games in which they scored first.*

Final Outlook Index figure: 800
Clean sheets: 16 (15 league)
Yellow cards: 64 Red cards: 3
Players used: 26
Leading scorer: Darren Byfield 8 (all league)

Outlook forecast: 12th

Your forecast:

BURNLEY

Nickname: The Clarets
Colours: Claret and blue

Ground: Turf Moor
Capacity: 22,546

Tel: 0871 221 1882

www.burnleyfootballclub.com

THERE'S been little to excite Burnley fans since they narrowly missed the Play-Off slots in 2001/02.

The Clarets have had no promotion drives since then, their cup runs have ended early and even their relegation scrapes have been minor.

Manager Steve Cotterill left midway through last season but his replacement, Owen Coyle, did well in keeping the club going forward after settling in.

It would, however, be a surprise if there was much improvement, as Burnley had the fourth leakiest defence in the Championship last term.

Strikers Kyle Lafferty, Andy Gray and Andy Cole all left during 2008, but Martin Paterson – 14 goals for relegated Scunthorpe last season – is an able replacement. Kevin McDonald and Christian Kalvenes are also good signings, and another solid season lies ahead.

Longest run without loss: 6
Longest run without win: 7
High – low league position: 6-15
High – low Outlook form figure: 60-35
Key Stat: *The Clarets won only one of their homes against the top nine.*

Outlook forecast: 14th

Final Outlook Index figure: 788
Clean sheets: 11 (10 league)
Yellow cards: 79 Red cards: 9
Players used: 27
Leading scorer: Andy Gray 13 (11 league)

Your forecast:

CARDIFF CITY

Nickname: The Bluebirds
Colours: Blue

Ground: Ninian Park
Capacity: 22,008

Tel: 02920 221 001

www.cardiffcityfc.co.uk

THE prize-money for Cardiff's FA Cup final appearance and the settlement of the Langston court case means the Bluebirds can concentrate on football this term, rather than worry about their finances.

However, that cup run was a mixed blessing as it put the likes of Aaron Ramsey and Joe Ledley in the shop window. Ramsey has already left for Arsenal, while Ledley's future remains unclear. The release of Trevor Sin-

clair and probable exit of Jimmy Floyd Hasselbaink leaves Dave Jones with work to do in reassembling his front-line.

Motherwell's Ross McCormack has come in but more firepower is still needed. However, the news that in-demand defender Roger Johnson is ready to extend his contract will be a relief to Jones.

In their last year at Ninian Park Cardiff can expect bumper home support, but they might fall short of promotion again.

Longest run without loss: 10
Longest run without win: 6
High – low league position: 7-20
High – low Outlook form figure: 64-39
Key Stat: *Second best first-half record, but only four sides worse after the break.*

Outlook forecast: 7th

Final Outlook Index figure: 797
Clean sheets: 18 (13 league)
Yellow cards: 56 Red cards: 3
Players used: 25
Leading scorer: Paul Parry 12 (11 league)

Your forecast:

CHARLTON ATHLETIC

Nickname: Addicks
Colours: Red and white

Ground: The Valley
Capacity: 27,111

Tel: 020 8333 4000

www.cafc.co.uk

CHARLTON'S season and Alan Pardew's future may be determined in the first couple of months of the new season.

Start slowly and restless fans will grow hostile. That would surely see the end of Pardew, and leave the Addicks' campaign in tatters.

Start well though, and Charlton have a squad capable of a promotion bid. Indeed, such is the bloated nature of Pardew's squad that it is probably working against him – the Charlton boss doesn't seem able to settle on his best XI and used a whopping 36 players in the league last season.

A quieter summer gives Pardew a chance to offload some dead wood and, as we went to press, he had only made two signings.

Mark Hudson will help stabilise a defence that was too leaky last term, while Stuart Fleetwood, the Conference top-scorer at Forest Green last term, will add bite to the Addicks' attack.

Longest run without loss: 6
Longest run without win: 6
High – low league position: 2-12
High – low Outlook form figure: 64-37
Key Stat: *The Addicks lost only two of their 12 games against the top six.*

Outlook forecast: 9th

Final Outlook Index figure: 793
Clean sheets: 13 (12 league)
Yellow cards: 72 Red cards: 6
Players used: 36
Leading scorer: Chris Iwelumo 10 (all league)

Your forecast:

COVENTRY CITY

Nickname: The Sky Blues
Colours: Sky blue

Ground: Ricoh Arena
Capacity: 32,609

Tel: 0870 421 1987

www.ccfc.co.uk

COVENTRY have endured a rocky ride in recent times but there is light at the end of the tunnel.

The Sky Blues nearly suffered both relegation and administration last season, but a takeover led by Ray Ranson has at least solved the latter concern.

The takeover was more about clearing debts than going on a spending spree, but new boss Chris Coleman does at least have some funds and doesn't have to offload swathes of his first team.

Captain Stephen Hughes has moved on, but Guillaume Beuzelin should prove a very capable replacement and Coleman will be looking to add a couple more solid signings to strengthen the team.

Progress may be steady rather than spectacular, but if Coleman can get some confidence back into his new side then mid-table will be an acceptable, and realistic, short-term goal.

Longest run without loss: 6
Longest run without win: 4
High – low league position: 1-21
High – low Outlook form figure: 65-39
Key Stat: *Twice as many second-half goals (35) as first-half goals (17).*

Outlook forecast: 16th

Final Outlook Index figure: 772
Clean sheets: 12 (9 league)
Yellow cards: 89 Red cards: 4
Players used: 30
Leading scorer: Michael Mifsud 17 (10 league)

Your forecast:

CRYSTAL PALACE

Nickname: The Eagles
Colours: Red and blue

Ground: Selhurst Park
Capacity: 26,309

Telephone: 0208 768 6000

www.cpfc.co.uk

NEIL WARNOCK has excelled at Palace, picking up the managerial reins in October with the side second-bottom and leading them into the Play-Offs.

That was on the back of an exceptional 16-13-7 record under Warnock, so no wonder the bookies fancy his chances of taking Palace up given a full season in charge.

They may not live up to expectations this term though, and odds as short as 9-1 in the outright betting make limited appeal after the summer departure of central defender Mark Hudson.

Tightening the defence was vital to Warnock's vision for turning Palace's fortunes around, and Hudson was the rock on which the rearguard was formed.

The signing of Paddy McCarthy will help fill that void, but Warnock faces an uphill struggle to hold on to other key players.

Longest run without loss: 13
Longest run without win: 9
High – low league position: 5-23
High – low Outlook form figure: 63-38
Key Stat: *Palace took just five points at home to other sides in the top eight.*

Final Outlook Index figure: 825
Clean sheets: 13 (all league)
Yellow cards: 70 Red cards: 1
Players used: 37
Leading scorer: Clinton Morrison 16 (all league)

Outlook forecast: 5th

Your forecast:

DERBY COUNTY

Nickname: The Rams
Colours: White and black

Ground: Pride Park
Capacity: 33,597

Tel: 0871 472 1884

www.dcfc.co.uk

DERBY set all kinds of records last season as the worst ever Premier League side, and they would be mistaken in thinking a drop to a lower level will solve all of their problems.

Paul Jewell hardly bolstered the Rams' morale last term by constantly bemoaning his players' lack of quality and some lurid tabloid headlines undermined his authority.

However, he has had a productive summer, committing himself to Derby amid reports of offers from Premier League sides, and bringing in a host of fresh faces.

Kris Commons is a promising addition, but Jewell's recent record in the transfer market has been less than spectacular and the likes of Nathan Ellington arriving don't inspire great confidence.

It's noticeable that the likes of Kenny Miller and Robert Earnshaw couldn't get out of Derby quickly enough – rebuilding team spirit looks a massive task.

Longest run without loss: 2
Longest run without win: 35
High – low league position: 19-20
High – low Outlook form figure: 48-25
Key Stat: *They salvaged one point from the 27 games in which they fell behind.*

Final Outlook Index figure: 776
Clean sheets: 3 (all league)
Yellow cards: 69 Red cards: 2
Players used: 36
Leading scorer: Kenny Miller 6 (4 league)

Outlook forecast: 17th

Your forecast:

Sponsored by Stan James

DONCASTER ROVERS

Nickname: Rovers
Colours: Red and white

Ground: Keepmoat Stadium
Capacity: 15,231

Tel: 01302 764 664

www.doncasterroversfc.co.uk

AFTER winning promotion through the Play-Offs last term, Doncaster have now gone from the Conference to the Championship in just five years.

Impressive as that is, the fairy-tale run will surely end this year – Sean O'Driscoll's side face a long season fighting relegation.

Not that Rovers are certainties for the drop, and with decent financial backing and a competent manager they will make a fight of it at the very least.

However, that Paul Green, their star midfielder and the longest-serving member of the club, left for Derby in the summer sums up O'Driscoll's plight.

Regardless of the size and splendour of the Keepmoat Stadium, there's no disguising that Donny are small fish in a big pond.

Rovers' patchy form last term is a concern – they failed to take six points from any top-half League 1 sides last term and look set to struggle at this level.

Longest run without loss: 11
Longest run without win: 4
High – low league position: 2-21
High – low Outlook form figure: 66-42
Key Stat: *Nine players scored six or more for Rovers in 2007/08.*

Outlook forecast: 23rd

Final Outlook Index figure: 753
Clean sheets: 23 (20 league)
Yellow cards: 57 Red cards: 4
Players used: 24
Leading scorer: James Hayter 11 (7 league)

Your forecast:

IPSWICH TOWN

Nickname: Town / Tractor Boys
Colours: Blue and white

Ground: Portman Road
Capacity: 30,311

Tel: 01473 400500

www.itfc.co.uk

IPSWICH only just missed out on the Play-Offs last term, but it was events off the pitch that got supporters excited.

After years of penny-pinching, the emergence of Marcus Evans and his millions has changed the Suffolk landscape. He took over the club in December, wiped out £32m of debt and handed Jim Magilton a hefty war chest in the summer.

Despite a shoestring budget, Ipswich have gone close to promotion in four of their

six seasons since leaving the top flight, so the cash could make all the difference.

The defence needs beefing up. Ipswich are fine when setting the pace and pushing forward – as shown by their 15-7-1-44-14 home record last term – but they struggle under pressure on the road.

Only two teams conceded more on their travels than Town last term, but some decent defensive summer signings could turn Ipswich into genuine contenders.

Longest run without loss: 6
Longest run without win: 4
High – low league position: 2-18
High – low Outlook form figure: 62-42
Key Stat: *Ipswich won their first eight at Portman Road.*

Outlook forecast: 3rd

Final Outlook Index figure: 803
Clean sheets: 12 (all league)
Yellow cards: 56 Red cards: 6
Players used: 29
Leading scorers: Counago, Lee and Walters 12 (all league bar one Lee Cup goal)

Your forecast:

NORWICH CITY

Nickname: The Canaries
Colours: Yellow and green

Ground: Carrow Road
Capacity: 26,164

Tel: 01603 760 760

www.canaries.co.uk

SINCE taking the Norwich job in October, Glenn Roeder has been busy rebuilding the squad and restructuring behind the scenes. Those are sensible long-term plans, but it may make 2008/09 a struggle.

Canaries supporters must be praying that Roeder can end his unfortunate habit of getting clubs relegated in his second season.

The fans are optimistic though and are voting with their feet – 20,000 season tickets have already been sold for 2008/09 and, while Carrow Road was the twelfth-largest ground in the section last term, they averaged the second highest gate.

However, only relegated Scunthorpe and Leicester scored fewer goals than the Canaries last term, and with Ched Evans' loan spell over, Dion Dublin retired, and Darren Huckerby released, Norwich have lost three of their top four scorers from 2007/08.

Longest run without loss: 9
Longest run without win: 12
High – low league position: 12-24
High – low Outlook form figure: 61-36
Key Stat: *They gathered two points from their aways at the top 11.*

Outlook forecast: 18th

Final Outlook Index figure: 780
Clean sheets: 12 (all league)
Yellow cards: 76 Red cards: 7
Players used: 35
Leading scorer: Jamie Cureton 14 (12 league)

Your forecast:

NOTTINGHAM FOREST

Nickname: Forest
Colours: Red and white

Ground: City Ground
Capacity: 30,576

Tel: 0115 9824444

www.nottinghamforest.co.uk

AFTER two near misses Forest bounced back to the Championship last term, but their chances of heading straight back down are greater than the odds would have you believe.

Colin Calderwood's men are 8-1 for an immediate return – double the price of a Swansea side who bagged ten more points than Forest last term – suggesting that the boys from the City Ground are priced up on their history and reputation.

Facing a tough start to the season, they certainly appeal as a back-to-lay prospect in the relegation market – they face Reading, Swansea, Watford and Wolves in their first four games.

The loss of Junior Agogo is a big blow – last term's top scorer has a decent pedigree, with the Ghanaian scoring twice at the 2008 African Cup Of Nations.

His replacement, Robert Earnshaw, will need to find his form of old – and quickly.

Longest run without loss: 7
Longest run without win: 6
High – low league position: 2-21
High – low Outlook form figure: 67-45
Key Stat: *Forest lost only once away at others in the top 11.*

Outlook forecast: 20th

Final Outlook Index figure: 772
Clean sheets: 25 (24 league)
Yellow cards: 58 Red cards: 4
Players used: 26
Leading scorer: Junior Agogo 13 (all league)

Your forecast:

PLYMOUTH ARGYLE

Nickname: The Pilgrims
Colours: Green and white

Ground: Home Park
Capacity: 29,922

Tel: 01752 562561

www.pafc.co.uk

PAUL STURROCK knows how to get the best out of a limited bunch of players, having achieved promotion with four unfashionable clubs.

Another promotion will be beyond him in his first full season back at Plymouth, though.

The Pilgrims have finished comfortably in mid-table for the past three seasons and even flirted with the Play-Offs briefly last term, but 2008/09 could be hard work.

After selling Sylvain Ebanks-Blake in January, Plymouth struggled for goals and tailed off badly, winning just twice against teams outside of the bottom six.

Home Park remains a tough venue though, and Plymouth's direct style should see them win ugly enough to keep their heads above water. If new signings Jermaine Easter and Jason Puncheon settle quickly, survival will be assured.

Longest run without loss: 5
Longest run without win: 5
High – low league position: 5-18
High – low Outlook form figure: 61-42
Key Stat: *Pilgrims won just one home game against top-half teams.*

Outlook forecast: 13th

Final Outlook Index figure: 789
Clean sheets: 15 (14 league)
Yellow cards: 76 Red cards: 2
Players used: 33
Leading scorer: Sylvain Ebanks-Blake 13 (11 league)

Your forecast:

PRESTON NORTH END

Nickname: North End / Lillywhites
Colours: White and navy blue

Ground: Deepdale
Capacity: 20,600

Tel: 0870 442 1964

www.pnefc.premiumtv.co.uk

NORTH END'S FA Cup exit summarised their season – lots of possession and neat passing, but no goals even when presented with a penalty.

The loss of David Nugent hurt Preston, with the side struggling to find an end product last term. They netted just 50 league goals – outside of the relegated sides, only Norwich scored fewer.

The January sale of Patrick Agyemang didn't help, but the year ahead will be about

consolidation for Alan Irvine in his first full season as first-team manager.

He certainly made an impressive start, dragging North End up from second from bottom after his arrival in November to finish 15th.

Irvine helped ensure Deepdale remained a tough venue for opposition teams to visit – all three promoted sides lost at Preston last term – but a lack of transfer activity suggests that another season of struggle lays ahead.

Longest run without loss: 7
Longest run without win: 6
High – low league position: 15-24
High – low Outlook form figure: 62-33
Key Stat: *1.25 points per game vs top-half teams but 1.18 vs the bottom half.*

Outlook forecast: 21st

Final Outlook Index figure: 787
Clean sheets: 14 (13 league)
Yellow cards: 76 Red cards: 4
Players used: 29
Leading scorer: Neil Mellor 10 (9 league)

Your forecast:

QUEENS PARK RANGERS

Nickname: The R's
Colours: Blue and white hoops

Ground: Loftus Road
Capacity: 19,128

Tel: 020 8743 0262

www.qpr.co.uk

QPR's end of 2008/09 season summary may turn out to be 'the club that had everything but signed Iain Dowie'.

With Lakshmi Mittal, the fourth-richest man in the world, throwing his financial clout in with Bernie Ecclestone and Flavio Briatore, it's no wonder the bookies fancy them, but what inspired the new consortium to hire a journeyman?

Dowie did well at Palace but he also spent heavily at Oldham and Charlton without suc-cess and only narrowly avoided relegation as Coventry boss last term.

That said, assuming he doesn't upset the board and that the fans give him time, fitness-fanatic Dowie can get QPR into shape and playing to their potential.

There have been some solid signings, with Peter Ramage and Radek Cerny bringing top-flight experience. The Play-Offs are a realistic aim, but the outright prices of 9-2 are too short.

Longest run without loss: 7
Longest run without win: 9
High – low league position: 12-24
High – low Outlook form figure: 60-32
Key Stat: *Rangers had the best first half-record but the worst second-half record.*

Final Outlook Index figure: 796
Clean sheets: 14 (all league)
Yellow cards: 84 Red cards: 6
Players used: 36
Leading scorer: Akos Buzsaky 10 (all league)

Outlook forecast: 6th

Your forecast:

READING

Nickname: The Royals
Colours: Blue and white

Ground: Madejski Stadium
Capacity: 24,161

Tel: 0118 968 1100

www.readingfc.co.uk

PSYCHOLOGY will play a big part in whether Reading bounce straight back up to the Premier League or whether they get bogged down in mid-table.

The manner of the Royals' late slide to relegation last season led to hints of dressing room unrest and, with the players at a low ebb, it may suggest that the latter scenario is more likely.

However, Steve Coppell was halted en route to the exit by the pleas of fans and chairman for him to stay – and unity counts for plenty in the wake of relegation.

Copple has spoken out about agents unsettling his players, although he is hopeful of keeping the bulk of his squad together, albeit with the probable loss of the odd star name such as Nicky Shorey.

Restoring confidence looks like Coppell's toughest task, but he should manage it in time for a decent season.

Longest run without loss: 5
Longest run without win: 11
High – low league position: 10-18
High – low Outlook form figure: 57-35
Key Stat: *Marcus Hahnemann made the most saves in the top flight (152).*

Final Outlook Index figure: 841
Clean sheets: 8 (7 league)
Yellow cards: 69 Red cards: 6
Players used: 26
Leading scorer: Dave Kitson 10 (all league)

Outlook forecast: 8th

Your forecast:

Sponsored by Stan James

SHEFFIELD UNITED

Nickname: The Blades
Colours: Red and white

Ground: Bramall Lane
Capacity: 32,609

Tel: 0871 222 1899

www.sufc.co.uk

KEVIN BLACKWELL turned Sheffield United's season around upon his arrival at Bramall Lane in February and, given a full season at the helm, he can take them even further.

Before his arrival, United averaged 1.22 points per game, but under Blackwell that figure shot up to 1.93 – sustained over a whole season, that level of performance would see the Blades with 89 points and almost certainly automatic promotion.

Much depends on James Beattie – much maligned at Everton, he is dynamite at this level, with 22 goals at Bramall Lane last term.

With Beattie back in the goals and enjoying his football, it seems more than likely that he will stay.

The club have no need to sell, and a few decent signings – they've already bought Sun Jihai and Greg Halford arrives on loan – would make them serious promotion candidates.

Longest run without loss: 7
Longest run without win: 9
High – low league position: 8-20
High – low Outlook form figure: 65-41

Key Stat: *The Blades scored two or more in eight of their last ten games.*

Outlook forecast: Runners-up

Final Outlook Index figure: 820
Clean sheets: 18 (15 league)
Yellow cards: 72 Red cards: 4
Players used: 31
Leading scorer: James Beattie 22 (all league)

Your forecast:

SHEFFIELD WEDNESDAY

Nickname: The Owls
Colours: Blue and white

Ground: Hillsborough
Capacity: 39,814

Tel: 0870 999 1867

www.swfc.co.uk

THE best policy regarding Wednesday in the short term is wait and see. Brian Laws currently has little to spend on his squad, but that may change if a proposed takeover goes ahead.

For now, Laws has had to trim his squad before bringing new players in but that off-loading could be to the benefit of the team.

Wednesday suffered a swathe of injuries last term, particularly up front.

As a result, the Owls relied heavily on loan signings and that seemed to disrupt the team, leading to a scramble for survival rather than a promotion bid.

Add one or two more in midfield – James O'Connor has signed from Burnley and they've taken Chelsea youngster Jimmy Smith on loan – and factor in a more settled side this year, and survival shouldn't be a problem.

If a mooted takeover goes ahead, then the Owls will set their sights much higher.

Longest run without loss: 9
Longest run without win: 8
High – low league position: 14-24
High – low Outlook form figure: 64-36

Key Stat: *The Owls had the worst first-half record in the section – 7-21-18.*

Outlook forecast: 11th

Final Outlook Index figure: 794
Clean sheets: 11 (all league)
Yellow cards: 74 Red cards: 3
Players used: 33
Leading scorer: Deon Burton 9 (7 league)

Your forecast:

SOUTHAMPTON

Nickname: The Saints
Colours: Red and white

Ground: St Mary's Stadium
Capacity: 32,689

Tel: 0845 688 9448

www.saintsfc.co.uk

SOUTHAMPTON endured a season of turmoil in 2007/08, avoiding relegation only on the final day of the season.

That was the result of financial mismanagement in the pursuit of a swift return to the Premier League, but more optimistic Saints fans will be hoping Rupert Lowe's return to the boardroom may bring stability back to the club.

However, Lowe is no Russian oligarch and Saints' financial strife will continue to hamper their progress on the pitch. Nor is Lowe doing himself any PR favours, having sacked Nigel Pearson – the caretaker manager who oversaw Saints' survival – and announcing Jan Poortvliet as his replacement, despite the Dutchman still being under contract in Holland.

Saints fans would probably be happy to simply keep their heads above water this season, but even that might prove to be beyond them.

Longest run without loss: 5
Longest run without win: 10
High – low league position: 10-22
High – low Outlook form figure: 58-38

Key Stat: *Saints were unbeaten against all the other teams in the bottom six.*

Outlook forecast: 22nd

Final Outlook Index figure: 787
Clean sheets: 12 (10 league)
Yellow cards: 55 Red cards: 4
Players used: 37

Leading scorer: Stern John 19 (all league)

Your forecast:

SWANSEA CITY

Nickname: The Swans
Colours: White

Ground: Liberty Stadium
Capacity: 20,532

Tel: 01792 616 600

www.swanseacity.net

SWANSEA look set to impress this season, but may fall just short of the Play-Offs.

After a slow start last term the Swans ended up blitzing League 1, holding top spot from February and finishing ten points clear. They arrive in the Championship with momentum, belief, solid finances and decent support.

The slight concern for Roberto Martinez is that he lost one of last year's star performers, Andy Robinson, during the summer, and key midfielder Ferrie Bodde is also itching to move on.

However, captain Garry Monk did extend his contract and last season's top scorer in League 1, Jason Scotland, looks settled.

Back the Swans to ruffle some feathers on the road – Martinez's men won more points away from home than at the Liberty Stadium last term, while Scotland also scored comfortably more on his travels than at home.

Longest run without loss: 12
Longest run without win: 3
High – low league position: 1-15
High – low Outlook form figure: 70-47

Key Stat: *They scored 29 times in the final 15 minutes last season.*

Outlook forecast: 10th

Final Outlook Index figure: 774
Clean sheets: 21 (17 league)
Yellow cards: 74 Red cards: 6
Players used: 26

Leading scorer: Jason Scotland 29 (24 league)

Your forecast:

WATFORD

Nickname: The Hornets
Colours: Yellow and red

Ground: Vicarage Road
Capacity: 22,000

Tel: 0845 442 1881

www.watfordfc.co.uk

HAVING led the Championship for much of 2007, Watford tailed off badly in 2008 – the second half of the season yielded just 27 points for the Hornets compared to 43 in the first 23 league games.

Winter saw the departure of assistant boss, Keith Burkinshaw, and the sale of top scorer, Marlon King.

Those losses, along with Watford's rivals sussing out their route-one football, all played their part, but the big question is whether Boothroyd can stop the rot.

It's a big ask. He has to tighten the purse strings and slash the wage bill, so it's unlikely star players will be brought in to fill the gaps in quality left by the likes of King, Hameur Bouazza and Ashley Young, and Danny Shittu is a target for both Old Firm clubs.

The Hornets are a big price for the drop at 16-1, and it might be worth taking a back-to-lay approach with them.

Longest run without loss: 11
Longest run without win: 8
High – low league position: 1-6
High – low Outlook form figure: 67-36
Key Stat: *Watford won one of their last 16 games.*

Final Outlook Index figure: 796
Clean sheets: 15 (13 league)
Yellow cards: 67 Red cards: 6
Players used: 28
Leading scorer: Darius Henderson 13 (12 league)

Outlook forecast: 15th

Your forecast:

WOLVES

Nickname: Wolves
Colours: Gold and black

Ground: Molineux
Capacity: 29,277

Tel: 0871 880 8442

www.wolves.co.uk

IN SIX seasons from 2001/02 – excluding their year in the top flight – Wolves have either finished in the Play-Offs or one place short of them five times.

They were promoted only once in that spell, but Wolves have a good chance of success this time.

Mick McCarthy is a very capable manager at this level and he has more spending power than when he first took his place in the Molineux dugout.

Last season his team missed out on the Play-Offs only on goal difference and, while Wolves had the fourth-best defensive record in the division last term, scoring goals was their problem.

McCarthy addressed that by signing Sylvain Ebanks-Blake, who got 12 goals in 20 league games, but regular showings from Michael Kightly and Matt Jarvis will be of equal importance.

They were injured for much of 2007/08 and their returns may make a big difference.

Longest run without loss: 6
Longest run without win: 7
High – low league position: 3-17
High – low Outlook form figure: 61-40
Key Stat: *Wolves took one point at home to the five that finished ahead of them.*

Final Outlook Index figure: 807
Clean sheets: 19 (all league)
Yellow cards: 63 Red cards: 0
Players used: 26
Leading scorer: Sylvain Ebanks-Blake 12 (all league)

Outlook forecast: 4th

Your forecast:

BRIGHTON & HOVE ALBION

Nickname: The Seagulls
Colours: Blue and white

Ground: Withdean Stadium
Capacity: 8,850

Tel: 01273 695 400

www.seagulls.co.uk

ANYONE sympathising with Sven-Goran Eriksson this summer should spare a thought for Dean Wilkins.

Albion were regarded by many as relegation fodder last term, yet Wilkins steered them to within a whisker of a Play-Off place.

His reward? Being eased out by the offer of a coaching role – which he turned down – to make way for the return of Micky Adams, who steered Brighton to promotion in 2001 but has had a mixed managerial record since then.

The ingredients are in place for a successful season, with the signing of Colin Hawkins increasing competition at the back and with Nicky Forster keeping the goals flowing. Confirmation of a new stadium being ready by 2010 is also a boost.

However, Wilkins had worked wonders at getting the best out of an inexperienced squad and he may prove a tougher act to follow than expected.

Longest run without loss: 10
Longest run without win: 5
High - low league position: 6-17
High - low Outlook form figure: 61-39
Key Stat: *Brighton came from behind to win or draw ten times.*

Final Outlook Index figure: 746
Clean sheets: 15 (14 league)
Yellow cards: 66 Red cards: 4
Players used: 33
Leading scorer: Nicky Forster 19 (15 league)

Outlook forecast: 12th

Your forecast:

BRISTOL ROVERS

Nickname: The Pirates / The Gas
Colours: Blue and white

Ground: The Memorial Stadium
Capacity: 11,916

Tel: 0117 909 6648

www.bristolrovers.co.uk

ROVERS were just one game away from Wembley last season after their fairytale run to the FA Cup quarter-finals, but reality is likely to hit hard this time.

It's been a summer of upheaval for the Pirates, who had hoped to redevelop the Memorial Stadium while groundsharing with Cheltenham, but were forced to shelve those plans when their preferred developer for the scheme pulled out, laying the blame on the credit crunch.

That may sound like a blessing in disguise as far as their prospects on the pitch are concerned but, while the dire quality of the playing surface upset classier rivals in the cup, it also contributed to the second-worst home record in the league.

Cost-cutting by pulling the reserves out of competitive football and releasing their head of youth development are worrying signs that hint at a downward spiral leading back into League 2.

Longest run without loss: 11
Longest run without win: 11
High - low league position: 7-20
High - low Outlook form figure: 63-34
Key Stat: *Got seven more points against top-half teams than bottom-half sides.*

Final Outlook Index figure: 705
Clean sheets: 15 (12 league)
Yellow cards: 58 Red cards: 2
Players used: 25
Leading scorer: Rickie Lambert 19 (13 league)

Outlook forecast: 22nd

Your forecast:

CARLISLE UNITED

Nickname: Cumbrians / Blues
Colours: Blue, white and red

Ground: Brunton Park
Capacity: 16,981

Tel: 01228 526 237

www.carlisleunited.co.uk

CLUBS of Carlisle's stature don't get too many shots at the big time so you could understand any feelings of gloom around Brunton Park after they blew their chance of promotion in spectacular fashion last season.

With eight games left, Carlisle were the form team in League 1. They were set to challenge for the title and second place looked a formality, but John Ward's side fell apart, winning just one more match against dis-

mal Yeovil and finishing three points off automatic promotion.

And, while they beat Leeds 2-1 in the first leg of their Play-Off semi-final, they let that chance go begging too, losing the return 2-0.

Ward faces an almighty task in raising his troops again and the top half of the table looks a more reaslisic target this time, particularly as their star man, keeper Keiren Westwood, has left for Coventry.

Longest run without loss: 12
Longest run without win: 5
High - low league position: 1-6
High - low Outlook form figure: 66-39
Key Stat: *Carlisle failed to hold on to a lead in ten games.*

Outlook forecast: 11th

Final Outlook Index figure: 749
Clean sheets: 19 (18 league)
Yellow cards: 67 Red cards: 2
Players used: 27
Leading scorer: Danny Graham 17 (14 league)

Your forecast:

CHELTENHAM TOWN

Nickname: The Robins
Colours: Red and white

Ground: Whaddon Road
Capacity: 7,066

Tel: 01242 573558

www.cheltenhamtownfc.premiumtv.co.uk

EVER since their promotion in 2006 Cheltenham have been relegation favourites, and this season is no exception, but their escapology skills should not be underestimated.

Nothing went right for Town early last season, with boss John Ward tempted away by Carlisle at a time when the club was on the way to winning just two of their opening 16 games. However, a tremendous run in the new year took them to safety and the rel-

atively dizzy heights of 19th place.

Despite another blow when the collapse of a proposed groundshare with Bristol Rovers put a hole in the transfer budget, Keith Downing has succeeded in hanging on to several key players – though he has lost top scorer Steven Gillespie to Colchester.

The proceeds are going straight back into the squad and there are better relegation bets than the underrated Robins.

Longest run without loss: 5
Longest run without win: 9
High - low league position: 12-24
High - low Outlook form figure: 59-37
Key Stat: *Eight of their ten home wins were by 1-0 and the other two by 2-1.*

Outlook forecast: 20th

Final Outlook Index figure: 708
Clean sheets: 10 (all league)
Yellow cards: 47 Red cards: 4
Players used: 28
Leading scorer: Steven Gillespie 16 (14 league)

Your forecast:

COLCHESTER UNITED

Nickname: The U's
Colours: Blue and white

Ground: Weston Homes Community Stadium
Capacity: 10,000

Tel: 0871 226 2161

www.cu-fc.com

IT'S a new era for Colchester as they move out of Layer Road, their home for 70 years, and into a new sStadium.

The club would have loved to begin life in their new home in the Championship but that never looked likely last season, as they failed to follow up a strong first campaign in the second tier by finishing 15 points short of safety.

The problems lay at the back, with the U's shipping 86 goals. Geraint Williams made strengthening the defence his priority over the summer with Forest left-back Matt Lockwood the first to arrive but he also spent a club-record fee to get striker Steven Gillespie from Cheltenham.

However, skipper Karl Duguid has departed and Williams faces a struggle to hang on to other key men, goalkeeper Dean Gerken and forward Mark Yeates – Colchester may have rediscovered their true level.

Longest run without loss: 4
Longest run without win: 10
High - low league position: 6-24
High - low Outlook form figure: 55-34
Key Stat: *Had no clean sheet between the end of August and the start of April.*

Outlook forecast: 13th

Final Outlook Index figure: 754
Clean sheets: 2 (both league)
Yellow cards: 57 Red cards: 5
Players used: 29
Leading scorer: Kevin Lisbie 17 (all league)

Your forecast:

CREWE ALEXANDRA

Nickname: The Railwaymen
Colours: Red and white

Ground: Gresty Road
Capacity: 10,107

Tel: 01270 213014

www.crewealex.net

DARIO GRADI'S move from manager to technical director was always going to be tough for Crewe but few predicted just how hard they would find it.

Only Bournemouth's ten-point deduction saved the Railwaymen from the drop and, unless more unlikely salvation comes their way, justice may be done this time.

Crewe survive on their ability to cash in on young talent but, judging by last year's efforts, there aren't many marketable assets in the current squad. However, Steve Holland will be desperate to hold on to 15-goal striker Nicky Maynard, having failed to land Stevenage frontman Steve Morison.

He bought Calvin Zola, but the Congolese striker scored only five goals in 35 games for Tranmere last term, and Holland suffered another blow when key defender Danny Woodards was transfer-listed having refused a contract extension.

Longest run without loss: 6
Longest run without win: 8
High - low league position: 10-21
High - low Outlook form figure: 63-33
Key Stat: *Crewe gained just three points from their games against the top six.*

Outlook forecast: 23rd

Final Outlook Index figure: 710
Clean sheets: 13 (all league)
Yellow cards: 25 Red cards: 1
Players used: 37
Leading scorer: Nicky Maynard 15 (all league)

Your forecast:

HARTLEPOOL UNITED

Nickname: Pools / Monkey Hangers
Colours: White and blue

Ground: Victoria Park
Capacity: 7,691

Tel: 01429 272584

www.hartlepoolunited.co.uk

IF POINTS were awarded for glowing references from rival managers then few clubs would have finished ahead of Hartlepool last season.

Instead, a weak defence meant that Pools often failed to pick up the points their flowing football deserved, while a squad light on numbers led to them tailing off badly at the end of the campaign.

Hartlepool took just five points from their last 27, leaving them down in 15th place.

Manager Danny Wilson has recognised the team's shortcomings and said his priority this summer was to bring in reinforcements at the back, but getting in the right faces was always likely to be difficult for a club of Hartlepool's stature, and business has been slow.

At the other end, in-demand Australian striker Joel Porter should continue to earn rave reviews, but mid-table could be the extent of their ambitions.

Longest run without loss: 3
Longest run without win: 6
High - low league position: 3-17
High - low Outlook form figure: 61-37
Key Stat: *Lost away at all the top seven, conceding two or more in six of those.*

Outlook forecast: 16th

Final Outlook Index figure: 707
Clean sheets: 10 (9 league)
Yellow cards: 56 Red cards: 5
Players used: 28
Leading scorer: Richie Barker 15 (12 league)

Your forecast:

HEREFORD

Nickname: The Bulls
Colours: Black and white

Ground: Edgar Street
Capacity: 8,843

Tel: 08442 761939

www.herefordunited.co.uk

HEREFORD'S resurrection gathered pace last season when they won promotion to League 1 having been in the Conference just two years ago.

However, such a rapid rise is often followed by a fall and Hereford may well have reached the limit of their potential. Survival would be a great achievement, but may prove just out of reach.

It's been a tricky summer for Graham Turner, who identified some much-needed

quality in the transfer market, but has struggled to compete with the financial clout of bigger clubs in the division.

It looks like they will miss out on their number one transfer target, Southend's Gary Hooper, who has also been stalling over a move. That's a massive concern as Hooper scored a crucial 11 goals for the Bulls while on loan last season. Teenage winger Matty Done has signed, but it may take more to save Hereford.

Longest run without loss: 11
Longest run without win: 4
High - low league position: 2-9
High - low Outlook form figure: 69-42
Key Stat: *Won 22 of the 23 league games where they took the lead.*

Outlook forecast: 21st

Final Outlook Index figure: 720
Clean sheets: 24 (19 league)
Yellow cards: 43 Red cards: 1
Players used: 26
Leading scorer: Theo Robinson 16 (13 league)

Your forecast:

HUDDERSFIELD TOWN

Nickname: The Terriers
Colours: Blue and white

Ground: Galpharm Stadium
Capacity: 24,554

Tel: 0870 444 4677

www.htafc.com

SUCCESSIVE mid-table finishes were bitterly disappointing for ambitious Huddersfield, but everything is now in place for a promotion push.

After parting company with Andy Ritchie in April, the club took 14 points from their last 18, including a 1-0 win over Leeds.

Stan Ternent is the man charged with getting the best out of an underachieving squad and he has been busy in the transfer market over the summer.

He signed Blackpool striker Keigan Parker to give the forward line a more potent look, while ex-Scunthorpe midfielder Jim Goodwin has also joined the ranks.

That the Galpham Stadium is almost guaranteed to be a sell-out every match – Huddersfield had sold 16,000 season tickets by June after charging just £100 to mark their centenary – should also work in their favour. The Terriers won't be too far away this time.

Longest run without loss: 6
Longest run without win: 5
High - low league position: 5-18
High - low Outlook form figure: 64-37
Key Stat: *It's 456 minutes since Huddersfield last conceded a goal.*

Outlook forecast: 6th

Final Outlook Index figure: 743
Clean sheets: 18 (16 league)
Yellow cards: 64 Red cards: 7
Players used: 28
Leading scorer: Luke Beckett 12 (8 league)

Your forecast:

LEEDS UNITED

Nickname: United
Colours: White

Ground: Elland Road
Capacity: 40,242

Tel: 0113 367 6000

www.leedsunited.com

HAVING overcome a 15-point deduction to come within 90 minutes of promotion, Leeds went into many books as bankers to put things right this season by going up as champions.

It's unlikely to work out quite as easily as that – even with their points given back they would still have finished second to Swansea.

It's also worth remembering that once their look of invincibility had worn off – Leeds picked up 35 points from the first

39 available – they were far from bulletproof, losing nine times in all.

However, they finished 2007/08 strongly under Gary McAllister and have real quality in the likes of Jermaine Beckford and fast-emerging midfield star Jonny Howson.

They also had the second-best defence in League 1 last term, and, with no club looking capable of doing a Swansea in League 1 this season, Leeds look the most likely winners.

Longest run without loss: 11
Longest run without win: 7
High - low league position: 3-24
High - low Outlook form figure: 66-42
Key Stat: *Leeds scored 17 goals in the last five minutes of league games.*

Outlook forecast: Winners

Final Outlook Index figure: 774
Clean sheets: 24 (20 league)
Yellow cards: 84 Red cards: 4
Players used: 35
Leading scorer: Jermaine Beckford 20 (all league)

Your forecast:

Sponsored by Stan James

LEICESTER CITY

Nickname: The Foxes
Colours: Blue

Ground: The Walkers Stadium
Capacity: 32,500

Tel: 0844 815 6000

www.lcfc.co.uk

LEICESTER became the latest big club to find themselves in the third tier of English football after an astonishingly turbulent year.

Though Sheffield Wednesday, Man City and Forest all struggled to adapt in their first season – only City landed place money – Leicester start from a stronger footing.

Their 52-point total last term is the most that a club has been relegated with since 1996.

A bigger worry is that Milan Mandaric still seems to think rotating managers is the way forward. Ian Holloway – sacked at the end of the season – was the Foxes' fourth boss in six months.

On paper, Nigel Pearson has a strong squad at his disposal but most of his career has been spent as an assistant.

It will be interesting to see how he copes when things don't go his way – and how Mandaric reacts.

Longest run without loss: 6
Longest run without win: 7
High - low league position: 9-22
High - low Outlook form figure: 59-37
Key Stat: *Leicester didn't win two on the trot at any time last season.*

Final Outlook Index figure: 776
Clean sheets: 19 (17 league)
Yellow cards: 73 Red cards: 4
Players used: 39
Leading scorer: Iain Hume 11 (all league)

Outlook forecast: 3rd

Your forecast:

LEYTON ORIENT

Nickname: The O's
Colours: Red

Ground: Brisbane Road
Capacity: 9,271

Tel: 0871 310 1881

www.leytonorient.com

ORIENT find themselves in a familiar position this summer – written off as likely strugglers despite a comfortable mid-table finish last season.

It was the same story last year but Martin Ling's side seemed to have silenced their critics by winning five of their first six matches of 2007/08 and staying in the promotion hunt until the new year.

However, four points from the last eight games had relegation written all over it.

Nonetheless, we recommended a points buy of Orient last year and the feeling persists that they have the quality to hit back and reward the same ploy.

Ling tied down key men Paul Terry and Alton Thelwell to new deals and signed left-back Danny Granville. The partnership between strikers Adam Boyd and Wayne Gray will grow stronger as they gain more playing time together, too.

The O's should easily avoid relegation.

Longest run without loss: 6
Longest run without win: 7
High - low league position: 1-14
High - low Outlook form figure: 60-33
Key Stat: *Picked up just two points from their games against the top five.*

Final Outlook Index figure: 710
Clean sheets: 14 (13 league)
Yellow cards: 50 Red cards: 5
Players used: 22
Leading scorer: Adam Boyd 16 (13 league)

Outlook forecast: 15th

Your forecast:

MILLWALL

Nickname: The Lions
Colours: Blue and white

Ground: The New Den
Capacity: 20,146

Tel: 020 7232 1222

www.millwallfc.co.uk

AMONG the favourites 12 months ago, Millwall wound up enduring a disastrous season, finishing just four points above the drop zone.

It's hard to see them improving much now because, having invested significantly under Nigel Spackman and Willie Donachie, the well seems to have run dry for Kenny Jackett, who has a massive rebuilding job on his hands.

Jackett made an excellent start at the New Den in November, with four wins in his first six games. He has struggled to maintain that form, though, and his fruitless quest for the winning formula was shown by the club's colossal player turnover.

Man City youngster Ashley Grimes could be a good signing, but the Lions have struggled to bring in new faces and have had to downgrade their youth system as a cost-cutting measure, which doesn't bode well.

Longest run without loss: 4
Longest run without win: 7
High - low league position: 13-24
High - low Outlook form figure: 59-34
Key Stat: *Scored more goals against top half sides than against bottom half sides.*

Outlook forecast: 18th

Final Outlook Index figure: 712
Clean sheets: 14 (13 league)
Yellow cards: 77 Red cards: 5
Players used: 43
Leading scorers: Gary Alexander, Jay Simpson 8 (7 & 6 league respectively)

Your forecast:

MILTON KEYNES DONS

Nickname: The Dons
Colours: White

Ground: stadium:mk
Capacity: 32,000

Tel: 01908 622922

www.mkdons.com

THE record of League 2 champions in this division has been good in recent years with Walsall, Carlisle and Doncaster all finishing in the top half in the last four seasons. MK Dons have the quality and the resources to do even better than that.

Paul Ince's move to Blackburn is a major blow, but Roberto Di Matteo can begin his managerial career full of optimism.

The Dons went up with a whopping 97 points last season and added the Johnstone's Paint Trophy to the cabinet as well, knocking out three League 1 clubs along the way – including champions Swansea.

Their team is full of ability, with midfield general Keith Andrews capable of a big season and, if they can add a regular source of goals up front, which seems likely given their transfer budget, a Play-Off place should be within their compass.

Longest run without loss: 14
Longest run without win: 5
High - low league position: 1-12
High - low Outlook form figure: 68-38
Key Stat: *MK Dons won 18 games away from home.*

Outlook forecast: 5th

Final Outlook Index figure: 746
Clean sheets: 23 (20 league)
Yellow cards: 86 Red cards: 4
Players used: 28
Leading scorer: Mark Wright 15 (13 league)

Your forecast:

NORTHAMPTON TOWN

Nickname: The Cobblers
Colours: Claret and white

Ground: Sixfields Stadium
Capacity: 7,653

Tel: 01604 683700

www.ntfc.co.uk

NORTHAMPTON have one of the most progressive profiles in the division and they are expected to finish on the fringes of the Play-Off race again.

Promoted in 2006, the Cobblers struggled initially under John Gorman but his replacement, Stuart Gray, led them to a mid-table finish in 06/07 and steered them to ninth place last term with just three defeats in their last 21 matches.

There is money at Sixfields, with Coven-try winger Liam Davis and Gretna midfielder Abdul Osman early summer buys.

But perhaps the club's biggest coup has been warding off a string of suitors for promising young striker Adebayo Akinfenwa. He scored seven goals in 15 games after signing for Northampton in January and he is joined up front by Leon Constantine from Leeds – he spent most of last term injured but got 26 goals for Port Vale in 2006/07.

Longest run without loss: 6
Longest run without win: 6
High - low league position: 9-22
High - low Outlook form figure: 63-40
Key Stat: *They lost none of the 22 games in which they scored first.*

Final Outlook Index figure: 750
Clean sheets: 12 (11 in league)
Yellow cards: 84 Red cards: 1
Players used: 28
Leading scorer: Poul Hubertz 13 (all league)

Outlook forecast: 8th

Your forecast:

OLDHAM ATHLETIC

Nickname: The Latics
Colours: Blue

Ground: Boundary Park
Capacity: 13,624

Tel: 08712 262235

www.oldhamathletic.co.uk

JOHN SHERIDAN is quietly doing one of the best jobs in the Football League at Oldham and he should steer them to another strong finish.

Operating on a shoestring budget in his two seasons at the helm, Sheridan has opted for experience to see the Latics through to placings of sixth and eighth.

For the first time he has now been given money to spend and the summer has seen a succession of new faces come through the door at Boundary Park.

Man United youngster Kieran Lee is probably the most well-known among them, but Danny Whitaker, the highly sought after ex-Port Vale player, could form a powerful midfield pairing with Latics favourite Mark Allott. Oldham also won the race for in-demand Rotherham striker Chris O'Grady.

With more quality at his disposal Sheridan is destined for another Play-Off push.

Longest run without loss: 11
Longest run without win: 7
High - low league position: 8-24
High - low Outlook form figure: 60-39
Key Stat: *Oldham haven't lost successive league games since September 15th.*

Final Outlook Index figure: 742
Clean sheets: 15 (13 league)
Yellow cards: 64 Red cards: 3
Players used: 32
Leading scorer: Craig Davies 13 (10 league)

Outlook forecast: 7th

Your forecast:

PETERBOROUGH UNITED

Nickname: Posh
Colours: Blue

Ground: London Road
Capacity: 15,152

Tel: 01733 563 947

www.theposh.com

IN EACH of the previous four seasons, the 92 points with which Peterborough finished would have been enough to claim the League 2 title.

MK Dons pipped them to that honour, but it shows the strong platform from which Posh start the new campaign and helps to explain why bookmakers have them in as third-favourites for the title.

The other factor is the burgeoning reputation of young manager Darren Fergu-

son, who is starting to suggest he has inherited his father's skill.

He has taken his side off to Marbella for a gruelling pre-season but, from a value perspective, the Ferguson factor has perhaps been overplayed.

Much of the summer has been spent discussing Aaron McLean's future. His 33 goals were vital to Posh's promotion but the club are asking for big money from any prospective buyers.

Longest run without loss: 16
Longest run without win: 3
High - low league position: 1-15
High - low Outlook form figure: 70-42
Key Stat: *Had best second-half record (26-11-9) with 56 scored after the break.*

Outlook forecast: 9th

Final Outlook Index figure: 728
Clean sheets: 17 (16 league)
Yellow cards: 72 Red cards: 2
Players used: 30
Leading scorer: Aaron McLean 33 (29 league)

Your forecast:

SCUNTHORPE UNITED

Nickname: The Iron
Colours: Claret and blue

Ground: Glanford Park
Capacity: 9,088

Tel: 0871 2211899

www.scunthorpe-united.co.uk

WITH two promotions in three years followed by immediate relegation, Scunthorpe start the season in a fresh division yet again.

Southend, who had a similar background, finished sixth in League 1 last year, but Scunny will struggle to emulate that and may finish outside the Play-Off places.

Nigel Adkins' side were well short of safety in May, and seven points from their last three games still didn't bring them close.

They also face life without top scorer Martin Paterson, who has earned a £1m move to Burnley, leaving them looking for a striker again after losing Billy Sharp the previous summer.

That said, several of the squad who won this division in 2006/07 are still at Glanford Park, and Morecambe winger Garry Thompson adds to their attacking strength.

A decent top-half finish remains within their capabilities.

Longest run without loss: 4
Longest run without win: 11
High - low league position: 4-24
High - low Outlook form figure: 53-34
Key Stat: *Scunny scored only six times in the final 20 minutes of all games.*

Outlook forecast: 10th

Final Outlook Index figure: 761
Clean sheets: 10 (all league)
Yellow cards: 61 Red cards: 10
Players used: 29
Leading scorer: Martin Paterson 14 (13 league)

Your forecast:

Sponsored by Stan James

SOUTHEND UNITED

Nickname: The Shrimpers
Colours: Blue

Ground: Roots Hall
Capacity: 12,306

Tel: 01702 304050

www.southendunited.co.uk

SOUTHEND'S season finished on a real low when they were humbled 5-1 by Doncaster in the Play-Offs but their form had been strong for some time before that and they look the each-way value for the title.

The Shrimpers looked set for mid-table in January, but a run of 11 wins in 17 matches – just one defeat – booked sixth place and that form carries more clout than a single game against an inspired Doncaster.

Manager Steve Tilson finally replaced Freddy Eastwood with the signing of Lee Barnard – he was a goal machine for Tottenham reserves, and scored nine in 18 games after joining Southend.

Barnard caps a strong attacking unit with Alan McCormack and Nick Bailey scoring 17 league goals between them from central midfield last season, while behind them, Peter Clarke is one of the top defenders at this level.

Longest run without loss: 13
Longest run without win: 5
High - low league position: 3-20
High - low Outlook form figure: 62-43
Key Stat: *Southend didn't concede more than one goal in their last 15 games.*

Final Outlook Index figure: 761
Clean sheets: 16 (12 league)
Yellow cards: 71 Red cards: 7
Players used: 32
Leading scorer: Nick Bailey 12 (9 league)

Outlook forecast: Runners-up

Your forecast:

STOCKPORT COUNTY

Nickname: The Hatters
Colours: Blue

Ground: Edgeley Park
Capacity: 10,799

Tel: 0161 286 8888

www.stockportcounty.com

STOCKPORT are as short as 7-4 for the drop this season, but they are a young side full of promise and can prove the layers wrong.

County finished last year on a roll, picking up 55 points from their last 24 matches at an average of 2.29 per game – a rate good enough to romp to the title over the whole season – before beating Wycombe and Rochdale in the Play-Offs.

Jim Gannon has a very young squad at his disposal, with the average age of their Wembley team just 21.

Nine squad players were allowed to leave in June, but the club's outstanding youth system should see them through – the way in which striker Liam Dickinson (now at Derby) filled the void left by Anthony Elding's exit is certainly a good sign for the future.

Teenage midfielder Tommy Rowe may be the next one destined for bigger things.

Longest run without loss: 10
Longest run without win: 6
High - low league position: 4-17
High - low Outlook form figure: 65-37
Key Stat: *Came back to win or draw ten league games in which they fell behind.*

Final Outlook Index figure: 718
Clean sheets: 21 (17 league)
Yellow cards: 53 Red cards: 3
Players used: 35
Leading scorer: Liam Dickinson 21 (19 league)

Outlook forecast: 17th

Your forecast:

SWINDON TOWN

Nickname: The Robins
Colours: Red and white

Ground: County Ground
Capacity: 15,728

Tel: 0871 4236433

www.swindontownfc.co.uk

IN EACH of the last three League 1 seasons a club has made the top four in their second year after promotion, and Swindon look likely to build on a strong first campaign back in the division.

The Robins acquitted themselves well to finish just outside the top half last year, and the future looks bright after their January takeover by local businessman Andrew Fitton.

Fitton is backing manager Maurice Malpas – a January appointment – in the transfer market with Swansea's Kevin Amankwaah their first signing and Wolves defender Charlie Mulgrew an ambitious target.

The Robins took 29 points from 22 games under Malpas, compared with 32 from the previous 24, and it's never easy to come in halfway through a season. Given time to make his mark the Scot can guide Swindon to a Play-Off spot.

Longest run without loss: 11
Longest run without win: 5
High - low league position: 6-17
High - low Outlook form figure: 64-40
Key Stat: *Swindon failed to hold on to a lead in 11 league games.*

Outlook forecast: 4th

Final Outlook Index figure: 726
Clean sheets: 10 (all league)
Yellow cards: 70 Red cards: 8
Players used: 32
Leading scorer: Simon Cox 15 (14 league)

Your forecast:

TRANMERE ROVERS

Nickname: Rovers
Colours: White

Ground: Prenton Park
Capacity: 16,789

Tel: 0870 460 3333

www.tranmererovers.co.uk

RONNIE MOORE has steered Tranmere to a top-half finish in each of his two seasons at the helm and has high hopes of pushing into a Play-Off spot this time. However, Rovers seem more likely to head the other way.

The top six looked achievable in February after they beat Leeds 2-0 for their fourth win in succession but, after that, their challenge petered out as five wins in their final 16 games saw them slip back down the standings.

Once again Tranmere used among the fewest players of any club in League 1, and that looked a key factor in their weak finish – as Moore doesn't have the budget to bring in lots of new faces, the same problem may hold them back again.

The first team – spearheaded by Chris Greenacre – is strong however, and if they can steer clear of injuries Rovers should win enough games to comfortably reach mid-table.

Longest run without loss: 8
Longest run without win: 5
High - low league position: 1-12
High - low Outlook form figure: 64-36
Key Stat: *Rovers won only four of their last 16 games.*

Outlook forecast: 14th

Final Outlook Index figure: 724
Clean sheets: 17 (16 league)
Yellow cards: 70 Red cards: 7
Players used: 24
Leading scorer: Chris Greenacre 14 (11 league)

Your forecast:

WALSALL

Nickname: The Saddlers
Colours: Red and white

Ground: Bescot Stadium
Capacity: 11,300

Tel: 0871 2210442

www.saddlers.co.uk

A TOP-HALF finish in their first season in League 1 should have been a rock-solid platform for Walsall to launch a concerted promotion push this time, but their hopes of progress were rocked in April by the resignation of highly rated Richard Money.

He had been frustrated by the club's eagerness to cash in on Danny Fox and Scott Dann in the January transfer window, and Walsall's season fell apart after the pair left, with nine points from their last 12 matches seeing them slide out of the Play-Off spots.

The Walsall board opted for continuity by replacing Money with his former assistant Jimmy Mullen, but the new man spent the summer struggling to get new players in.

The Saddlers released 11 players at the end of the season and it will be an uphill struggle for Mullen to rebuild the side and get them ready for the new season.

Longest run without loss: 18
Longest run without win: 7
High - low league position: 4-24
High - low Outlook form figure: 61-37
Key Stat: *Walsall won only once at home against the top nine.*

Final Outlook Index figure: 726
Clean sheets: 19 (16 league)
Yellow cards: 69 Red cards: 3
Players used: 31
Leading scorer: Tommy Mooney 12 (11 league)

Outlook forecast: 19th

Your forecast:

YEOVIL TOWN

Nickname: The Glovers
Colours: Green and white

Ground: Huish Park
Capacity: 9,978

Tel: 01935 423662

www.ytfc.net

REGULAR League 1 viewers will have seen enough of Yeovil to last them a lifetime, but they may not have to endure the Glovers for much longer.

Yeovil's pitiful return of just 38 goals last season saw them edge dangerously close to relegation, with only a solid defence keeping them afloat. It's not just the ageing forward line of Lloyd Owusu and Marcus Stewart that must take the blame either – they were forced to feed on scraps.

Since the turn of the year, Yeovil's form had relegation written all over it, as they finished with a record of 4-5-14 for the second half of the campaign.

It seems as though Russell Slade's negative brand of football – built around eking out, and clinging onto, narrow leads – may well have caught up with them.

Glovers fans had already turned on Slade last season and the protests could build as they head for the drop.

Longest run without loss: 5
Longest run without win: 8
High - low league position: 4-18
High - low Outlook form figure: 60-37
Key Stat: *Their second half of the season record was 4-5-14.*

Final Outlook Index figure: 704
Clean sheets: 10 (8 league)
Yellow cards: 75 Red cards: 6
Players used: 40
Leading scorer: Lloyd Owusu 11 (9 league)

Outlook forecast: 24th

Your forecast:

ACCRINGTON STANLEY

Nickname: Stanley
Colours: Red, white and black

Ground: The Fraser Eagle Stadium
Capacity: 5,057

Tel: 01254 356 950

www.accringtonstanley.co.uk

THE FAMOUS name of Accrington Stanley has been dragged through the mud during an FA probe into allegations of unusual betting patterns prior to the last game of last season.

The investigation centres on betting being suspended in the build-up to Stanley's 2-0 home defeat to Bury after a flood of money for an away win and manager John Coleman has angrily branded match-fixing suggestions as "rubbish" and fervently defended the tarnished name of the club.

It's been a tough time for Accy and the loss of a shirt sponsorship deal gives the cash-strapped club more cause for concern.

Despite culling 11 players, the budget is as tight as ever and it will take all of Coleman's nous to keep them afloat.

Stanley's sieve-like defence has shipped 164 goals in the last two seasons, so over 2.5 goals is always a runner.

Longest run without loss: 3
Longest run without win: 6
High – low league position: 10-24
High – low Outlook form figure: 59-28
Key Stat: *Stanley took one point from 36 against the top six, conceding 32 goals.*

Final Outlook Index figure: 640
Clean sheets: 8 (all league)
Yellow cards: 76 Red cards: 5
Players used: 35
Leading scorer: Paul Mullin 13 (12 league)

Outlook forecast: 22nd

Your forecast:

ALDERSHOT TOWN

Nickname: The Shots
Colours: Red and blue

Ground: EBB Stadium
Capacity: 7,500

Tel: 01252 320 211

www.theshots.co.uk

AUGUST 9 will be an emotional day for all connected with Aldershot.

The first fixture back in the league will signal the rebirth of the club after they folded and were dumped into the Isthmian league in 1992.

Ironically, Aldershot's opening fixture is away to Accrington Stanley, another club that would not die, and, after charging to the Conference title, there's no reason why they shouldn't make their presence felt.

Manager Gary Waddock had a dream first year in charge at The Rec, winning 39 games out of 60, and he's likely to have some cash available after Joel Grant's £130,000 move to Crewe.

Woking player of the season Marvin Morgan has been added to a wealth of attacking options and Nikki Bull, who's gone back on his decision to leave, has the potential to be one of the section's top goalkeepers.

Longest run without loss: 18
Longest run without win: 4
High – low league position: 1-10
High – low Outlook form figure: 68-47
Key Stat: *The Shots won all 26 league games in which they took the lead.*

Final Outlook Index figure: 693
Clean sheets: 16 (14 league)
Yellow cards: 72 Red cards: 6
Players used: 24
Leading scorer: John Grant 28 (23 league)

Outlook forecast: 15th

Your forecast:

BARNET

Nickname: The Bees
Colours: Amber and black

Ground: Underhill Stadium
Capacity: 5,560

Tel: 020 8441 6932

www.barnetfc.com

THERE aren't too many lower league scouting networks better than Barnet's.

Time and time again in recent years they've gambled on rough diamonds and turned them into gems, banking a tidy profit.

The latest is Jason Puncheon, who's been sold to Plymouth for £250,000 and follows the likes of Simon King, Nicky Bailey, Dean Sinclair and Liam Hatch by moving up the league ladder in the last year or so.

With manager Paul Fairclough's knowledge of the non-league scene, cheap replacements have been brought in with no adverse effects.

The likes of Albert Adomah and Cliff Akurang, recruited from Harrow and Histon respectively, should fill the void left by Puncheon – if they stick around.

Midfielder Neal Bishop and 15-goal Adam Birchall are staying and the Bees look set for a comfortable campaign.

Longest run without loss: 7
Longest run without win: 5
High – low league position: 5-21
High – low Outlook form figure: 63-35
Key Stat: *Only 15 of their 53 league goals came before the break.*
Outlook forecast: 13th

Final Outlook Index figure: 676
Clean sheets: 12 (11 league)
Yellow cards: 63 Red cards: 10
Players used: 27
Leading scorer: Adam Birchall 15 (11 league)
Your forecast:

BOURNEMOUTH

Nickname: The Cherries
Colours: Red and black

Ground: The Fitness First Stadium
Capacity: 10,700

Tel: 01202 726300

www.afcb.co.uk

LAST season a ten-point penalty ultimately cost the Cherries their League 1 place and the expected 15-point penalty for this term could seriously undermine their efforts to bounce back straight away.

Although a consortium is waiting in the wings to take over, Bournemouth's administrator believes the club will suffer the same fate as Leeds for breaking insolvency rules.

This would be a cruel blow for manag-

er Kevin Bond, particularly as his side finished as the form team in the country.

A final-day draw at Carlisle sealed relegation but, prior to that, Bond's side made the great escape possible by winning six on the spin.

The core of last season's squad have signed new deals, although promising striker Sam Vokes has left for Wolves. Jo Kuffour – five goals in his last seven games – will be a handful at this level if the Cherries hang onto him.

Longest run without loss: 7
Longest run without win: 5
High – low league position: 11-24
High – low Outlook form figure: 66-33
Key Stat: *The Cherries were 2-2-0 away at the top four in League 1.*
Outlook forecast: 4th

Final Outlook Index figure: 737
Clean sheets: 8 (all league)
Yellow cards: 61 Red cards: 3
Players used: 36
Leading scorer: Jo Kuffour 13 (12 league)
Your forecast:

BRADFORD CITY

Nickname: The Bantams
Colours: Claret and amber

Ground: Valley Parade
Capacity: 25,136

Tel: 01274 773 355

www.bradfordcityfc.co.uk

NOW MK Dons and Peterborough have climbed out of the league, Bradford may be the biggest club left in League 2.

Stuart McCall's first full season in charge was always going to be about rebuilding and a shaky start put paid to any lofty ambitions.

But, thanks to an innovative season-ticket scheme, crowds at Valley Parade averaged 13,692, the highest in the division.

Finances are stable with the club expected to break even for the first time since their Premier League days eight years ago and, at this level, Bradford have plenty of clout when it comes to attracting new players.

Links with the likes of Darren Moore and Luke Beckett show the club's ambition and the signings made so far are encouraging.

Everything is in place for City to improve on their tenth-place finish, if McCall can harness the fans' expectations.

Longest run without loss: 6
Longest run without win: 8
High - low league position: 7-21
High - low Outlook form figure: 63-34
Key Stat: *Away at bottom-half teams, they lost just once.*

Outlook forecast: Runnners-up

Final Outlook Index figure: 680
Clean sheets: 10 (9 league)
Yellow cards: 52 Red cards: 4
Players used: 32
Leading scorer: Peter Thorne 15 (14 league)

Your forecast:

BRENTFORD

Nickname: The Bees
Colours: Red, white and black

Ground: Griffin Park
Capacity: 12,763

Tel: 0845 3456 442

www.brentfordfc.co.uk

ANDY SCOTT had been threatening a clearout since the day he took full control at Griffin Park and will use the summer to transform his squad.

Scott, who stepped up to the plate following Terry Butcher's sacking in December, emphasised his lack of trust in the players he inherited by dabbling in the loan market more often than an out-of-pocket gambler.

Both Scott and his assistant Terry Bulli-vant have signed long contracts after learning of the club's budget and now they've cleared out the dead wood, the pressure is on to show they can recruit the right players.

Marcus Bean and Adam Newton look the pick of the new arrivals so far but there have been plenty of comings and goings and the players will need time to gel.

Regardless of who arrives, opposing Brentford early on could be a wise move.

Longest run without loss: 9
Longest run without win: 7
High – low league position: 5-19
High – low Outlook form figure: 62-27
Key Stat: *Home defeats to the top seven, conceding two or more each time.*

Outlook forecast: 14th

Final Outlook Index figure: 664
Clean sheets: 7 (all league)
Yellow cards: 55 Red cards: 5
Players used: 35
Leading scorer: Kevin Poole 14 (all league)

Your forecast:

BURY

Nickname: The Shakers
Colours: White and blue

Ground: Gigg Lane
Capacity: 11,669

Tel: 0161 764 4881

www.buryfc.co.uk

BURY are indebted to new boss Alan Knill, who took over from Chris Casper in February and steered the club to a 13th-place finish.

Playing out time was an unexpected luxury for Bury – they were staring down the relegation barrel for much of the season – but 26 points out of a possible 36 in the last two months of the season shows the transformation under Knill.

Persuading keeper Wayne Brown, who kept 21 clean sheets during Hereford's promotion campaign, to stay down in League 2 is a real coup.

There's plenty of optimism in the Gigg Lane air but Bury's progress seems to have slipped off the bookies' radar – they are out at 40-1 for the title in places.

Rather than steam in at fancy prices though, a shrewder way to keep Bury onside would be a points buy or an each-way nibble on the handicaps.

Longest run without loss: 9
Longest run without win: 9
High – low league position: 10-23
High – low Outlook form figure: 65-31
Key Stat: *Got same number of wins from the top and bottom halves of League 2.*
Outlook forecast: 7th

Final Outlook Index figure: 678
Clean sheets: 9 (8 league)
Yellow cards: 60 Red cards: 3
Players used: 28
Leading scorer: Andy Bishop 25 (19 league)
Your forecast:

CHESTER CITY

Nickname: The Blues / City
Colours: Blue and white

Ground: Deva Stadium
Capacity: 5,367

Tel: 01244 371376

www.chestercityfc.net

IT WAS a real season of two halves at the Deva. Under Bobby Williamson the Blues started like a house on fire and were second behind champions MK Dons in early November.

In last year's annual, we advised a back-to-lay strategy on Chester and this was the time to lock in a profit because the wheels came off big time after Christmas.

Ongoing wage problems came to a head, morale nose-dived and, in the end, it was left to former head of youth Simon Davies to assure safety in the penultimate game.

Although Davies has signed a two-year-contract, the wage problem resurfaced in June and the Football League slapped a transfer embargo on the club.

The ban has since been lifted and new players have been signed, but two wins from Boxing Day onwards is shoddy form and Chester look like banker material for relegation.

Longest run without loss: 6
Longest run without win: 12
High – low league position: 2-22
High – low Outlook form figure: 58-34
Key Stat: *Chester lost at home to all the others in the bottom four.*
Outlook forecast: 24th

Final Outlook Index figure: 632
Clean sheets: 9 (8 league)
Yellow cards: 71 Red cards: 4
Players used: 28
Leading scorer: Kevin Ellison 11 (all league)
Your forecast:

CHESTERFIELD

Nickname: Spireites
Colours: Blue and white

Ground: Recreation Ground
Capacity: 8,502

Tel: 01246 209765

www.chesterfield-fc.co.uk

PLANS are in the pipeline that will see Saltergate become the latest ground packed with charm and character consigned to the history books.

The club have got permission for a 10,000 capacity stadium on a site in Whittington Moor and work could start in early 2009.

This could be the last full season playing in the shadow of the crooked spire and it would be the ideal time to get out of the division, particularly as relocations sometimes have an adverse effect on form.

Last term ended disappointingly and questions were asked of manager Lee Richardson after the club frittered away a Play-Off place.

Richardson has added Robert Page and Kevin Austin to his defensive ranks, but captain Peter Leven has joined MK Dons and, up front, keeping hold of Jack Lester and Jamie Ward will be as crucial as any new additions.

Longest run without loss: 7
Longest run without win: 6
High - low league position: 2-10
High - low Outlook form figure: 61-41
Key Stat: *They conceded nine in the five minutes before the interval.*

Outlook forecast: 6th

Final Outlook Index figure: 682
Clean sheets: 11 (all league)
Yellow cards: 79 Red cards: 1
Players used: 32
Leading scorer: Jack Lester 27 (25 league)

Your forecast:

DAGENHAM & REDBRIDGE

Nickname: Daggers
Colours: Red and white

Ground: LB of Barking & Dagenham Stadium
Capacity: 6,000

Tel: 020 8592 1549

www.daggers.co.uk

IN THE current climate of non-league clubs with professional playing squads, it comes as a surprise to know there was a semi-pro player at a Football League club last season.

The man in question was Daggers part-timer Dave Rainford, who combined his playing duties with teaching at a local school.

The lure of a senior teaching post has proved too much and he has hung up his full-time boots to join Chelmsford.

Let's hope his pupils appreciate him because his goals from the heart of midfield will be missed and John Still has more problems in the engine room after Glen Southam voiced his desire to move on as well.

Championship clubs are sniffing around defender Scott Griffiths and his exit would be another blow but, in Ben Strevens and Paul Benson, injured for most of last season, they have the firepower to beat the drop – just.

Longest run without loss: 5
Longest run without win: 9
High - low league position: 12-24
High - low Outlook form figure: 71-35
Key Stat: *Won only two homes against the top 14, but beat five of them away.*

Outlook forecast: 21st

Final Outlook Index figure: 659
Clean sheets: 13 (11 league)
Yellow cards: 38 Red cards: 3
Players used: 28
Leading scorer: Ben Strevens 20 (15 league)

Your forecast:

DARLINGTON

Nickname: The Quakers
Colours: Black and white

Ground: The Darlington Arena
Capacity: 25,000

Tel: 01325 387000

www.darlington-fc.net

DARLO can count themselves unfortunate to still be in this division after a spate of injuries to their strikers crippled their promotion challenge.

The Quakers went into the second leg of the Play-Offs with midfielder Michael Cummins pushed into an emergency striker role and, despite matching opponents Rochdale for most of the tie, they finally went out on penalties.

For many, Dave Penney is the best man-ager in the section and he has wielded the axe this summer – Clarke Keltie and Julian Joachim are two of nine to have been shown the door recently.

Rumours of a cut in the playing budget is a worry, as are dwindling crowds, but Penney plays the transfer market shrewdly.

With moneybags MK Dons and Peterborough out of the section, a repeat of last season's form should see them as prime movers in the race for the title.

Longest run without loss: 5
Longest run without win: 8
High – low league position: 1-7
High – low Outlook form figure: 69-40
***Key Stat:** Darlo had the best first-half record (24-14-8) in the division.*

Outlook forecast: Winners

Final Outlook Index figure: 689
Clean sheets: 24 (all league)
Yellow cards: 90 Red cards: 6
Players used: 40
Leading scorer: Tommy Wright 15 (13 league)

Your forecast:

EXETER CITY

Nickname: The Grecians
Colours: Black and white

Ground: St James Park
Capacity: 9,036

Tel: 0871 855 1904

www.exetercityfc.co.uk

AFTER five years in the wilderness and a close shave with extinction, Exeter are back in the Football League.

The Grecians deserve tremendous credit for bouncing back from the disappointment of a Play-Off final defeat in 2006/07 to beat Cambridge 1-0 at Wembley last season, and the fans who took over running the club's finances five years ago will go into the new season full of optimism after the joys of promotion.

Cravat-wearing manager Paul Tisdale has persuaded England 'C' international Dean Moxey to stay and has done his pre-season shopping early, snapping up a trio of new signings, including York captain Emmanuel Panther.

No newly-promoted League 2 team has gone straight back down in the last six years, and with the current feel-good factor at St James Park, Exeter should be able to stay out of trouble.

Longest run without loss: 10
Longest run without win: 4
High – low league position: 1-11
High – low Outlook form figure: 66-43
***Key Stat:** Five Exeter players scored ten or more goals last term.*

Outlook forecast: 20th

Final Outlook Index figure: 680
Clean sheets: 16 (14 league)
Yellow cards: 59 Red cards: 2
Players used: 22
Leading scorer: Richard Logan 19 (18 league)

Your forecast:

GILLINGHAM

Nickname: The Gills
Colours: Blue and white

Ground: Priestfield Stadium
Capacity: 11,582

Tel: 01634 300000

www.gillinghamfootballclub.co.uk

THE GILLS need to stop a rot going back to the turn of the year if they are going to make an impact in League 2.

Since the 3-0 mauling of Notts Forest in the last game of 2007, the Kent outfit have won four league games out of 24 and conceded 36 goals.

It's up to Mark Stimson to lift the general malaise around Priestfield Stadium but, to be fair to the manager – who joined the club last November after three consecutive FA Trophy wins in charge of Grays and Stevenage – he showed the players he means business by hauling them in for twice-weekly training sessions even before pre-season started in July.

A fast start could be crucial if the manager does not want the fans to turn against him.

And, if Stimson can add a prolific striker to the squad, the Gills should be competing at the business end of the table.

Longest run without loss: 5
Longest run without win: 7
High – low league position: 16-23
High – low Outlook form figure: 58-34
Key Stat: *Won five after falling behind, but lost five after taking the lead.*

Final Outlook Index figure: 700
Clean sheets: 8 (all league)
Yellow cards: 69 Red cards: 9
Players used: 40
Leading scorer: Chris Dickson 11 (7 league)

Outlook forecast: 5th

Your forecast:

GRIMSBY TOWN

Nickname: The Mariners
Colours: Black and white

Ground: Blundell Park
Capacity: 9,106

Tel: 01472 605050

www.grimsby-townfc.premiumtv.co.uk

THE MARINERS always have their each-way supporters and in a division as wide open as this they are likely to attract the value-seekers once again.

A word of caution though – they finished the most out-of-sorts team in the country with an *Outlook Index* form rating of -1.83%.

Maybe the effects of the Johnstone's Paint Trophy final defeat to MK Dons took its toll but Alan Buckley needs to freshen up the playing staff.

Defenders Robbie Stockdale, Richard Hope and Matt Heywood have joined the club and former striker Michael Boulding, who's on every League 2 shopping list after his 25 goals for relegated Mansfield last term, has been linked with a return.

Whether Boulding arrives or not, getting goals out of talented striker Danny North could be the difference between another mediocre season and a top-ten finish.

Longest run without loss: 11
Longest run without win: 11
High – low league position: 9-23
High – low Outlook form figure: 65-33
Key Stat: *They lost nine of their last 11 games, including the final seven.*

Final Outlook Index figure: 654
Clean sheets: 13 (10 league)
Yellow cards: 54 Red cards: 6
Players used: 25
Leading scorer: Danny North 10 (9 league)

Outlook forecast: 18th

Your forecast:

LINCOLN CITY

Nickname: The Imps
Colours: Red, white and black

Ground: Sincil Bank
Capacity: 10,127

Tel: 0870 899 2005

www.redimps.com

THE POOR health of manager Peter Jackson put City's season of struggle into some sort of perspective.

After a poor start that left the club bottom of the pile, John Schofield was sacked in October and Jackson came in to turn the tide.

Jackson was instantly hailed as the club's saviour but, in February, he was diagnosed with throat cancer.

Assistant boss Iffy Onuora took charge, steering the club to a comfortable 15th place. The pair are back in tandem now Jackson has received the all-clear and, as we went to press, they were actively looking to bolster the squad.

Key areas need reinforcing, as Lincoln shipped 77 league goals last term and striker Jamie Forrester has joined Notts County.

The Imps are difficult to weigh up but there are more likely candidates for the Play-Offs and a repeat of last term is on the cards.

Longest run without loss: 5
Longest run without win: 15
High – low league position: 4-24
High – low Outlook form figure: 67-34
Key Stat: *From Aug 25 to Jan 5, they went 24 games without a clean sheet.*

Final Outlook Index figure: 677
Clean sheets: 6 (all league)
Yellow cards: 47 Red cards: 8
Players used: 29
Leading scorer: Jamie Forrester 14 (12 league)

Outlook forecast: 16th

Your forecast:

LUTON TOWN

Nickname: The Hatters
Colours: White and black

Ground: Kenilworth Road
Capacity: 10,191

Tel: 01582 411622

www.lutontown.co.uk

JUST when Hatters fans thought things couldn't get any worse, they face the harsh reality of League 2 with a points deduction after the FA found the club guilty of misconduct.

Luton already have a ten-point deduction for charges relating to bung allegations but things could get 15 points worse if they are also found guilty of breaking rules on leaving administration.

It's feasible that they could wipe out ten points with a good early run, but 25 points would be a mountain to climb and would leave the Hatters in big trouble.

The Nick Owen-led LTFC2020 takeover consortium is fighting the crisis club's cause but these issues take time to resolve and will not have helped Mick Harford's pre-season plans.

With the current squad a mid-table finish is attainable – but only without a second points penalty.

Longest run without loss: 7
Longest run without win: 15
High – low league position: 4-24
High – low Outlook form figure: 60-32
Key Stat: *Luton never came from behind to win last season.*

Final Outlook Index figure: 686
Clean sheets: 12 (8 league)
Yellow cards: 64 Red cards: 6
Players used: 33
Leading scorer: Paul Furlong 12 (8 league) and Matthew Spring (9 league)

Outlook forecast: 19th

Your forecast:

MACCLESFIELD TOWN

Nickname: The Silkmen
Colours: Blue

Ground: Moss Rose
Capacity: 6,335

Tel: 01625 264686

www.mtfc.co.uk

MACC must be on any ante-post punter's relegation shortlist after loitering in the nether regions of League 2 for the past three seasons.

However, Town fans could argue that last season was a slight improvement and, in former Lincoln and Peterborough boss Keith Alexander, they have a man with a proven track record at this level.

Alexander's methods are old school – he's an advocate of the dated 5-3-2 formation – but his substance-over-style approach saved the Silkmen from the drop.

A way to approach them from a punting perspective would be to back under 2.5 goals in their games, particularly with Alexander at the helm – this bet copped in nine of his 12 games in charge.

Quotes of 5-1 for Macc to be relegated are tempting, and if Luton avoid a 25-point penalty, the Cheshire club could find themselves in real danger.

Longest run without loss: 4
Longest run without win: 9
High – low league position: 10-22
High – low Outlook form figure: 63-30
Key Stat: *In only four league games were they winning at half time.*

Outlook forecast: 23rd

Final Outlook Index figure: 655
Clean sheets: 12 (11 league)
Yellow cards: 91 Red cards: 1
Players used: 36
Leading scorer: Francis Green 11 (all league)

Your forecast:

MORECAMBE

Nickname: The Shrimps
Colours: Red and white

Ground: Christie Park
Capacity: 6,400

Tel: 01524 411797

www.morecambefc.com

A MID-TABLE finish and a couple of good cup runs meant Morecambe's debut season in the Football League was a resounding success.

With two wins in the last 14 games they tailed off badly but, back at the start of the year, manager Sammy McIlroy said: "I would have snapped people's hands off if I'd been awarded 50 points before the end of February."

Fresh blood has arrived ahead of the new season and, off the pitch, the club's commercial activities have moved up a notch with a new shirt sponsor and a four-year kit deal with Puma.

Plans for a move away from the antiquated Christie Park may have been put on hold but the Shrimps should continue to move forward.

Keep an eye out for defender Jim Bentley in the goalscorer markets as he can be a real menace from set-pieces.

Longest run without loss: 5
Longest run without win: 6
High – low league position: 6-17
High – low Outlook form figure: 67-37
Key Stat: *Five cup wins aginst teams from a higher division, four away.*

Outlook forecast: 11th

Final Outlook Index figure: 659
Clean sheets: 10 (7 league)
Yellow cards: 58 Red cards: 2
Players used: 27
Leading scorer: Carl Baker, Matt Blinkhorn 11 (both 10 league)

Your forecast:

NOTTS COUNTY

Nickname: The Magpies
Colours: Black and white

Ground: Meadow Lane
Capacity: 20,300

Tel: 0115 9529000

www.nottscountyfc.co.uk

WHILE the red half of Nottingham were gearing up for life in the Championship, the black and white half were fearing a drop to the Conference.

In the end though, the Magpies made sure of their league status with a game to spare.

Yet another new regime was installed at Meadow Lane last October when former player Ian McParland became the fifth manager in four years.

County are relaunching their Centre of Excellence – axed two years ago – but, in the short-term, the manager must rely on experience.

Veteran keeper Russell Hoult will add to an already miserly defence and, to arrest a chronic lack of firepower, 33-year-old poacher Jamie Forrester has signed from Lincoln. Despite Forrester's guile, it's hard to get too excited about their prospects – the Magpies were the division's lowest scorers last term.

Longest run without loss: 5
Longest run without win: 7
High – low league position: 11-22
High – low Outlook form figure: 60-36
Key Stat: *The worst League 2 attack – just two players scored more than three.*

Final Outlook Index figure: 660
Clean sheets: 15 (14 league)
Yellow cards: 56 Red cards: 2
Players used: 30
Leading scorer: Richard Butcher 12 (all league)

Outlook forecast: 17th

Your forecast:

PORT VALE

Nickname: The Valiants
Colours: White and black

Ground: Vale Park
Capacity: 22,356

Tel: 01782 655800

www.port-vale.co.uk

FOOTBALL, like any other industry, is feeling the squeeze of the credit crunch and it's refreshing to see a small club like Port Vale reacting in a positive way.

A discounted season-ticket scheme, similar to Bradford's, saw over 5,000 season tickets sold before the end of May.

That's good going for the relegated side, particularly when you consider their average attendance in League 1 last term was 4,417.

There will be plenty of new faces at Vale Park as Lee Sinnott rebuilds a squad shorn of over a dozen players.

The club have been busy in the transfer market but most crucial is having a fully-fit Luke Rodgers leading the attack.

Last term the hitman scored 12 goals in a struggling side and he will be potent at this level, as long as he recovers from a hernia operation that's likely to see him miss the start of the season.

Longest run without loss: 4
Longest run without win: 10
High – low league position: 15-24
High – low Outlook form figure: 66-34
Key Stat: *From mid-October, conceded three or more in 30% of league games.*

Final Outlook Index figure: 694
Clean sheets: 7 (6 league)
Yellow cards: 65 Red cards: 5
Players used: 39
Leading scorer: Luke Rodgers 12 (9 league)

Outlook forecast: 10th

Your forecast:

ROCHDALE

Nickname: The Dale
Colours: Blue and black

Ground: Spotland Stadium
Capacity: 10,249

Tel: 0870 822 1907

www.rochdaleafc.co.uk

ROCHDALE looked destined for promotion as they set off on a first trip to Wembley for the League 2 Play-Off final in their centenary year but local rivals Stockport had not read the script.

Dale have been resident in the basement division since relegation from the old Division Three in 1973/74 but, after their 3-2 reverse in the Play-Off final, colourful gaffer Keith Hill signalled his intention to escape the division in 2008/09.

Hill's record at Spotland stands up to close scrutiny and his side not only ended the season with 24 points from their last ten games, but they also finished with the best away record in the section.

Dale are not the most fashionable club and may struggle to compete in the transfer market, but if Hill can keep the squad together, there's no reason why they cannot gear up for another crack at promotion.

Longest run without loss: 10
Longest run without win: 5
High – low league position: 4-23
High – low Outlook form figure: 66-37
Key Stat: *Dale won or drew half of the 20 games in which they fell behind.*

Outlook forecast: 3rd

Final Outlook Index figure: 712
Clean sheets: 12 (all league)
Yellow cards: 72 Red cards: 5
Players used: 33
Leading scorer: Adam Le Fondre 16 (15 league)

Your forecast:

ROTHERHAM UNITED

Nickname: The Millers
Colours: Red and white

Ground: Don Valley Stadium
Capacity: 25,000

Tel: 08714 231 884

www.themillers.co.uk

ROTHERHAM face an anxious wait to find out if they'll start 2008/09 docked 15 points for their financial problems.

The Millers were saved from liquidation in 2006 but the last two campaigns have been wrecked by successive ten-point deductions for entering administration.

In 2006/07, the penalty led to relegation from League 1 and last term's punishment hampered a Play-Off charge.

Under the new ownership of Tony Stewart, the club are looking to the future, but this season's move away from Millmoor may see attendances drop.

In the circumstances, rookie boss Mark Robins is doing a sterling job. He has tied up deals for several of last season's first-team players and recruited wisely.

Without a points penalty the Millers would be genuine Play-Off contenders but, until their fate is known, hold all bets.

Longest run without loss: 10
Longest run without win: 5
High – low league position: 2-14
High – low Outlook form figure: 62-37
Key Stat: *Record at the bottom ten was 8-2-0 but won only one other away game.*

Outlook forecast: 12th

Final Outlook Index figure: 689
Clean sheets: 14 (13 league)
Yellow cards: 43 Red cards: 0
Players used: 28
Leading scorer: Derek Holmes 11 (all league)

Your forecast:

Sponsored by Stan James

SHREWSBURY TOWN

Nickname: The Shrews
Colours: Blue and amber

Ground: New Meadow
Capacity: 10,000

Tel: 0871 811 8800

www.shrewsburytown.co.uk

PAUL SIMPSON rebuffed a number of approaches before signing at Oteley Road in March but, after one win in ten games under his stewardship, Town fans must be wondering what all the fuss was about.

With the pressure on to make a fast start, Simpson arranged a four-day boot camp in Almeria to get his players up for the new campaign.

The net has been cast far and wide for new arrivals and the £170,000 club-record signing of striker Grant Holt from Notts Forest shows they mean business.

But, while they are spending money, they haven't had the £500,000 bonus for ex-keeper Joe Hart's first England cap – that won't come until he starts a competitive game.

The Shrews were the worst travellers in League 2 last season and must reverse their wretched away form if they are going to make their presence felt anywhere near the summit.

Longest run without loss: 3
Longest run without win: 15
High – low league position: 2-19
High – low Outlook form figure: 62-35
Key Stat: *They did not concede a goal at home to other sides in the bottom eight.*
Outlook forecast: 9th

Final Outlook Index figure: 652
Clean sheets: 14 (13 league)
Yellow cards: 62 Red cards: 1
Players used: 31
Leading scorer: Dave Hibbert 12 (all league)
Your forecast:

WYCOMBE WANDERERS

Nickname: The Chairboys
Colours: Sky and navy blue

Ground: Adams Park
Capacity: 10,000

Tel: 01494 472100

www.wycombewanderers.premiumtv.co.uk

PETER TAYLOR'S stock has fallen so far that murmurs of discontent greeted his appointment at Wycombe.

The former England U-21 boss – who took charge of the full England side for a game in 2000 – has been sliding down the managerial ladder over the past few years and failed to get Stevenage into the Conference Play-Offs last season.

He takes over from Paul Lambert, who stepped down despite guiding the Chairboys to a League Cup semi-final and the Play-Offs in his two seasons in charge.

First-team regulars Russell Martin and Stefan Oakes rejected new deals and followed seven other players out the door, leaving Taylor with a blank canvas and the manager has had a busy summer.

The new arrivals include Millwall pair Chris Zebroski and Gavin Grant, Brazilian striker Magno Silva Vieira and former Palace youngster Lewwis Spence.

Longest run without loss: 6
Longest run without win: 4
High – low league position: 5-19
High – low Outlook form figure: 65-39
Key Stat: *Wycombe never lost successive league games last term.*
Outlook forecast: 8th

Final Outlook Index figure: 709
Clean sheets: 19 (all league)
Yellow cards: 64 Red cards: 2
Players used: 32
Leading scorer: Scott McGleish 25 (all league)
Your forecast:

CELTIC

Nickname: The Bhoys
Colours: Green and white
Ground: Celtic Park
Capacity: 60,832
Tel: 0871 226 1888
www.celticfc.net

CELTIC'S latest title triumph was sweeter than most because it seemed so unlikely. That they ended up winning the SPL highlights what a great spirit Gordon Strachan has instilled in his squad.

Most Celtic fans will tell you the current team is way short of being in the same class as some of their illustrious predecessors, but don't bet against them making it four in a row this season.

That's because whatever they lack in genuine class, Strachan's squad more than make up for in belief and determination.

Sure, Rangers' fixture congestion contributed to the Bhoys' title success last term, but all but the most die-hard of Rangers fans would have to take their hat off to Celtic for refusing to give up when the league seemed well out of reach. Beating the Gers twice in the final few weeks of the season highlighted their never-say-die attitude.

They'll be keen to have a better start to the season this time out as Rangers are unlikely to face the same backlog of fixtures and will be fully focused on top spot in the SPL from start to finish.

It'll be a close run thing between the two clubs, but Celtic still have an edge over their rivals. In Scott McDonald and Jan Vennegoor of Hesselink, Celtic had the top two scorers in the SPL – the pair helped the Bhoys score the same number of goals as Rangers, but Celtic conceded fewer.

The Gers aren't far behind, but this Celtic side know how to win titles and should be able to nose ahead of their Glasgow neighbours once again.

Longest run without loss: 14
Longest run without win: 3
High – low league position: 1-3
High – low Outlook form figure: 76-44
Final Outlook Index figure: 905
Key Stat: *The Hoops were behind at half time in seven league games last season.*

2007/08 SPL Stats

	Apps	Gls	YC	RC
B Balde	4	0	0	0
A Boruc	30	0	3	0
M Brown	8	0	0	0
S Brown	31 (3)	3	7	0
P Caddis	0 (2)	0	0	0
G Caldwell	35	1	1	0
R Conroy	2	0	0	0
M Donati	22 (3)	3	8	0
P Hartley	23 (4)	0	4	0
A Hinkel	16	1	0	0
B Hutchinson	0 (2)	0	0	0
J Jarosik	6 (2)	1	1	0
J Kennedy	5 (2)	0	4	0
C Killen	2 (18)	1	0	0
S McDonald	35 (1)	25	5	0
A McGeady	35 (1)	7	9	0
P McGowan	0 (1)	0	0	0
S McManus	37	5	4	0
K Miller	1 (1)	3	0	0
S Nakamura	24 (2)	6	2	0
L Naylor	33	1	4	0
J O'Brien	0 (1)	0	0	0
D O'Dea	3 (3)	0	1	0
J-J Perrier Doumbe	2	0	0	0
S Pressley	5	0	0	0
D Riordan	2 (6)	1	0	0
B Robson	11 (6)	2	2	1
G Samaras	5 (11)	5	1	0
C Sheridan	0 (1)	0	0	0
E Sno	3 (9)	0	0	0
J Vennegoor	31 (1)	15	5	0
M Wilson	8 (3)	0	1	0
M Zurawski	1 (4)	0	0	0

League Stats
Clean sheets: 21 (19 league)
Yellow cards: 36 Red cards: 0
Players used: 33
Leading scorer: Scott McDonald 31 (25 league)

Outlook forecast: Champions

Your forecast:

RANGERS

Nickname: The Gers
Colours: Blue, white and black
Ground: Ibrox Stadium
Capacity: 51,082
Tel: 0871 702 1972
www.rangers.co.uk

RANGERS fans will never forget their rollercoaster 2007/08 season.

The club could have made history by winning four trophies, but ultimately ended up with just two and missed out on the ones that really mattered.

Blowing the SPL title race and losing the Uefa Cup final to Zenit St Petersburg really hurt and the key to Rangers' 2008/09 campaign will be how they react to that disappointment.

The club will probably never face such a demanding fixture list again, but Walter Smith was quick to set about the task of strengthening his squad for the rigours ahead, adding three new strikers – Kenny Miller, Kyle Lafferty and Andrius Velicka – to the payroll by the middle of June. More new players will arrive over the summer.

It's hard to escape the conclusion that the fixture backlog cost Rangers last season – they simply ran out of steam towards the end. While they were able to muddle through at Ibrox, they fared less well on the road, winning just one of their last seven away matches in the SPL.

Two of those games were losses at Parkhead and they proved to be pivotal. With little to separate the Old Firm, it's likely that results between the pair will prove to be equally decisive this season.

Glasgow's big two are on a level footing in terms of quality, but Celtic have got into the habit of winning titles and that alone may give them the edge in another close race. Rangers will be battling all the way but may fall just short again.

Longest run without loss: 27
Longest run without win: 4
High – low league position: 1-3
High – low Outlook form figure: 70-48
Final Outlook Index figure: 880
Key Stat: *68 games last season and clean sheets in more than half.*

2007/08 SPL Stats

	Apps	Gls	YC	RC
C Adam	12 (4)	2	1	0
N Alexander	7 (1)	0	0	0
D Beasley	8 (3)	2	2	0
K Boyd	17 (11)	14	2	0
K Broadfoot	14 (1)	1	2	0
T Buffel	0 (1)	0	0	0
C Burke	10 (1)	2	2	0
D Cousin	20 (6)	10	1	0
C Cuellar	36	5	5	1
C Dailly	12	2	2	0
J Darcheville	14 (16)	12	0	0
S Davis	11 (1)	0	2	0
A Faye	2 (2)	0	0	0
B Ferguson	37 (1)	7	0	0
J Fleck	0 (1)	0	0	0
D Furman	0 (1)	0	0	0
B Hemdani	12	0	1	0
A Hutton	20	0	6	0
L McCulloch	19 (3)	3	4	1
A McGregor	31	0	2	0
S Naismith	13 (9)	5	1	0
N Novo	10 (18)	10	1	1
S Papac	22	0	0	0
K Thomson	25 (1)	1	8	0
A Webster	1	1	0	0
D Weir	37	2	2	0
S Whittaker	29 (1)	4	4	1

League Stats
Clean sheets: 35 (17 league)
Yellow cards: 32 Red cards: 1
Players used: 27
Leading scorer: Kris Boyd 25
(14 league)

Outlook forecast: Runners-up
Your forecast:

ABERDEEN

Nickname: The Dons
Colours: Red

Ground: Pittodrie
Capacity: 22,474

Tel: 01224 650400

www.afc.co.uk

AS WELL as a respectable fourth place in the SPL, Aberdeen enjoyed some high times in Europe last season, reaching the last 32 of the Uefa Cup.

Now fans want the board to strengthen manager Jimmy Calderwood's hand by ploughing some of the money generated in Europe back into the team.

There are funds available, and that investment is certainly needed if the Dons are to move forward.

Calderwood admits that he needs to strengthen in every department if Aberdeen are to go one better than last season and take third place in the league, but at least the lack of any European distractions this time around leaves the Dons free to concentrate on the SPL.

They'll be one of a clutch of clubs challenging for that Uefa Cup spot but they may find that, just as they did last season, they fall slightly short.

Longest run without loss: 7
Longest run without win: 7
High – low league position: 4-10
High – low Outlook form figure: 63-36
Key Stat: *Dons conceded three or more 16 times in all games last season.*

Outlook forecast: 5th

Final Outlook Index figure: 828
Clean sheets: 14 (9 league)
Yellow cards: 41 Red cards: 0
Players used: 28
Leading scorer: Lee Miller 13 (12 league)

Your forecast:

DUNDEE UNITED

Nickname: The Terrors
Colours: Orange and black

Ground: Tannadice Park
Capacity: 14,223

Tel: 01382 833166

www.dundeeunitedfc.co.uk

CRAIG LEVEIN'S Dundee United played some of the best football in the SPL last season and were desperately unlucky not to put some silverware in the trophy cabinet after losing the CIS Cup final to Rangers on penalties.

After all that Levein could be forgiven for resting on his laurels, but the events of last season seem only to have inspired him.

The Terrors boss has made it clear that he wants the club to push on and has been hard at work in the transfer market during the close season.

With a stronger squad the Terriers can make a real push for European football this season.

They face some stiff competition for third place but, if they can add some defensive grit to their undoubted attacking ability it would be no surprise to see them doing well again this season.

Longest run without loss: 7
Longest run without win: 7
High – low league position: 3-6
High – low Outlook form figure: 66-39
Key Stat: *United took just three points away to other top-seven sides.*

Outlook forecast: 3rd

Final Outlook Index figure: 803
Clean sheets: 16 (13 league)
Yellow cards: 35 Red cards: 8
Players used: 30
Leading scorer: Noel Hunt 18 (13 league)

Your forecast:

Sponsored by Stan James

FALKIRK

Nickname: The Bairns
Colours: Dark blue and white

Ground: Falkirk Stadium
Capacity: 8,000

Tel: 01324 624121

www.falkirkfc.co.uk

FALKIRK did as well as they could have hoped to last season and survival is the priority again – although there are hopes that the club can push on for a top-half finish.

That might be a bit optimistic, but the Bairns should be good enough to stay out of trouble.

Manager John Hughes is working on a tight budget, but he has freshened things up over the summer with a few new faces and is optimistic about pushing up the SPL table.

The loss of Pedro Moutinho, probably their most creative player, will be keenly felt. However, the experienced trio of Jackie McNamara, Lee Bullen and Neil McCann should add some steel to the side.

The presence of those three gives Falkirk a more solid look than many of their rivals, which should stand them in good stead – a comfortable season in mid-table beckons.

Longest run without loss: 7
Longest run without win: 6
High – low league position: 6-11
High – low Outlook form figure: 65-35
Key Stat: *The Bairns won all eight games where they led at half time.*

Final Outlook Index figure: 806
Clean sheets: 15 (all league)
Yellow cards: 32 Red cards: 6
Players used: 28
Leading scorer: Michael Higdon 9 (8 league)

Outlook forecast: 8th

Your forecast:

HAMILTON ACADEMICAL

Nickname: The Accies
Colours: Red and white

Ground: New Douglas Park
Capacity: 5,396

Tel: 01698 368 652

www.acciesfc.co.uk

HAMILTON won promotion to the SPL by playing good football on the deck – they'll try to stick to their footballing principles in the top flight, but they'll have to scrap too, if they are to stay up.

The Accies have an excellent manager in Billy Reid and a board willing to invest in new talent but everyone at the club accepts that avoiding an immediate return to Division One is going to be tough.

Reid can call on an exciting crop of young players, such as promising defender James Gibson and the highly rated James McCarthy, who has reputedly attracted the eye of several Premier League scouts.

They served the club well last season and, with a few experienced new additions to play alongside them, the Accies will be in with a chance. It'll be a close run thing, but they can stay up.

Longest run without loss: 11
Longest run without win: 3
High – low league position: 1-3
High – low Outlook form figure: 70-45
Key Stat: *Between Aug 11 and Boxing Day, Accies conceded one first-half goal.*

Final Outlook Index figure: 774
Clean sheets: 22 (20 league)
Yellow cards: 42 Red cards: 0
Players used: 32
Leading scorer: Richard Offiong 21 (19 league)

Outlook forecast: 11th

Your forecast:

HEARTS

Nickname: Jambos
Colours: Claret and white

Ground: Tynecastle
Capacity: 17,420

Tel: 0871 663 1874

www.heartsfc.co.uk

NEW season, same old chaotic muddle at Tynecastle. As we go to press, it's difficult to make a prediction for Hearts as we still have no idea who will be the manager in 2008/09.

One thing we do know is that anyone who does take the job will have to contend with the demands of owner Vladimir Romanov.

Romanov needs to back off if Hearts are to progress, but it's likely that he'll still want to meddle in team selection and, as we have seen before, unless he appoints a yes man, his meddling can only hinder the job of the manager.

While it's difficult to see the club having as bad a time as they did last season, things are still not right at Tynecastle.

As long as the club remains a media circus it's difficult to see the team making any real progress on the pitch. Another season of mid-table mediocrity beckons.

Longest run without loss: 7
Longest run without win: 10
High – low league position: 5-11
High – low Outlook form figure: 66-36
Key Stat: *No SPL clean sheets between Sept 3 and Jan 19 (17 games).*

Final Outlook Index figure: 802
Clean sheets: 12 (10 league)
Yellow cards: 57 Red cards: 8
Players used: 34
Leading scorer: Andrius Velicka 14 (11 league)

Outlook forecast: 7th

Your forecast:

HIBERNIAN

Nickname: Hibees
Colours: Green and white

Ground: Easter Road
Capacity: 17,458

Tel: 0131 661 2159

www.hibs.co.uk

HIBS' season started early in the Intertoto Cup but, as we went to press, a European run was looking unlikely.

In any case, the priority must be improving on last season's sixth-place finish in the SPL.

Mixu Paatelainen has had six months in the hotseat now and will be looking to stamp his authority on the club in the coming year.

He's already started shaking up the squad, but he will still need to bring in a few new signings before the big kick-off.

The manager needs to address the club's away form if they are to move forward – only the bottom three scored fewer goals on the road last season and Hibernian's only win away from Easter Road under Paatelainen was at Falkirk, way back in February.

No doubt the Hibees will be in the mix for third place, but they may fall short once again.

Longest run without loss: 8
Longest run without win: 8
High – low league position:
High – low Outlook form figure: 63-41
Key Stat: *Quick starters – Hibs scored ten goals in the first five minutes.*

Final Outlook Index figure: 805
Clean sheets: 13 (11 league)
Yellow cards: 41 Red cards: 4
Players used: 30
Leading scorer: Steven Fletcher 14 (13 league)

Outlook forecast: 6th

Your forecast:

INVERNESS CT

Nickname: Caley
Colours: Blue and red

Ground: Caledonian Stadium
Capacity: 7,500

Tel: 01463 222880

www.caleythistleonline.com

INVERNESS scored plenty of goals last season – more than third-placed Motherwell – but they were very poor defensively, conceding more goals than every SPL team bar Gretna. They must tighten up at the back if they are to stay in the top flight.

With no obvious relegation favourites this season, Caley will be nervously looking over their shoulders, but they took some notable scalps after Craig Brewster took over as manager and they will hope to do just enough to avoid the drop again.

Home form will be the key, as no other side in the bottom half of the table won as many games at home as Caley last season. It was a good job too, as only Gretna lost more away matches.

They could struggle to repeat that 9-2-8 home record this time around, though, and that could spell trouble. It might even see them drop out of the SPL.

Longest run without loss: 5
Longest run without win: 11
High – low league position: 7-12
High – low Outlook form figure: 66-34
Key Stat: *Their record against the top six was 3-1-14. Only Gretna fared worse.*

Final Outlook Index figure: 782
Clean sheets: 8 (7 league)
Yellow cards: 30 Red cards: 3
Players used: 26
Leading scorer: Marius Niculae 10 (8 league)

Outlook forecast: 12th

Your forecast:

KILMARNOCK

Nickname: Killie
Colours: Blue and white

Ground: Rugby Park
Capacity: 18,128

Tel: 01563 545 300

www.kilmarnockfc.co.uk

KILMARNOCK had a disappointing season in 2007/08 and must be wary of the drop going into the new campaign.

Consistency was Jim Jefferies' main worry. His side took seven out of the first nine points on offer, but then had to wait until their final two games of the season to earn their next back-to-back wins.

Jefferies badly needs to freshen up his squad, particularly up front where goals proved hard to come by.

The gaffer has already shipped a couple of forwards out of the club and is looking to add some fresh striking talent to the roster before the new season starts.

Whoever comes in, Killie are likely to be fighting at the wrong end of the table again but they have the experience to see them through. They look stronger than several of the other sides likely to be involved in the relegation battle.

Longest run without loss: 3
Longest run without win: 7
High – low league position: 4-11
High – low Outlook form figure: 62-36
Key Stat: *Didn't win successive league games between August 18 and May 17.*

Final Outlook Index figure: 792
Clean sheets: 9 (7 league)
Yellow cards: 50 Red cards: 3
Players used: 32
Leading scorer: Colin Nish 9 (7 league)

Outlook forecast: 10th

Your forecast:

MOTHERWELL

Nickname: The Well / The Steelmen
Colours: Amber and claret

Ground: Fir Park
Capacity: 13,742

Tel: 01698 333 333

www.motherwellfc.co.uk

MARK MCGHEE has been courted by the likes of Hearts and Scotland over the past few months, but has chosen to remain at Fir Park for at least one more year and that can only be good news for Motherwell.

McGhee did a fantastic job in his first season at the helm, steering the club through a difficult time after the tragic death of skipper Phil O'Donnell and leading them to a remarkable third-place finish which will see them compete in this season's Uefa Cup.

That has allowed them to keep hold of players who may have left in other years, such as Mark Reynolds, the subject of a rejected £750,000 bid from Rangers in June.

It's a small squad though, and progress in Europe – while welcome – may affect their league form.

A repeat of last term's third place would be an incredible achievement, but it's more likely that they will fall back a bit.

Longest run without loss: 6
Longest run without win: 5
High – low league position: 3-6
High – low Outlook form figure: 70-40
Key Stat: *Well never lost more than two games in a row last term.*

Outlook forecast: 4th

Final Outlook Index figure: 820
Clean sheets: 11 (10 league)
Yellow cards: 37 Red cards: 0
Players used: 27
Leading scorer: Chris Porter 18 (14 league)

Your forecast:

ST MIRREN

Nickname: The Saints
Colours: Black and white

Ground: St Mirren Park
Capacity: 10,752

Tel: 0141 889 2558

www.saintmirren.net

ST MIRREN have spent the last two seasons battling near the foot of the SPL and will once again have to work hard to stay up.

Scoring goals was the Saints' problem last season. They scored fewer than relegated Gretna, so watching their games was a painful experience at times.

Gus MacPherson has been busy in the transfer market and looks to have made a few useful signings.

The boss has already brought in Dennis Wyness to address their goal-scoring problem and, with several other attack-minded players joining the squad, St Mirren should be a bit more potent this season.

The Saints face another hard campaign though, and they'll be in the relegation mix to the bitter end. They know what it takes to stay up and can fend off the drop for a third successive season.

Longest run without loss: 4
Longest run without win: 8
High – low league position: 7-11
High – low Outlook form figure: 58-35
Key Stat: *Saints won one of their games against the top five.*

Outlook forecast: 9th

Final Outlook Index figure: 779
Clean sheets: 14 (12 league)
Yellow cards: 38 Red cards: 4
Players used: 28
Leading scorer: Billy Mehmet 8 (6 league)

Your forecast:

Sponsored by Stan James

Dark Blues can return to the promised land

THE DEMISE of Gretna opens up a spot for a new club to enter the Scottish football league and it's safe to say that Annan won't be enjoying the same meteoric rise that Gretna did, *writes Dominic Sutton*.

But, while it's unlikely that another benefactor in the mould of Brooks Mileson will roll up at any of the league's 30 clubs, most will agree that this is probably for the best and it's to be hoped that Annan are run along more sensible lines.

Promotion is not beyond the realms of possibility for the league's new members, as there is little to separate many of the teams in the third tier from some of their non-league counterparts.

However, **Montrose** are vying for favouritism with **Dumbarton** after Stranraer went up, following Gretna's exit from the league.

The Gable Endies finished 11 points clear of fifth-placed Stenhousemuir, and look stronger than most other teams in the division.

Despite a poor season last time out, Dumbarton have been busy in the transfer market during the summer and could also have a say in the title race.

However, relegated Berwick were poor in finishing bottom of the second division, winning just three games all season – they are unlikely to make an immediate return.

In Division Two, promoted **East Fife** will look to make good on their triumphant finish to last season by securing a second successive promotion.

They walked Division Three, eventually winning the title by a mammoth 23 points and scoring 77 goals.

If they can maintain the form which took them up they are capable of challenging at this level.

They are joined in the second division by Play-Off winners Arbroath and runners-up Stranraer, who lost out to Arbroath in the Play-Offs but go up because of the space left by Gretna. Both teams will be happy to stay up.

Raith, who finished third in Division Two last season, will be many punters' fancies to win the division this year, but they have no significant advantage over their rivals.

Relegated Stirling won just four games in Division One last season. They've ditched plenty of the players who got them relegated, but could well be in for another season of struggle.

Dundee were streets ahead of everyone except for promoted Hamilton in Division One last term.

They've lost a couple of key players – notably influential midfielder Scott Robertson and out-of-contract defender Paul Dixon, who

ALEX RAE: does his work from the touchline these days – he can lead Dundee to promotion

have both defected to local rivals Dundee United – but player-manager Alex Rae has also brought in a few new faces and look the outstanding bet to win the division this time around.

The Dark Blues could well face a strong challenge from **Queen Of The South**, who will doubtless put some of the money earned in their Scottish Cup run to use in the transfer market.

Dunfermline and Partick both see their rightful place as the SPL and will be determined to make up for poor seasons in 2007/08 by pushing hard this time.

At the other end of Division One, Morton and Clyde will be worried after poor seasons last term.

Ross County, who went up as Division Two champions, could struggle too now that 29-goal Andy Barrowman has left for Inverness, while Airdrie, who went up following Gretna's demise, are a decent side at the back but will struggle for goals in the First Division.

They look likely make a rapid return to Division Two.

Ratings are the perfect antidote to tabloid hype

MY BETTING life is based solely around numbers and they come from the RFO's very own rating system, the Outlook Index, writes Alex Deacon.

Our rating system looks objectively at the relative strengths of teams in the hope of finding inconsistencies in the betting in the 1X2 markets and, increasingly, the outright markets.

While my horseracing counterparts work in a sport where ratings and the quantification of a horse's ability is part and parcel of the whole business, the ratings-based football tipster lives on the margins of society. And, to be honest, it probably suits most of us that way.

Nevertheless, it's still galling to work in a world where no-one believes a word you say – or at least relates to it in the same way that you do.

Of course, everyone with even the vaguest interest in football is a self-proclaimed expert on the sport.

Part of being a supporter is the right to express an opinion and those opinions are, naturally, if usually incorrectly, applied to each and every supporter's betting.

When the average football punter has a bet, you know that the majority of them haven't looked at anything more sophisticated than the back pages of whatever their newspaper is.

If they're a little bit more on the ball, then it's six-match form either of the league table or the line-by-line variety.

Compare that with the average racing punter. Even stood among the waifs and strays of all human existence on a typical weekday afternoon in the local bookies, a substantial proportion use a rating of some kind, whether it's the type of 1-100 that the tabloids use, or maybe those from the Outlook or the Racing Post.

Ratings are part of the furniture in racing, but they will probably always remain an irrelevance to most football bettors.

It's this reluctance to think about ratings, however, that can give those football punters willing to give them a try that vital edge.

Time and again, every season, I make the point that in football betting we must be objective above everything else.

Football is the subject of more hype and media overreaction than almost any other sport and ratings will continue to be useful as long as most punters think they're going to learn all they can about football betting simply by studying the team sheets and such like, when they would get closer to the truth by adopting some of the rigour of the horseracing form student.

Their ignorance is good news for ratings-based punters and it's where the most profitable football bets can be found, season in, season out – and that's worth bearing in mind with nine months of punting ahead of you.

Rant over and finally on to my predictions for the coming season. Last year's crop of picks netted me a decent enough strike-rate with more than half of the predictions right – this year I'm aiming for a 75 per cent success rate.

Kevin Keegan will not finish the year as Newcastle manager – Alex Ferguson will announce his retirement before the end of the season – England will continue to struggle on the international stage with Fabio Capello's reign not

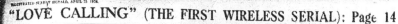

ILLUSTRATED Sunday Herald ILLUSTRATED

No. 579—LONDON, SUNDAY, APRIL 25, 1926. — Telephone:—Museum 9881. (Registered as a Newspaper.) TWOPENCE.

MAKING THE BUDGET
By RT. HON. W. GRAHAM, M.P.
(Page 5)

GOAL THAT WON THE CUP

The decisive moment at the Wembley Stadium, where Bolton Wanderers yesterday carried off the English Cup by 1 goal to 0, avenging their defeat by Manchester City 22 years ago, when the two great Lancashire rivals last met as Cup finalists. David Jack, on the ground, scoring the only goal with a low shot 32 minutes after half time. The tension of the multitude packing the Stadium broke into tremendous cheers, which were renewed when later Jack was carried off the field shoulder high.—(Illustrated Sunday Herald.)

TABLOID HYPE: Bolton win the cup in 1926 – the Outlook tipped them for their 1929 win

heralding a quick turnaround in the form of the national team – England will still be favourites to win their World Cup qualifying group – Alan Shearer will still not have dipped his toe into the managerial water – Steve McClaren will return to English club management after a brief but successful stint in the Dutch league – Russian sides will continue to improve at a rapid rate in both the Champions League and Uefa Cup – only one of the sides promoted from last season's Championship will be relegated from the Premier League – an English side will not win this season's Champions League final – Martin O'Neill will bring about further improvement in Aston Villa's final league position – David O'Leary's comeback to management will be thankfully another year in the waiting – an ex-Premier League team will again be relegated to League 1 – Rafa Benitez will leave Liverpool at some point in the season – former Swindon and England midfielder Paul Ince will improve on Blackburn's league position of last season – another former Football League side will be promoted from the Conference – Liverpool will once again find themselves finishing out of the top three in the Premier League and without a trophy – Newcastle will finish outside the top ten.

Sponsored by Stan James

League tables are, quite simply, one of the most deceptive tools a punter can employ in making selections each week, showing as they do the state of a competition at any given point in time.

In their usual format they reveal nothing as to the quality of the opponents each side has met until then. That's where the *Outlook Index* comes in, showing as it does the relative strength of each side determined by the results of over 38,000 matches and weighted by the strength of the opposition.

Detailed 60-match form is also given for each side so that trends in any side's playing strength can be readily identified. Each week of the football season, the *Outlook* prints updated *Index* ratings with the best analysis to help your football betting.

CHAMPIONS OF EUROPE: but Chelsea are top of the Outlook Index ratings

premier league 2007/08

| | Curr | Previous match form | | | | | | | | | | Home | Away | Trend |
		1-6	7-12	13-18	19-24	25-30	31-36	37-42	43-48	49-54	55-60			
Chelsea	969	963	955	955	952	950	955	960	963	957	962	988	943	8
Man Utd	950	952	948	954	956	958	948	962	967	964	968	961	923	-1
Liverpool	937	932	923	915	924	926	923	924	929	934	924	965	880	8
Arsenal	934	928	936	935	928	935	927	922	925	923	916	980	892	2
Everton	895	897	909	900	891	879	884	878	874	874	872	891	855	-3
Blackburn	885	888	892	887	888	903	894	886	886	888	878	898	878	-2
Aston Villa	880	884	890	889	883	880	874	869	855	852	860	878	853	-4
Tottenham	873	875	878	875	868	871	882	892	885	876	889	903	832	-1
Portsmouth	871	889	888	882	892	888	873	870	866	872	876	910	848	-11
West Ham	862	865	878	880	870	861	861	846	825	828	841	861	860	-6
Middlesbrough	860	855	856	854	852	848	858	858	868	866	856	887	843	4
Man City	860	868	876	880	878	872	859	850	852	853	849	873	843	-9
Newcastle Utd	856	856	840	849	856	861	860	861	872	880	877	907	816	5
Bolton	852	842	841	850	859	849	858	876	886	893	890	882	829	5
Wigan	852	846	841	837	834	830	844	839	847	843	855	851	852	7
Fulham	846	830	829	828	839	841	840	841	850	854	859	878	809	11
Sunderland	842	848	840	840	836	842	849	851	840	820	803	868	824	0
Reading	841	843	844	850	857	861	869	873	871	873	864	862	825	-3
Birmingham	832	830	830	828	826	830	832	833	836	840	848	904	805	2
Derby	776	782	788	792	802	815	816	824	831	833	833	823	792	-7

Sponsored by Stan James

championship 2007/08

	Curr	1-6	7-12	13-18	19-24	25-30	31-36	37-42	43-48	49-54	55-60	Home	Away	Trend
					Previous match form									
WBA	827	818	815	820	828	826	817	818	811	818	830	839	831	6
C Palace	825	818	808	814	810	790	786	798	806	805	802	823	826	8
Stoke	824	819	825	822	820	809	813	813	813	804	797	842	812	2
Sheff Utd	820	817	804	801	809	820	814	824	838	840	841	859	804	8
Hull	820	822	808	804	794	789	781	777	774	774	771	839	813	6
Wolves	807	804	802	798	802	817	813	809	812	814	819	819	804	4
Ipswich	803	796	794	795	795	796	800	797	795	784	780	875	764	6
Bristol City	800	802	817	811	809	795	795	788	773	771	768	837	784	-6
Cardiff	797	800	796	806	797	784	777	774	772	794	798	850	784	-1
Watford	796	809	818	816	817	829	842	831	820	811	813	818	835	-11
QPR	796	800	791	789	780	771	772	762	772	767	754	849	793	2
Sheff Weds	794	787	787	784	791	800	790	789	808	798	781	836	803	5
Charlton	793	796	810	817	822	833	832	842	838	848	836	844	800	-9
Plymouth	789	793	802	794	799	798	797	792	794	780	789	854	782	-5
Burnley	788	791	798	796	792	800	787	791	784	773	767	831	801	-4
Southampton	787	780	779	786	794	802	804	802	805	801	812	836	791	4
Preston	787	796	785	773	773	772	786	786	797	814	829	851	772	1
Blackpool	784	788	791	784	778	774	783	789	780	758	747	844	791	-2
Norwich	780	785	794	798	781	760	757	776	784	790	784	840	788	-6
Leicester	776	776	776	780	775	782	784	778	772	773	791	804	824	0
Barnsley	772	773	773	772	782	784	778	770	761	755	752	839	764	-1
Coventry	772	774	766	766	776	784	785	788	780	788	778	843	781	2
Scunthorpe	761	753	760	757	762	772	785	789	785	782	782	810	760	3
Colchester	754	755	764	776	772	783	790	796	800	793	794	806	778	-6

league 1 2007/08

	Curr	1-6	7-12	13-18	19-24	25-30	31-36	37-42	43-48	49-54	55-60	Home	Away	Trend
					Previous match form									
Swansea	774	773	783	792	784	771	762	750	750	746	736	798	792	-4
Leeds	774	768	759	763	782	795	800	793	776	772	762	820	786	6
Nottm Forest	772	762	754	759	765	772	767	761	762	758	750	823	764	9
Southend	761	762	742	733	730	745	749	745	745	763	761	800	774	10
Doncaster	753	760	768	765	750	736	732	723	727	733	747	798	764	-6
Northampton	750	742	744	734	719	714	729	726	728	728	721	798	762	8
Carlisle	749	761	767	749	745	750	747	741	740	738	726	812	730	-6
Brighton	746	745	743	733	730	735	726	716	712	729	726	771	805	4
Huddersfield	743	729	723	732	726	732	728	738	740	729	730	803	754	11
Oldham	742	736	735	738	740	733	722	729	738	744	753	786	754	4
Bournemouth	737	720	702	700	693	696	700	707	720	727	717	794	751	20
Swindon	726	718	723	730	730	722	728	724	718	715	714	803	725	2
Walsall	726	735	744	748	746	738	725	711	717	719	714	761	765	-10
Tranmere	724	729	733	735	725	729	742	742	728	730	738	787	725	-4
Millwall	712	712	713	713	720	720	722	733	753	751	751	779	746	0
Crewe	710	715	711	708	711	722	717	723	728	725	735	780	752	-1
Leyton Orient	710	711	725	725	724	732	731	735	722	724	719	774	750	-6
Cheltenham	708	710	707	711	711	706	702	715	718	708	701	795	720	0
Hartlepool	707	712	715	716	720	724	735	740	736	746	745	781	731	-5
Bristol Rovers	705	716	722	733	724	709	713	720	704	686	680	766	749	-11
Yeovil	704	708	712	719	736	740	744	753	748	742	749	770	730	-6
Gillingham	700	700	698	710	721	714	712	710	716	713	715	816	698	-2
Port Vale	694	690	673	680	688	691	695	706	714	725	724	784	726	8
Luton	686	697	696	706	728	728	729	730	738	742	762	785	714	-10

OUTLOOK INDEX RATINGS

league 2 2007/08

	Curr	1-6	7-12	13-18	19-24	25-30	31-36	37-42	43-48	49-54	55-60	Home	Away	Trend
MK Dons	746	741	732	722	738	729	728	714	710	708	714	745	797	8
Peterborough	728	733	727	710	693	697	688	674	675	671	661	759	765	4
Hereford	720	713	711	709	701	696	684	670	659	664	678	733	755	7
Stockport	718	723	715	700	687	679	679	689	693	698	712	756	760	4
Rochdale	712	711	696	700	709	699	690	692	698	693	682	750	746	6
Wycombe	709	706	698	694	695	682	681	673	666	681	690	776	740	6
Rotherham	689	677	689	707	718	713	695	692	695	704	700	744	738	-1
Darlington	689	690	710	713	712	710	699	694	688	686	688	747	731	-9
Chesterfield	682	688	690	689	702	704	700	698	690	692	702	745	730	-5
Bradford	680	686	679	682	678	675	675	696	701	704	714	740	736	-1
Bury	678	669	654	644	643	664	668	650	656	645	650	746	733	15
Lincoln	677	676	675	665	651	653	657	674	687	695	708	734	724	4
Barnet	676	672	664	666	677	677	698	682	673	671	665	772	687	5
Brentford	664	672	669	684	669	662	672	679	681	690	704	728	728	-6
Notts Co	660	654	654	658	652	660	666	674	668	666	663	738	731	4
Morecambe	659	665	668	684	691	680	671	672	674	673	676	705	685	-8
Dagenham	659	652	668	653	652	658	671	680	684	695	691	690	692	2
Macclesfield	655	656	646	652	653	665	666	668	663	670	670	748	692	3
Grimsby	654	666	680	679	670	656	660	672	680	679	672	720	712	-12
Shrewsbury	652	652	660	669	677	677	675	694	691	689	692	751	690	-5
Mansfield	642	646	641	648	641	642	645	650	654	665	676	714	697	-1
Accrington	640	645	654	650	665	665	665	658	664	660	654	698	694	-7
Wrexham	638	635	645	644	629	640	643	650	656	644	639	747	684	0
Chester	632	629	632	644	662	678	684	670	661	665	675	709	718	-2

conference 2007/08

	Curr	1-6	7-12	13-18	19-24	25-30	31-36	37-42	43-48	49-54	55-60	Home	Away	Trend
Aldershot	693	700	700	684	684	679	668	648	636	644	635	730	661	-1
Exeter	680	679	677	673	667	665	667	673	665	660	668	720	656	3
Cambridge	671	662	675	669	665	666	665	654	640	623	620	704	682	3
Oxford Utd	664	648	640	637	647	653	656	666	659	656	661	712	678	14
Burton	660	658	660	662	669	669	666	659	655	654	652	690	643	0
Torquay	658	670	668	681	676	669	664	647	632	633	634	722	673	-9
Histon	657	653	648	648	648	648	641	638	-	-	-	647	666	5
Grays	653	651	653	642	643	630	626	633	628	625	624	690	657	3
Stevenage	650	657	664	664	676	672	677	672	660	658	670	690	654	-8
Salisbury	650	648	654	650	636	632	640	645	-	-	-	672	637	1
Forest Green	647	645	648	656	660	665	651	645	642	632	626	678	666	-1
Kidderminster	646	651	636	634	646	636	639	633	631	642	646	677	669	3
Ebbsfleet Utd	645	649	651	659	646	654	650	650	650	645	650	703	628	-4
Crawley	638	632	636	642	648	643	641	635	631	642	644	692	633	1
Rushden	635	640	640	633	632	634	642	636	641	639	645	698	661	-1
York	633	638	655	662	657	649	644	653	663	660	653	640	675	-11
Woking	625	622	620	637	630	628	627	632	632	624	618	685	632	0
Northwich	624	621	608	587	586	575	580	598	620	637	629	665	650	12
Halifax	620	619	624	625	627	638	640	636	631	632	643	721	604	-1
Weymouth	611	603	597	592	606	618	619	618	622	624	629	665	627	8
Altrincham	607	604	598	599	593	598	596	595	609	620	606	657	624	5
Farsley Celtic	591	604	610	605	606	618	629	635	-	-	-	625	625	-10
Stafford R	573	569	577	586	579	588	588	593	612	622	622	591	644	-1
Droylsden	570	576	573	578	586	591	598	621	-	-	-	618	595	-4v

94

Sponsored by Stan James

scottish premier league 2007/08

Previous match form

	Curr	1-6	7-12	13-18	19-24	25-30	31-36	37-42	43-48	49-54	55-60	Home	Away	Trend
Celtic	905	897	895	890	886	888	892	892	912	917	918	918	888	8
Rangers	880	888	899	890	881	875	884	887	884	869	868	927	839	-7
Aberdeen	828	820	810	832	836	837	837	846	846	838	844	850	798	5
Motherwell	820	810	805	809	804	786	784	777	790	796	790	821	810	9
Falkirk	806	809	811	816	802	788	794	792	780	788	779	827	795	-2
Hibernian	805	813	816	799	814	827	818	807	814	822	821	864	770	-4
Dundee Utd	803	809	809	797	802	800	788	782	782	777	774	850	775	-1
Hearts	802	817	813	804	823	837	840	844	842	838	832	828	785	-7
Kilmarnock	792	786	785	792	803	819	828	816	814	811	817	824	774	3
Inverness CT	782	782	793	812	806	792	786	801	802	811	812	818	773	-7
St Mirren	779	778	779	781	769	772	769	766	764	774	778	804	771	1
Gretna	737	728	734	735	731	732	737	742	751	762	752	767	745	4

scottish division one 2007/08

Previous match form

	Curr	1-6	7-12	13-18	19-24	25-30	31-36	37-42	43-48	49-54	55-60	Home	Away	Trend
Hamilton	774	771	763	761	759	760	746	741	740	739	750	798	748	6
Dundee	754	756	749	752	753	747	738	726	727	717	715	811	727	1
St Johnstone	749	755	765	758	756	762	759	752	750	752	754	794	734	-6
Dunfermline	749	744	743	743	733	749	759	769	753	757	764	777	761	5
Queen Of Sth	734	735	736	720	709	713	719	731	716	702	699	792	717	3
Partick	709	722	715	709	706	698	704	695	705	710	721	786	713	-4
Clyde	707	705	709	717	717	717	719	734	737	741	741	739	732	-1
Livingston	702	702	706	709	715	707	708	720	721	730	734	754	732	-2
Morton	702	692	689	704	712	707	715	720	721	730	720	740	728	5
Stirling	664	663	673	679	693	690	690	704	694	694	696	740	683	-5

scottish division two 2007/08

Previous match form

	Curr	1-6	7-12	13-18	19-24	25-30	31-36	37-42	43-48	49-54	55-60	Home	Away	Trend
Ross County	708	718	733	727	717	713	706	712	714	718	720	754	734	-10
Airdrie Utd	705	701	714	710	706	705	710	704	705	700	696	738	724	-1
Brechin	681	681	680	666	650	655	669	672	678	678	673	714	699	5
Raith	680	682	680	693	693	690	691	680	674	658	644	703	728	-3
Peterhead	670	661	664	655	657	656	646	649	650	651	658	716	684	7
Alloa	668	663	655	658	668	650	645	640	652	648	649	722	685	6
Ayr	658	661	650	640	650	662	657	650	638	644	657	690	700	4
Queen's Park	637	642	628	633	633	629	636	616	607	591	595	686	678	2
Cowdenbeath	631	626	630	644	648	647	641	640	633	637	634	695	672	-1
Berwick	593	600	604	620	619	631	644	646	643	646	636	684	656	-9

scottish division three 2007/08

Previous match form

	Curr	1-6	7-12	13-18	19-24	25-30	31-36	37-42	43-48	49-54	55-60	Home	Away	Trend
East Fife	649	648	641	635	630	617	613	604	587	588	593	690	694	5
Stranraer	619	614	622	625	636	646	647	639	639	639	653	697	658	-1
Arbroath	588	594	596	601	605	610	605	627	626	613	604	652	665	-6
Montrose	576	580	575	576	563	559	541	530	530	543	635	633	0	
Stenhousemuir	568	563	575	566	557	558	568	565	572	590	600	653	626	1
Elgin	560	572	565	559	552	542	534	550	548	543	547	646	607	-3
Dumbarton	559	558	564	561	574	591	598	597	601	611	607	684	598	-2
Forfar	555	563	555	548	555	563	581	601	612	612	612	653	621	-1
Albion	546	546	553	555	562	553	567	553	564	558	547	634	631	-3
East Stirling	522	508	505	516	518	516	505	500	508	514	514	619	571	9

primera liga 2007/08

Previous match form

	Curr	1-6	7-12	13-18	19-24	25-30	31-36	37-42	43-48	49-54	55-60	Home	Away	Trend
R Madrid	987	984	981	998	995	989	992	982	967	958	968	998	960	0
Villarreal	984	973	971	960	959	968	964	948	924	926	931	976	961	11
Seville	959	948	944	939	936	944	952	962	957	962	968	982	916	11
R Mallorca	953	937	924	917	918	927	924	926	918	908	908	961	934	18
Barcelona	949	954	968	981	976	979	980	974	969	972	978	998	910	-11
Atl Madrid	940	939	940	943	950	944	933	932	938	942	944	952	919	0
Deportivo	932	938	921	902˙	901	906	908	911	921	923	910	951	923	7
R Santander	930	931	934	924	928	923	915	918	938	924	918	950	912	0
R Betis	922	928	923	912	901	900	902	906	915	918	900	933	920	1
Valencia	922	909	920	928	940	958	960	958	954	958	960	940	916	2
Almeria	921	926	925	931	915	912	919	-	-	-	-	940	912	-3
Getafe	919	916	924	918	918	910	906	923	927	932	926	964	899	0
Ath Bilbao	918	922	918	909	909	909	909	906	904	909	917	950	910	1
Valladolid	916	917	912	920	916	906	916	-	-	-	-	944	912	0
Recreativo	912	909	908	906	914	906	918	919	928	927	930	933	912	3
R Zaragoza	906	908	906	918	915	927	922	928	933	929	927	989	857	-2
Osasuna	897	904	910	904	907	908	913	914	916	920	931	938	898	-6
Espanyol	893	904	920	931	944	934	916	913	918	920	914	923	890	-16
Levante	870	876	874	872	868	874	885	899	890	899	888	920	880	-2
R Murcia	863	873	874	888	896	891	891	882	887	898	906	924	872	-10

serie a 2007/08

Previous match form

	Curr	1-6	7-12	13-18	19-24	25-30	31-36	37-42	43-48	49-54	55-60	Home	Away	Trend
Inter Milan	966	969	976	996	998	992	994	993	996	995	987	986	962	-8
Roma	957	957	956	954	956	956	949	945	952	952	958	990	939	1
AC Milan	926	924	930	937	933	935	944	962	963	962	955	961	942	-2
Fiorentina	916	914	922	929	928	945	951	949	942	944	936	980	896	-3
Sampdoria	907	905	894	888	885	885	887	892	888	890	886	967	904	8
Juventus	905	903	890	890	875	853	844	858	886	886	898	1066	868	8
Udinese	884	890	884	881	894	886	870	877	884	885	888	906	911	-1
Lazio	883	885	895	889	904	917	932	940	942	928	925	936	882	-5
Reggina	880	867	868	871	870	878	890	893	887	891	886	948	868	8
Cagliari	878	868	852	845	847	860	872	882	885	883	888	953	854	15
Siena	878	878	881	867	861	866	864	870	876	882	885	920	909	2
Atalanta	876	875	884	890	893	908	907	899	888	890	884	948	868	-4
Palermo	876	873	878	887	893	900	906	899	908	923	924	918	888	-2
Torino	866	865	878	876	876	877	874	871	867	864	878	895	884	-4
Empoli	860	862	867	876	878	886	893	904	909	909	900	931	880	-5
Parma	852	857	865	865	878	887	893	894	877	865	872	920	846	-7
Catania	851	851	852	859	870	877	875	870	870	890	904	918	846	-2
Napoli	841	837	820	804	798	780	770	752	767	786	809	1047	748	14
Livorno	831	844	857	862	867	852	859	873	877	877	880	914	851	-15
Genoa	815	822	804	793	762	752	732	731	741	749	791	932	753	7

Sponsored by Stan James

bundesliga 2007/08

Previous match form

	Curr	1-6	7-12	13-18	19-24	25-30	31-36	37-42	43-48	49-54	55-60	Home	Away	Trend
B Munich	966	962	955	951	953	949	938	938	939	950	944	985	927	7
Schalke	947	938	934	941	937	945	940	942	951	946	934	960	918	7
W Bremen	944	932	930	945	945	937	938	946	944	953	948	943	926	6
Wolfsburg	921	908	895	880	878	869	873	886	878	878	873	939	909	17
Stuttgart	914	922	925	918	924	929	941	926	922	913	909	953	876	-5
Hamburg	906	910	931	928	933	920	916	907	895	889	908	914	889	-10
Hannover	899	894	888	896	895	890	887	888	892	882	872	915	891	5
B Leverkusen	897	907	923	925	915	918	908	913	908	912	908	914	888	-12
H Berlin	891	882	881	878	884	888	881	884	902	910	906	920	873	7
B Dortmund	888	891	889	888	889	893	892	881	891	908	913	919	871	-1
E Frankfurt	885	890	902	892	886	887	878	872	867	872	875	910	878	-5
Bochum	883	890	895	890	887	896	901	883	874	876	871	902	880	-5
E Cottbus	882	881	868	874	866	868	881	885	872	869	878	914	872	6
A Bielefeld	876	869	856	863	874	883	887	865	866	882	880	912	860	8
Karlsruhe	870	881	895	900	904	895	886	880	886	892	897	915	860	-14
Nuremburg	866	869	863	870	878	886	894	901	909	899	894	928	852	-1
Hansa Rostock	851	853	862	866	866	858	866	867	856	858	867	892	848	-5
Duisburg	846	850	840	839	841	847	850	848	852	848	847	878	867	2

ligue 1 2007/08

Previous match form

	Curr	1-6	7-12	13-18	19-24	25-30	31-36	37-42	43-48	49-54	55-60	Home	Away	Trend
Lyon	938	935	935	932	942	943	932	942	947	945	961	952	919	2
Bordeaux	922	918	906	902	892	893	890	893	892	892	895	930	875	9
Marseille	905	908	904	894	884	876	896	900	882	887	891	916	864	3
Lille	895	891	882	874	868	871	870	868	884	902	904	912	856	9
Rennes	894	884	873	872	886	904	896	895	886	889	888	908	860	11
St Etienne	892	886	868	860	867	866	862	864	870	876	879	929	850	13
Nice	884	874	877	892	881	878	876	877	876	869	865	924	840	4
Lorient	882	878	878	881	876	867	881	871	876	872	863	912	846	3
Nancy	874	881	884	883	888	892	881	863	852	862	871	915	819	-6
Sochaux	872	884	874	860	860	864	869	879	878	881	888	879	876	-1
Le Mans	871	876	878	874	884	884	884	874	876	877	878	907	845	-4
Caen	868	867	857	877	872	850	844	851	845	840	842	896	836	1
Paris St-G	864	856	863	874	873	877	874	878	861	864	862	893	863	1
Toulouse	864	865	862	868	869	870	871	866	877	867	859	902	856	0
Monaco	860	858	865	881	880	880	890	883	882	877	869	881	857	-4
Auxerre	859	866	879	872	872	871	872	884	884	876	877	898	842	-8
Lens	854	857	870	874	869	870	870	883	894	904	904	927	840	-7
Valenciennes	848	860	865	875	879	877	877	870	874	870	874	908	829	-12
Strasbourg	821	831	854	860	857	857	850	844	853	849	849	859	844	-16
Metz	816	811	814	801	809	820	821	830	844	832	845	833	840	5

EUROPEAN INDEX RATINGS

There's so much more to Man United than Ronaldo

LAST year I ducked the Chelsea/**Man United** issue here before plumping for United in the *Outlook* Premier League pullout but this time I have little doubt that Fergie's men are value to land the title treble.

Cristiano Ronaldo? By the time you are reading this, I hope they've sold him. If they haven't, they will have kept not only him, but all the speculation surrounding him and he will have lost not only his dream move to Madrid but some of his popularity with the fans.

Because of all the hype around celebrities now, fans and pundits so often over-estimate the impact of one player's departure. People forget it's a team game – as Ronaldo himself seemed to in his award acceptance speeches.

Everton improved after losing Wayne Rooney and, as predicted here last year, Arsenal were better in 2007/08 without Thierry Henry than with him in 2006/07.

Despite the wonderful attacking play, United's Champions League and title double was built from the back on the twin towers of Nemanja Vidic and Rio Ferdinand. Patrice Evra was outstanding too and United should have Gary Neville back this term for a last hurrah.

Apart from the kind of contributions you would expect from established internationals like Carlos Tevez and Owen Hargreaves on their debut season, the players bought for the future, Anderson and Nani, were outstanding and are already clearly equipped to step into the shoes of the fading Paul Scholes and Ryan Giggs.

The sale of Ronaldo should fund the purchase of a new goalkeeper, winger and central striker, and so the next United jigsaw will begin to take shape.

They have mastered evolution to such an extent that they are forcing their main rivals Chelsea to attempt revolution. Roman Abramovic may give his managers money but, unlike the Glazers at Old Trafford, he doesn't allow them time and independence.

Luiz Felipe Scolari is a fascinating appointment – can Big Phil fill the big hole left by Jose Mourinho?

Portuguese star Deco is another interesting arrival at Stamford Bridge, but the little Portuguese playmaker might just find the pace and power of the Premier League a bit hot to handle – in fact just like the English players in the squad might find Scolari.

Arsenal remain enigmatic but Arsene Wenger remains a magician.

If Emmanuel Adebayor goes, Robin van Persie will surely step up to the plate, while at the end of last season Theo Walcott was beginning to justify the fee and

RONALDO: United's star man, but the defence was the bedrock of their success last term

the fuss. Cesc Fabregas just gets better and better. The Gunners have a goalkeeping problem, though, and William Gallas has not kept all his toys in the pram as captain.

The loss of Mathieu Flamini to Milan was a blow and, if Alexandr Hleb is also lost across the English Channel, the lack of depth in this squad will be even further exposed.

This time, **Liverpool** could well emerge as United's closest challengers, especially if they get Gareth Barry from Aston Villa.

That will be two goal-scoring midfielders behind **Fernando Torres** and an extra supply line for the pacey front man to pick up. Given that foreign strikers often do better in their second season here, the Spaniard looks a cracking bet for the Golden Boot.

There were signs towards the end of last season that Rafa Benitez was not only becoming both less feverish with his squad ro-

tation but also more of a fixture at Anfield – maybe not a rock around which the owners and chief executive were fighting their private battles, but at least a rapidly solidifying blob.

As we went to press, the other ante-post markets looked even more volatile and dangerous than usual.

I'm still not quite sure how Bolton and Fulham managed to avoid the drop, nor is it easy to spot which of West Brom, Hull and Stoke stand the best chance of staying up.

All three showed commendable determination to sign players in May and June only to be rebuffed, mainly by unreasonable contract demands.

For a rank outsider in this market, I am not sure that Paul Ince is quite ready to step up from League 2 management and the news that the Jack Walker Trust Fund will not be providing a transfer kitty for **Blackburn** is a blow.

If Mark Hughes takes one or two players with him to Man City, the 14-1 that Ladbrokes offer against Blackburn being relegated could look silly.

One or two other relegation issues are interesting. Points deductions played a big part in determining who dropped out of League 1 last term and, with so many fans feeling the pinch at the moment, it would be a surprise if some clubs did not as well, so others may go into administration I am afraid.

Formwise, three clubs dropped like stones after Christmas – Yeovil in League 1, and **Chester** and Shrewsbury in League 2. Of that trio, Shrewsbury have been taking the biggest steps to redress their problems. There is new money in the club and some of it has already been spent wisely.

Yeovil and Chester (traditionally a place where rich footballers live and poor footballers play) could be in trouble though.

The League 1 relegation market is extraordinary with half the clubs 4-1 or less in the early quotes. Both Leyton Orient and Crewe are in that mix, but the O's have improved every year under Martin Ling and both they and Alex have made some good summer signings.

If they are still being quoted at around 5-2 for the drop when you read this, they should be a lay on the betting exchanges. Yeovil, though, are backable at that price and Chester even more so.

Promotion issues in the lower leagues are hardly clearcut either.

We tipped QPR for promotion from the Championship on the *Hotline* back in May, but they are plenty short enough at 5-1. There's a ton of cash at the club, of course, but the arrival of three Italian players suggests new boss Iain Dowie may not be as free to organise the squad as he might wish.

Derby will be unrecognisable from last year but that will be no bad thing.

Reading, however, seem to be keeping hold of the nucleus of a squad arguably a little unfortunate to go down. In fact, several of the side that took them up so easily from this level three seasons ago are still there, as well as the same boss, so they are a fair price at 9-1.

When Ladbrokes are the shortest about a favourite for League 1 you tend to sit up and take notice, but their 11-4 against Leeds is hardly dwarfed by the best quote of 7-2. We'll use them in the acca.

For an outsider here, Coral could be taking a risk offering 22-1 against **Brighton**. Micky Adams won promotion with Albion the last time he was at the Withdean, and so did Adam Virgo, Brighton's Player of the Year before his unhappy move to Celtic from whence he has returned.

With the new stadium at last going ahead, Brighton are a progressive club who finished last season well and could kick on.

The League 2 title race is a nightmare with nine clubs on offer at a best price of between 7-1 and 12-1 as we went to press.

Without question the strongest finishers in the set were Bournemouth – they collected 19 points from their last seven games – but a team with none of the Cherries' financial problems appeal more.

Bradford will continue to have massive support because of their imaginative pricing policies and manager Stuart McCall has recruited well with ex-Doncaster skipper Graeme Lee turning down League 1 teams to join them and Tranmere playmaker Paul McLaren happy to step down a level as well.

And so to Scotland. Celtic or Rangers? I haven't a clue or a view this year I'm afraid! But Old Firm betting is discussed in detail in my analysis piece on page 12.

In Division One, Dundee and St Johnstone are predictably at the head of affairs but with 1-5 the odds available against finishing in the top three, **Queen Of The South** look interesting at 6-1 if they can repeat any of last season's cup heroics in the league.

Recommended bets

20pts on Man United at 11-8 (Boylesports, Skybet).

11pts on Liverpool for a top two finish.

5pts on Man United-Liverpool straight forecast.

5pts on Fernando Torres for the Golden Boot.

5pts on Blackburn to be relegated at 14-1 (Ladbrokes).

10pts on Reading at 9-1 (generally).

3pts each-way on Brighton at 22-1 (Coral).

10pts on Bradford at 9-1 (generally).

10pts on Chester to be relegated.

5pts each-way on Queen Of The South at 6-1 (Ladbrokes).

Yankee: Man United, Reading, Leeds and East Fife = 11 bets, stake 2pts per bet.

BIG REPUTATION: but can Big Phil shake Man United from the top of the tree?

Premier League 2008/09

	B365	BDIR	BFRED	BLSQ	BOYLES	CORAL	HILLS	LADS	POWER	SKY	SJAMES	TOTE	VC
Man Utd	5-4	11-10	11-10	13-10	11-8	5-4	5-4	11-10	5-4	11-8	11-10	11-10	5-4
Chelsea	2	2	9-4	15-8	15-8	15-8	7-4	2	15-8	13-8	2	21-10	7-4
Arsenal	9-2	9-2	9-2	9-2	9-2	5	4	5	5	5	9-2	5	11-2
Liverpool	7	7	8	7	13-2	13-2	15-2	11-2	7	13-2	7	7	8
Tottenham	66	66	80	50	50	66	50	50	66	66	66	50	50
Aston Villa	100	200	200	150	200	100	150	150	200	100	200	125	200
Everton	200	200	200	150	200	150	200	150	200	200	200	200	200
Man City	200	200	250	200	200	250	200	200	200	150	200	250	200
Newcastle	200	250	250	200	300	200	200	125	200	250	250	400	250
Portsmouth	500	500	500	400	500	250	300	350	500	500	500	400	500
Blackburn	500	500	500	750	500	500	500	350	750	1000	500	500	750
West Ham	1000	1000	1000	1000	1000	1000	1000	750	1000	1000	1000	1000	1000
Middlesbrough	750	1000	1000	1500	1000	1000	1000	750	1500	1500	1000	1000	1000
Sunderland	2000	1000	2500	1500	1500	1500	1000	1250	1500	2000	1000	2000	1500
Bolton	2000	1000	2500	2000	1500	2500	2000	2500	2500	3000	1000	2000	5000
Fulham	2500	2000	5000	2500	3000	2500	2000	3500	2500	2500	2000	3000	5000
Wigan	2000	1000	5000	2500	2000	2500	2000	2500	2500	2500	1000	2500	5000
West Brom	1500	2000	7500	2000	2500	3000	2000	2500	3000	5000	2000	3000	2500
Stoke	7500	7500	7500	5000	5000	5000	5000	7500	5000	7500	7500	5000	5000
Hull	7500	10000	10000	6000	4000	5000	5000	7500	5000	7500	10000	7500	5000

☆ Win or each-way (see individual bookmakers for terms)

Sponsored by Stan James

Championship 2008/09

	B365	BDIR	BFRED	BLSQ	BOYLES	CORAL	HILLS	LADS	POWER	SKY	SJAMES	TOTE	VC
QPR	13-2	11-2	6	6	5	6	6	6	6	9-2	11-2	6	11-2
Birmingham	13-2	6	7	6	15-2	7	7	6	7	6	6	6	6
Reading	8	8	8	9	8	9	8	6	15-2	9	8	8	9
C Palace	10	10	12	11	11	12	11	9	14	14	10	11	11
Wolves	10	12	14	11	12	12	14	14	12	9	12	12	14
Derby	14	14	14	12	14	12	12	14	12	10	14	10	14
Sheff Utd	14	11	10	11	14	12	11	12	12	16	11	11	12
Watford	14	14	16	12	16	16	16	14	16	16	14	16	16
Charlton	16	14	16	12	16	14	14	18	16	20	14	16	16
Ipswich	16	16	16	18	16	16	12	20	20	16	16	18	12
Cardiff	20	20	20	22	25	20	20	18	20	25	20	25	20
Bristol City	20	16	20	18	20	25	25	12	25	20	16	20	20
Nottm Forest	25	25	25	28	33	25	25	25	33	33	25	28	25
Norwich	25	33	33	22	25	22	20	33	20	33	33	33	33
Swansea	33	33	33	33	33	40	40	33	33	33	33	28	25
Southampton	33	33	40	33	33	33	40	33	33	33	33	33	33
Coventry	33	33	33	33	40	40	25	33	33	33	33	33	33
Sheff Weds	40	33	33	40	40	40	40	25	40	33	33	40	33
Preston	33	33	40	40	40	28	33	25	40	40	33	28	33
Plymouth	40	40	40	33	50	40	40	33	50	50	40	50	50
Burnley	50	40	40	33	66	40	50	40	50	40	40	50	50
Doncaster	50	33	50	50	50	50	50	40	66	50	33	50	50
Barnsley	100	66	66	80	80	80	80	66	100	100	66	80	80
Blackpool	100	80	66	80	80	80	80	80	100	100	80	80	100

☆ Win or each-way (see individual bookmakers for terms)

League 1 2008/09

	B365	BDIR	BFRED	BLSQ	BOYLES	CORAL	HILLS	LADS	POWER	SKY	SJAMES	TOTE	VC
Leeds	10-3	10-3	7-2	10-3	3	7-2	3	11-4	3	7-2	10-3	3	7-2
Leicester	5	5	11-2	9-2	11-2	5	5	5	5	9-2	5	5	5
Peterborough	10	10	12	10	11	11	9	11	11	10	10	11	8
MK Dons	12	12	12	14	12	12	11	12	14	10	12	11	12
Carlisle	14	12	14	12	11	14	16	12	16	16	12	16	14
Southend	16	14	14	16	18	14	20	16	18	16	14	18	20
Colchester	16	12	16	16	18	16	20	20	18	16	12	16	20
Brighton	20	16	20	16	18	22	20	20	20	16	16	18	14
Huddersfield	14	14	20	16	18	16	16	22	18	16	14	16	16
Tranmere	20	18	20	18	20	20	20	25	20	20	18	20	20
Scunthorpe	20	14	16	18	22	16	25	16	20	20	14	18	20
Oldham	20	20	20	22	22	20	25	28	22	25	20	20	20
Millwall	33	28	33	33	28	33	33	33	28	25	28	33	33
Swindon	33	33	33	33	33	33	33	40	33	33	33	33	33
Northampton	25	28	33	28	33	33	33	40	33	33	28	33	33
Bristol Rovers	33	33	33	40	40	40	33	33	40	33	33	33	33
Hartlepool	33	33	40	40	40	33	33	40	40	33	33	33	40
Leyton Orient	33	33	40	40	40	50	40	33	40	33	33	33	33
Walsall	50	33	33	33	33	40	33	33	33	33	33	33	33
Yeovil	40	40	40	40	40	40	50	50	40	40	40	40	40
Hereford	40	40	50	40	50	66	40	40	50	50	40	40	50
Stockport	66	40	40	40	66	40	50	33	50	40	40	40	50
Crewe	40	50	66	40	80	50	66	100	66	66	50	66	66
Cheltenham	100	66	66	80	90	80	80	80	80	150	66	66	66

☆ Win or each-way (see individual bookmakers for terms)

League 2 2008/09

	B365	BDIR	BFRED	BLSQ	BOYLES	CORAL	HILLS	LADS	POWER	SKY	SJAMES	TOTE	VC
Bradford	17-2	8	8	9	8	8	9	9	9	8	8	8	13-2
Darlington	10	9	8	8	9	10	9	9	10	7	9	9	9
Gillingham	11	9	10	8	11	9	9	10	9	8	9	9	8
Rochdale	12	10	12	10	11	11	9	12	11	12	10	11	10
Chesterfield	12	10	12	10	12	10	11	12	12	12	10	10	11
Shrewsbury	11	9	10	12	11	12	11	12	12	10	9	12	12
Bournemouth	12	10	10	11	12	14	10	11	11	12	10	12	10
Port Vale	12	12	10	12	12	14	10	14	12	12	12	14	14
Wycombe	10	10	14	12	12	10	12	12	11	12	10	11	12
Brentford	16	14	16	18	20	20	20	16	18	16	14	20	16
Rotherham	16	18	20	20	18	18	20	16	20	20	18	16	16
Aldershot	18	16	25	22	20	25	20	14	20	20	16	18	20
Lincoln City	20	20	20	20	20	20	20	25	20	20	20	20	20
Grimsby	20	20	25	20	28	33	33	28	28	20	20	25	25
Notts County	28	25	33	33	25	28	25	28	25	25	25	28	33
Barnet	16	25	33	28	20	28	25	25	33	33	25	20	25
Bury	40	33	33	25	33	28	33	33	33	40	33	22	25
Luton	33	28	33	22	33	40	33	33	25	25	28	28	33
Morecambe	33	33	33	33	33	28	40	25	33	40	33	33	33
Chester	40	40	50	50	40	50	50	50	50	50	40	50	50
Exeter	22	25	40	40	33	25	25	25	40	50	25	25	40
Macclesfield	40	40	50	40	40	50	66	50	50	50	40	40	50
Dag & Red	50	50	50	66	66	80	80	50	66	50	50	50	50
Accrington Stanley	50	50	66	66	80	80	66	50	66	100	50	66	50

☆ Win or each-way (see individual bookmakers for terms)

Conference 2008/09

	B365	BDIR	BFRED	BLSQ	BOYLES	CORAL	LADS	POWER	SKY	SJAMES	TOTE	VC
Stevenage	13-2	6	13-2	11-2	6	6	6	6	4	6	11-2	6
Torquay	6	7	7	6	7	13-2	6	7	7	7	13-2	11-2
Wrexham	7	7	8	7	8	9	7	9	9	7	15-2	9
Rushden	13-2	7	9	9	9	15-2	9	8	6	7	8	7
Oxford	10	8	9	9	9	8	8	8	8	8	9	9
Cambridge Utd	8	7	7	11	9	10	10	8	10	7	8	13-2
Mansfield	10	9	10	10	11	14	11	11	14	9	10	11
Burton	14	14	16	14	16	16	14	14	16	14	12	14
Ebsfleet	16	14	14	14	16	16	18	14	16	14	16	16
Grays	20	20	25	14	20	20	18	22	16	20	20	20
Kidderminster	20	20	20	25	25	20	20	25	20	20	22	25
York	28	25	25	25	25	25	20	25	25	25	25	33
Histon	28	33	33	33	33	33	33	33	33	33	33	33
Forest Green	28	33	25	28	33	33	25	28	33	33	33	33
Crawley	33	28	40	33	33	20	25	20	40	28	33	40
Salisbury	33	40	33	40	40	40	33	40	40	40	40	40
Kettering	33	33	33	33	40	50	33	33	40	33	33	40
Woking	50	50	40	50	50	50	50	50	50	50	50	50
Northwich	50	50	50	50	50	40	40	40	50	50	66	66
Weymouth	66	50	50	66	66	40	50	50	66	50	50	66
Barrow	66	50	66	66	66	66	66	50	66	50	66	66
Eastbourne B	66	66	50	80	66	50	66	66	66	66	66	66
Altrincham	80	80	125	80	100	100	100	100	100	80	100	100
Lewes	66	66	66	125	100	125	66	66	125	66	80	80

☆ Win or each-way (see individual bookmakers for terms)

GLORY DAYS: Portsmouth celebrate Kanu's winning goal against Cardiff

FA Cup 2008/09

	B365	BDIR	BFRED	BLSQ	BOYLES	CORAL	HILLS	LADS	POWER	SKY	S.JAMES	TOTE
Chelsea	4	9-2	9-2	4	9-2	4	4	9-2	9-2	4	9-2	9-2
Man Utd	9-2	4	5	4	4	4	4	7-2	4	4	4	4
Liverpool	15-2	15-2	7	15-2	7	11-2	11-2	6	13-2	7	15-2	15-2
Arsenal	8	7	6	7	7	6	5	7	6	6	7	13-2
Tottenham	11	12	12	14	12	14	12	10	11	16	12	12
Everton	20	20	20	16	20	20	16	14	16	20	20	20
Man City	25	20	25	20	16	20	20	14	20	20	20	22
Portsmouth	25	20	25	20	20	22	22	20	20	25	20	25
Aston Villa	20	20	20	25	25	16	16	14	20	25	20	18
Newcastle	25	25	25	28	25	25	25	16	22	25	25	25
West Ham	33	33	25	33	33	33	33	33	33	25	33	33
Blackburn	40	33	25	28	33	33	28	33	25	25	33	33
Middlesbrough	33	40	33	40	40	33	40	33	40	25	40	40
Sunderland	50	40	40	50	50	40	40	50	40	40	40	50
Bolton	80	66	66	66	66	66	80	50	50	40	66	66
Fulham	80	66	66	66	66	80	66	66	66	66	66	80
West Brom	66	80	80	80	80	80	80	50	80	66	80	80
Wigan	100	66	80	66	66	100	66	50	66	50	66	80
Birmingham	125	100	100	125	80	125	100	-	100	80	100	125
Reading	100	-	100	100	100	100	100	-	100	80	-	125
QPR	100	100	100	100	100	150	100	-	100	100	100	100
Sheff Utd	125	125	100	150	150	125	100	-	150	100	125	150
Derby County	125	125	150	150	150	150	-	-	150	150	125	150
Hull City	150	100	150	150	150	150	100	-	150	100	100	150
Wolves	125	150	150	150	100	125	125	-	150	100	150	150
Watford	175	175	150	150	150	150	150	-	150	100	175	150
Charlton	150	175	150	150	150	150	125	-	150	150	175	200
C Palace	150	175	150	125	100	150	125	-	150	100	175	200
Stoke	200	150	150	150	150	150	100	100	150	100	150	125
Cardiff	200	200	150	150	150	150	150	-		200	200	200
Bristol City	250	200	150	200	200	150	200	-	150	100	200	200
Ipswich	250	200	200	-	200	250	125	-	200	250	200	200

☆ Win or each-way (see individual bookmakers for terms). Others available.

EARLY NIGHT: United fans vote with their feet as Coventry put Red Devils out

League Cup 2008/09

	B365	BFRED	BLSQ	BOYLES	CORAL	HILLS	LADS	POWER	SKY	TOTE
Chelsea	**11-2**	5	9-2	5	9-2	9-2	9-2	9-2	5	5
Man Utd	6	6	6	13-2	6	13-2	6	6	**7**	6
Liverpool	6	8	7	7	11-2	8	7	15-2	**10**	7
Arsenal	12	10	7	10	8	8	**12**	8	10	9
Tottenham	8	10	9	10	11	10	6	10	**12**	9
Everton	16	14	14	16	14	11	14	14	14	14
Aston Villa	16	14	14	16	16	11	12	16	**20**	16
Newcastle	20	**20**	16	**20**	**20**	16	14	18	**20**	**20**
Portsmouth	22	20	20	18	20	16	16	18	20	20
Man City	25	20	14	16	16	16	12	16	20	16
Blackburn	25	20	25	25	**28**	20	20	22	20	25
West Ham	25	20	**28**	25	**28**	22	20	22	20	25
Middlesbrough	28	25	**33**	**33**	28	22	25	28	20	28
Sunderland	50	33	40	**50**	40	33	**50**	33	33	40
Bolton	80	50	66	66	**80**	66	40	50	33	66
Fulham	80	50	66	66	66	50	40	66	50	66
Wigan	66	66	66	66	**80**	40	40	50	40	66
West Brom	80	66	66	**80**	66	50	50	50	50	66
Birmingham	100	80	100	100	100	80	-	100	66	100
QPR	100	80	100	100	125	80	-	100	80	100
Reading	100	100	100	100	100	125	-	100	66	100
Cardiff	150	125	150	150	150	125	-	-	150	150
Derby	150	125	150	150	125	-	-	125	125	150
Hull	150	125	125	125	125	80	-	100	80	125
Stoke	150	125	125	100	125	80	50	100	80	125
Charlton	175	125	150	150	125	100	-	150	100	150
C Palace	175	125	125	125	150	100	-	150	80	150
Watford	175	125	150	150	150	125	-	150	80	150

☆ *Win or each-way (see individual bookmakers for terms). Others available*

Scottish Premier League 2008/09

	B365	BDIR	BFRED	BLSQ	BOYLES	CORAL	HILLS	LADS	POWER	SKY	SJAMES	TOTE	VC
Celtic	5-6	5-6	4-5	5-6	4-5	8-11	8-11	5-6	4-5	5-6	5-6	4-5	4-5
Rangers	5-6	5-6	Evs	5-6	Evs	Evs	Evs	5-6	10-11	5-6	5-6	10-11	10-11
Aberdeen	200	150	150	200	150	125	150	100	200	100	150	200	150
Hearts	125	125	125	150	100	200	150	150	150	66	125	150	100
Hibernian	150	200	150	250	200	150	200	150	200	100	200	150	200
Motherwell	250	200	200	200	200	200	200	200	200	150	200	200	200
Dundee Utd	200	200	250	150	200	150	300	200	300	150	200	250	250
Kilmarnock	1000	1500	1000	1500	1000	750	1000	750	1000	1500	1500	1000	750
Falkirk	1500	1000	1000	1000	1000	1000	1500	2000	1000	1000	1000	1500	1000
Inverness CT	2500	2000	2500	2500	2500	2500	2000	2500	2000	2000	2000	2500	1500
Hamilton	5000	5000	5000	5000	5000	5000	2500	5000	5000	5000	5000	5000	2500
St Mirren	5000	2500	5000	5000	5000	2500	2500	2500	2500	2500	2500	5000	2000

☆ Win or each-way (see individual bookmakers for terms)

CELTIC: clinch their third title in a row

Scottish Division One 2008/09

	B365	BDIR	CORAL	HILLS	LADS	SJAMES
St Johnstone	15-8	9-4	2	7-4	9-4	9-4
Dundee	5-2	2	2	15-8	2	2
Queen Of Sth	13-2	6	11-2	7	6	6
Dunfermline	11-2	13-2	10	9	6	13-2
Partick Thistle	10	12	10	14	10	12
Livingston	14	14	14	14	14	14
Ross County	14	14	16	12	10	14
Morton	20	20	20	20	20	20
Clyde	25	25	22	25	20	25
Airdrie Utd	25	33	25	40	20	33

☆ Win or each-way (see individual bookmakers for terms)

Scottish Division Two 2008/09

	B365	BDIR	CORAL	HILLS	LADS	SJAMES
East Fife	3	3	3	7-2	3	3
Raith	3	4	7-2	10-3	3	4
Ayr	13-2	6	5	9-2	6	6
Alloa	15-2	7	7	8	6	7
Peterhead	13-2	6	15-2	13-2	6	6
Brechin	7	7	13-2	11-2	9	7
Stirling	15-2	8	8	9	8	8
Stanraer	20	25	25	20	16	20
Arbroath	25	14	20	22	20	14
Queen's Park	25	18	25	28	14	18

☆ Win or each-way (see individual bookmakers for terms)

Scottish Division Three 2008/09

	B365	BDIR	CORAL	HILLS	LADS	SJAMES
Montrose	4	7-2	7-2	7-2	3	7-2
Dumbarton	4	7-2	7-2	7-2	4	7-2
Stenhousemuir	4	9-2	9-2	9-2	9-2	9-2
Cowdenbeath	7-2	9-2	9-2	9-2	4	9-2
Berwick	6	11-2	6	11-2	5	11-2
Forfar	12	12	8	12	12	12
East Stirling	14	10	12	11	12	10
Elgin	14	14	16	16	12	14
Albion	16	20	28	22	16	20
Annan	20	28	33	20	25	28

☆ Win or each-way (see individual bookmakers for terms)

Spanish Primera Liga

	B365	BDIR	CORAL	HILLS	LADS	SJAMES
R Madrid	5-6	4-5	5-6	9-10	4-5	4-5
Barcelona	5-4	5-4	5-4	6-5	11-8	5-4
Seville	16	25	16	20	16	25
Villarreal	25	20	20	20	25	20
Atl Madrid	20	22	20	20	20	22
Valencia	25	50	25	33	25	50
Deportivo	200	300	150	250	150	300
Getafe	200	300	150	150	200	300
R Mallorca	200	300	150	250	200	300
R Santander	300	200	300	250	250	200
Espanyol	250	350	250	250	250	350
Ath Bilbao	400	350	400	250	300	350
Almeria	500	400	500	300	500	400
R Betis	300	500	300	300	250	500
Osasuna	400	500	500	400	500	500
Valladolid	500	500	500	400	500	500
Gijon	750	1000	750	400	750	1000
Malaga	500	1000	750	400	750	1000
Numancia	750	1000	750	750	750	1000
Recreativo	750	1000	750	400	750	1000

☆ Win or each-way (see individual bookmakers for terms)

Italian Serie A

	B365	BDIR	CORAL	HILLS	LADS	SJAMES
Inter Milan	Evs	11-10	6-5	Evs	5-6	11-10
AC Milan	11-4	5-2	11-4	9-4	7-2	5-2
Juventus	11-2	9-2	9-2	5	5	9-2
Roma	9-2	9-2	5	4	9-2	9-2
Fiorentina	50	40	50	40	50	40
Sampdoria	150	100	100	100	150	100
Udinese	150	150	150	125	150	150
Lazio	250	200	250	150	250	200
Napoli	200	250	150	150	200	250
Genoa	500	250	250	250	500	250
Palermo	500	350	300	250	500	350
Atalanta	500	400	300	250	500	400
Cagliari	500	500	500	500	500	500
Torino	500	400	500	500	500	400
Bologna	1000	500	500	500	750	500
Catania	1000	750	1000	500	1000	750
Chievo	750	1000	500	1000	750	1000
Lecce	1000	1000	500	1000	1000	1000
Reggina	1000	1000	1000	1000	1000	1000
Siena	1000	1000	500	500	750	1000

☆ Win or each-way (see individual bookmakers for terms)

German Bundesliga

	B365	BFRED	CORAL	HILLS	LADS	TOTE
B Munich	4-11	4-9	2-5	2-5	4-9	2-5
Werder Bremen	13-2	5	7	6	5	13-2
Schalke	15-2	13-2	7	9	8	15-2
Hamburg	22	16	20	16	14	18
Stuttgart	28	20	25	25	20	28
Wolfsburg	33	14	16	20	28	28
B Leverkusen	40	40	50	33	33	33
B Dortmund	50	66	80	66	66	50
Hannover	125	100	100	150	100	100
Hertha Berlin	150	100	150	100	100	150
B M'Gladbach	100	100	150	100	150	100
E Frankfurt	200	150	150	100	150	150
Hoffenheim	150	150	100	100	150	200
Cologne	250	200	250	250	250	250
Bochum	500	500	500	250	500	400
Karlsruhe	500	250	500	500	300	400
A Bielefeld	1000	750	750	1000	750	750
E Cottbus	1000	750	750	1000	750	750

☆ Win or each-way (see individual bookmakers for terms)

French Ligue 1

	B365	BFRED	CORAL	HILLS	LADS	POWER
Lyon	4-6	4-6	8-13	8-11	4-7	4-6
Marseille	7-2	7-2	4	5-2	9-2	7-2
Bordeaux	9-2	9-2	11-2	9-2	5	9-2
Paris-SG	25	33	28	20	25	22
St-Etienne	25	16	33	25	33	33
Monaco	33	40	40	33	25	40
Lille	33	40	40	40	50	28
Rennes	50	50	50	40	50	40
Nancy	50	33	50	66	40	33
Auxerre	150	150	150	150	100	150
Nantes	200	100	150	150	150	150
Nice	150	150	200	150	150	66
Le Mans	200	150	200	250	200	150
Sochaux	200	100	200	250	200	150
Toulouse	300	200	300	500	300	125
Valenciennes	300	250	300	500	250	200
Lorient	400	150	500	500	300	150
Caen	500	250	500	250	500	200
Le Havre	500	500	500	1000	500	500
Grenoble	1000	1000	1000	1000	750	750

☆ Win or each-way (see individual bookmakers for terms)

Lyon's Ligue dominance could finally be at an end

THE guillotine looks set to fall on Lyon's track record of domination in Le Championnat – revolt against the French title-holders!

Lyon are seeking an eighth straight championship in France but there's enough evidence to suggest that feat might be beyond them this season, which means we need to find an alternative to Les Gones, who will go off at odds-on for the title.

Let's start with the stats. While Lyon won the league for the seventh time last term, the race for the title was a much closer affair than in recent years, with Lyon winning by just four points.

That was a marked loosening of their stranglehold over Ligue 1 compared to previous campaigns – prior to last term, the Stade Gerland crew had been winning Le Championnat by ever-increasing margins since 2004, with the gap peaking at 17 points in 2006/07.

This recent downturn puts a very different spin on last season's triumph, but it's not the only concern for would-be Lyon backers – despite their latest success, the board still felt the need to ditch Alain Perrin and have hired Claude Puel to manage the side.

You may remember that Puel tried to encourage his Lille outfit to leave the pitch against Man United in the Champions League a while back, so he's hardly calmness personified, and his trophy haul in recent years has been limited too.

Perrin's departure means it's now four managers in four years for Lyon and, with the Champions League success the goal, it's easy to see them losing their domestic focus for a while.

In the circumstances, back **Marseille** and **Bordeaux** to take advantage – both are over-priced to do so.

The Italian close season has been dominated by the arrival of Jose Mourinho at **Inter Milan**.

The Italian champions are seeking a fourth Scudetto in a row, and the appointment of the 'special one' certainly makes them hard to oppose.

Inter were our headline bet last year, and they duly obliged at 7-5. They didn't have it all their own way though, as the Nerazzurri almost blew a huge lead towards the end of the campaign, before finally bringing home the bacon on the last day of the season.

Had Mourinho not been appointed Inter would have been a lay this time, precisely because of that decline during the latter stages of 2008.

However, his appointment suggests that they will be back with renewed vigour this season. It might be wise to

MARSEILLE: Mathieu Valbuena's team are well set to take advantage of a Lyon stumble

wait for a couple of weeks before diving in though, just to see if Inter require time to shake off a few cobwebs – if so, their price might drift a touch in our favour.

In Germany, there might be a little mileage in picking a fight with Bayern Munich – whether they should be in at odds-on to win the title is debatable.

At face value, you might say 1-2 is fair enough. After all, the Bavarian giants won the league last season by ten points, and made the semi-finals of the Uefa Cup too.

However, some of Bayern's high-profile players are a bit frustrated with life at the Allianz Arena, and may not stay.

Bastian Schweinsteiger and Lukas Podolski are known to be unhappy, while France's Franck Ribery is out injured. You should certainly tread carefully before remortgaging the house and lumping on.

Jurgen Klinsmann has agreed to coach the side, but don't forget he's been sunning himself in California since quitting as Germany boss, so you'll also be taking the risk that the world-renowned diver will hit the ground running if you're backing Bayern.

It probably makes better sense to try a small bet on **Werder Bremen** at this stage.

As usual, Bremen were scoring for fun last season and, if they tighten up at the back, they could go close – have a punt on them in the short term whilst we see how things

progress in Munich.

Staying in the Bundesliga, keep an eye on **Wolfsburg** in the first couple of months – they should be worth following regularly.

Felix Magath has just taken the Wolves into the Uefa Cup during his first year in charge, a stint that saw them rise from 15th to fifth in the table.

The club, backed by Volkswagen, have made some big signings this summer and should go well, so stay on the right side of these dark horses.

In Spain, it's hard to see past **Real Madrid**, who are available at Evens in places.

Los Merengues sluiced in last year, winning La Liga with a whopping 84 goals, and heading arch rivals Barcelona by 18 points.

That makes 13-10 about Barca look ridiculous, because the Nou Camp is a hotbed of discontent.

Apart from an exodus of players, the club have also appointed reserve team coach Pep Guardiola to replace Frank Rijkaard. He may be a popular choice with the fans, but it's unlikely that he will have enough experience to influence Barca's broader decline.

Villarreal secured their highest ever league finish last term, but they will be missing Turkish striker Nihat Kahveci for some time following an operation on his thigh. Not that Real Madrid need a leg up anyway – La Liga is theirs for the taking.

premier league

Champions:	Man United
Runners-up:	Chelsea
Relegated:	Reading
	Birmingham
	Derby

championship

Champions:	West Brom
Runners-up:	Stoke
Play-off champions:	Hull
Relegated:	Leicester
	Scunthorpe
	Colchester

league 1

Champions:	Swansea
Runners-up:	Nottingham F
Play-off champions:	Doncaster
Relegated:	Bournemouth
	Gillingham
	Port Vale
	Luton Town

league 2

Champions:	MK Dons
Runners-up:	Peterborough
Third:	Hereford
Play-off champions:	Stockport
Relegated:	Mansfield
	Wrexham

conference

Champions:	Aldershot Town
Play-off champions:	Exeter City
Relegated:	Halifax
	Farsley Celtic
	Stafford
	Droylsden

conference north

Champions:	Kettering
Play-off champions:	Barrow
Relegated:	Nuneaton
	Boston United
	Leigh RMI

conference south

Champions:	Lewes
Play-off champions:	Eastbourne
Relegated:	Cambridge
	Sutton United

scottish premier league

Champions:	Celtic
Runners-up:	Rangers
Relegated:	Gretna

scottish division one

Champions:	Hamilton
Runners-up:	Dundee
Relegated:	Stirling Albion

scottish division two

Champions:	Ross County
Promoted:	Airdrie United
Relegated:	Cowdenbeath
	Berwick

scottish division three

Champions:	East Fife
Play-off champions:	Arbroath
Promoted:	Stranraer
Bottom:	Forfar Athletic

fa cup

Winners:	Portsmouth
Runners-up:	Cardiff City

league cup

Winners:	Tottenham
Runners-up:	Chelsea

johnstone's paint trophy

Winners:	MK Dons
Runners-up:	Grimsby Town

fa trophy

Winners:	Ebbsfleet
Runners-up:	Torquay

setanta shield

Winners:	Aldershot
Runners-up:	Rushden & D

scotttish cup

Winners:	Rangers
Runners-up:	Queen of South

scottish league cup

Winners:	Rangers
Runners-up:	Dundee United

scottish challenge cup

Winners:	St Johnstone
Runners-up:	Dunfermline

Referees can be the bane of players and managers alike but the bookings market is increasingly where spread betting and fixed odds punters look to make some profit.

Below are the stats for last season's select group of referees. Their card counts are exclusive to the Premier League and you should bear that in mind when weighing up their final scores.

		Games	Y	R	Pts	Ave
Martin Atkinson	West Yorkshire	42	109	6	1240	**29.52**
Steve Bennett	Kent	45	143	9	1655	**36.78**
Mark Clattenburg	Tyne & Wear	39	124	10	1490	**38.21**
Mike Dean	Wirral	45	154	10	1790	**39.78**
Phil Dowd	Staffordshire	45	124	11	1515	**33.67**
Chris Foy	Merseyside	37	116	6	1310	**35.41**
Mark Halsey	Lancashire	44	91	5	1035	**23.52**
Andre Marriner	West Midlands	39	118	6	1330	**34.10**
Lee Mason	Lancashire	31	114	4	1240	**40.00**
Lee Probert	Gloucestershire	37	82	3	895	**24.19**
Uriah Rennie	South Yorkshire	24	66	7	835	**34.79**
Mike Riley	West Yorkshire	42	149	8	1690	**40.24**
Keith Stroud	Hampshire	36	117	7	1345	**37.36**
Rob Styles	Hampshire	37	124	15	1615	**43.65**
Steve Tanner	Somerset	34	103	3	1105	**32.50**
Peter Walton	Northamptonshire	44	130	5	1425	**32.39**
Howard Webb	South Yorkshire	46	166	4	1760	**38.26**
Alan Wiley	Staffordshire	44	135	3	1425	**32.39**

MEN IN BLACK: Rob Styles racked up the most cards per games last season

PREMIER LEAGUE

Team	Pld	W	D	L	F	GFA	PGA	Pts
1 Man Utd (1)	38	27	6	5	80	**2.11**	2.3	87
2 Arsenal (3)	38	24	11	3	74	**1.95**	2.2	83
3 Aston Villa (6)	38	16	12	10	71	**1.87**	1.6	60
4 Liverpool (4)	38	21	13	4	67	**1.76**	2.0	76
5 Tottenham (11)	38	11	13	14	66	**1.74**	1.2	46
6 Chelsea (2)	38	25	10	3	65	**1.71**	2.2	85
7 Everton (5)	38	19	8	11	55	**1.45**	1.7	65
8 Blackburn (7)	38	15	13	10	50	**1.32**	1.5	58
9 Portsmouth (8)	38	16	9	13	48	**1.26**	1.5	57
10 Birmingham (19)	38	8	11	19	46	**1.21**	0.9	35
11 Man City (9)	38	15	10	13	45	**1.18**	1.4	55
12 Newcastle (12)	38	11	10	17	45	**1.18**	1.1	43
13 Middlesbro (13)	38	10	12	16	43	**1.13**	1.1	42
14 West Ham (10)	38	13	10	15	42	**1.11**	1.3	49
15 Reading (18)	38	10	6	22	41	**1.08**	0.9	36
16 Fulham (18)	38	8	12	18	38	**1.00**	0.9	36
17 Sunderland (15)	38	11	6	21	36	**0.95**	1.0	39
18 Bolton (16)	38	9	10	19	36	**0.95**	1.0	37
19 Wigan (14)	38	10	10	18	34	**0.89**	1.1	40
20 Derby (20)	38	1	8	29	20	**0.53**	0.3	11

- Number in brackets refers to final league finishing position
- GFA: Goals for average per match
- PGA: Average points gained per match

CHAMPIONSHIP

Team	Pld	W	D	L	F	GFA	PGA	Pts
1 West Brom (1)	46	23	12	11	88	**1.91**	1.8	81
2 Stoke (2)	46	21	16	9	69	**1.50**	1.7	79
3 Hull City (3)	46	21	12	13	65	**1.41**	1.6	75
4 Ipswich (8)	46	18	15	13	65	**1.41**	1.5	69
5 Charlton (12)	46	17	13	16	63	**1.37**	1.4	64
6 Watford (7)	46	18	16	12	62	**1.35**	1.5	70
7 Colchester (24)	46	7	17	22	62	**1.35**	0.8	38
8 Plymouth (12)	46	17	13	16	60	**1.30**	1.4	64
9 Burnley (13)	46	16	14	16	60	**1.30**	1.3	62
10 QPR (14)	46	14	16	16	60	**1.30**	1.3	58
11 Cardiff (12)	46	16	16	14	59	**1.28**	1.4	64
12 Blackpool (20)	46	12	18	16	59	**1.28**	1.2	54
13 C Palace (5)	46	18	17	11	58	**1.26**	1.5	71
14 Sheff Utd (9)	46	17	15	14	56	**1.22**	1.4	66
15 Southampton (20)	46	13	15	18	56	**1.22**	1.2	54
16 Bristol C (4)	46	20	14	12	54	**1.17**	1.6	74
17 Sheff Wed (18)	46	14	13	19	54	**1.17**	1.2	55
18 Wolves (7)	46	18	16	12	53	**1.15**	1.5	70
19 Barnsley (18)	46	14	13	19	52	**1.13**	1.2	55
20 Coventry (21)	46	14	11	21	52	**1.13**	1.2	53
21 Preston (15)	46	15	11	20	50	**1.09**	1.2	56
22 Norwich (18)	46	15	10	21	49	**1.07**	1.2	55
23 Scunthorpe (23)	46	11	13	22	46	**1.00**	1.0	46
24 Leicester (22)	46	12	16	18	42	**0.91**	1.1	52

TOP SCORERS 2007/08

PREMIER LEAGUE

Team	Pld	W	D	L	A	GAA	PGA	Pts
1 Man Utd (1)	38	27	6	5	22	**0.58**	2.3	87
2 Chelsea (2)	38	25	10	3	26	**0.68**	2.2	85
3 Liverpool (4)	38	21	13	4	28	**0.74**	2.0	76
4 Arsenal (3)	38	24	11	3	31	**0.82**	2.2	83
5 Everton (5)	38	19	8	11	33	**0.87**	1.7	65
6 Portsmouth (8)	38	16	9	13	40	**1.05**	1.5	57
7 Blackburn (7)	38	15	13	10	48	**1.26**	1.5	58
8 West Ham (10)	38	13	10	15	50	**1.32**	1.3	49
9 Aston Villa (6)	38	16	12	10	51	**1.34**	1.6	60
10 Wigan (14)	38	10	10	18	51	**1.34**	1.1	40
11 Man City (9)	38	15	10	13	53	**1.39**	1.4	55
12 Middlesbro (13)	38	10	12	16	53	**1.39**	1.1	42
13 Bolton (16)	38	9	10	19	54	**1.42**	1.0	37
14 Sunderland (15)	38	11	6	21	59	**1.55**	1.0	39
15 Fulham (18)	38	8	12	18	60	**1.58**	0.9	36
16 Tottenham (11)	38	11	13	14	61	**1.61**	1.2	46
17 Birmingham (19)	38	8	11	19	62	**1.63**	0.9	35
18 Newcastle (12)	38	11	10	17	65	**1.71**	1.1	43
19 Reading (18)	38	10	6	22	66	**1.74**	0.9	36
20 Derby (20)	38	1	8	29	89	**2.34**	0.3	11

- Number in brackets refers to final league finishing position
- GAA: Goals against average per match
- PGA: Average points gained per match

CHAMPIONSHIP

Team	Pld	W	D	L	A	GAA	PGA	Pts
1 C Palace (5)	46	18	17	11	42	**0.91**	1.5	71
2 Leicester (22)	46	12	16	18	45	**0.98**	1.1	52
3 Hull City (3)	46	21	12	13	47	**1.02**	1.6	75
4 Wolves (7)	46	18	16	12	48	**1.04**	1.5	70
5 Plymouth (12)	46	17	13	16	50	**1.09**	1.4	64
6 Sheff Utd (9)	46	17	15	14	51	**1.11**	1.4	66
7 Bristol C (4)	46	20	14	12	53	**1.15**	1.6	74
8 West Brom (1)	46	23	12	11	55	**1.20**	1.8	81
9 Stoke (2)	46	21	16	9	55	**1.20**	1.7	79
10 Cardiff (12)	46	16	16	14	55	**1.20**	1.4	64
11 Sheff Wed (18)	46	14	13	19	55	**1.20**	1.2	55
12 Watford (7)	46	18	16	12	56	**1.22**	1.5	70
13 Ipswich (8)	46	18	15	13	56	**1.22**	1.5	69
14 Preston (15)	46	15	11	20	56	**1.22**	1.2	56
15 Charlton (12)	46	17	13	16	58	**1.26**	1.4	64
16 Norwich (18)	46	15	10	21	59	**1.28**	1.2	55
17 Blackpool (20)	46	12	18	16	64	**1.39**	1.2	54
18 Coventry (21)	46	14	11	21	64	**1.39**	1.2	53
19 Barnsley (18)	46	14	13	19	65	**1.41**	1.2	55
20 QPR (14)	46	14	16	16	66	**1.43**	1.3	58
21 Burnley (13)	46	16	14	16	67	**1.46**	1.3	62
22 Scunthorpe (23)	46	11	13	22	69	**1.50**	1.0	46
23 Southampton (20)	46	13	15	18	72	**1.57**	1.2	54
24 Colchester (24)	46	7	17	22	86	**1.87**	0.8	38

BEST DEFENCE 2007/08

TOP SCORERS 2007/08

LEAGUE 1

Team	Pld	W	D	L	F	GFA	PGA	Pts
1 Swansea (1)	46	27	11	8	82	**1.78**	2.0	92
2 Leeds (2)	46	27	10	9	72	**1.57**	2.0	91
3 Southend (6)	46	22	10	14	70	**1.52**	1.7	76
4 Doncaster (5)	46	23	11	12	65	**1.41**	1.7	80
5 Nottm Forest (3)	46	22	16	8	64	**1.39**	1.8	82
6 Carlisle (5)	46	23	11	12	64	**1.39**	1.7	80
7 Swindon (13)	46	16	13	17	63	**1.37**	1.3	61
8 Hartlepool (16)	46	15	9	22	63	**1.37**	1.2	54
9 Bournemouth (15)	46	17	7	22	62	**1.35**	1.3	58
10 Northampton (10)	46	17	15	14	60	**1.30**	1.4	66
11 Brighton (7)	46	19	12	15	58	**1.26**	1.5	69
12 Oldham (8)	46	18	13	15	58	**1.26**	1.5	67
13 Tranmere (11)	46	18	11	17	52	**1.13**	1.4	65
14 Walsall (12)	46	16	16	14	52	**1.13**	1.4	64
15 Huddersfield (10)	46	20	6	20	50	**1.09**	1.4	66
16 Leyton Orient (14)	46	16	12	18	49	**1.07**	1.3	60
17 Crewe (21)	46	12	14	20	47	**1.02**	1.1	50
18 Port Vale (24)	46	9	11	26	47	**1.02**	0.8	38
19 Bristol R (17)	46	12	17	17	45	**0.98**	1.2	53
20 Millwall (19)	46	14	10	22	45	**0.98**	1.1	52
21 Gillingham (22)	46	11	13	22	44	**0.96**	1.0	46
22 Luton (23)	46	11	10	25	43	**0.93**	0.9	43
23 Cheltenham (20)	46	13	12	21	42	**0.91**	1.1	51
24 Yeovil (19)	46	14	10	22	38	**0.83**	1.1	52

LEAGUE 2

Team	Pld	W	D	L	F	GFA	PGA	Pts
1 Peterborough (2)	46	28	8	10	84	**1.83**	2.0	92
2 MK Dons (1)	46	29	10	7	82	**1.78**	2.1	97
3 Rochdale (5)	46	23	11	12	77	**1.67**	1.7	80
4 Chesterfield (9)	46	19	12	15	76	**1.65**	1.5	69
5 Hereford (3)	46	26	10	10	72	**1.57**	1.9	88
6 Stockport (4)	46	24	10	12	72	**1.57**	1.8	82
7 Darlington (7)	46	22	12	12	67	**1.46**	1.7	78
8 Bradford (10)	46	17	11	18	63	**1.37**	1.3	62
9 Rotherham (8)	46	21	11	14	62	**1.35**	1.6	74
10 Lincoln (15)	46	18	4	24	61	**1.33**	1.3	58
11 Morecambe (12)	46	16	12	18	59	**1.28**	1.3	60
12 Bury (14)	46	16	11	19	58	**1.26**	1.3	59
13 Wycombe (7)	46	22	12	12	56	**1.22**	1.7	78
14 Barnet (12)	46	16	12	18	56	**1.22**	1.3	60
15 Shrewsbury (19)	46	12	14	20	56	**1.22**	1.1	50
16 Grimsby (16)	46	15	10	21	55	**1.20**	1.2	55
17 Brentford (14)	46	17	8	21	52	**1.13**	1.3	59
18 Chester (22)	46	12	11	23	51	**1.11**	1.0	47
19 Accrington (17)	46	16	3	27	49	**1.07**	1.1	51
20 Dag & Red (20)	46	13	10	23	49	**1.07**	1.1	49
21 Mansfield (23)	46	11	9	26	48	**1.04**	0.9	42
22 Macclesfield (19)	46	11	17	18	47	**1.02**	1.1	50
23 Wrexham (24)	46	10	10	26	38	**0.83**	0.9	40
24 Notts Co (21)	46	10	18	18	37	**0.80**	1.0	48

Sponsored by Stan James

LEAGUE 1

Team	Pld	W	D	L	A	GAA	PGA	Pts
1 Nott'm Forest (3)	46	22	16	8	32	**0.70**	1.8	82
2 Leeds (2)	46	27	10	9	38	**0.83**	2.0	91
3 Doncaster (5)	46	23	11	12	41	**0.89**	1.7	80
4 Swansea (1)	46	27	11	8	42	**0.91**	2.0	92
5 Carlisle (5)	46	23	11	12	46	**1.00**	1.7	80
6 Oldham (8)	46	18	13	15	46	**1.00**	1.5	67
7 Walsall (12)	46	16	16	14	46	**1.00**	1.4	64
8 Tranmere (11)	46	18	11	17	47	**1.02**	1.4	65
9 Brighton (7)	46	19	12	15	50	**1.09**	1.5	69
10 Bristol R (17)	46	12	17	17	53	**1.15**	1.2	53
11 Southend (6)	46	22	10	14	55	**1.20**	1.7	76
12 Northampton (10)	46	17	15	14	55	**1.20**	1.4	66
13 Swindon (13)	46	16	13	17	56	**1.22**	1.3	61
14 Yeovil (19)	46	14	10	22	59	**1.28**	1.1	52
15 Millwall (19)	46	14	10	22	60	**1.30**	1.1	52
16 Huddersfield (10)	46	20	6	20	62	**1.35**	1.4	66
17 Leyton Orient (14)	46	16	12	18	63	**1.37**	1.3	60
18 Luton (23)	46	11	10	25	63	**1.37**	0.9	43
19 Cheltenham (20)	46	13	12	21	64	**1.39**	1.1	51
20 Crewe (21)	46	12	14	20	65	**1.41**	1.1	50
21 Hartlepool (16)	46	15	9	22	66	**1.43**	1.2	54
22 Bournemouth (15)	46	17	7	22	72	**1.57**	1.3	58
23 Gillingham (22)	46	11	13	22	73	**1.59**	1.0	46
24 Port Vale (24)	46	9	11	26	81	**1.76**	0.8	38

LEAGUE 2

Team	Pld	W	D	L	A	GAA	PGA	Pts
1 MK Dons (1)	46	29	10	7	37	**0.80**	2.1	97
2 Darlington (7)	46	22	12	12	40	**0.87**	1.7	78
3 Hereford (3)	46	26	10	10	41	**0.89**	1.9	88
4 Wycombe (7)	46	22	12	12	42	**0.91**	1.7	78
5 Peterborough (2)	46	28	8	10	43	**0.93**	2.0	92
6 Notts Co (21)	46	10	18	18	53	**1.15**	1.0	48
7 Stockport (4)	46	24	10	12	54	**1.17**	1.8	82
8 Rochdale (5)	46	23	11	12	54	**1.17**	1.7	80
9 Chesterfield (9)	46	19	12	15	56	**1.22**	1.5	69
10 Rotherham (8)	46	21	11	14	58	**1.26**	1.6	74
11 Bradford (10)	46	17	11	18	61	**1.33**	1.3	62
12 Bury (14)	46	16	11	19	61	**1.33**	1.3	59
13 Barnet (12)	46	16	12	18	63	**1.37**	1.3	60
14 Morecambe (12)	46	16	12	18	63	**1.37**	1.3	60
15 Macclesfield (19)	46	11	17	18	64	**1.39**	1.1	50
16 Shrewsbury (19)	46	12	14	20	65	**1.41**	1.1	50
17 Grimsby (16)	46	15	10	21	66	**1.43**	1.2	55
18 Chester (22)	46	12	11	23	68	**1.48**	1.0	47
19 Mansfield (23)	46	11	9	26	68	**1.48**	0.9	42
20 Brentford (14)	46	17	8	21	70	**1.52**	1.3	59
21 Dag & Red (20)	46	13	10	23	70	**1.52**	1.1	49
22 Wrexham (24)	46	10	10	26	70	**1.52**	0.9	40
23 Lincoln (15)	46	18	4	24	77	**1.67**	1.3	58
24 Accrington (17)	46	16	3	27	83	**1.80**	1.1	51

BLUE SQUARE PREMIER

Team	Pld	W	D	L	F	GFA	PGA	Pts
1 Torquay (3)	46	26	8	12	83	**1.80**	19	86
2 Exeter (4)	46	22	17	7	83	**1.80**	1.8	83
3 Aldershot (1)	46	31	8	7	82	**1.78**	2.2	101
4 Stevenage (6)	46	24	7	15	82	**1.78**	1.7	79
5 Burton (5)	46	23	12	11	79	**1.72**	1.8	81
6 Histon (7)	46	20	12	14	76	**1.65**	1.6	72
7 Forest Green (9)	46	19	14	13	76	**1.65**	1.5	71
8 Kidderminster (13)	46	19	10	17	74	**1.61**	1.5	67
9 Crawley (14)	46	19	9	18	73	**1.59**	1.4	66
10 York (15)	46	17	11	18	71	**1.54**	1.3	62
11 Salisbury (12)	46	18	14	14	70	**1.52**	1.5	68
12 Cambridge (3)	46	25	11	10	68	**1.48**	1.9	86
13 Ebbsfleet (11)	46	19	12	15	65	**1.41**	1.5	69
14 Halifax (18)	46	12	16	18	61	**1.33**	1.1	52
15 Grays (10)	46	19	13	14	58	**1.26**	1.5	70
16 Oxford (9)	46	20	11	15	56	**1.22**	1.5	71
17 Altrincham (21)	46	9	14	23	56	**1.22**	0.9	41
18 Rushden (16)	46	15	14	17	55	**1.20**	1.3	59
19 Woking (17)	46	12	17	17	53	**1.15**	1.2	53
20 Weymouth (19)	46	11	13	22	53	**1.15**	1.0	46
21 Northwich (20)	46	11	11	24	52	**1.13**	1.0	44
22 Farsley (22)	46	10	9	27	48	**1.04**	0.8	39
23 Droylsden (24)	46	5	9	32	46	**1.00**	0.5	24
24 Stafford (23)	46	5	10	31	42	**0.91**	0.5	25

SCOTTISH PREMIER LEAGUE

Team	Pld	W	D	L	F	GFA	PGA	Pts
1 Celtic (1)	38	28	5	5	84	**2.21**	2.3	89
2 Rangers (2)	38	27	5	6	84	**2.21**	2.3	86
3 Dundee Utd (6)	38	14	10	14	53	**1.39**	1.4	52
4 Inverness CT (9)	38	13	4	21	51	**1.34**	1.1	43
5 Motherwell (3)	38	18	6	14	50	**1.32**	1.6	60
6 Aberdeen (4)	38	15	8	15	50	**1.32**	1.4	53
7 Hibernian (6)	38	14	10	14	49	**1.29**	1.4	52
8 Hearts (8)	38	13	9	16	47	**1.24**	1.3	48
9 Falkirk (7)	38	13	10	15	45	**1.18**	1.3	49
10 Kilmarnock (11)	38	10	10	18	39	**1.03**	1.1	40
11 Gretna (12)	38	5	8	25	32	**0.84**	0.6	23

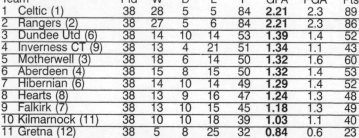

UNSTOPPABLE: Scott McDonald scores yet another goal in Celtic's title charge

Sponsored by Stan James

BLUE SQUARE PREMIER

Team	Pld	W	D	L	A	GAA	PGA	Pts
1 Cambridge (3)	46	25	11	10	41	**0.89**	1.9	86
2 Grays (10)	46	19	13	14	47	**1.02**	1.5	70
3 Aldershot (1)	46	31	8	7	48	**1.04**	2.2	101
4 Oxford (9)	46	20	11	15	48	**1.04**	1.5	71
5 Stevenage (6)	46	24	7	15	55	**1.20**	1.7	79
6 Rushden (16)	46	15	14	17	55	**1.20**	1.3	59
7 Burton (5)	46	23	12	11	56	**1.22**	1.8	81
8 Torquay (3)	46	26	8	12	57	**1.24**	1.9	86
9 Kidderminster (13)	46	19	10	17	57	**1.24**	1.5	67
10 Exeter (4)	46	22	17	7	58	**1.26**	1.8	83
11 Forest Green (9)	46	19	14	13	59	**1.28**	1.5	71
12 Salisbury (12)	46	18	14	14	60	**1.30**	1.5	68
13 Ebbsfleet (11)	46	19	12	15	61	**1.33**	1.5	69
14 Woking (17)	46	12	17	17	61	**1.33**	1.2	53
15 Histon (7)	46	20	12	14	67	**1.46**	1.6	72
16 Crawley (14)	46	19	9	18	67	**1.46**	1.4	66
17 Halifax (18)	46	12	16	18	70	**1.52**	1.1	52
18 Weymouth (19)	46	11	13	22	73	**1.59**	1.0	46
19 York (15)	46	17	11	18	74	**1.61**	1.3	62
20 Northwich (20)	46	11	11	24	78	**1.70**	1.0	44
21 Altrincham (21)	46	9	14	23	82	**1.78**	0.9	41
22 Farsley (22)	46	10	9	27	86	**1.87**	0.8	39
23 Stafford (23)	46	5	10	31	99	**2.15**	0.5	25
24 Droylsden (24)	46	5	9	32	103	**2.24**	0.5	24

SCOTTISH PREMIER LEAGUE

Team	Pld	W	D	L	A	GAA	PGA	Pts
1 Celtic (1)	38	28	5	5	26	**0.68**	2.3	89
2 Rangers (2)	38	27	5	6	33	**0.87**	2.3	86
3 Hibernian (6)	38	14	10	14	45	**1.18**	1.4	52
4 Motherwell (3)	38	18	6	14	46	**1.21**	1.6	60
5 Dundee Utd (6)	38	14	10	14	47	**1.24**	1.4	52
6 Falkirk (7)	38	13	10	15	49	**1.29**	1.3	49
7 Kilmarnock (11)	38	10	10	18	52	**1.37**	1.1	40
8 St Mirren (10)	38	10	11	17	54	**1.42**	1.1	41
9 Hearts (8)	38	13	9	16	55	**1.45**	1.3	48
10 Aberdeen (4)	38	15	8	15	58	**1.53**	1.4	53
11 Inverness CT (9)	38	13	4	21	62	**1.63**	1.1	43

ARTUR BORUC: safe hands for Celtic last term, here keeping Colin Nish at bay

SCOTTISH DIVISION ONE

	Team	Pld	W	D	L	F	GFA	PGA	Pts
1	Hamilton (1)	36	23	7	6	62	**1.72**	2.1	76
2	St Johnstone (3)	36	15	13	8	60	**1.67**	1.6	58
3	Dundee (2)	36	20	9	7	58	**1.61**	1.9	69
4	Livingston (7)	36	10	9	17	55	**1.53**	1.1	39
5	Queen of Sth (4)	36	14	10	12	47	**1.31**	1.4	52
6	Stirling (10)	36	4	12	20	41	**1.14**	0.7	24
7	Partick (6)	36	11	12	13	40	**1.11**	1.3	45
8	Clyde (9)	36	9	10	17	40	**1.11**	1.0	37
9	Morton (9)	36	9	10	17	40	**1.11**	1.0	37
10	Dunfermline (5)	36	13	12	11	36	**1.00**	1.4	51

SCOTTISH DIVISION TWO

	Team	Pld	W	D	L	F	GFA	PGA	Pts
1	Ross County (1)	36	22	7	7	78	**2.17**	2.0	73
2	Peterhead (5)	36	16	7	13	65	**1.81**	1.5	55
3	Airdrie Utd (2)	36	20	6	10	64	**1.78**	1.8	66
4	Brechin (6)	36	13	13	10	63	**1.75**	1.4	52
5	Raith (3)	36	19	3	14	60	**1.67**	1.7	60
6	Alloa (4)	36	16	8	12	57	**1.58**	1.6	56
7	Ayr (7)	36	13	7	16	51	**1.42**	1.3	46
8	Queen's Park (8)	36	13	5	18	48	**1.33**	1.2	44
9	Cowdenbeath (9)	36	10	7	19	47	**1.31**	1.0	37
10	Berwick (10)	36	3	7	26	40	**1.11**	0.4	16

SCOTTISH DIVISION THREE

	Team	Pld	W	D	L	F	GFA	PGA	Pts
1	East Fife (1)	36	28	4	4	77	**2.14**	24	88
2	Stranraer (2)	36	19	8	9	65	**1.81**	1.8	65
3	Montrose (3)	36	17	8	11	59	**1.64**	1.6	59
4	Elgin City (6)	36	13	8	15	56	**1.56**	1.3	47
5	Arbroath (4)	36	14	10	12	54	**1.50**	1.4	52
6	Albion (8)	36	9	10	17	51	**1.42**	1.0	37
7	Stenh'semuir (5)	36	13	9	14	50	**1.39**	1.3	48
8	East Stirling (9)	36	10	4	22	48	**1.33**	0.9	34
9	Forfar (10)	36	8	9	19	35	**0.97**	0.9	33
10	Dumbarton (8)	36	9	10	17	31	**0.86**	1.0	37

RICHARD OFFIONG: he led the charge in Hamilton's goal rush during 2007/08

Sponsored by Stan James

SCOTTISH DIVISION ONE

Team	Pld	W	D	L	A	GAA	PGA	Pts
1 Hamilton (1)	36	23	7	6	27	**0.75**	2.1	76
2 Dundee (2)	36	20	9	7	30	**0.83**	1.9	69
3 Partick (6)	36	11	12	13	39	**1.08**	1.3	45
4 Dunfermline (5)	36	13	12	11	41	**1.14**	1.4	51
5 Queen of Sth (4)	36	14	10	12	43	**1.19**	1.4	52
6 St Johnstone (3)	36	15	13	8	45	**1.25**	1.6	58
7 Morton (9)	36	9	10	17	58	**1.61**	1.0	37
8 Clyde (9)	36	9	10	17	59	**1.64**	1.0	37
9 Livingston (7)	36	10	9	17	66	**1.83**	1.1	39
10 Stirling (10)	36	4	12	20	71	**1.97**	0.7	24

SCOTTISH DIVISION TWO

Team	Pld	W	D	L	A	GAA	PGA	Pts
1 Airdrie Utd (2)	36	20	6	10	34	**0.94**	1.8	66
2 Ross County (1)	36	22	7	7	44	**1.22**	2.0	73
3 Brechin (6)	36	13	13	10	48	**1.33**	1.4	52
4 Raith (3)	36	19	3	14	50	**1.39**	1.7	60
5 Queen's Park (8)	36	13	5	18	51	**1.42**	1.2	44
6 Peterhead (5)	36	16	7	13	54	**1.50**	1.5	55
7 Alloa (4)	36	16	8	12	56	**1.56**	1.6	56
8 Ayr (7)	36	13	7	16	62	**1.72**	1.3	46
9 Cowdenbeath (9)	36	10	7	19	73	**2.03**	1.0	37
10 Berwick (10)	36	3	7	26	101	**2.81**	0.4	16

SCOTTISH DIVISION THREE

Team	Pld	W	D	L	A	GAA	PGA	Pts
1 East Fife (1)	36	28	4	4	24	**0.67**	2.4	88
2 Montrose (3)	36	17	8	11	36	**1.00**	1.6	59
3 Stranraer (2)	36	19	8	9	43	**1.19**	1.8	65
4 Arbroath (4)	36	14	10	12	47	**1.31**	1.4	52
5 Dumbarton (8)	36	9	10	17	48	**1.33**	1.0	37
6 Stenh'semuir (5)	36	13	9	14	59	**1.64**	1.3	48
7 Forfar (10)	36	8	9	19	62	**1.72**	0.9	33
8 Elgin City (6)	36	13	8	15	68	**1.89**	1.3	47
9 Albion (8)	36	9	10	17	68	**1.89**	1.0	37
10 East Stirling (9)	36	10	4	22	71	**1.97**	0.9	34

EAST FIFE: a tight defence helped the boys from Bayview to Div Three promotion

PREMIER LEAGUE

	Team	Pld	CS	CS%
1	Chelsea (2)	38	21	**55.3**
2	Man Utd (1)	38	21	**55.3**
3	Liverpool (4)	38	18	**47.4**
4	Portsmouth (8)	38	16	**42.1**
5	Arsenal (3)	38	15	**39.5**
6	Everton (5)	38	14	**36.8**
7	Wigan (14)	38	12	**31.6**
8	Bolton (16)	38	12	**31.6**
9	Man City (9)	38	11	**28.9**
10	Tottenham (11)	38	9	**23.7**
11	Aston Villa (6)	38	9	**23.7**
12	Reading (18)	38	8	**21.1**
13	Blackburn (7)	38	8	**21.1**
14	West Ham (10)	38	8	**21.1**
15	Newcastle (12)	38	8	**21.1**
16	Middlesbro (13)	38	8	**21.1**
17	Fulham (18)	38	7	**18.4**
18	Sunderland (15)	38	7	**18.4**
19	Derby (20)	38	3	**7.9**
20	Birmingham (19)	38	3	**7.9**

NO SURPRISES: Petr Cech kept the most clean sheets

RECORD WHEN KEEPING A CLEAN SHEET

	Team	Pld	W	D	L	F	GFA	PGA	Pts
1	Man Utd (1)	21	20	1	0	45	2.14	**2.9**	61
2	Tottenham (11)	9	8	1	0	21	2.33	**2.8**	25
3	Aston Villa (6)	9	8	1	0	24	2.67	**2.8**	25
4	West Ham (10)	8	7	1	0	15	1.88	**2.8**	22
5	Middlesbro (13)	8	7	1	0	9	1.13	**2.8**	22
6	Chelsea (2)	21	18	3	0	33	1.57	**2.7**	57
7	Arsenal (3)	15	13	2	0	26	1.73	**2.7**	41
8	Sunderland (15)	7	6	1	0	9	1.29	**2.7**	19
9	Everton (5)	14	11	3	0	19	1.36	**2.6**	36
10	Wigan (14)	12	9	3	0	14	1.17	**2.5**	30
11	Liverpool (4)	18	13	5	0	34	1.89	**2.4**	44
12	Portsmouth (8)	16	10	6	0	16	1.00	**2.3**	36
13	Bolton (16)	12	8	4	0	14	1.17	**2.3**	28
14	Man City (9)	11	7	4	0	9	0.82	**2.3**	25
15	Reading (18)	8	5	3	0	9	1.13	**2.3**	18
16	Newcastle (12)	8	5	3	0	9	1.13	**2.3**	18
17	Birmingham (19)	3	2	1	0	4	1.33	**2.3**	7
18	Fulham (18)	7	4	3	0	6	0.86	**2.1**	15
19	Blackburn (7)	8	4	4	0	4	0.50	**2.0**	16
20	Derby (20)	3	1	2	0	1	0.33	**1.7**	5

- Number in brackets refers to final league finishing position
- GFA: Goals for average per match
- PGA: Average points gained per match

Sponsored by Stan James

CHAMPIONSHIP

	Team	Pld	CS	CS%
1	Wolves (7)	46	19	**41.3**
2	Leicester (22)	46	17	**37.0**
3	Bristol C (4)	46	15	**32.6**
4	Hull City (3)	46	15	**32.6**
5	Sheff Utd (9)	46	15	**32.6**
6	QPR (14)	46	14	**30.4**
7	Plymouth (12)	46	14	**30.4**
8	West Brom (1)	46	14	**30.4**
9	Watford (7)	46	13	**28.3**
10	Cardiff (12)	46	13	**28.3**
11	C Palace (5)	46	13	**28.3**
12	Preston (15)	46	13	**28.3**
13	Ipswich (8)	46	12	**26.1**
14	Norwich (18)	46	12	**26.1**
15	Barnsley (18)	46	12	**26.1**
16	Charlton (12)	46	12	**26.1**
17	Stoke (2)	46	11	**23.9**
18	Blackpool (20)	46	11	**23.9**
19	Sheff Wed (18)	46	11	**23.9**
20	Burnley (13)	46	10	**21.7**
21	Scunthorpe (23)	46	10	**21.7**
22	Southampton (20)	46	10	**21.7**
23	Coventry (21)	46	9	**19.6**
24	Colchester (24)	46	2	**4.3**

MICK MCCARTHY: at Wolves he's able to run a tight ship

RECORD WHEN KEEPING A CLEAN SHEET

	Team	Pld	W	D	L	F	GFA	PGA	Pts
1	Colchester (24)	2	2	0	0	5	2.50	**3.0**	6
2	Hull City (3)	15	14	1	0	29	1.93	**2.9**	43
3	Charlton (12)	12	11	1	0	19	1.58	**2.8**	34
4	Plymouth (12)	14	11	3	0	21	1.50	**2.6**	36
5	West Brom (1)	14	11	3	0	29	2.07	**2.6**	36
6	Sheff Utd (9)	15	11	4	0	17	1.13	**2.5**	37
7	Norwich (18)	12	9	3	0	13	1.08	**2.5**	30
8	Watford (7)	13	9	4	0	17	1.31	**2.4**	31
9	Cardiff (12)	13	9	4	0	12	0.92	**2.4**	31
10	C Palace (5)	13	9	4	0	20	1.54	**2.4**	31
11	Burnley (13)	10	7	3	0	10	1.00	**2.4**	24
12	Southampton (20)	10	7	3	0	13	1.30	**2.4**	24
13	Bristol C (4)	15	10	5	0	16	1.07	**2.3**	35
14	Ipswich (8)	12	8	4	0	18	1.50	**2.3**	28
15	Blackpool (20)	11	7	4	0	13	1.18	**2.3**	25
16	Wolves (7)	19	11	8	0	17	0.89	**2.2**	41
17	Leicester (22)	17	10	7	0	18	1.06	**2.2**	37
18	Preston (15)	13	8	5	0	12	0.92	**2.2**	29
19	Barnsley (18)	12	7	5	0	14	1.17	**2.2**	26
20	Scunthorpe (23)	10	6	4	0	7	0.70	**2.2**	22
21	QPR (14)	14	8	6	0	15	1.07	**2.1**	30
22	Sheff Wed (18)	11	6	5	0	11	1.00	**2.1**	23
23	Coventry (21)	9	5	4	0	9	1.00	**2.1**	19
24	Stoke (2)	11	5	6	0	7	0.64	**1.9**	21

LEAGUE 1

	Team	Pld	CS	CS%
1	Nottm Forest (3)	46	24	**52.2**
2	Leeds (2)	46	20	**43.5**
3	Doncaster (5)	46	20	**43.5**
4	Carlisle (5)	46	18	**39.1**
5	Swansea (1)	46	17	**37.0**
6	Walsall (12)	46	16	**34.8**
7	Tranmere (11)	46	16	**34.8**
8	Huddersfield (10)	46	16	**34.8**
9	Brighton (7)	46	14	**30.4**
10	Crewe (21)	46	13	**28.3**
11	Oldham (8)	46	13	**28.3**
12	Millwall (19)	46	13	**28.3**
13	Leyton Orient (14)	46	13	**28.3**
14	Southend (6)	46	12	**26.1**
15	Bristol R (17)	46	12	**26.1**
16	Northampton (10)	46	11	**23.9**
17	Swindon (13)	46	10	**21.7**
18	Cheltenham (20)	46	10	**21.7**
19	Hartlepool (16)	46	9	**19.6**
20	Luton (23)	46	8	**17.4**
21	Yeovil (19)	46	8	**17.4**
22	Gillingham (22)	46	8	**17.4**
23	Bournemouth (15)	46	8	**17.4**
24	Port Vale (24)	46	6	**13.0**

IAN BRECKIN: was part of a rock-solid Forest backline

RECORD WHEN KEEPING A CLEAN SHEET

	Team	Pld	W	D	L	F	GFA	PGA	Pts
1	Southend (6)	12	12	0	0	21	1.75	**3.0**	36
2	Leeds (2)	20	19	1	0	34	1.70	**2.9**	58
3	Huddersfield (10)	16	15	1	0	20	1.25	**2.9**	46
4	Northampton (10)	11	10	1	0	19	1.73	**2.8**	31
5	Swindon (13)	10	9	1	0	22	2.20	**2.8**	28
6	Cheltenham (20)	10	9	1	0	10	1.00	**2.8**	28
7	Hartlepool (16)	9	8	1	0	18	2.00	**2.8**	25
8	Bournemouth (15)	8	7	1	0	12	1.50	**2.8**	22
9	Carlisle (5)	18	15	3	0	26	1.44	**2.7**	48
10	Doncaster (5)	20	16	4	0	30	1.50	**2.6**	52
11	Swansea (1)	17	13	4	0	27	1.59	**2.5**	43
12	Tranmere (11)	16	12	4	0	21	1.31	**2.5**	40
13	Millwall (19)	13	10	3	0	18	1.38	**2.5**	33
14	Leyton Orient (14)	13	10	3	0	14	1.08	**2.5**	33
15	Bristol R (17)	12	9	3	0	13	1.08	**2.5**	30
16	Walsall (12)	16	11	5	0	23	1.44	**2.4**	38
17	Oldham (8)	13	9	4	0	20	1.54	**2.4**	31
18	Nottm Forest (3)	24	16	8	0	34	1.42	**2.3**	56
19	Crewe (21)	13	8	5	0	15	1.15	**2.2**	29
20	Brighton (7)	14	8	6	0	16	1.14	**2.1**	30
21	Luton (23)	8	4	4	0	6	0.75	**2.0**	16
22	Port Vale (24)	6	3	3	0	6	1.00	**2.0**	12
23	Yeovil (19)	8	3	5	0	3	0.38	**1.8**	14
24	Gillingham (22)	8	3	5	0	5	0.63	**1.8**	14

LEAGUE 2

	Team	Pld	CS	CS%
1	Darlington (7)	46	24	**52.2**
2	MK Dons (1)	46	20	**43.5**
3	Wycombe (7)	46	19	**41.3**
4	Hereford (3)	46	19	**41.3**
5	Stockport (4)	46	17	**37.0**
6	Peterborough (2)	46	16	**34.8**
7	Notts Co (21)	46	14	**30.4**
8	Rotherham (8)	46	13	**28.3**
9	Shrewsbury (19)	46	13	**28.3**
10	Rochdale (5)	46	12	**26.1**
11	Wrexham (24)	46	12	**26.1**
12	Barnet (12)	46	11	**23.9**
13	Dag & Red (20)	46	11	**23.9**
14	Chesterfield (9)	46	11	**23.9**
15	Macclesfield (19)	46	11	**23.9**
16	Grimsby (16)	46	10	**21.7**
17	Bradford (10)	46	9	**19.6**
18	Bury (14)	46	8	**17.4**
19	Chester (22)	46	8	**17.4**
20	Mansfield (23)	46	8	**17.4**
21	Accrington (17)	46	8	**17.4**
22	Brentford (14)	46	7	**15.2**
23	Morecambe (12)	46	7	**15.2**
24	Lincoln (15)	46	6	**13.0**

INCE: didn't mess about as a player or as MK Dons boss

RECORD WHEN KEEPING A CLEAN SHEET

	Team	Pld	W	D	L	F	GFA	PGA	Pts
1	Lincoln (15)	6	6	0	0	11	1.83	**3.0**	18
2	MK Dons (1)	20	19	1	0	38	1.90	**2.9**	58
3	Stockport (4)	17	15	2	0	26	1.53	**2.8**	47
4	Peterborough (2)	16	14	2	0	32	2.00	**2.8**	44
5	Rotherham (8)	13	12	1	0	19	1.46	**2.8**	37
6	Bury (14)	8	7	1	0	14	1.75	**2.8**	22
7	Accrington (17)	8	7	1	0	9	1.13	**2.8**	22
8	Wycombe (7)	19	16	3	0	24	1.26	**2.7**	51
9	Rochdale (5)	12	10	2	0	20	1.67	**2.7**	32
10	Brentford (14)	7	6	1	0	10	1.43	**2.7**	19
11	Morecambe (12)	7	6	1	0	9	1.29	**2.7**	19
12	Darlington (7)	24	19	5	0	42	1.75	**2.6**	62
13	Dag & Red (20)	11	9	2	0	15	1.36	**2.6**	29
14	Chesterfield (9)	11	9	2	0	20	1.82	**2.6**	29
15	Grimsby (16)	10	8	2	0	14	1.40	**2.6**	26
16	Bradford (10)	9	7	2	0	10	1.11	**2.6**	23
17	Hereford (3)	19	14	5	0	24	1.26	**2.5**	47
18	Macclesfield (19)	11	8	3	0	10	0.91	**2.5**	27
19	Shrewsbury (19)	13	9	4	0	20	1.54	**2.4**	31
20	Wrexham (24)	12	7	5	0	10	0.83	**2.2**	26
21	Notts Co (21)	14	8	6	0	9	0.64	**2.1**	30
22	Barnet (12)	11	6	5	0	11	1.00	**2.1**	23
23	Chester (22)	8	4	4	0	10	1.25	**2.0**	16
24	Mansfield (23)	8	4	4	0	10	1.25	**2.0**	16

BLUE SQUARE PREMIER

	Team	Pld	CS	CS%
1	Oxford (9)	46	19	**41.3**
2	Burton (5)	46	16	**34.8**
3	Torquay (3)	46	16	**34.8**
4	Cambridge (3)	46	16	**34.8**
5	Stevenage (6)	46	16	**34.8**
6	Kidderminster (13)	46	15	**32.6**
7	Exeter (4)	46	14	**30.4**
8	Grays (10)	46	14	**30.4**
9	Aldershot (1)	46	14	**30.4**
10	Salisbury (12)	46	14	**30.4**
11	Rushden (16)	46	12	**26.1**
12	Histon (7)	46	11	**23.9**
13	Weymouth (19)	46	11	**23.9**
14	Forest Green (9)	46	11	**23.9**
15	York (15)	46	10	**21.7**
16	Woking (17)	46	10	**21.7**
17	Halifax (18)	46	10	**21.7**
18	Farsley (22)	46	9	**19.6**
19	Northwich (20)	46	9	**19.6**
20	Ebbsfleet (11)	46	8	**17.4**
21	Altrincham (21)	46	6	**13.0**
22	Crawley (14)	46	5	**10.9**
23	Droylsden (24)	46	4	**8.7**
24	Stafford (23)	46	2	**4.3**

DARREN PATTERSON: Oxford boss has his side well drilled

RECORD WHEN KEEPING A CLEAN SHEET

	Team	Pld	W	D	L	F	GFA	PGA	Pts
1	Crawley (14)	5	5	0	0	12	2.40	**3.0**	15
2	Histon (7)	11	10	1	0	14	1.27	**2.8**	31
3	Ebbsfleet (11)	8	7	1	0	9	1.13	**2.8**	22
4	Kidderminster (13)	15	13	2	0	30	2.00	**2.7**	41
5	Exeter (4)	14	12	2	0	22	1.57	**2.7**	38
6	Aldershot (1)	14	11	3	0	22	1.57	**2.6**	36
7	York (15)	10	8	2	0	18	1.80	**2.6**	26
8	Woking (17)	10	8	2	0	12	1.20	**2.6**	26
9	Torquay (3)	16	12	4	0	20	1.25	**2.5**	40
10	Cambridge (3)	16	12	4	0	24	1.50	**2.5**	40
11	Forest Green (9)	11	8	3	0	17	1.55	**2.5**	27
12	Burton (5)	16	11	5	0	23	1.44	**2.4**	38
13	Stevenage (6)	16	11	5	0	29	1.81	**2.4**	38
14	Salisbury (12)	14	10	4	0	19	1.36	**2.4**	34
15	Oxford (9)	19	12	7	0	20	1.05	**2.3**	43
16	Rushden (16)	12	8	4	0	14	1.17	**2.3**	28
17	Farsley (22)	9	6	3	0	13	1.44	**2.3**	21
18	Northwich (20)	9	6	3	0	10	1.11	**2.3**	21
19	Altrincham (21)	6	4	2	0	6	1.00	**2.3**	14
20	Halifax (18)	10	6	4	0	14	1.40	**2.2**	22
21	Grays (10)	14	8	6	0	12	0.86	**2.1**	30
22	Weymouth (19)	11	6	5	0	10	0.91	**2.1**	23
23	Droylsden (24)	4	2	2	0	3	0.75	**2.0**	8
24	Stafford (23)	2	0	2	0	0	0.00	**1.0**	2

SCOTTISH PREMIER LEAGUE

	Team	Pld	CS	CS%
1	Celtic (1)	38	19	**50.0**
2	Rangers (2)	38	17	**44.7**
3	Falkirk (7)	38	15	**39.5**
4	Dundee Utd (6)	38	13	**34.2**
5	St Mirren (10)	38	12	**31.6**
6	Hibernian (6)	38	11	**28.9**
7	Hearts (8)	38	10	**26.3**
8	Motherwell (3)	38	10	**26.3**
9	Aberdeen (4)	38	9	**23.7**
10	Kilmarnock (11)	38	7	**18.4**
11	Inverness CT (9)	38	7	**18.4**
12	Gretna (12)	38	5	**13.2**

GORDON STRACHAN: plots another defensive masterplan

KILLIE: why the leaky defence? Keeper on the wrong side of the net wouldn't help

RECORD WHEN KEEPING A CLEAN SHEET

	Team	Pld	W	D	L	F	GFA	PGA	Pts
1	Rangers (2)	17	16	1	0	39	2.29	**2.9**	49
2	Celtic (1)	19	17	2	0	43	2.26	**2.8**	53
3	Motherwell (3)	10	9	1	0	16	1.60	**2.8**	28
4	Aberdeen (4)	9	8	1	0	16	1.78	**2.8**	25
5	Inverness CT (9)	7	6	1	0	14	2.00	**2.7**	19
6	Hibernian (6)	11	9	2	0	13	1.18	**2.6**	29
7	Hearts (8)	10	8	2	0	12	1.20	**2.6**	26
8	Dundee Utd (6)	13	10	3	0	22	1.69	**2.5**	33
9	Falkirk (7)	15	9	6	0	20	1.33	**2.2**	33
10	St Mirren (10)	12	7	5	0	8	0.67	**2.2**	26
11	Gretna (12)	5	2	3	0	3	0.60	**1.8**	9
12	Kilmarnock (11)	7	2	5	0	3	0.43	**1.6**	11

SCOTTISH DIVISION ONE

	Team	Pld	CS	CS%
1	Hamilton (1)	36	20	**55.6**
2	Dundee (2)	36	12	**33.3**
3	Partick (6)	36	11	**30.6**
4	Dunfermline (5)	36	11	**30.6**
5	Queen of Sth (4)	36	10	**27.8**
6	St Johnstone (3)	36	9	**25.0**
7	Clyde (9)	36	7	**19.4**
8	Morton (9)	36	7	**19.4**
9	Stirling (10)	36	6	**16.7**
10	Livingston (7)	36	6	**16.7**

GLUM: poor defence didn't help Proctor's Livi prospects

RECORD WHEN KEEPING A CLEAN SHEET

	Team	Pld	W	D	L	F	GFA	PGA	Pts
1	Dundee (2)	12	11	1	0	20	1.67	**2.8**	34
2	Hamilton (1)	20	17	3	0	36	1.80	**2.7**	54
3	Livingston (7)	6	5	1	0	12	2.00	**2.7**	16
4	Dunfermline (5)	11	8	3	0	14	1.27	**2.5**	27
5	Partick (6)	11	7	4	0	18	1.64	**2.3**	25
6	Queen of Sth (4)	10	6	4	0	9	0.90	**2.2**	22
7	St Johnstone (3)	9	5	4	0	9	1.00	**2.1**	19
8	Clyde (9)	7	4	3	0	7	1.00	**2.1**	15
9	Morton (9)	7	4	3	0	8	1.14	**2.1**	15
10	Stirling (10)	6	2	4	0	4	0.67	**1.7**	10

SCOTTISH DIVISION TWO

	Team	Pld	CS	CS%
1	Airdrie Utd (2)	36	14	**38.9**
2	Ross County (1)	36	12	**33.3**
3	Raith (3)	36	9	**25.0**
4	Peterhead (5)	36	9	**25.0**
5	Alloa (4)	36	8	**22.2**
6	Brechin (6)	36	7	**19.4**
7	Queen's Park (8)	36	7	**19.4**
8	Ayr (7)	36	6	**16.7**
9	Cowdenbeath (9)	36	6	**16.7**
10	Berwick (10)	36	1	**2.8**

BERWICK: fewer clean sheets than (insert smutty joke here)

RECORD WHEN KEEPING A CLEAN SHEET

	Team	Pld	W	D	L	F	GFA	PGA	Pts
1	Raith (3)	9	9	0	0	14	1.56	**3.0**	27
2	Peterhead (5)	9	9	0	0	18	2.00	**3.0**	27
3	Queen's Park (8)	7	7	0	0	11	1.57	**3.0**	21
4	Cowdenbeath (9)	6	6	0	0	7	1.17	**3.0**	18
5	Berwick (10)	1	1	0	0	2	2.00	**3.0**	3
6	Airdrie Utd (2)	14	13	1	0	32	2.29	**2.9**	40
7	Ross County (1)	12	11	1	0	22	1.83	**2.8**	34
8	Ayr (7)	6	5	1	0	13	2.17	**2.7**	16
9	Alloa (4)	8	6	2	0	13	1.63	**2.5**	20
10	Brechin (6)	7	4	3	0	14	2.00	**2.1**	15

SCOTTISH DIVISION THREE

	Team	Pld	CS	CS%
1	East Fife (1)	36	20	**55.6**
2	Arbroath (4)	36	13	**36.1**
3	Montrose (3)	36	13	**36.1**
4	Dumbarton (8)	36	11	**30.6**
5	Stranraer (2)	36	11	**30.6**
6	Forfar (10)	36	9	**25.0**
7	Elgin City (6)	36	7	**19.4**
8	Stenh'semuir (5)	36	7	**19.4**
9	Albion (8)	36	5	**13.9**
10	East Stirling (9)	36	5	**13.9**

EAST STIRLING: they usually obliged for opposition strikers

RECORD WHEN KEEPING A CLEAN SHEET

	Team	Pld	W	D	L	F	GFA	PGA	Pts
1	East Fife (1)	20	18	2	0	45	2.25	**2.8**	56
2	Stenh'semuir (5)	7	6	1	0	12	1.71	**2.7**	19
3	Stranraer (2)	11	9	2	0	21	1.91	**2.6**	29
4	East Stirling (9)	5	4	1	0	9	1.80	**2.6**	13
5	Arbroath (4)	13	10	3	0	21	1.62	**2.5**	33
6	Dumbarton (8)	11	7	4	0	9	0.82	**2.3**	25
7	Forfar (10)	9	6	3	0	9	1.00	**2.3**	21
8	Montrose (3)	13	8	5	0	22	1.69	**2.2**	29
9	Albion (8)	5	3	2	0	4	0.80	**2.2**	11
10	Elgin City (6)	7	4	3	0	12	1.71	**2.1**	15

YOU'LL NEVER CATCH IT! the Albion defence again fail to stem the flow of goals

PREMIER LEAGUE

	Team	Pld	FS	FS%
1	Man Utd (1)	38	**28**	73.7
2	Arsenal (3)	38	**26**	68.4
3	Chelsea (2)	38	**25**	65.8
4	Everton (5)	38	**23**	60.5
5	Liverpool (4)	38	**23**	60.5
6	Tottenham (11)	38	**22**	57.9
7	Middlesbro (13)	38	**20**	52.6
8	Man City (9)	38	**18**	47.4
9	West Ham (10)	38	**17**	44.7
10	Aston Villa (6)	38	**17**	44.7
11	Fulham (18)	38	**16**	42.1
12	Wigan (14)	38	**15**	39.5
13	Bolton (16)	38	**15**	39.5
14	Blackburn (7)	38	**14**	36.8
15	Newcastle (12)	38	**14**	36.8
16	Birmingham (19)	38	**14**	36.8
17	Reading (18)	38	**13**	34.2
18	Portsmouth (8)	38	**13**	34.2
19	Sunderland (15)	38	**13**	34.2
20	Derby (20)	38	**8**	21.1

DEADLY DUO: usual suspects struck in the Premier League

RECORD WHEN FIRST TO SCORE

	Team	Pld	W	D	L	F	GFA	PGA	Pts
1	Portsmouth (8)	13	13	0	0	31	7	**3.0**	39
2	Man Utd (1)	28	25	2	1	68	10	**2.8**	77
3	Chelsea (2)	25	20	5	0	49	11	**2.6**	65
4	Everton (5)	23	19	3	1	49	16	**2.6**	60
5	Liverpool (4)	23	17	6	0	53	12	**2.5**	57
6	Arsenal (3)	26	19	5	2	54	18	**2.4**	62
7	Reading (18)	13	10	1	2	23	10	**2.4**	31
8	Sunderland (15)	13	9	4	0	23	9	**2.4**	31
9	Man City (9)	18	12	4	2	29	16	**2.2**	40
10	Aston Villa (6)	17	12	1	4	44	19	**2.2**	37
11	Blackburn (7)	14	9	4	1	24	12	**2.2**	31
12	Wigan (14)	15	10	2	3	25	14	**2.1**	32
13	Newcastle (12)	14	9	2	3	27	18	**2.1**	29
14	West Ham (10)	17	9	7	1	30	13	**2.0**	34
15	Tottenham (11)	22	11	7	4	50	29	**1.8**	40
16	Bolton (16)	15	8	2	5	22	15	**1.7**	26
17	Middlesbro (13)	20	9	5	6	31	23	**1.6**	32
18	Birmingham (19)	14	6	5	3	28	20	**1.6**	23
19	Fulham (18)	16	6	5	5	24	20	**1.4**	23
20	Derby (20)	8	1	4	3	11	15	**0.9**	7

- Number in brackets refers to final league finishing position
- GFA: Goals for average per match
- PGA: Average points gained per match

FIRST TO SCORE 2007/08

Sponsored by Stan James

CHAMPIONSHIP

	Team	Pld	FS	FS%
1	Charlton (12)	46	**25**	54.3
2	QPR (14)	46	**24**	52.2
3	Wolves (7)	46	**24**	52.2
4	Watford (7)	46	**24**	52.2
5	Cardiff (12)	46	**24**	52.2
6	Hull City (3)	46	**24**	52.2
7	West Brom (1)	46	**24**	52.2
8	Blackpool (20)	46	**24**	52.2
9	Burnley (13)	46	**23**	50.0
10	Sheff Utd (9)	46	**23**	50.0
11	Ipswich (8)	46	**22**	47.8
12	C Palace (5)	46	**22**	47.8
13	Plymouth (12)	46	**22**	47.8
14	Colchester (24)	46	**22**	47.8
15	Stoke (2)	46	**21**	45.7
16	Preston (15)	46	**20**	43.5
17	Bristol C (4)	46	**20**	43.5
18	Norwich (18)	46	**19**	41.3
19	Scunthorpe (23)	46	**19**	41.3
20	Southampton (20)	46	**19**	41.3
21	Barnsley (18)	46	**17**	37.0
22	Coventry (21)	46	**16**	34.8
23	Leicester (22)	46	**15**	32.6
24	Sheff Wed (18)	46	**12**	26.1

SHOCKER: Charlton were the fast starters of the second tier

RECORD WHEN FIRST TO SCORE

	Team	Pld	W	D	L	F	GFA	PGA	Pts
1	Bristol C (4)	20	18	1	1	36	12	**2.8**	55
2	Hull City (3)	24	21	2	1	51	13	**2.7**	65
3	West Brom (1)	24	18	3	3	56	19	**2.4**	57
4	Watford (7)	24	16	8	0	44	18	**2.3**	56
5	Ipswich (8)	22	15	6	1	47	20	**2.3**	51
6	C Palace (5)	22	14	8	0	42	15	**2.3**	50
7	Barnsley (18)	17	12	3	2	37	22	**2.3**	39
8	Leicester (22)	15	10	4	1	26	8	**2.3**	34
9	Wolves (7)	24	16	5	3	40	20	**2.2**	53
10	Norwich (18)	19	13	2	4	31	16	**2.2**	41
11	Coventry (21)	16	10	5	1	31	13	**2.2**	35
12	Charlton (12)	25	15	8	2	44	19	**2.1**	53
13	Burnley (13)	23	14	7	2	41	25	**2.1**	49
14	Sheff Utd (9)	23	14	7	2	39	20	**2.1**	49
15	Plymouth (12)	22	14	5	3	39	17	**2.1**	47
16	Stoke (2)	21	13	6	2	41	24	**2.1**	45
17	Preston (15)	20	13	3	4	34	17	**2.1**	42
18	Cardiff (12)	24	13	8	3	37	22	**2.0**	47
19	Southampton (20)	19	10	6	3	33	20	**1.9**	36
20	Blackpool (20)	24	12	7	5	41	29	**1.8**	43
21	Sheff Wed (18)	12	6	3	3	20	12	**1.8**	21
22	QPR (14)	24	12	5	7	44	32	**1.7**	41
23	Scunthorpe (23)	19	9	4	6	27	25	**1.6**	31
24	Colchester (24)	22	5	8	9	35	44	**1.0**	23

FIRST TO SCORE 2007/08

LEAGUE 1

	Team	Pld	FS	FS%
1	Leeds (2)	46	**29**	63.0
2	Southend (6)	46	**28**	60.9
3	Carlisle (5)	46	**27**	58.7
4	Swansea (1)	46	**26**	56.5
5	Doncaster (5)	46	**26**	56.5
6	Tranmere (11)	46	**25**	54.3
7	Huddersfield (10)	46	**24**	52.2
8	Oldham (8)	46	**23**	50.0
9	Nottm Forest (3)	46	**23**	50.0
10	Northampton (10)	46	**23**	50.0
11	Swindon (13)	46	**21**	45.7
12	Walsall (12)	46	**21**	45.7
13	Hartlepool (16)	46	**21**	45.7
14	Cheltenham (20)	46	**20**	43.5
15	Gillingham (22)	46	**20**	43.5
16	Leyton Orient (14)	46	**20**	43.5
17	Bristol R (17)	46	**19**	41.3
18	Millwall (19)	46	**18**	39.1
19	Bournemouth (15)	46	**18**	39.1
20	Crewe (21)	46	**17**	37.0
21	Luton (23)	46	**17**	37.0
22	Brighton (7)	46	**17**	37.0
23	Yeovil (19)	46	**16**	34.8
24	Port Vale (24)	46	**15**	32.6

ELLAND ROAD: lots of early goals in Leeds last term

RECORD WHEN FIRST TO SCORE

	Team	Pld	W	D	L	F	GFA	PGA	Pts
1	Leeds (2)	29	24	4	1	56	15	**2.6**	76
2	Bournemouth (15)	18	14	4	0	40	14	**2.6**	46
3	Doncaster (5)	26	21	3	2	49	14	**2.5**	66
4	Nottm Forest (3)	23	18	4	1	45	11	**2.5**	58
5	Swansea (1)	26	19	5	2	56	19	**2.4**	62
6	Northampton (10)	23	16	7	0	45	17	**2.4**	55
7	Southend (6)	28	20	4	4	53	25	**2.3**	64
8	Huddersfield (10)	24	18	2	4	35	16	**2.3**	56
9	Oldham (8)	23	16	5	2	48	19	**2.3**	53
10	Leyton Orient (14)	20	13	6	1	29	12	**2.3**	45
11	Tranmere (11)	25	17	3	5	42	19	**2.2**	54
12	Walsall (12)	21	14	4	3	38	16	**2.2**	46
13	Brighton (7)	17	12	2	3	31	13	**2.2**	38
14	Carlisle (5)	27	17	7	3	46	21	**2.1**	58
15	Swindon (13)	21	13	6	2	43	17	**2.1**	45
16	Millwall (19)	18	12	2	4	29	14	**2.1**	38
17	Crewe (21)	17	10	6	1	30	12	**2.1**	36
18	Luton (23)	17	11	2	4	29	18	**2.1**	35
19	Yeovil (19)	16	10	4	2	24	16	**2.1**	34
20	Hartlepool (16)	21	13	1	7	42	27	**1.9**	40
21	Cheltenham (20)	20	11	5	4	24	17	**1.9**	38
22	Bristol R (17)	19	10	7	2	28	16	**1.9**	37
23	Gillingham (22)	20	8	6	6	30	27	**1.5**	30
24	Port Vale (24)	15	6	3	6	24	24	**1.4**	21

Sponsored by Stan James

LEAGUE 2

	Team	Pld	FS	FS%
1	MK Dons (1)	46	**34**	73.9
2	Wycombe (7)	46	**28**	60.9
3	Darlington (7)	46	**28**	60.9
4	Peterborough (2)	46	**27**	58.7
5	Rotherham (8)	46	**26**	56.5
6	Stockport (4)	46	**26**	56.5
7	Shrewsbury (19)	46	**25**	54.3
8	Grimsby (16)	46	**24**	52.2
9	Chesterfield (9)	46	**23**	50.0
10	Hereford (3)	46	**22**	47.8
11	Lincoln (15)	46	**22**	47.8
12	Bradford (10)	46	**22**	47.8
13	Rochdale (5)	46	**21**	45.7
14	Brentford (14)	46	**21**	45.7
15	Macclesfield (19)	46	**21**	45.7
16	Morecambe (12)	46	**19**	41.3
17	Accrington (17)	46	**18**	39.1
18	Bury (14)	46	**17**	37.0
19	Notts Co (21)	46	**17**	37.0
20	Mansfield (23)	46	**17**	37.0
21	Barnet (12)	46	**16**	34.8
22	Wrexham (24)	46	**16**	34.8
23	Dag & Red (20)	46	**16**	34.8
24	Chester (22)	46	**14**	30.4

HEREFORD: not quite the '72 vintage but good with a lead

RECORD WHEN FIRST TO SCORE

	Team	Pld	W	D	L	F	GFA	PGA	Pts
1	Hereford (3)	22	21	1	0	52	13	**2.9**	64
2	Peterborough (2)	27	23	2	2	66	19	**2.6**	71
3	Barnet (12)	16	13	2	1	36	14	**2.6**	41
4	Stockport (4)	26	21	3	2	49	16	**2.5**	66
5	Bury (14)	17	13	3	1	33	11	**2.5**	42
6	MK Dons (1)	34	26	5	3	70	23	**2.4**	83
7	Darlington (7)	28	21	4	3	57	16	**2.4**	67
8	Wycombe (7)	28	20	6	2	45	18	**2.4**	66
9	Rotherham (8)	26	19	6	1	43	18	**2.4**	63
10	Lincoln (15)	22	16	4	2	43	19	**2.4**	52
11	Rochdale (5)	21	16	3	2	47	20	**2.4**	51
12	Chesterfield (9)	23	15	7	1	50	18	**2.3**	52
13	Brentford (14)	21	14	6	1	35	18	**2.3**	48
14	Dag & Red (20)	16	11	3	2	30	13	**2.3**	36
15	Morecambe (12)	19	11	6	2	35	20	**2.1**	39
16	Accrington (17)	18	12	1	5	32	23	**2.1**	37
17	Grimsby (16)	24	15	4	5	42	23	**2.0**	49
18	Bradford (10)	22	13	3	6	37	24	**1.9**	42
19	Notts Co (21)	17	9	5	3	19	13	**1.9**	32
20	Wrexham (24)	16	10	1	5	24	19	**1.9**	31
21	Chester (22)	14	8	3	3	30	19	**1.9**	27
22	Mansfield (23)	17	9	4	4	32	22	**1.8**	31
23	Macclesfield (19)	21	9	9	3	27	20	**1.7**	36
24	Shrewsbury (19)	25	11	5	9	42	32	**1.5**	38

BLUE SQUARE PREMIER

	Team	Pld	FS	FS%
1	Exeter (4)	46	**30**	65.2
2	Torquay (3)	46	**28**	60.9
3	Aldershot (1)	46	**27**	58.7
4	Kidderminster (13)	46	**27**	58.7
5	Histon (7)	46	**26**	56.5
6	Cambridge (3)	46	**26**	56.5
7	Oxford (9)	46	**25**	54.3
8	Burton (5)	46	**24**	52.2
9	Stevenage (6)	46	**24**	52.2
10	Ebbsfleet (11)	46	**24**	52.2
11	Crawley (14)	46	**23**	50.0
12	Forest Green (9)	46	**23**	50.0
13	York (15)	46	**21**	45.7
14	Salisbury (12)	46	**21**	45.7
15	Grays (10)	46	**20**	43.5
16	Halifax (18)	46	**20**	43.5
17	Woking (17)	46	**19**	41.3
18	Weymouth (19)	46	**19**	41.3
19	Rushden (16)	46	**17**	37.0
20	Northwich (20)	46	**17**	37.0
21	Farsley (22)	46	**16**	34.8
22	Altrincham (21)	46	**15**	32.6
23	Droylsden (24)	46	**12**	26.1
24	Stafford (23)	46	**10**	21.7

ALTRINCHAM: a long time since they held Ossie's mob

RECORD WHEN FIRST TO SCORE

	Team	Pld	W	D	L	F	GFA	PGA	Pts
1	Aldershot (1)	27	26	0	1	60	22	**2.9**	78
2	Torquay (3)	28	23	3	2	60	25	**2.6**	72
3	Burton (5)	24	20	2	2	55	22	**2.6**	62
4	Grays (10)	20	16	4	0	43	15	**2.6**	52
5	Stevenage (6)	24	20	1	3	59	20	**2.5**	61
6	Salisbury (12)	21	16	4	1	46	15	**2.5**	52
7	Cambridge (3)	26	20	3	3	49	17	**2.4**	63
8	Oxford (9)	25	19	4	2	49	19	**2.4**	61
9	Forest Green (9)	23	17	4	2	54	25	**2.4**	55
10	Rushden (16)	17	12	4	1	31	12	**2.4**	40
11	Exeter (4)	30	20	9	1	66	33	**2.3**	69
12	Histon (7)	26	18	6	2	48	27	**2.3**	60
13	Ebbsfleet (11)	24	16	7	1	44	22	**2.3**	55
14	Crawley (14)	23	15	5	3	53	24	**2.2**	50
15	Kidderminster (13)	27	17	6	4	59	21	**2.1**	57
16	York (15)	21	14	2	5	45	24	**2.1**	44
17	Woking (17)	19	10	8	1	31	18	**2.0**	38
18	Halifax (18)	20	9	8	3	43	28	**1.8**	35
19	Northwich (20)	17	9	4	4	32	24	**1.8**	31
20	Weymouth (19)	19	10	3	6	32	23	**1.7**	33
21	Farsley (22)	16	6	5	5	24	21	**1.4**	23
22	Altrincham (21)	15	5	6	4	23	23	**1.4**	21
23	Stafford (23)	10	4	2	4	17	18	**1.4**	14
24	Droylsden (24)	12	4	3	5	20	21	**1.3**	15

SCOTTISH PREMIER LEAGUE

	Team	Pld	FS	FS%
1	Rangers (2)	38	**28**	73.7
2	Celtic (1)	38	**24**	63.2
3	Dundee Utd (6)	38	**21**	55.3
4	Motherwell (3)	38	**21**	55.3
5	Aberdeen (4)	38	**19**	50.0
6	Hibernian (6)	38	**19**	50.0
7	Hearts (8)	38	**17**	44.7
8	Falkirk (7)	38	**16**	42.1
9	Inverness CT (9)	38	**15**	39.5
10	St Mirren (10)	38	**14**	36.8
11	Kilmarnock (11)	38	**11**	28.9
12	Gretna (12)	38	**7**	18.4

KRIS BOYD: kept the goals coming for Rangers last term

RECORD WHEN FIRST TO SCORE

	Team	Pld	W	D	L	F	GFA	PGA	Pts
1	Rangers (2)	28	26	2	0	71	14	**2.9**	80
2	Celtic (1)	24	22	1	1	63	12	**2.8**	67
3	Inverness CT (9)	15	12	1	2	37	15	**2.5**	37
4	St Mirren (10)	14	10	3	1	20	9	**2.4**	33
5	Motherwell (3)	21	15	3	3	39	17	**2.3**	48
6	Falkirk (7)	16	12	1	3	32	12	**2.3**	37
7	Dundee Utd (6)	21	14	5	2	44	17	**2.2**	47
8	Aberdeen (4)	19	12	4	3	33	19	**2.1**	40
9	Hearts (8)	17	11	3	3	31	18	**2.1**	36
10	Hibernian (6)	19	11	5	3	32	19	**2.0**	38
11	Kilmarnock (11)	11	6	3	2	18	11	**1.9**	21
12	Gretna (12)	7	4	1	2	15	12	**1.9**	13

GRETNA: managed to take the lead occasionally – but then threw it all away

SCOTTISH DIVISION ONE

	Team	Pld	FS	FS%
1	Hamilton (1)	36	**28**	77.8
2	Clyde (9)	36	**20**	55.6
3	Dundee (2)	36	**20**	55.6
4	Dunfermline (5)	36	**16**	44.4
5	Queen of Sth (4)	36	**16**	44.4
6	Morton (9)	36	**15**	41.7
7	St Johnstone (3)	36	**15**	41.7
8	Partick (6)	36	**13**	36.1
9	Livingston (7)	36	**13**	36.1
10	Stirling (10)	36	**9**	25.0

BILLY REID: Hamilton boss is all smiles as the goals flow

RECORD WHEN FIRST TO SCORE

	Team	Pld	W	D	L	F	GFA	PGA	Pts
1	Hamilton (1)	28	22	3	3	58	18	**2.5**	69
2	Dundee (2)	20	16	1	3	40	13	**2.5**	49
3	Dunfermline (5)	16	11	5	0	25	8	**2.4**	38
4	Partick (6)	13	9	4	0	27	7	**2.4**	31
5	St Johnstone (3)	15	9	4	2	29	17	**2.1**	31
6	Queen of Sth (4)	16	9	4	3	29	17	**1.9**	31
7	Livingston (7)	13	7	3	3	31	20	**1.8**	24
8	Morton (9)	15	7	5	3	26	17	**1.7**	26
9	Clyde (9)	20	6	6	8	30	34	**1.2**	24
10	Stirling (10)	9	3	2	4	16	17	**1.2**	11

SCOTTISH DIVISION TWO

	Team	Pld	FS	FS%
1	Ross County (1)	36	**24**	66.7
2	Ayr (7)	36	**22**	61.1
3	Airdrie Utd (2)	36	**22**	61.1
4	Alloa (4)	36	**20**	55.6
5	Cowdenbeath (9)	36	**18**	50.0
6	Raith (3)	36	**17**	47.2
7	Peterhead (5)	36	**16**	44.4
8	Queen's Park (8)	36	**15**	41.7
9	Brechin (6)	36	**14**	38.9
10	Berwick (10)	36	**8**	22.2

ROSS COUNTY: usually got their noses in front in 2007/08

RECORD WHEN FIRST TO SCORE

	Team	Pld	W	D	L	F	GFA	PGA	Pts
1	Raith (3)	17	15	1	1	39	17	**2.7**	46
2	Ross County (1)	24	19	4	1	57	20	**2.5**	61
3	Alloa (4)	20	16	2	2	44	18	**2.5**	50
4	Airdrie Utd (2)	22	17	2	3	50	14	**2.4**	53
5	Peterhead (5)	16	12	2	2	40	18	**2.4**	38
6	Brechin (6)	14	9	5	0	38	16	**2.3**	32
7	Queen's Park (8)	15	10	3	2	28	13	**2.2**	33
8	Ayr (7)	22	13	4	5	45	29	**2.0**	43
9	Cowdenbeath (9)	18	9	4	5	28	28	**1.7**	31
10	Berwick (10)	8	2	4	2	15	16	**1.3**	10

SCOTTISH DIVISION THREE

	Team	Pld	FS	FS%
1	East Fife (1)	36	**27**	75.0
2	Stenh'semuir (5)	36	**20**	55.6
3	Montrose (3)	36	**19**	52.8
4	Arbroath (4)	36	**18**	50.0
5	Albion (8)	36	**15**	41.7
6	Forfar (10)	36	**14**	38.9
7	Dumbarton (8)	36	**14**	38.9
8	Stranraer (2)	36	**14**	38.9
9	Elgin City (6)	36	**13**	36.1
10	East Stirling (9)	36	**13**	36.1

EAST FIFE: smooching after scoring first again

RECORD WHEN FIRST TO SCORE

	Team	Pld	W	D	L	F	GFA	PGA	Pts
1	Stranraer (2)	14	13	1	0	34	7	**2.9**	40
2	East Fife (1)	27	25	1	1	66	11	**2.8**	76
3	Montrose (3)	19	15	3	1	49	16	**2.5**	48
4	Arbroath (4)	18	13	2	3	38	15	**2.3**	41
5	Elgin City (6)	13	9	3	1	31	13	**2.3**	30
6	Dumbarton (8)	14	9	3	2	20	10	**2.1**	30
7	Stenh'semuir (5)	20	11	5	4	40	27	**1.9**	38
8	Albion (8)	15	7	5	3	37	26	**1.7**	26
9	Forfar (10)	14	7	3	4	21	18	**1.7**	24
10	East Stirling (9)	13	6	1	6	26	21	**1.5**	19

STAIR PARK: Stranraer supporters would be well advised to get to the ground early

FINAL

CARDIFF	0-1	PORTSMOUTH

SEMI-FINALS

BARNSLEY	0-1	CARDIFF
WEST BROM	0-1	PORTSMOUTH

SIXTH-ROUND

BRISTOL R	1-5	WEST BROM
MIDDLESBRO	0-2	CARDIFF
BARNSLEY	1-0	CHELSEA
MAN UTD	0-1	PORTSMOUTH

FIFTH-ROUND REPLAY

MIDDLESBRO	1-0	SHEFF UTD

(aet, 0-0 after 90 minutes)

FIFTH ROUND

PRESTON	0-1	PORTSMOUTH
SHEFF UTD	0-0	MIDDLESBRO
BRISTOL R	1-0	SOUTHAMPTON
CARDIFF	2-0	WOLVES
CHELSEA	3-1	HUDDERSFIELD
COVENTRY	0-5	WEST BROM
LIVERPOOL	1-2	BARNSLEY
MAN UTD	4-0	ARSENAL

FOURTH ROUND

HEREFORD	1-2	CARDIFF
MAN UTD	3-1	TOTTENHAM
SHEFF UTD	2-1	MAN CITY
ARSENAL	3-0	NEWCASTLE
BARNET	0-1	BRISTOL R
COVENTRY	2-1	MILLWALL
DERBY	1-4	PRESTON
LIVERPOOL	5-2	HAVANT & W
MANSFIELD	0-2	MIDDLESBRO
OLDHAM	0-1	HUDDERSFIELD
PETERBOROUGH	0-3	WEST BROM
PORTSMOUTH	2-1	PLYMOUTH
SOUTHAMPTON	2-0	BURY
WATFORD	1-4	WOLVES
WIGAN	1-2	CHELSEA
SOUTHEND	0-1	BARNSLEY

THIRD-ROUND REPLAYS

BARNET	1-1	SWINDON

(aet, 1-1 after 90 mins, Barnet won 2-0 on pens)

BRISTOL R	0-0	FULHAM

(aet, 0-0 after 90 mins, Bristol R won 5-3 on pens)

SHEFF WED	1-1	DERBY

(aet, 1-1 after 90 mins, Sheff Weds won 4-2 on pens)

HAVANT & W	4-2	SWANSEA
HEREFORD	1-0	TRANMERE
MAN CITY	1-0	WEST HAM
NEWCASTLE	4-1	STOKE
BURY	2-1	NORWICH
LIVERPOOL	5-0	LUTON
MILLWALL	2-1	WALSALL
READING	0-1	TOTTENHAM
WEST BROM	2-2	CHARLTON

(aet, 2-2 after 90 mins, West Brom won 4-3 on pens)

THIRD ROUND

BURNLEY	0-2	ARSENAL
DERBY	2-2	SHEFF WED
FULHAM	2-2	BRISTOL R
LUTON	1-1	LIVERPOOL

STOKE	0-0	NEWCASTLE
ASTON VILLA	0-2	MAN UTD
BARNSLEY	2-1	BLACKPOOL
BLACKBURN	1-4	COVENTRY
BOLTON	0-1	SHEFF UTD
BRIGHTON	1-2	MANSFIELD
BRISTOL C	1-2	MIDDLESBRO
CHARLTON	1-1	WEST BROM
CHASETOWN	1-3	CARDIFF
CHELSEA	1-0	QPR
COLCHESTER	1-3	PETERBOROUGH
EVERTON	0-1	OLDHAM
HUDDERSFIELD	2-1	BIRMINGHAM
IPSWICH	0-1	PORTSMOUTH
NORWICH	1-1	BURY
PLYMOUTH	3-2	HULL CITY
PRESTON	1-0	SCUNTHORPE
SOUTHAMPTON	2-0	LEICESTER
SOUTHEND	5-2	DAG & RED
SUNDERLAND	0-3	WIGAN
SWANSEA	1-1	HAVANT & W
SWINDON	1-1	BARNET
TOTTENHAM	2-2	READING
TRANMERE	2-2	HEREFORD
WALSALL	0-0	MILLWALL
WATFORD	2-0	C PALACE
WEST HAM	0-0	MAN CITY
WOLVES	2-1	CAMBRIDGE

SECOND-ROUND REPLAYS

BARNET	1-0	BURTON
CHASETOWN	1-0	PORT VALE
SOUTHEND	3-0	OXFORD
WALSALL	1-0	NORTHAMPTON
LUTON	1-0	NOTTM FOREST
SWANSEA	6-2	HORSHAM

SECOND ROUND

HARROGATE R	2-3	MANSFIELD
PORT VALE	1-1	CHASETOWN
BRADFORD	0-3	TRANMERE
BRISTOL R	5-1	RUSHDEN
BURTON	1-1	BARNET
BURY	1-0	EXETER
CAMBRIDGE	1-0	WEYMOUTH
DAG & RED	3-1	KIDDERMINSTER
HEREFORD	2-0	HARTLEPOOL
HUDDERSFIELD	3-0	GRIMSBY
MILLWALL	2-1	BOURNEMOUTH
NORTHAMPTON	1-1	WALSALL
NOTTS CO	0-1	HAVANT & W
OLDHAM	1-0	CREWE
OXFORD	0-0	SOUTHEND
STAINES	0-5	PETERBOROUGH
SWINDON	3-2	FOREST GREEN
TORQUAY	0-2	BRIGHTON
HORSHAM	1-1	SWANSEA

FIRST-ROUND REPLAYS

BRENTFORD	0-2	LUTON
BRISTOL R	3-3	LEYTON ORIENT

(aet, 2-2 after 90 mins, Bristol R won 6-5 on pens)

DONCASTER	1-2	OLDHAM
NOTTM FOREST	3-1	LINCOLN

Sponsored by Stan James

SUCCESS AT LAST: Harry Redknapp finally gets his hands on the FA Cup

STAINES	1-1	STOCKPORT

(aet, 1-1 after 90 mins, Staines won 4-3 on pens)

BOURNEMOUTH	3-2	BARROW

(aet, 2-2 after 90 mins)

BRIGHTON	2-1	CHELTENHAM
GRIMSBY	1-0	CARLISLE
LEEDS	0-1	HEREFORD
NORTHAMPTON	2-1	DARLINGTON
ROTHERHAM	0-3	FOREST GREEN

FIRST ROUND

FOREST GREEN	2-2	ROTHERHAM
GAINSBOROUGH	0-6	HARTLEPOOL
TORQUAY	4-1	YEOVIL
ACCRINGTON	2-3	HUDDERSFIELD
ALTRINCHAM	1-2	MILLWALL
BARNET	2-1	GILLINGHAM
BARROW	1-1	BOURNEMOUTH
BILLERICAY	1-2	SWANSEA
BRADFORD	1-0	CHESTER
BURY	4-1	WORKINGTON
CAMBRIDGE	2-1	ALDERSHOT
CARLISLE	1-1	GRIMSBY
CHELTENHAM	1-1	BRIGHTON
CHESTERFIELD	1-2	TRANMERE
CREWE	2-1	MK DONS
DARLINGTON	1-1	NORTHAMPTON
EASTBOURNE	0-4	WEYMOUTH
EXETER	4-0	STEVENAGE
HALIFAX	0-4	BURTON
HAMPTON & R	0-3	DAG & RED
HARROGATE R	2-0	DROYLSDEN
HORSHAM	4-1	MAIDENHEAD
LEYTON ORIENT	1-1	BRISTOL R

LINCOLN	1-1	NOTTM FOREST
LUTON	1-1	BRENTFORD
MANSFIELD	3-0	LEWES
MORECAMBE	0-2	PORT VALE
NOTTS CO	3-0	HISTON
OLDHAM	2-2	DONCASTER
OXFORD	3-1	NORTHWICH
PETERBOROUGH	4-1	WREXHAM
RUSHDEN	3-1	MACCLESFIELD
SOUTHEND	2-1	ROCHDALE
STOCKPORT	1-1	STAINES
TEAM BATH	0-2	CHASETOWN
WALSALL	2-0	SHREWSBURY
WARE	0-2	KIDDERMINSTER
WYCOMBE	1-2	SWINDON
YORK	0-1	HAVANT & W
HEREFORD	0-0	LEEDS

FOURTH QUALIFYING ROUND REPLAYS

LEWES	2-0	GRAYS
ALDERSHOT	1-0	CRAWLEY
BARROW	2-1	FARSLEY
CAMBRIDGE	5-1	STAFFORD
FOREST GREEN	4-1	EASTLEIGH
HALIFAX	2-1	EVESHAM
HITCHIN	0-1	WEYMOUTH
STEVENAGE	1-0	SALISBURY

FOURTH QUALIFYING ROUND

BATH CITY	0-2	TORQUAY
BRADFORD PA	0-4	GAINSBOROUGH
BURTON	2-1	TAMWORTH
CHASETOWN	2-1	NUNEATON
CHIPPENHAM	2-3	HORSHAM
CORBY	1-2	DROYLSDEN
CRAWLEY	1-1	ALDERSHOT
EASTBOURNE	2-1	BROMLEY
EASTLEIGH	3-3	FOREST GREEN
EBBSFLEET	1-3	EXETER
EVESHAM	0-0	HALIFAX
FARSLEY	1-1	BARROW
FOLKESTONE	0-2	BILLERICAY
GRAYS	2-0	LEWES
HAMPTON & R	1-0	WEALDSTONE
HARROGATE R	2-1	HARROGATE T
HAVANT & W	3-0	LEIGHTON
HISTON	4-1	BAMBER BR.
HORNCHURCH	0-1	TEAM BATH
KENDAL TOWN	0-1	ALTRINCHAM
KIDDERMINSTER	3-1	VAUXHALL M
MAIDENHEAD	1-0	HAYES & Y
MERTHYR	1-2	OXFORD
RUSHDEN	5-0	SOLIHULL M
SALISBURY	0-0	STEVENAGE
SOUTHPORT	1-3	NORTHWICH
STAFFORD	1-1	CAMBRIDGE
WARE	3-1	TONBRIDGE
WEYMOUTH	1-1	HITCHIN
WOKING	0-1	STAINES
WORKINGTON	1-0	BOSTON UTD
YORK	6-0	RUSHALL O

FINAL

TOTTENHAM	2-1	CHELSEA

(aet, 1-1 after 90 mins)

SEMI-FINAL SECOND LEGS

EVERTON	0-1	CHELSEA
TOTTENHAM	5-1	ARSENAL

SEMI-FINAL FIRST LEGS

ARSENAL	1-1	TOTTENHAM
CHELSEA	2-1	EVERTON

QUARTER-FINALS

CHELSEA	2-0	LIVERPOOL
BLACKBURN	2-3	ARSENAL

(aet, 2-2 after 90 mins)

MAN CITY	0-2	TOTTENHAM
WEST HAM	1-2	EVERTON

FOURTH ROUND

BOLTON	0-1	MAN CITY
CHELSEA	4-3	LEICESTER
LIVERPOOL	2-1	CARDIFF
LUTON	0-1	EVERTON

(aet, 0-0 after 90 mins)

PORTSMOUTH	1-2	BLACKBURN
SHEFF UTD	0-3	ARSENAL
TOTTENHAM	2-0	BLACKPOOL
COVENTRY	1-2	WEST HAM

THIRD ROUND

ASTON VILLA	0-1	LEICESTER
BLACKBURN	3-0	BIRMINGHAM
FULHAM	1-2	BOLTON

(aet, 1-1 after 90 mins)

HULL CITY	0-4	CHELSEA
MAN UTD	0-2	COVENTRY
SHEFF WED	0-3	EVERTON
TOTTENHAM	2-0	MIDDLESBRO
WEST HAM	1-0	PLYMOUTH
ARSENAL	2-0	NEWCASTLE
BLACKPOOL	2-1	SOUTHEND

(aet, 1-1 after 90 mins)

BURNLEY	0-1	PORTSMOUTH
LUTON	3-1	CHARLTON

(aet, 1-1 after 90 mins)

MAN CITY	1-0	NORWICH
READING	2-4	LIVERPOOL
SHEFF UTD	5-0	MORECAMBE
WEST BROM	2-4	CARDIFF

SECOND ROUND

NOTTM FOREST	2-3	LEICESTER
BRISTOL C	1-2	MAN CITY
MIDDLESBRO	2-0	NORTHAMPTON
NEWCASTLE	2-0	BARNSLEY
BIRMINGHAM	2-1	HEREFORD
BRISTOL R	1-2	WEST HAM
BURNLEY	3-0	OLDHAM
CARDIFF	1-0	LEYTON ORIENT
CARLISLE	0-2	COVENTRY
CHARLTON	4-3	STOCKPORT
DERBY	2-2	BLACKPOOL

(aet, 1-1 after 90 mins, Blackpool won 7-6 on pens)

LUTON	3-0	SUNDERLAND
MK DONS	2-3	SHEFF UTD

(aet, 2-2 after 90 mins)

PETERBOROUGH	0-2	WEST BROM
PLYMOUTH	2-0	DONCASTER
PORTSMOUTH	3-0	LEEDS
ROCHDALE	1-1	NORWICH

(aet, 1-1 after 90 mins, Norwich won 4-3 on pens)

SHEFF WED	2-1	HARTLEPOOL

(aet, 1-1 after 90 mins)

SHREWSBURY	0-1	FULHAM
SOUTHEND	2-0	WATFORD
SWANSEA	0-1	READING

(aet, 0-0 after 90 mins)

WIGAN	0-1	HULL CITY
WOLVES	1-3	MORECAMBE

(aet, 1-1 after 90 mins)

WREXHAM	0-5	ASTON VILLA

FIRST ROUND

ROTHERHAM	1-3	SHEFF WED
CREWE	0-3	HULL CITY
WOLVES	2-1	BRADFORD
ACCRINGTON	0-1	LEICESTER
BARNSLEY	2-1	DARLINGTON
BLACKPOOL	1-0	HUDDERSFIELD
BRENTFORD	0-3	BRISTOL C
BRISTOL R	1-1	C PALACE

(aet, 1-1 after 90 mins, Bristol R won 4-1 on pens)

BURY	0-1	CARLISLE
CARDIFF	1-0	BRIGHTON

(aet, 0-0 after 90 mins)

CHESTER	0-0	NOTTM FOREST

(aet, 0-0 after 90 mins, Nottm Forest won 4-2 on pens)

COVENTRY	3-0	NOTTS CO
DAG & RED	1-2	LUTON
DONCASTER	4-1	LINCOLN
GRIMSBY	1-1	BURNLEY

(aet, 0-0 after 90 mins, Burnley won 4-2 on pens)

HEREFORD	4-1	YEOVIL
MK DONS	3-3	IPSWICH

(aet, 2-2 after 90 mins, MK Dons won 5-3 on pens)

MACCLESFIELD	0-1	LEEDS
NORTHAMPTON	2-0	MILLWALL
NORWICH	5-2	BARNET
OLDHAM	4-1	MANSFIELD
PLYMOUTH	2-1	WYCOMBE
PORT VALE	1-1	WREXHAM

(aet, 1-1 after 90 mins, Wrexham won 5-3 on pens)

PRESTON	1-2	MORECAMBE
QPR	1-2	LEYTON ORIENT
ROCHDALE	2-2	STOKE

(aet, 1-1 after 90 mins, Rochdale won 4-2 on pens)

SCUNTHORPE	1-2	HARTLEPOOL
SHEFF UTD	3-1	CHESTERFIELD
SHREWSBURY	1-0	COLCHESTER

(aet, 0-0 after 90 mins)

SOUTHEND	4-1	CHELTENHAM

(aet, 1-1 after 90 mins)

STOCKPORT	1-0	TRANMERE
SWANSEA	2-0	WALSALL
SWINDON	0-2	CHARLTON
WATFORD	3-0	GILLINGHAM
WEST BROM	1-0	BOURNEMOUTH
PETERBOROUGH	2-1	SOUTHAMPTON

JONATHAN WOODGATE: headed Tottenham to League Cup glory over Chelsea

FINAL

GRIMSBY	0-2	MK DONS

NORTHERN FINAL

MORECAMBE	0-1	GRIMSBY
GRIMSBY	0-0	MORECAMBE

SOUTHERN FINAL

SWANSEA	0-1	MK DONS
MK DONS	0-1	SWANSEA

(aet, 1-1 agg score, MK Dons won 5-4 on pens)

NORTHERN SECTION SEMI-FINAL

MORECAMBE	2-0	BURY
STOCKPORT	1-2	GRIMSBY

SOUTHERN SECTION SEMI-FINAL

GILLINGHAM	1-1	MK DONS

(aet, 1-1 after 90 mins, MK Dons won 5-4 on pens)

SWANSEA	1-0	BRIGHTON

NORTHERN SECTION QUARTERS

CARLISLE	0-3	STOCKPORT
GRIMSBY	2-2	DONCASTER

(aet, 2-2 after 90 mins, Grimsby won 5-4 on pens)

HARTLEPOOL	1-1	MORECAMBE

(aet, 1-1 after 90 mins, Morecambe won 4-2 on pens)

LEEDS	1-2	BURY

SOUTHERN SECTION QUARTERS

BRIGHTON	4-1	CHELTENHAM
BOURNEMOUTH	0-2	MK DONS
GILLINGHAM	4-0	DAG & RED
SWANSEA	1-0	YEOVIL

NORTHERN SECTION 2ND ROUND

MACCLESFIELD	0-1	STOCKPORT
CARLISLE	4-2	CHESTER
MORECAMBE	2-2	PORT VALE

(Morecambe won 4-2 on pens)

ROCHDALE	1-3	BURY

DONCASTER	3-0	OLDHAM
DARLINGTON	0-1	LEEDS
LINCOLN	2-5	HARTLEPOOL
ROTHERHAM	1-1	GRIMSBY

(Grimsby won 4-2 on pens)

SOUTHERN SECTION 2ND ROUND

HEREFORD	0-0	YEOVIL

(Yeovil won 4-2 on pens)

BRISTOL R	0-1	BOURNEMOUTH
SWINDON	1-3	CHELTENHAM
SWANSEA	2-0	WYCOMBE
MK DONS	3-1	PETERBOROUGH
BRIGHTON	2-1	BARNET
LEYTON ORIENT	0-1	DAG & RED
GILLINGHAM	4-3	LUTON

NORTHERN SECTION 1ST ROUND

TRANMERE	0-1	MORECAMBE
CHESTER	1-1	CREWE

(Chester won 4-3 on pens)

WREXHAM	0-1	MACCLESFIELD
ACCRINGTON	2-3	OLDHAM
CHESTERFIELD	1-3	HARTLEPOOL
MANSFIELD	0-1	ROTHERHAM
DONCASTER	5-1	BRADFORD
GRIMSBY	4-1	HUDDERSFIELD

SOUTHERN SECTION 1ST ROUND

BOURNEMOUTH	2-0	WALSALL
SWANSEA	3-2	MILLWALL
SWINDON	4-1	BRENTFORD
YEOVIL	1-0	SHREWSBURY
LUTON	2-0	NORTHAMPTON
NOTTM FOREST	2-3	PETERBOROUGH
NOTTS CO	0-1	LEYTON ORIENT
SOUTHEND	2-2	DAG & RED

(Dagenham & Redbridge won 7-6 on pens)

FA TROPHY 2007/08

FINAL
| EBBSFLEET | 1-0 | TORQUAY |

SEMI-FINAL SECOND LEGS
| ALDERSHOT | 1-1 | EBBSFLEET |
| YORK | 1-0 | TORQUAY |

SEMI-FINAL FIRST LEGS
| EBBSFLEET | 3-1 | ALDERSHOT |
| TORQUAY | 2-0 | YORK |

FOURTH ROUND REPLAY
| EBBSFLEET | 1-0 | BURTON |

(aet, 0-0 after 90 mins)

FOURTH ROUND
BURTON	0-0	EBBSFLEET
RUSHDEN	0-1	YORK
TAMWORTH	1-2	ALDERSHOT
TORQUAY	4-1	CRAWLEY

THIRD ROUND REPLAYS
| HISTON | 0-1 | BURTON |
| TAMWORTH | 2-1 | STAFFORD |

THIRD ROUND
FARSLEY	0-2	YORK
ALDERSHOT	3-0	BRAINTREE
BURTON	2-2	HISTON
CRAWLEY	8-0	DROYLSDEN
EBBSFLEET	1-0	WEYMOUTH
HALIFAX	0-2	RUSHDEN
STAFFORD	2-2	TAMWORTH
WIMBLEDON	0-2	TORQUAY

SECOND ROUND REPLAYS
ALFRETON	0-2	FARSLEY
HALIFAX	4-1	BISHOP'S ST
KIDDERMINSTER	2-2	WEYMOUTH

(aet, 1-1 after 90 mins, Weymouth won 3-0 on pens)

| WORKINGTON | 1-2 | BRAINTREE |
| GRAYS | 1-4 | YORK |

SECOND ROUND
HISTON	2-0	CAMBRIDGE
BISHOP'S ST	2-2	HALIFAX
BLYTH SPTNS	0-1	TAMWORTH
BRAINTREE	1-1	WORKINGTON
CRAWLEY	2-1	EASTLEIGH
DORCHESTER	0-2	EBBSFLEET
DROYLSDEN	1-0	CAMBRIDGE C
FARSLEY	1-1	ALFRETON
NEWPORT CO	1-2	TORQUAY
RUSHDEN	3-0	EXETER
STAFFORD	2-1	FOREST GREEN
TONBRIDGE	0-4	WIMBLEDON
VAUXHALL M	1-4	BURTON
WEYMOUTH	0-0	KIDDERMINSTER
WOKING	2-4	ALDERSHOT
YORK	1-1	GRAYS

FIRST ROUND REPLAYS
| TONBRIDGE | 1-0 | OXFORD |
| FARSLEY | 4-1 | GATESHEAD |

FIRST ROUND
| HALIFAX | 2-1 | LEAMINGTON |
| ALFRETON | 1-0 | SOUTHPORT |

FROM TINY ACORNS: the FA Trophy helped launch O'Neill as a manager

GUISELEY	1-2	KIDDERMINSTER
HUCKNALL	0-1	TAMWORTH
ALTRINCHAM	1-3	YORK
BAMBER BR	2-3	RUSHDEN
BISHOP'S ST	8-0	CANVEY ISL
CAMBRIDGE	5-0	KING'S LYNN
CAMBRIDGE C	3-2	KETTERING
COLWYN BAY	1-2	BURTON
CRAWLEY	1-0	BROMLEY
DORCHESTER	2-1	STEVENAGE
DROYLSDEN	2-1	REDDITCH
EASTLEIGH	1-0	BOGNOR REGIS
EBBSFLEET	4-1	CARSHALTON
EXETER	3-0	SALISBURY
GATESHEAD	1-1	FARSLEY
GLOUCESTER	0-2	BRAINTREE
GRAYS	3-0	LEWES
HAYES & Y	0-5	ALDERSHOT
HEMEL	0-1	WOKING
HISTON	5-2	RETFORD UTD
LEIGH RMI	1-3	WORKINGTON
MAIDENHEAD	0-2	WIMBLEDON
NEWPORT CO	3-0	BATH CITY
OXFORD	0-0	TONBRIDGE
STAFFORD	3-1	OSSETT TOWN
SUTTON UTD	1-4	FOREST GREEN
TELFORD	1-2	BLYTH SPTNS
TORQUAY	1-0	BASHLEY
VAUXHALL M	2-1	NORTHWICH
WEALDSTONE	0-1	WEYMOUTH

142

Sponsored by Stan James

FINAL
QUEEN OF STH 2-3 RANGERS
SEMI-FINALS
ST JOHNSTONE 1-1 RANGERS
(aet, 0-0 after 90 mins, Rangers won 4-3 on pens)
QUEEN OF STH 4-3 ABERDEEN
QUARTER-FINAL REPLAYS
PARTICK 0-2 RANGERS
CELTIC 0-1 ABERDEEN ST
MIRREN 1-3 ST JOHNSTONE
QUARTER-FINALS
RANGERS 1-1 PARTICK
ABERDEEN 1-1 CELTIC
QUEEN OF STH 2-0 DUNDEE
ST JOHNSTONE 1-1 ST MIRREN
FIFTH-ROUND REPLAYS
RANGERS 1-0 HIBERNIAN
DUNDEE UTD 0-1 ST MIRREN
PARTICK 1-1 LIVINGSTON
(aet, 1-1 after 90 mins, Partick won 5-4 on pens)
FIFTH ROUND
ROSS COUNTY 0-1 ST JOHNSTONE
MOTHERWELL 1-2 DUNDEE
HIBERNIAN 0-0 RANGERS
ABERDEEN 1-0 HAMILTON
KILMARNOCK 1-5 CELTIC
LIVINGSTON 0-0 PARTICK
MORTON 0-2 QUEEN OF STH
ST MIRREN 0-0 DUNDEE UTD
FOURTH-ROUND REPLAYS
ABERDEEN 3-1 FALKIRK
MOTHERWELL 1-0 HEARTS
BRECHIN 2-1 HAMILTON
(aet, 1-1 after 90 mins)
GRETNA 0-3 MORTON
FOURTH ROUND
AIRDRIE UTD 0-2 KILMARNOCK
COVE RANGERS 2-4 ROSS COUNTY
RANGERS 6-0 EAST STIRLING
PARTICK 2-1 DUNFERMLINE
CLYDE 0-1 DUNDEE UTD
HUNTLY 1-3 DUNDEE
LIVINGSTON 2-0 COWDENBEATH
ST JOHNSTONE 3-1 RAITH
CELTIC 3-0 STIRLING
FALKIRK 2-2 ABERDEEN
HAMILTON 0-0 BRECHIN
HEARTS 2-2 MOTHERWELL
HIBERNIAN 3-0 INVERNESS CT
MORTON 2-2 GRETNA
QUEEN OF STH 4-0 LINLITHGOW R
ST MIRREN 3-0 DUMBARTON
THIRD-ROUND REPLAYS
EAST FIFE 1-2 BRECHIN
QUEEN'S PARK 2-4 AIRDRIE UTD
THIRD ROUND
AIRDRIE UTD 1-1 QUEEN'S PARK
ALBION 1-5 EAST STIRLING
ARBROATH 0-1 COWDENBEATH
BRECHIN 1-1 EAST FIFE
CLYDE 2-0 MONTROSE
COVE RANGERS 1-0 EDINBURGH UNI
CULTER 1-3 HUNTLY
DUMBARTON 2-0 BERWICK
LINLITHGOW R 1-0 DALBEATTIE S

DAVID V GOLIATH: minnows Queen Of The South pushed Rangers all the way

LIVINGSTON 4-0 ALLOA
MORTON 3-2 BUCKIE THISTLE
PARTICK 2-1 AYR
PETERHEAD 0-5 QUEEN OF STH
ROSS COUNTY 4-0 WHITEHILL W
STRANRAER 0-6 STIRLING
THREAVE ROVERS 0-5 RAITH
SECOND-ROUND REPLAYS
DUMBARTON 3-0 FORFAR
POLLOK 0-1 MONTROSE
SECOND ROUND
ALBION 8-0 BURNTISLAND S
ANNAN 2-5 HUNTLY
ARBROATH 5-0 ELGIN CITY
BUCKIE THISTLE 4-1 NAIRN COUNTY
COVE RANGERS 3-0 KEITH
CULTER 2-1 VALE OF LEITHEN
EDINBURGH C 1-2 EAST STIRLING
EDINBURGH UNI 3-1 DEVERONVALE
FORFAR 1-1 DUMBARTON
GIRVAN 1-2 STRANRAER
INVERURIE L 0-2 EAST FIFE
LINLITHGOW R 4-1 SPARTANS
MONTROSE 2-2 POLLOK
SELKIRK 0-2 DALBEATTIE S
THREAVE R 1-0 STENH'SEMUIR
WHITEHILL W 6-1 GOLSPIE
FIRST-ROUND REPLAYS
EDINBURGH C 1-0 CLACHNACUDDIN
HUNTLY 2-0 FRASERBURGH
FIRST ROUND
BRORA RANGERS 0-5 COVE RANGERS
CIVIL SERV STROL 1-2 SELKIRK
CLACHNACUDDIN 2-2 EDINBURGH C
COLDSTREAM 0-4 DALBEATTIE S
CULTER 7-0 HAWICK ROYAL A
FORT WILLIAM 0-6 SPARTANS
FRASERBURGH 1-1 HUNTLY
GIRVAN 2-0 FORRES M
GLASGOW UNIV 1-2 BUCKIE THISTLE
GOLSPIE 3-1 PRESTON ATH.
LOSSIEMOUTH 1-3 WHITEHILL W
NEWTON S 0-6 LINLITHGOW R
ROTHES 1-4 NAIRN COUNTY
ST CUTHBERT'S 2-6 POLLOK
VALE OF LEITHEN 3-1 GALA FAIRYDEAN
WICK ACADEMY 0-5 DEVERONVALE
WIGTOWN & B 3-5 BURNTISLAND S

CIS & CHALLENGE CUPS 2007/08

CIS CUP FINAL

DUNDEE UTD	2-2	RANGERS

(aet, 1-1 after 90 mins, Rangers won 3-2 on pens)

SEMI-FINALS

ABERDEEN	1-4	DUNDEE UTD
RANGERS	2-0	HEARTS

QUARTER-FINALS

ABERDEEN	4-1	INVERNESS CT
CELTIC	0-2	HEARTS
DUNDEE UTD	3-1	HAMILTON
MOTHERWELL	1-2	RANGERS

THIRD ROUND

DUNDEE	1-2	CELTIC
EAST FIFE	0-4	RANGERS
HIBERNIAN	2-4	MOTHERWELL
PARTICK	0-2	ABERDEEN
FALKIRK	0-1	DUNDEE UTD
HAMILTON	2-0	KILMARNOCK
HEARTS	4-1	DUNFERMLINE

(aet, 1-1 after 90 mins)

INVERNESS CT	3-0	GRETNA

SECOND ROUND

DUNDEE UTD	2-1	ROSS COUNTY
MOTHERWELL	3-1	RAITH
BERWICK	2-3	HAMILTON
DUNDEE	2-2	LIVINGSTON

(aet, 2-2 after 90 mins, Dundee won 6-5 on pens)

GRETNA	3-1	COWDENBEATH
INVERNESS CT	3-1	ARBROATH
MONTROSE	1-2	FALKIRK
PARTICK	0-0	ST JOHNSTONE

(aet, 0-0 after 90 mins, Partick won 5-4 on pens)

PETERHEAD	0-3	KILMARNOCK
QUEEN'S PARK	1-2	HIBERNIAN
ST MIRREN	0-1	EAST FIFE
STIRLING	0-2	HEARTS

FIRST ROUND

ARBROATH	4-2	ALBION
EAST FIFE	1-0	QUEEN OF STH
PARTICK	2-1	AIRDRIE UTD
STRANRAER	1-2	MONTROSE
BERWICK	3-1	STENH'SEMUIR

(aet, 1-1 after 90 mins)

BRECHIN	0-1	STIRLING
CLYDE	0-3	RAITH
COWDENBEATH	2-0	DUMBARTON
DUNDEE	2-0	MORTON
FORFAR	0-1	PETERHEAD
HAMILTON	2-1	EAST STIRLING
LIVINGSTON	5-0	AYR
QUEEN'S PARK	2-1	ALLOA
ROSS COUNTY	3-1	ELGIN CITY

CHALLENGE CUP FINAL

DUNFERMLINE	2-3	ST JOHNSTONE

SEMI-FINALS

DUNFERMLINE	1-0	AYR
MORTON	1-3	ST JOHNSTONE

QUARTER-FINALS

ST JOHNSTONE	4-1	BRECHIN
AIRDRIE UTD	0-2	DUNFERMLINE
AYR	2-1	PARTICK

(aet, 1-1 after 90 mins)

EAST STIRLING	0-4	MORTON

SECOND ROUND

CLYDE	1-4	DUNFERMLINE
ROSS COUNTY	0-2	ST JOHNSTONE
AIRDRIE UTD	5-1	ARBROATH
EAST STIRLING	1-0	QUEEN'S PARK
FORFAR	0-2	AYR
MONTROSE	1-2	BRECHIN

(aet, 0-0 after 90 mins)

PARTICK	3-1	BERWICK
PETERHEAD	0-1	MORTON

FIRST ROUND

ARBROATH	2-0	ALLOA
ALBION	1-1	BERWICK

(aet, 1-1 after 90 mins, Berwick won 4-3 on pens)

CLYDE	1-0	QUEEN OF STH
DUNDEE	1-2	ROSS COUNTY
EAST STIRLING	4-2	DUMBARTON
ELGIN CITY	1-4	BRECHIN
FORFAR	3-2	EAST FIFE
HAMILTON	1-2	AYR
MONTROSE	5-1	STIRLING
MORTON	1-0	LIVINGSTON
PETERHEAD	1-0	COWDENBEATH
QUEEN'S PARK	1-0	STRANRAER
RAITH	1-1	ST JOHNSTONE

(aet, 1-1 after 90 mins, St Johnstone won 5-4 on pens)

STENH'SEMUIR	1-3	AIRDRIE UTD

COMETH THE HOUR: Allan McGregor was Rangers' hero in CIS Cup final

FINAL

MAN UTD	1-1	CHELSEA

(aet, 1-1 after 90 mins, Man Utd won 6-5 on pens)

SEMI-FINALS SECOND LEGS

CHELSEA	3-2	LIVERPOOL

(aet, 2-2 on agg after 90 mins)

MAN UTD	1-0	BARCELONA

SEMI-FINALS FIRST LEGS

BARCELONA	0-0	MAN UTD
LIVERPOOL	1-1	CHELSEA

QUARTER-FINALS SECOND LEGS

BARCELONA	1-0	SCHALKE
MAN UTD	1-0	ROMA
CHELSEA	2-0	FENERBAHCE
LIVERPOOL	4-2	ARSENAL

QUARTER-FINALS FIRST LEGS

ARSENAL	1-1	LIVERPOOL
FENERBAHCE	2-1	CHELSEA
ROMA	0-2	MAN UTD
SCHALKE	0-1	BARCELONA

LAST 16 SECOND LEGS

INTER MILAN	0-1	LIVERPOOL
CHELSEA	3-0	OLYMPIAKOS
PORTO	1-0	SCHALKE

(aet, 1-1 on agg, Schalke won 4-1 on pens)

REAL MADRID	1-2	ROMA
BARCELONA	1-0	CELTIC
MAN UTD	1-0	LYON
AC MILAN	0-2	ARSENAL
SEVILLE	3-2	FENERBAHCE

(aet, 5-5 on agg, Fenerbahce won 3-2 on pens)

LAST 16 FIRST LEGS

ARSENAL	0-0	AC MILAN
CELTIC	2-3	BARCELONA
FENERBAHCE	3-2	SEVILLE
LYON	1-1	MAN UTD
LIVERPOOL	2-0	INTER MILAN
OLYMPIAKOS	0-0	CHELSEA
ROMA	2-1	REAL MADRID
SCHALKE	1-0	PORTO

GROUP A

MARSEILLE	0-4	LIVERPOOL
PORTO	2-0	BESIKTAS
BESIKTAS	2-1	MARSEILLE
LIVERPOOL	4-1	PORTO
LIVERPOOL	8-0	BESIKTAS
PORTO	2-1	MARSEILLE
BESIKTAS	2-1	LIVERPOOL
MARSEILLE	1-1	PORTO
BESIKTAS	0-1	PORTO
LIVERPOOL	0-1	MARSEILLE
MARSEILLE	2-0	BESIKTAS
PORTO	1-1	LIVERPOOL

GROUP B

CHELSEA	0-0	VALENCIA
SCHALKE	3-1	ROSENBORG
ROSENBORG	0-4	CHELSEA
VALENCIA	0-0	SCHALKE
SCHALKE	0-0	CHELSEA
VALENCIA	0-2	ROSENBORG
CHELSEA	2-0	SCHALKE
ROSENBORG	2-0	VALENCIA
ROSENBORG	0-2	SCHALKE
VALENCIA	1-2	CHELSEA
CHELSEA	1-1	ROSENBORG
SCHALKE	0-1	VALENCIA

TEARFUL TERRY: JT slips on the spot

GROUP C

OLYMPIAKOS	3-0	W BREMEN
REAL MADRID	3-1	LAZIO
LAZIO	1-2	OLYMPIAKOS
W BREMEN	3-2	REAL MADRID
LAZIO	2-1	W BREMEN
OLYMPIAKOS	0-0	REAL MADRID
REAL MADRID	4-2	OLYMPIAKOS
W BREMEN	2-1	LAZIO
LAZIO	2-2	REAL MADRID
W BREMEN	1-3	OLYMPIAKOS
OLYMPIAKOS	1-1	LAZIO
REAL MADRID	2-1	W BREMEN

GROUP D

AC MILAN	1-0	CELTIC
SHAKHTAR D	1-2	BENFICA
BENFICA	1-1	AC MILAN
CELTIC	2-1	SHAKHTAR D
CELTIC	1-0	BENFICA
SHAKHTAR D	0-3	AC MILAN
BENFICA	1-0	CELTIC
AC MILAN	4-1	SHAKHTAR D
BENFICA	0-1	SHAKHTAR D
CELTIC	2-1	AC MILAN
AC MILAN	2-1	BENFICA
SHAKHTAR D	2-0	CELTIC

GROUP E

BARCELONA	3-1	STUTTGART
RANGERS	0-3	LYON
LYON	2-2	BARCELONA
STUTTGART	3-2	RANGERS
BARCELONA	2-0	RANGERS
LYON	4-2	STUTTGART
RANGERS	0-0	BARCELONA
STUTTGART	0-2	LYON
LYON	0-3	RANGERS
STUTTGART	0-2	BARCELONA
BARCELONA	3-0	LYON
RANGERS	2-1	STUTTGART

GROUP F

ROMA	1-1	MAN UTD
S LISBON	3-0	DYNAMO KIEV
DYNAMO KIEV	1-4	ROMA
MAN UTD	2-1	S LISBON
MAN UTD	4-0	DYNAMO KIEV
S LISBON	2-2	ROMA
DYNAMO KIEV	2-4	MAN UTD
ROMA	2-1	S LISBON
DYNAMO KIEV	1-2	S LISBON
MAN UTD	1-0	ROMA
ROMA	2-0	DYNAMO KIEV
S LISBON	0-1	MAN UTD

GROUP G

FENERBAHCE	3-1	CSKA MOSCOW
PSV EINDHOVEN	0-1	INTER MILAN
CSKA MOSCOW	0-1	PSV EINDHOVEN
INTER MILAN	3-0	FENERBAHCE
FENERBAHCE	2-0	PSV EINDHOVEN
INTER MILAN	4-2	CSKA MOSCOW
CSKA MOSCOW	1-2	INTER MILAN
PSV EINDHOVEN	0-0	FENERBAHCE
CSKA MOSCOW	2-2	FENERBAHCE
INTER MILAN	2-0	PSV EINDHOVEN
FENERBAHCE	1-0	INTER MILAN
PSV EINDHOVEN	2-1	CSKA MOSCOW

GROUP H

ARSENAL	2-1	STEAUA
SLAVIA PRAGUE	0-3	SEVILLE
SEVILLE	3-1	ARSENAL
STEAUA	1-1	SLAVIA PRAGUE
SLAVIA PRAGUE	0-0	ARSENAL
STEAUA	0-2	SEVILLE
ARSENAL	7-0	SLAVIA PRAGUE
SEVILLE	2-1	STEAUA
SEVILLE	4-2	SLAVIA PRAGUE
STEAUA	0-1	ARSENAL
ARSENAL	3-0	SEVILLE
SLAVIA PRAGUE	2-1	STEAUA

THIRD QUALIFYING RD SECOND LEGS

AEK ATHENS	1-4	SEVILLE
ANDERLECHT	0-2	FENERBAHCE
ARSENAL	3-0	SPARTA PRAGUE
BESIKTAS	2-0	FC ZURICH
CELTIC	1-1	SPARTAK M
(aet, 2-2 on agg, Celtic won 4-3 on pens)		
DYN ZAGREB	2-3	W BREMEN
DYNAMO KIEV	3-0	SARAJEVO
ELFSBORG	1-2	VALENCIA
FC COPENHAGEN	0-1	BENFICA
ROSENBORG	2-0	TAMPERE UTD
SHAKHTAR D	3-1	SV SALZBURG
SLAVIA PRAGUE	2-1	AJAX
STEAUA	2-0	BATE BORISOV
DIN BUCHAREST	1-3	LAZIO
LIVERPOOL	4-0	TOULOUSE
RED STAR	0-0	RANGERS

THIRD QUALIFYING RD FIRST LEGS

AJAX	0-1	SLAVIA PRAGUE
BATE BORISOV	2-2	STEAUA
FC ZURICH	1-1	BESIKTAS
FENERBAHCE	1-0	ANDERLECHT
SV SALZBURG	1-0	SHAKHTAR D
SARAJEVO	0-1	DYNAMO KIEV
SEVILLE	2-0	AEK ATHENS
SPARTA PRAGUE	0-2	ARSENAL
SPARTAK M	1-1	CELTIC
TAMPERE UTD	0-3	ROSENBORG
TOULOUSE	0-1	LIVERPOOL
W BREMEN	2-1	DYN ZAGREB
BENFICA	2-1	COPENHAGEN
LAZIO	1-1	DIN BUCHAREST
RANGERS	1-0	RED STAR
VALENCIA	3-0	ELFSBORG

SECOND QUALIFYING RD SECOND LEGS

BATE BORISOV	1-1	HAFNARFJORDUR
ELFSBORG	0-0	DEBRECEN

FC SHERIFF	0-3	BESIKTAS
LEVADIA TALLINN	2-1	RED STAR
(Red Star Belgrade won on away goals)		
ROSENBORG	7-1	ZHENIS ASTANA
SV SALZBURG	4-0	VENTSPILS
SARAJEVO	0-1	GENK
(Sarajevo won on away goals)		
SHAKHTAR D	2-1	PYUNIK YEREVAN
SLAVIA PRAGUE	0-0	ZILINA
(aet, 0-0 on agg after 90 mins, Slavia won 4-3 on pens)		
STEAUA	2-1	ZAGLEBIE LUBIN
BEITAR J	1-1	COPENHAGEN
(aet, 1-0 after 90 mins, Copenhagen won 2-1 on agg)		
DYN ZAGREB	3-1	DOMZALE
LEVSKI SOFIA	0-1	TAMPERE UTD
ZETA	0-1	RANGERS

SECOND QUALIFYING RD FIRST LEGS

BESIKTAS	1-0	FC SHERIFF
DOMZALE	1-2	DYN ZAGREB
HAFNARFJORDUR	1-3	BATE BORISOV
RED STAR	1-0	LEVADIA TALLINN
VENTSPILS	0-3	SV SALZBURG
ZHENIS ASTANA	1-3	ROSENBORG
ZILINA	0-0	SLAVIA PRAGUE
DEBRECEN	0-1	ELFSBORG
FC COPENHAGEN	1-0	BEITAR J
GENK	1-2	SARAJEVO
PYUNIK YEREVAN	0-2	SHAKHTAR D
RANGERS	2-0	ZETA
TAMPERE UTD	1-0	LEVSKI SOFIA
ZAGLEBIE LUBIN	0-1	STEAUA

FIRST QUALIFYING RD SECOND LEGS

ELFSBORG	1-0	LINFIELD
HB TORSHAVN	0-0	HAFNARFJORDUR
LEVADIA TALLINN	0-0	FK POBEDA
PYUNIK YEREVAN	2-0	DERRY CITY
SK TIRANA	1-2	DOMZALE
TAMPERE UTD	2-0	MURATA
VENTSPILS	2-1	TNS
(Ventspils won on away goals)		
ZILINA	5-4	F91 DUDELANGE
BATE BORISOV	3-0	APOEL NICOSIA
(aet, 2-2 on aggregate after 90 mins)		
DYN ZAGREB	3-1	KHAZAR
(aet, 2-2 on aggregate after 90 mins)		
FBK KAUNAS	3-2	ZETA
R VENECIA	0-3	FC SHERIFF
SARAJEVO	3-1	MARSAXLOKK
ZHENIS ASTANA	3-0	OLIMPI RUSTAVI

FIRST QUALIFYING RD FIRST LEGS

DERRY CITY	0-0	PYUNIK YEREVAN
DOMZALE	1-0	SK TIRANA
F91 DUDELANGE	1-2	ZILINA
FC SHERIFF	2-0	R VENECIA
HAFNARFJORDUR	4-1	HB TORSHAVN
FK POBEDA	0-1	LEVADIA TALLINN
MARSAXLOKK	0-6	SARAJEVO
APOEL NICOSIA	2-0	BATE BORISOV
KHAZAR	1-1	DYN ZAGREB
LINFIELD	0-0	ELFSBORG
MURATA	1-2	TAMPERE UTD
OLIMPI RUSTAVI	0-0	ZHENIS ASTANA
TNS	3-2	VENTSPILS
ZETA	3-1	FBK KAUNAS

FINAL

ZENIT	2-0	RANGERS

SEMI-FINALS SECOND LEGS

FIORENTINA	0-0	RANGERS
(aet, 0-0 on agg, Rangers won 4-2 on pens)		
ZENIT	4-0	B MUNICH

SEMI-FINALS FIRST LEGS

B MUNICH	1-1	ZENIT
RANGERS	0-0	FIORENTINA

QUARTER-FINALS SECOND LEGS

GETAFE	3-3	B MUNICH
(aet, 1-1 after 90 mins, B Munich won on away goals)		
PSV EINDHOVEN	0-2	FIORENTINA
SPORTING LISBON	0-2	RANGERS
ZENIT	0-1	B LEVERKUSEN

QUARTER-FINALS FIRST LEGS

B LEVERKUSEN	1-4	ZENIT
B MUNICH	1-1	GETAFE
FIORENTINA	1-1	PSV EINDHOVEN
RANGERS	0-0	SP LISBON

LAST 16 SECOND LEGS

SP LISBON	1-0	BOLTON
W BREMEN	1-0	RANGERS
B MUNICH	1-2	ANDERLECHT
EVERTON	2-0	FIORENTINA
(aet, 2-0 after 90 mins, Fiorentina won 4-2 on pens)		
GETAFE	1-0	BENFICA
HAMBURG	3-2	B LEVERKUSEN
(B Leverkusen won on away goals)		
PSV EINDHOVEN	0-1	TOTTENHAM
(aet, 0-1 after 90 mins, PSV won 6-5 on pens)		
ZENIT	2-0	MARSEILLE
(Zenit won on away goals)		

LAST 16 FIRST LEGS

ANDERLECHT	0-5	B MUNICH
B LEVERKUSEN	1-0	HAMBURG
BENFICA	1-2	GETAFE
BOLTON	1-1	SP LISBON
FIORENTINA	2-0	EVERTON
MARSEILLE	3-1	ZENIT
RANGERS	2-0	W BREMEN
TOTTENHAM	0-1	PSV EINDHOVEN

LAST 32 SECOND LEGS

ATL MADRID	0-0	BOLTON
B LEVERKUSEN	5-1	GALATASARAY
B MUNICH	5-1	ABERDEEN
BASLE	0-3	SP LISBON
BORDEAUX	1-1	ANDERLECHT
BRAGA	0-1	W BREMEN
EVERTON	6-1	BRANN
FIORENTINA	2-1	ROSENBORG
GETAFE	3-0	AEK ATHENS
HAMBURG	0-0	FC ZURICH
HELSINGBORGS	1-2	PSV EINDHOVEN
NUREMBURG	2-2	BENFICA
PANATHINAIKOS	1-1	RANGERS
(Rangers won on away goals)		
SPARTAK M	2-0	MARSEILLE
TOTTENHAM	1-1	SLAVIA PRAGUE
VILLARREAL	2-1	ZENIT
(Zenit won on away goals)		

LAST 32 FIRST LEGS

ABERDEEN	2-2	B MUNICH
BENFICA	1-0	NUREMBURG
BOLTON	1-0	ATL MADRID
FC ZURICH	1-3	HAMBURG
ROSENBORG	0-1	FIORENTINA
SLAVIA PRAGUE	1-2	TOTTENHAM
AEK ATHENS	1-1	GETAFE

ANDERLECHT	2-1	BORDEAUX
BRANN	0-2	EVERTON
GALATASARAY	0-0	B LEVERKUSEN
MARSEILLE	3-0	SPARTAK M
PSV EINDHOVEN	2-0	HELSINGBORGS
RANGERS	0-0	PANATHINAIKOS
SPORTING LISBON	2-0	BASLE
W BREMEN	3-0	BRAGA
ZENIT	1-0	VILLARREAL

GROUP A

AZ ALKMAAR	2-3	EVERTON
LARISSA	1-3	NUREMBURG
EVERTON	1-0	ZENIT
NUREMBURG	2-1	AZ ALKMAAR
AZ ALKMAAR	1-0	LARISSA
ZENIT	2-2	NUREMBURG
LARISSA	2-3	ZENIT
NUREMBURG	0-2	EVERTON
EVERTON	3-1	LARISSA
ZENIT	1-1	AZ ALKMAAR

GROUP B

ABERDEEN	4-0	COPENHAGEN
ATL MADRID	2-1	PANATHINAIKOS
COPENHAGEN	0-2	ATL MADRID
PANATHINAIKOS	2-0	LOKOMOTIV MOS
ATL MADRID	2-0	ABERDEEN
LOKOMOTIV MOS	0-1	COPENHAGEN
ABERDEEN	1-1	LOKOMOTIV MOS
COPENHAGEN	0-1	PANATHINAIKOS
LOKOMOTIV MOS	3-3	ATL MADRID
PANATHINAIKOS	3-0	ABERDEEN

GROUP C

AEK ATHENS	1-2	VILLARREAL
FIORENTINA	2-1	MLADA B
MLADA B	0-1	AEK ATHENS
VILLARREAL	2-0	ELFSBORG
AEK ATHENS	1-1	FIORENTINA
ELFSBORG	1-3	MLADA B
FIORENTINA	6-1	ELFSBORG
MLADA B	1-2	VILLARREAL
ELFSBORG	1-1	AEK ATHENS
VILLARREAL	1-1	FIORENTINA

GROUP D

HAMBURG	1-1	BASLE
RENNES	1-1	DYN ZAGREB
BASLE	1-0	BRANN
DYN ZAGREB	0-2	HAMBURG
BRANN	2-1	DYN ZAGREB
HAMBURG	3-0	RENNES
DYN ZAGREB	0-0	BASLE
RENNES	1-1	BRANN
BASLE	1-0	RENNES
BRANN	0-1	HAMBURG

GROUP E

FC ZURICH	0-5	B LEVERKUSEN
TOULOUSE	2-1	SPARTAK M
B LEVERKUSEN	1-0	SPARTA PRAGUE
SPARTAK M	1-0	FC ZURICH
FC ZURICH	2-0	TOULOUSE
SPARTA PRAGUE	0-0	SPARTAK M
SPARTAK M	2-1	B LEVERKUSEN
TOULOUSE	2-3	SPARTA PRAGUE
B LEVERKUSEN	1-0	TOULOUSE
SPARTA PRAGUE	1-2	FC ZURICH

GROUP F

B MUNICH	6-0	ARIS SALONIKA
BRAGA	2-0	RED STAR BEL
ARIS SALONIKA	1-1	BRAGA

Sponsored by Stan James

RED STAR BEL	0-1	BOLTON
BOLTON	1-1	ARIS SALONIKA
BRAGA	1-1	B MUNICH
ARIS SALONIKA	3-0	RED STAR BEL
B MUNICH	2-2	BOLTON
BOLTON	1-1	BRAGA
RED STAR BEL	2-3	B MUNICH

GROUP G

GETAFE	2-1	ANDERLECHT
HAPOEL TEL AVIV	1-3	AALBORG
AALBORG	1-2	GETAFE
ANDERLECHT	1-1	TOTTENHAM
GETAFE	1-2	HAPOEL TEL AVIV
TOTTENHAM	3-2	AALBORG
AALBORG	1-1	ANDERLECHT
HAPOEL TEL AVIV	0-2	TOTTENHAM
ANDERLECHT	2-0	HAPOEL TEL AVIV
TOTTENHAM	1-2	GETAFE

GROUP H

GALATASARAY	0-0	AUSTRIA VIENNA
PANIONIOS	2-3	BORDEAUX
AUSTRIA VIENNA	0-1	PANIONIOS
BORDEAUX	2-1	HELSINGBORGS
HELSINGBORGS	3-0	AUSTRIA VIENNA
PANIONIOS	0-3	GALATASARAY
AUSTRIA VIENNA	1-2	BORDEAUX
GALATASARAY	2-3	HELSINGBORGS
BORDEAUX	2-1	GALATASARAY
HELSINGBORGS	1-1	PANIONIOS

FIRST ROUND SECOND LEGS

AIK SOLNA	0-1	HAPOEL TEL AVIV
AZ ALKMAAR	0-0	PACOS FERREIRA
AALBORG	0-0	SAMPDORIA

(Aalborg won on away goals)

AJAX	2-3	DYN ZAGREB

(aet, 0-1 after 90 mins, Zagreb won on away goals)

ANORTHOSIS	1-1	TOTTENHAM
BATE BORISOV	0-2	VILLARREAL
BASLE	6-0	SARAJEVO
BELENENSES	0-2	B MUNICH
BLACKBURN	2-1	LARISSA
BOLTON	1-0	RABOTNICKI
BORDEAUX	1-1	TAMPERE UTD
BRAGA	4-0	HAMMARBY
CSKA SOFIA	1-1	TOULOUSE

(Toulouse won on away goals)

DNIPRO	1-1	ABERDEEN

(Aberdeen won on away goals)

ELFSBORG	0-1	DIN BUCHAREST

(Elfsborg won on away goals)

ERCIYESSPOR	0-5	ATL MADRID
FC BRUGES	1-2	BRANN

(Brann won on away goals)

COPENHAGEN	2-1	LENS

(aet, 1-1 after 90 mins, Copenhagen won 3-2 on agg)

FC TWENTE	3-2	GETAFE

(Getafe won on away goals)

FC ZURICH	3-0	EMPOLI
FIORENTINA	1-1	FC GRONINGEN

(aet, 1-1 after 90 mins, Fiorentina won 4-3 on pens)

GALATASARAY	5-1	FC SION
HACKEN	1-3	SPARTAK M
HAMBURG	3-1	LITEX
HELSINGBORGS	5-1	HEERENVEEN
LOKOMOTIV MOS	2-0	MIDTJYLLAND
METALIST	2-3	EVERTON
OB ODENSE	0-0	SPARTA PRAGUE

(aet, 0-0 after 90 mins, S Prague won 4-3 on pens)

PALERMO	0-1	MLADA B

(aet, 0-1 after 90 mins, Palermo won 4-2 on pens)

PANIONIOS	0-1	SOCHAUX
R BUCHAREST	2-2	NUREMBURG

(Nuremburg won on away goals)

RAPID VIENNA	0-1	ANDERLECHT
RED STAR BEL	1-0	GROCLIN
RENNES	1-2	LOKO SOFIA
SV SALZBURG	1-0	AEK ATHENS
STANDARD LIEGE	1-1	ZENIT
UNIAO LEIRIA	3-2	B LEVERKUSEN
VALERENGA	2-2	AUSTRIA VIENNA
ZARAGOZA	2-1	ARIS SALONIKA

(Aris Salonika won on away goals)

PANATHINAIKOS	3-0	ARTMEDIA

FIRST ROUND FIRST LEGS

AEK ATHENS	3-0	SV SALZBURG
ABERDEEN	0-0	DNIPRO
ANDERLECHT	1-1	RAPID VIENNA
ARIS SALONIKA	1-0	ZARAGOZA
ARTMEDIA	1-2	PANATHINAIKOS
ATL MADRID	4-0	ERCIYESSPOR
AUSTRIA VIENNA	2-0	VALERENGA
B LEVERKUSEN	3-1	UNIAO LEIRIA
B MUNICH	1-0	BELENENSES
BRANN	0-1	FC BRUGES
DIN BUCHAREST	1-2	ELFSBORG
DYN ZAGREB	0-1	AJAX
EMPOLI	2-1	FC ZURICH
EVERTON	1-1	METALIST
FC GRONINGEN	1-1	FIORENTINA
FC SION	3-2	GALATASARAY
GETAFE	1-0	FC TWENTE
GROCLIN	0-1	RED STAR BEL
HAMMARBY	2-1	BRAGA
HAPOEL TEL AVIV	0-0	AIK SOLNA
HEERENVEEN	5-3	HELSINGBORGS
LARISSA	2-0	BLACKBURN
LOK SOFIA	1-3	RENNES
MIDTJYLLAND	1-3	LOKOMOTIV MOS
MLADA B	0-1	PALERMO
NUREMBURG	0-0	R BUCHAREST
PACOS FERREIRA	0-1	AZ ALKMAAR
RABOTNICKI	1-1	BOLTON
SAMPDORIA	2-2	AALBORG
SARAJEVO	1-2	BASLE
SOCHAUX	0-2	PANIONIOS
SPARTA PRAGUE	0-0	OB ODENSE
SPARTAK M	5-0	HACKEN
TAMPERE UTD	2-3	BORDEAUX
TOTTENHAM	6-1	ANORTHOSIS
TOULOUSE	0-0	CSKA SOFIA
VILLARREAL	4-1	BATE BORISOV
ZENIT	3-0	STANDARD LIEGE
LENS	1-1	COPENHAGEN
LITEX	0-1	HAMBURG

SECOND QUAL ROUND SECOND LEGS

AIK SOLNA	2-0	METALURGS
AALBORG	3-0	HJK HELSINKI
ANORTHOSIS FAM	0-0	CFR CLUJ
ARTMEDIA	2-0	FC MIKA
BELCHATOW	2-4	DNIPRO
BLACKBURN	2-0	MYPA-47
CSKA SOFIA	2-1	OMONIA NICOSIA
ERCIYESSPOR	3-1	M TEL AVIV
FC SION	3-0	RIED
FK SUDUVA	3-4	BRANN
FREDRIKSTAD	1-1	HAMMARBY
GALATASARAY	2-1	SLAVEN
GROCLIN	2-0	TOBOL
HACKEN	1-0	DUNFERMLINE

HAMBURG	4-0	HONVED
HAPOEL TEL AVIV	3-0	SIROKI BRIJEG
HELSINGBORGS	3-0	DROGHEDA
JABLONEC	1-1	AUSTRIA VIENNA
LENS	5-1	YOUNG BOYS
LITEX	3-0	BESA
MACCABI NET	0-1	UNIAO LEIRIA
MATTERSBURG	0-4	BASLE
MIDTJYLLAND	5-2	FC HAKA
OB ODENSE	4-0	DINAMO MINSK
OTELUL GALATI	0-0	LOK SOFIA
RAPID VIENNA	5-0	DYNAMO TBILISI
SAMPDORIA	1-1	HAJDUK SPLIT
STANDARD LIEGE	1-0	KAERJENG
VALERENGA	6-0	EKRANAS
VOJVODINA NS	1-2	ATL MADRID
ZENIT	3-0	ZLATE MORAVCE
ZRINJSKI MOSTAR	1-2	RABOTNICKI

SECOND QUAL ROUND FIRST LEGS

ATL MADRID	3-0	VOJVODINA NS
AUSTRIA VIENNA	4-3	JABLONEC
BASLE	2-1	MATTERSBURG
BESA	0-3	LITEX
BRANN	2-1	FK SUDUVA
CFR CLUJ	1-3	ANORTHOSIS
DINAMO MINSK	1-1	OB ODENSE
DNIPRO	1-1	BELCHATOW
DROGHEDA	1-1	HELSINGBORGS
DUNFERMLINE	1-1	HACKEN
DYNAMO TBILISI	0-3	RAPID VIENNA
EKRANAS	1-1	VALERENGA
FC HAKA	1-2	MIDTJYLLAND
FC MIKA	2-1	ARTMEDIA
HJK HELSINKI	2-1	AALBORG
HAJDUK SPLIT	0-1	SAMPDORIA
HAMMARBY	2-1	FREDRIKSTAD
HONVED	0-0	HAMBURG
KAERJENG	0-3	STANDARD LIEGE
LOK SOFIA	3-1	OTELUL GALATI
MACCABI TEL AVIV	1-1	ERCIYESSPOR
METALURGS	3-2	AIK SOLNA
MYPA-47	0-1	BLACKBURN
SIROKI BRIJEG	0-3	HAPOEL TEL AVIV
OMONIA NICOSIA	1-1	CSKA SOFIA
RABOTNICKI	0-0	ZRINJSKI
RIED	1-1	FC SION
SLAVEN	1-2	GALATASARAY
TOBOL	0-1	GROCLIN
UNIAO LEIRIA	0-0	MACCABI NET
ZLATE MORAVCE	0-2	ZENIT
YOUNG BOYS	1-1	LENS

FIRST QUAL ROUND SECOND LEGS

AIK SOLNA	4-0	GLENTORAN
ALMA ATA	1-1	ZLATE MORAVCE
AMERI TBILISI	2-0	BELCHATOW

(aet, 2-0 after 90 mins, Belchatow won 4-2 on pens)

ANORTHOSIS	1-0	VARDAR SKOPJE
BESA	0-0	BEZANIJA

(Besa won on away goals)

BRANN	6-3	CARMARTHEN
DINAMO BREST	1-2	METALURGS
DINAMO MINSK	2-0	SKONTO RIGA
DROGHEDA	3-0	LIBERTAS
EB STREYMUR	1-1	MYPA-47
EKRANAS	3-2	B36 TORSHAVN
ETZELLA	0-1	HJK HELSINKI
FC HAKA	2-0	RHYL

(FC Haka won on away goals)

FC MIKA	1-0	MTK BUDAPEST

(FC Mika won on away goals)

FC ZIMBRU	2-2	ARTMEDIA

(Artmedia won on away goals)

FK SUDUVA	4-0	DUNGANNON
GROCLIN	1-0	FK ARAZ
HAJDUK SPLIT	1-0	BUDUCNOST P
HIBERNIANS	0-2	VOJVODINA NS
HONVED	1-1	NISTRU OTACI

(aet, 1-1 after 90 mins, Honved won 5-4 on pens)

KR REYKJAVIK	0-1	HACKEN
KOPER	2-3	SIROKI BRIJEG
LITEX	4-0	SLIEMA W
MAC TEL AVIV	4-0	SANTA COLOMA
MATTERSBURG	4-2	AKTOBE LENTO
MIDTJYLLAND	2-1	IB KEFLAVIK

(Midtjylland won on away goals)

NEFTCHI BAKU	2-1	RIED
OB ODENSE	5-0	ST PATRICK'S
PARTIZAN BEL	5-0	ZRINJSKI

(Partizan Belgrade expelled following crowd trouble)

RABOTNICKI	2-1	ND HIT GORICA
RUDAR PLJEVLJA	0-2	OMONIA NICOSIA
TEUTA	2-2	SLAVEN
TRANS NARVA	0-3	HELSINGBORGS
VADUZ	0-0	DYNAMO TBILISI
VALERENGA	1-0	FLORA TALLINN
YOUNG BOYS	4-0	BANANTS
KAERJENG	1-0	LILLESTROM

(Kaerjeng won on away goals)

FIRST QUAL ROUND FIRST LEGS

AKTOBE LENTO	1-0	MATTERSBURG
ARTMEDIA	1-1	FC ZIMBRU
B36 TORSHAVN	1-3	EKRANAS
BANANTS	1-1	YOUNG BOYS
BELCHATOW	2-0	AMERI TBILISI
BEZANIJA	2-2	BESA
BUDUCNOST P	1-1	HAJDUK SPLIT
CARMARTHEN	0-8	BRANN
DUNGANNON	1-0	FK SUDUVA
DYNAMO TBILISI	2-0	VADUZ
FK ARAZ	0-0	GROCLIN
FLORA TALLINN	0-1	VALERENGA
GLENTORAN	0-5	AIK SOLNA
HJK HELSINKI	2-0	ETZELLA
HACKEN	1-1	KR REYKJAVIK
HELSINGBORGS	6-0	TRANS NARVA
IB KEFLAVIK	3-2	MIDTJYLLAND
LIBERTAS	1-1	DROGHEDA
LILLESTROM	2-1	KAERJENG
MTK BUDAPEST	2-1	FC MIKA
METALURGS	1-1	DINAMO BREST
MYPA-47	1-0	EB STREYMUR
ND HIT GORICA	1-2	RABOTNICKI
SIROKI BRIJEG	3-1	KOPER
NISTRU OTACI	1-1	HONVED
OMONIA NICOSIA	2-0	RUDAR PLJEVLJA
RHYL	3-1	FC HAKA
RIED	3-1	NEFTCHI BAKU
SANTA COLOMA	1-0	MAC TEL AVIV
SKONTO RIGA	1-1	DINAMO MINSK
SLAVEN	6-2	TEUTA
SLIEMA W	0-3	LITEX
ST PATRICK'S	0-0	OB ODENSE
VARDAR SKOPJE	0-1	ANORTHOSIS
ZLATE MORAVCE	3-1	ALMA ATA
VOJVODINA NS	5-1	HIBERNIANS
ZRINJSKI MOSTAR	1-6	PARTIZAN BEL

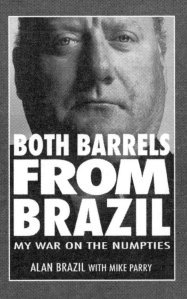

premiership		home					away						
Pos		P	W	D	L	F	A	W	D	L	F	A	Pts	GD
1	Man Utd	38	17	1	1	47	7	10	5	4	33	15	87	+58
2	Chelsea	38	12	7	0	36	13	13	3	3	29	13	85	+39
3	Arsenal	38	14	5	0	37	11	10	6	3	37	20	83	+43
4	Liverpool	38	12	6	1	43	13	9	7	3	24	15	76	+39
5	Everton	38	11	4	4	34	17	8	4	7	21	16	65	+22
6	Aston Villa	38	10	3	6	34	22	6	9	4	37	29	60	+20
7	Blackburn	38	8	7	4	26	19	7	6	6	24	29	58	+2
8	Portsmouth	38	7	8	4	24	14	9	1	9	24	26	57	+8
9	Man City	38	11	4	4	28	20	4	6	9	17	33	55	-8
10	West Ham	38	7	7	5	24	24	6	3	10	18	26	49	-8
11	Tottenham	38	8	5	6	46	34	3	8	8	20	27	46	+5
12	Newcastle	38	8	5	6	25	26	3	5	11	20	39	43	-20
13	Middlesbrough	38	7	5	7	27	23	3	7	9	16	30	42	-10
14	Wigan	38	8	5	6	21	17	2	5	12	13	34	40	-17
15	Sunderland	38	9	3	7	23	21	2	3	14	13	38	39	-23
16	Bolton	38	7	5	7	23	18	2	5	12	13	36	37	-18
17	Fulham	38	5	5	9	22	31	3	7	9	16	29	36	-22
18	Reading	38	8	2	9	19	25	2	4	13	22	41	36	-25
19	Birmingham	38	6	8	5	30	23	2	3	14	16	39	35	-16
20	Derby	38	1	5	13	12	43	0	3	16	8	46	11	-69

championship		home					away						
Pos		P	W	D	L	F	A	W	D	L	F	A	Pts	GD
1	WBA	46	12	8	3	51	27	11	4	8	37	28	81	+33
2	Stoke	46	12	7	4	36	27	9	9	5	33	28	79	+14
3	Hull	46	13	7	3	43	19	8	5	10	22	28	75	+18
4	Bristol City	46	13	7	3	33	20	7	7	9	21	33	74	+1
5	Crystal Palace	46	9	9	5	31	23	9	8	6	27	19	71	+16
6	Watford	46	8	7	8	26	29	10	9	4	36	27	70	+6
7	Wolves	46	11	6	6	31	25	7	10	6	22	23	70	+5
8	Ipswich	46	15	7	1	44	14	3	8	12	21	42	69	+9
9	Sheff Utd	46	10	8	5	32	24	7	7	9	24	27	66	+5
10	Plymouth	46	9	9	5	37	22	8	4	11	23	28	64	+10
11	Charlton	46	9	7	7	38	29	8	6	9	25	29	64	+5
12	Cardiff	46	12	4	7	31	21	4	12	7	28	34	64	+4
13	Burnley	46	7	9	7	31	31	9	5	9	29	36	62	-7
14	QPR	46	10	6	7	32	27	4	10	9	28	39	58	-6
15	Preston	46	11	5	7	29	20	4	6	13	21	36	56	-6
16	Sheff Weds	46	9	5	9	29	25	5	8	10	25	30	55	-1
17	Norwich	46	10	6	7	30	22	5	4	14	19	37	55	-10
18	Barnsley	46	11	7	5	35	26	3	6	14	17	39	55	-13
19	Blackpool	46	8	11	4	35	27	4	7	12	24	37	54	-5
20	Southampton	46	9	5	9	26	27	4	10	9	30	45	54	-16
21	Coventry	46	8	8	7	25	26	6	3	14	27	38	53	-12
22	Leicester	46	7	7	9	23	19	5	9	9	19	26	52	-3
23	Scunthorpe	46	7	8	8	31	33	4	5	14	15	36	46	-23
24	Colchester	46	4	8	11	31	41	3	9	11	31	45	38	-24

152

league 1

Pos		P	home W	D	L	F	A	away W	D	L	F	A	Pts	GD
1	Swansea	46	13	5	5	38	21	14	6	3	44	21	92	+40
2	Nottm F	46	13	8	2	37	13	9	8	6	27	19	82	+32
3	Doncaster	46	14	4	5	34	18	9	7	7	31	23	80	+24
4	Carlisle	46	17	3	3	39	16	6	8	9	25	30	80	+18
5	Leeds	46	15	4	4	41	18	12	6	5	31	20	76	+34
6	Southend	46	12	6	5	35	20	10	4	9	35	35	76	+15
7	Brighton	46	12	6	5	37	25	7	6	10	21	25	69	+8
8	Oldham	46	10	7	6	32	21	8	6	9	26	25	67	+12
9	Northampton	46	12	6	5	38	21	5	9	9	22	34	66	+5
10	Huddersfield	46	12	4	7	29	22	8	2	13	21	40	66	-12
11	Tranmere	46	13	4	6	32	18	5	7	11	20	29	65	+5
12	Walsall	46	7	9	7	27	26	9	7	7	25	20	64	+6
13	Swindon	46	12	5	6	41	24	4	8	11	22	32	61	+7
14	Leyton O	46	9	6	8	27	29	7	6	10	22	34	60	-14
15	Hartlepool	46	11	5	7	40	26	4	4	15	23	40	54	-3
16	Bristol R	46	5	10	8	25	30	7	7	9	20	23	53	-8
17	Millwall	46	9	4	10	30	26	5	6	12	15	34	52	-15
18	Yeovil	46	9	4	10	19	27	5	6	12	19	32	52	-21
19	Cheltenham	46	10	8	5	23	21	3	4	16	19	43	51	-22
20	Crewe	46	8	6	9	27	33	4	8	11	20	32	50	-18
21	Bournemouth	46	10	4	9	31	35	7	3	13	31	37	48	-10
22	Gillingham	46	9	9	5	26	22	2	4	17	18	51	46	-29
23	Port Vale	46	5	8	10	26	35	4	3	16	21	46	38	-34
24	Luton	46	10	5	8	29	25	1	5	17	14	38	33	-20

Leeds 15 points deducted, Bournemouth 10 points deducted, Luton 10 points deducted

league 2

Pos		P	home W	D	L	F	A	away W	D	L	F	A	Pts	GD
1	MK Dons	46	11	7	5	39	17	18	3	2	43	20	97	+45
2	Peterboro	46	14	4	5	46	20	14	4	5	38	23	92	+41
3	Hereford	46	11	6	6	34	19	15	4	4	38	22	88	+31
4	Stockport	46	11	5	7	40	30	13	5	5	32	24	82	+18
5	Rochdale	46	11	4	8	37	28	12	7	4	40	26	80	+23
6	Darlington	46	11	7	5	36	22	11	5	7	31	18	78	+27
7	Wycombe	46	13	6	4	29	15	9	6	8	27	27	78	+14
8	Chesterfield	46	9	8	6	42	29	10	4	9	34	27	69	+20
9	Rotherham	46	12	4	7	37	29	9	7	7	25	29	64	+4
10	Bradford	46	10	4	9	30	30	7	7	9	33	31	62	+2
11	Morecambe	46	9	6	8	33	32	7	6	10	26	31	60	-4
12	Barnet	46	10	6	7	37	30	6	6	11	19	33	60	-7
13	Bury	46	8	6	9	30	30	8	5	10	28	31	59	-3
14	Brentford	46	7	5	11	25	35	10	3	10	27	35	59	-18
15	Lincoln	46	9	3	11	33	38	9	1	13	28	39	58	-16
16	Grimsby	46	7	5	11	26	34	8	5	10	29	32	55	-14
17	Accrington	46	7	1	15	20	39	9	2	12	29	44	51	-34
18	Shrewsbury	46	9	6	8	31	22	3	8	12	25	43	50	-9
19	Macclesfield	46	6	8	9	27	31	5	9	9	20	33	50	-17
20	Dagenham & R	46	6	7	10	27	32	7	3	13	22	38	49	-21
21	Notts Co	46	8	5	10	19	23	2	13	8	18	30	48	-16
22	Chester	46	5	5	13	21	30	7	6	10	30	38	47	-17
23	Mansfield	46	6	3	14	30	39	5	6	12	18	29	42	-20
24	Wrexham	46	6	6	7	10	16	28	4	3	16	22	42	40	-32

Rotherham 10 points deducted

UNITED: topped the pile again after another season of scintillating attacking football

conference

Pos		P	home W	D	L	F	A	away W	D	L	F	A	Pts	GD
1	Aldershot	46	18	2	3	44	21	13	6	4	38	27	101	+34
2	Cambridge Utd	46	14	6	3	36	17	11	5	7	32	24	86	+27
3	Torquay	46	15	3	5	39	21	11	5	7	44	36	86	+26
4	Exeter	46	13	9	1	44	26	9	8	6	39	32	83	+25
5	Burton	46	15	3	5	48	31	8	9	6	31	25	81	+23
6	Stevenage	46	13	5	5	47	25	11	2	10	35	30	79	+27
7	Histon	46	10	7	6	42	36	10	5	8	34	31	72	+9
8	Forest Green	46	11	6	6	45	34	8	8	7	31	25	71	+17
9	Oxford Utd	46	10	8	5	32	21	10	3	10	24	27	71	+8
10	Grays	46	11	6	6	35	23	8	7	8	23	24	70	+11
11	Ebbsfleet U	46	14	3	6	40	29	5	9	9	25	32	69	+4
12	Salisbury	46	12	7	4	35	22	6	7	10	35	38	68	+10
13	Kidderminster	46	12	5	6	38	23	7	5	11	36	34	67	+17
14	York	46	8	5	10	33	34	9	6	8	38	40	62	-3
15	Crawley	46	12	5	6	47	31	7	4	12	26	36	60	+6
16	Rushden & D	46	7	10	6	26	22	8	4	11	29	33	59	0
17	Woking	46	7	9	7	28	27	5	8	10	25	34	53	-8
18	Weymouth	46	7	5	11	24	34	4	8	11	29	39	46	-20
19	Northwich	46	6	7	10	30	36	5	4	14	22	42	44	-26
20	Halifax	46	8	10	5	30	29	4	6	13	31	41	42	-9
21	Altrincham	46	6	6	11	32	44	3	8	12	24	38	41	-26
22	Farsley C	46	6	5	12	27	38	4	4	15	21	48	39	-38
23	Stafford	46	2	4	17	16	48	3	6	14	26	51	25	-57
24	Droylsden	46	4	5	14	27	45	1	4	18	19	58	24	-57

Crawley 6 points deducted, Halifax deducted 10 points and removed from Conference after financial problems

Sponsored by Stan James

conf north

Pos		P	W	D	L	F	A	W	D	L	F	A	Pts	GD
1	Kettering	42	17	1	3	57	19	13	6	2	36	15	97	+59
2	Telford	42	14	4	3	45	21	10	4	7	25	22	80	+27
3	Stalybridge	42	12	4	5	47	24	13	0	8	41	27	79	+37
4	Southport	42	10	8	3	38	21	12	3	6	39	29	77	+27
5	Barrow	42	13	4	4	40	18	8	9	4	30	21	76	+31
6	Harrogate	42	10	6	5	25	16	11	5	5	30	25	74	+14
7	Nuneaton	42	12	6	3	32	17	7	8	6	26	23	71	+18
8	Burscough	42	8	8	5	33	30	11	0	10	29	28	65	+4
9	Hyde	42	12	2	7	45	32	8	1	12	39	34	63	+18
10	Boston	42	12	3	6	39	22	5	5	11	26	35	59	+8
11	Gainsborough	42	8	8	5	35	26	7	4	10	27	39	57	-3
12	Worcester	42	8	7	6	27	30	6	5	10	21	38	54	-20
13	Redditch	42	10	4	7	28	24	5	4	12	13	34	53	-17
14	Workington	42	8	4	9	25	20	5	7	9	27	36	50	-4
15	Tamworth	42	9	6	6	31	20	4	5	12	22	39	50	-6
16	Alfreton	42	7	5	9	27	26	5	6	10	22	28	47	-5
17	Solihull M	42	7	5	9	29	36	5	6	10	21	40	47	-26
18	Blyth Sp	42	7	2	12	27	31	5	8	8	25	31	46	-10
19	Hinckley	42	7	4	10	24	28	4	8	9	24	41	45	-21
20	Hucknall T	42	4	4	13	25	36	7	2	12	28	39	39	-22
21	Vauxhall M	42	5	4	12	26	47	2	3	16	16	53	28	-58
22	Leigh RMI	42	5	4	12	21	38	1	4	16	15	49	26	-51

conf south

Pos		P	W	D	L	F	A	W	D	L	F	A	Pts	GD
1	Lewes	42	14	4	3	37	13	13	4	4	44	26	89	+42
2	Eastbourne	42	12	6	3	42	15	11	5	5	41	23	80	+45
3	Hampton	42	10	8	3	49	23	11	6	4	38	26	77	+38
4	Fisher	42	10	3	8	35	36	12	2	7	30	25	71	+4
5	Braintree	42	13	4	4	30	14	6	8	7	22	28	69	+10
6	Eastleigh	42	9	7	5	34	29	10	3	8	42	33	67	+14
7	Havant and W	42	14	3	4	33	16	5	7	9	26	37	67	+6
8	Bath	42	10	8	3	30	12	7	7	7	29	24	66	+23
9	Newport Co	42	9	5	7	37	27	9	7	5	27	22	66	+15
10	B Stortford	42	9	6	6	43	32	9	4	8	29	28	64	+12
11	Bromley	42	11	3	7	44	29	8	4	9	33	37	64	+11
12	Thurrock	42	13	4	4	39	26	5	5	11	24	38	63	-1
13	Hayes & Y	42	7	9	5	40	35	7	3	11	27	38	54	-6
14	Cambridge C	42	8	7	6	43	32	6	3	12	28	40	52	-1
15	Basingstoke	42	8	6	7	33	34	4	8	9	21	41	50	-21
16	Welling	42	6	5	10	23	34	7	2	12	18	30	46	-23
17	Maidenhead	42	2	6	13	24	34	9	6	6	32	25	45	-3
18	Bognor	42	6	5	10	21	31	5	6	10	28	36	44	-18
19	St Albans	42	5	5	11	21	35	5	7	9	22	34	42	-26
20	Weston SM	42	6	4	11	28	38	3	6	12	24	47	37	-33
21	Dorchester	42	5	4	12	17	33	3	6	12	19	37	34	-34
22	Sutton Utd	42	2	3	16	13	45	3	6	12	19	41	24	-54

spl

Pos		P	W	D	L	F	A	W	D	L	F	A	Pts	GD
			home						**away**					
1	Celtic	38	14	4	1	42	7	14	1	4	42	19	89	+58
2	Rangers	38	18	0	1	50	10	9	5	5	34	23	86	+51
3	Motherwell	38	9	4	6	30	26	9	2	8	20	20	60	+4
4	Aberdeen	38	11	5	4	33	21	4	3	11	17	37	53	-8
5	Dundee Utd	38	9	6	4	26	14	5	4	10	27	33	52	+6
6	Hibernian	38	10	5	4	34	22	4	5	10	15	23	52	+4
7	Falkirk	38	8	6	5	21	16	5	4	10	24	33	49	-4
8	Hearts	38	8	4	7	27	26	5	5	9	20	29	48	-8
9	Inv CT	38	9	2	8	32	28	4	2	13	19	34	43	-11
10	St Mirren	38	7	4	8	17	27	3	7	9	9	27	41	-28
11	Kilmarnock	38	7	5	7	26	23	3	5	11	13	29	40	-13
12	Gretna	38	4	3	11	18	34	1	5	14	14	49	13	-51

Gretna 10pts deducted

scot div one

Pos		P	W	D	L	F	A	W	D	L	F	A	Pts	GD
			home						**away**					
1	Hamilton	36	14	4	0	29	3	9	3	6	33	24	76	+35
2	Dundee	36	13	3	2	34	13	7	6	5	24	17	69	+28
3	St Johnstone	36	10	7	1	38	21	5	6	7	22	24	58	+15
4	Queen of Sth	36	9	6	3	29	20	5	4	9	18	23	52	+4
5	Dunfermline	36	7	5	6	19	20	6	7	5	17	21	51	-5
6	Partick	36	7	8	3	23	15	4	4	10	17	24	45	+1
7	Livingston	36	8	4	6	29	26	2	5	11	26	40	39	-11
8	Morton	36	4	5	9	22	29	5	5	8	18	29	37	-18
9	Clyde	36	5	3	10	22	32	4	7	7	18	27	37	-19
10	Stirling	36	3	7	8	22	33	1	5	12	19	38	24	-30

scot div two

Pos		P	W	D	L	F	A	W	D	L	F	A	Pts	GD
			home						**away**					
1	Ross Co	36	11	4	3	45	23	11	3	4	33	21	73	+34
2	Airdrie Utd	36	11	3	4	32	12	9	3	6	32	22	66	+30
3	Raith	36	8	3	7	28	27	11	0	7	32	23	60	+10
4	Alloa	36	12	1	5	32	27	4	7	7	25	29	56	+4
5	Peterhead	36	10	2	6	37	25	6	5	7	28	29	55	+11
6	Brechin	36	7	7	4	35	23	6	6	6	28	25	52	+15
7	Ayr	36	6	2	10	26	32	7	5	6	25	30	46	-11
8	Queen's Park	36	6	3	9	23	26	7	2	9	25	25	44	-3
9	Cowdenbeath	36	5	4	9	20	33	5	3	10	27	40	37	-26
10	Berwick	36	2	6	10	25	42	1	1	16	15	59	16	-61

scot div three

Pos		P	W	D	L	F	A	W	D	L	F	A	Pts	GD
			home						**away**					
1	East Fife	36	14	2	2	40	8	14	2	2	37	16	88	+53
2	Stranraer	36	10	3	5	29	21	9	5	4	36	22	65	+22
3	Montrose	36	9	3	6	31	22	8	5	5	28	14	59	+23
4	Arbroath	36	6	7	5	24	20	8	3	7	30	27	52	+7
5	Stenhousemuir	36	6	5	7	23	27	7	4	7	27	32	48	-9
6	Elgin	36	9	2	7	35	33	4	6	8	21	35	47	-12
7	Albion	36	4	7	7	29	35	5	3	10	22	33	37	-17
8	Dumbarton	36	7	5	6	17	19	2	5	11	14	29	37	-17
9	East Stirling	36	6	3	9	32	35	4	1	13	16	36	34	-23
10	Forfar	36	6	3	9	20	26	2	6	10	15	36	33	-27

primera liga	home						away						
Pos	P	W	D	L	F	A	W	D	L	F	A	Pts	GD
1 Real Madrid	38	17	0	2	53	18	10	4	5	31	18	48	85
2 Villarreal	38	12	5	2	33	15	12	0	7	30	25	23	77
3 Barcelona	38	14	2	3	46	12	5	8	6	30	31	33	67
4 Atl Madrid	38	12	2	5	45	26	7	5	7	21	21	19	64
5 Seville	38	13	1	5	46	20	7	3	9	29	29	26	64
6 R Santander	38	11	3	5	24	18	6	6	7	18	23	1	60
7 R Mallorca	38	9	6	4	35	22	6	8	5	34	32	15	59
8 Almeria	38	9	5	5	18	14	5	5	9	24	31	-3	52
9 Deportivo	38	9	3	7	24	23	6	4	9	22	24	-1	52
10 Valencia	38	7	3	9	24	31	8	3	8	24	31	-14	51
11 Ath Bilbao	38	7	8	4	22	14	6	3	10	18	29	-3	50
12 Espanyol	38	8	3	8	21	23	5	6	8	22	30	-10	48
13 Real Betis	38	7	4	8	27	26	5	7	7	18	25	-6	47
14 Getafe	38	7	7	5	24	22	5	4	10	20	26	-4	47
15 Valladolid	38	6	9	4	19	18	5	3	11	23	39	-15	45
16 Recreativo	38	6	7	6	24	25	5	4	10	16	35	-20	44
17 Osasuna	38	8	4	7	25	21	4	3	12	12	23	-7	43
18 R Zaragoza	38	9	7	3	36	24	1	5	13	14	37	-11	42
19 R Murcia	38	6	4	9	21	26	1	5	13	15	39	-29	30
20 Levante	38	5	4	10	22	34	2	1	16	11	41	-42	26

serie a	home						away						
Pos	P	W	D	L	F	A	W	D	L	F	A	Pts	GD
1 Inter Milan	38	15	3	1	41	14	10	7	2	28	12	43	85
2 Roma	38	15	3	1	43	20	9	7	3	29	17	35	82
3 Juventus	38	12	5	2	39	12	8	7	4	33	25	35	72
4 Fiorentina	38	12	4	3	35	18	7	5	7	20	21	16	66
5 AC Milan	38	8	7	4	31	18	10	3	6	35	20	28	64
6 Sampdoria	38	10	7	2	35	18	7	2	10	21	28	10	60
7 Udinese	38	9	4	6	30	29	7	5	7	18	24	-5	57
8 Napoli	38	11	4	4	27	16	3	4	12	23	37	-3	50
9 Atalanta	38	8	7	4	36	28	4	5	10	16	28	-4	48
10 Genoa	38	8	4	7	23	22	5	5	9	21	30	-8	48
11 Palermo	38	8	7	4	25	21	4	4	11	22	36	-10	47
12 Lazio	38	9	4	6	28	23	2	9	8	19	28	-4	46
13 Siena	38	6	9	4	24	17	3	8	8	16	28	-5	44
14 Cagliari	38	8	5	6	22	20	3	4	12	18	36	-16	42
15 Torino	38	5	7	7	19	19	3	9	7	17	30	-13	40
16 Reggina	38	8	5	6	24	19	1	8	10	13	37	-19	40
17 Catania	38	8	6	5	21	14	0	7	12	12	31	-12	37
18 Empoli	38	5	7	7	18	21	4	2	13	11	31	-23	36
19 Parma	38	7	6	6	28	26	0	7	12	14	36	-20	34
20 Livorno	38	3	8	8	18	28	3	4	12	17	32	-25	30

Cagliari 3pts deducted

bundesliga		home					away						
Pos		P	W	D	L	F	A	W	D	L	F	A	Pts	GD
1	B Munich	34	12	5	0	41	8	10	5	2	27	13	47	76
2	W Bremen	34	13	0	4	48	19	7	6	4	27	26	30	66
3	Schalke	34	10	4	3	29	13	8	6	3	26	19	23	64
4	Hamburg	34	9	5	3	30	11	5	7	5	17	15	21	54
5	Wolfsburg	34	7	6	4	28	17	8	3	6	30	29	12	54
6	Stuttgart	34	12	2	3	39	19	4	2	11	18	38	0	52
7	B Leverkusen	34	9	4	4	32	13	6	2	9	25	27	17	51
8	Hannover	34	8	5	4	32	27	5	5	7	22	29	-2	49
9	E Frankfurt	34	8	4	5	24	24	4	6	7	19	26	-7	46
10	Hertha Berlin	34	9	3	5	21	18	3	5	9	18	26	-5	44
11	Karlsruhe	34	6	6	5	23	22	5	4	8	15	31	-15	43
12	Bochum	34	5	9	3	32	28	5	2	10	16	26	-6	41
13	B Dortmund	34	7	5	5	29	24	3	5	9	21	38	-12	40
14	E Cottbus	34	8	2	7	25	20	1	7	9	10	36	-21	36
15	A Bielefeld	34	7	4	6	21	18	1	6	10	14	42	-25	34
16	Nuremberg	34	5	7	5	21	18	2	3	12	14	33	-16	31
17	Hansa Rostock	34	5	4	8	17	21	3	2	12	13	31	-22	30
18	Duisburg	34	3	3	11	19	29	5	2	10	17	26	-19	29

ligue 1		home					away						
Pos		P	W	D	L	F	A	W	D	L	F	A	Pts	GD
1	Lyon	38	14	4	1	44	16	10	3	6	30	21	37	79
2	Bordeaux	38	13	4	2	38	17	9	5	5	27	21	27	75
3	Marseille	38	11	3	5	34	21	6	8	5	24	24	13	62
4	Nancy	38	13	5	1	31	11	2	10	7	13	19	14	60
5	St Etienne	38	12	6	1	30	4	4	4	11	17	30	13	58
6	Rennes	38	10	2	7	27	19	6	8	5	20	25	3	58
7	Lille	38	8	7	4	29	18	5	11	3	16	14	13	57
8	Nice	38	8	7	4	20	14	5	9	5	15	16	5	55
9	Le Mans	38	9	6	4	23	16	5	5	9	23	33	-3	53
10	Lorient	38	9	7	3	18	12	3	9	7	14	23	-3	52
11	Caen	38	10	5	4	31	19	3	7	9	17	34	-5	51
12	Monaco	38	7	5	7	22	24	6	3	10	18	24	-8	47
13	Valenciennes	38	11	4	4	33	13	1	5	13	9	27	2	45
14	Sochaux	38	3	9	7	13	21	7	5	7	21	22	-9	44
15	Auxerre	38	8	4	7	20	17	4	4	11	13	35	-19	44
16	Paris St-G	38	4	8	7	22	23	6	5	8	15	22	-8	43
17	Toulouse	38	4	11	4	14	15	5	4	10	22	27	-6	42
18	Lens	38	5	11	3	26	22	4	2	13	17	30	-9	40
19	Strasbourg	38	5	5	9	19	20	4	3	12	15	35	-21	35
20	Metz	38	3	3	13	18	34	2	6	11	10	30	-36	24

PREMIER LEAGUE 2007/08 RESULTS

	Arsenal	Aston Villa	Birmingham	Blackburn	Bolton	Chelsea	Derby	Everton	Fulham	Liverpool	Man City	Man Utd	Middlesboro	Newcastle	Portsmouth	Reading	Sunderland	Tottenham	West Ham	Wigan
Arsenal	*	1-1	1-1	2-0	2-0	1-0	5-0	1-0	2-1	1-1	1-0	2-2	1-1	3-0	3-1	2-0	3-2	2-1	2-0	2-0
Aston Villa	1-2	*	5-1	1-1	4-0	2-0	2-0	2-0	2-1	1-2	1-1	1-4	1-1	4-1	1-3	3-1	0-1	2-1	1-0	0-2
Birmingham	2-2	1-2	*	4-1	1-0	0-1	1-1	1-1	1-1	2-2	3-1	0-1	3-0	1-1	0-2	1-1	2-2	4-1	0-1	3-2
Blackburn	1-1	0-4	2-1	*	4-1	0-1	3-1	0-0	1-1	0-0	1-0	1-1	1-1	3-1	0-1	4-2	1-0	1-1	0-1	3-1
Bolton	2-3	1-1	3-0	1-2	*	0-1	1-0	1-2	0-0	1-3	0-0	1-0	0-0	1-3	0-1	3-0	2-0	1-1	1-0	4-1
Chelsea	2-1	4-4	3-2	0-0	1-1	*	6-1	1-1	0-0	0-0	6-0	2-1	1-0	2-1	1-0	1-0	2-0	2-0	1-0	1-1
Derby	2-6	0-6	1-2	1-2	1-1	0-2	*	0-2	2-2	1-2	1-1	0-1	0-1	1-0	2-2	0-4	0-0	2-0	0-5	0-1
Everton	1-4	2-2	3-1	1-1	2-0	0-1	1-0	*	3-0	1-2	1-0	0-1	2-0	3-1	3-1	1-0	7-1	0-3	1-1	2-1
Fulham	0-3	2-1	2-0	2-2	2-1	1-2	0-0	1-0	*	0-2	3-3	0-3	1-2	0-1	0-2	3-1	1-3	0-0	0-1	1-1
Liverpool	1-1	2-2	0-0	3-1	4-0	1-1	6-0	1-0	2-0	*	1-0	0-1	3-2	3-0	4-1	2-1	3-0	2-2	4-0	1-1
Man City	1-3	1-0	1-0	2-2	4-2	0-2	1-0	0-2	2-3	0-0	*	1-0	3-1	3-1	3-1	0-0	1-0	2-1	1-1	0-0
Man Utd	2-1	4-0	1-0	2-0	2-0	2-0	4-1	2-1	2-0	3-0	1-2	*	4-1	6-0	2-0	2-0	1-0	1-0	4-1	4-0
Middlesboro	2-1	0-3	2-0	1-2	0-1	0-2	1-0	0-2	1-0	1-1	8-1	2-2	*	2-2	2-0	0-1	2-2	1-1	1-2	1-0
Newcastle	1-1	0-0	2-1	0-1	0-0	0-2	2-2	3-2	2-0	0-3	0-2	1-5	1-1	*	1-4	3-0	2-0	3-1	3-1	1-0
Portsmouth	0-0	2-0	4-2	0-1	3-1	1-1	3-1	0-0	0-1	0-0	0-0	1-1	0-1	0-0	*	7-4	1-0	0-1	0-0	2-0
Reading	1-3	1-2	2-1	0-0	0-2	1-2	1-0	1-0	0-2	3-1	2-0	0-2	1-1	2-1	0-2	*	2-1	0-1	0-3	2-1
Sunderland	0-1	1-1	2-0	1-2	0-1	4-4	1-0	0-1	1-1	0-2	1-2	0-4	3-2	1-1	0-2	2-1	*	1-0	2-1	2-0
Tottenham	1-3	4-4	2-3	1-2	1-1	4-4	4-0	1-3	5-1	0-2	2-1	1-1	1-1	1-4	2-0	6-4	2-0	*	4-0	1-1
West Ham	0-1	2-2	1-1	2-1	1-1	0-4	2-1	0-2	2-1	1-0	0-2	2-1	3-0	2-2	0-1	1-1	3-1	1-1	*	1-1
Wigan	0-0	1-2	2-0	5-3	1-0	0-2	2-0	1-2	1-1	0-1	1-1	0-2	1-0	1-0	0-2	0-0	3-0	1-1	1-0	*

CHAMPIONSHIP 2007/08 RESULTS

	Barnsley	Blackpool	Bristol C	Burnley	Cardiff	Charlton	Colchester	Coventry	Crystal P	Hull	Ipswich	Leicester	Norwich	Plymouth	Preston	QPR	Scunthorpe	Sheff Utd	Sheff Wed	S'hampton	Stoke	WBA	Watford	Wolves
Barnsley	*	2-1	3-0	1-1	1-1	3-0	0-0	1-4	0-0	1-3	4-1	0-1	1-3	3-2	1-0	0-0	2-0	0-1	0-0	2-2	3-3	2-1	3-2	1-1
Blackpool	1-1	*	1-0	3-0	0-1	5-3	2-2	4-0	1-1	2-1	1-1	2-1	1-3	0-0	0-0	1-0	1-0	2-2	2-1	2-2	2-3	1-3	1-1	0-0
Bristol C	3-2	0-1	*	2-2	1-0	0-1	1-1	2-1	1-1	2-1	2-0	0-2	2-1	1-2	3-0	2-2	2-1	2-0	2-1	2-1	1-0	1-1	0-0	0-0
Burnley	2-1	2-2	2-2	*	3-3	1-0	1-1	2-0	2-0	0-1	2-2	1-1	2-1	1-0	2-3	0-2	2-0	1-2	1-1	2-3	0-0	2-1	2-2	1-3
Cardiff	3-0	3-1	2-1	2-1	*	0-2	4-1	0-1	2-0	1-0	1-0	0-1	1-2	1-2	2-2	3-1	1-1	0-3	3-2	1-0	0-1	0-0	1-2	2-3
Charlton	1-1	0-2	1-1	1-3	3-0	*	1-2	4-1	0-2	1-3	3-1	2-0	2-0	1-1	1-2	0-1	0-1	2-2	1-2	1-1	0-1	1-1	2-2	2-3
Colchester	2-2	1-2	0-3	2-3	1-1	1-0	*	1-1	1-0	1-1	2-0	1-1	2-1	1-1	2-0	4-2	0-1	0-1	0-0	1-1	0-1	3-2	2-3	1-1
Coventry	4-0	0-1	2-0	1-2	0-0	1-2	1-5	*	0-2	1-1	2-1	2-0	1-0	3-1	2-1	0-0	2-0	3-2	2-1	1-1	1-2	0-4	0-3	0-2
Crystal P	2-0	0-0	2-0	5-0	0-1	0-1	1-0	1-1	*	1-1	0-1	2-2	1-1	2-1	2-1	1-1	2-0	1-1	1-0	1-1	1-3	1-1	0-2	2-0
Hull	3-0	2-2	6-0	2-0	0-0	1-2	2-1	1-0	2-1	*	3-1	2-0	2-1	2-3	3-0	1-0	3-2	1-1	4-1	5-0	1-1	1-3	3-0	3-0
Ipswich	0-0	0-1	0-0	0-0	2-2	2-0	3-1	4-1	1-0	1-0	*	3-1	2-1	0-0	2-1	0-0	1-0	0-1	1-3	2-0	1-1	2-0	1-2	0-0
Leicester	2-0	1-2	2-0	0-1	0-0	1-1	1-1	2-0	1-0	0-2	2-0	*	4-0	2-1	0-1	1-1	3-0	0-1	0-1	1-2	0-1	1-2	4-1	1-1
Norwich	1-0	3-0	1-3	2-0	1-2	1-1	5-1	2-0	1-0	1-1	2-2	4-0	*	2-1	1-0	3-0	0-1	0-1	3-0	2-1	2-2	1-2	1-3	1-1
Plymouth	3-0	3-0	1-1	3-1	2-2	1-2	4-1	1-0	1-0	1-1	1-1	0-0	3-0	*	2-2	2-1	3-0	2-2	1-2	1-1	3-0	2-1	1-1	2-1
Preston	1-2	0-1	0-0	0-1	1-2	0-2	0-3	1-2	0-1	3-0	1-2	1-1	0-1	2-1	*	0-0	0-1	2-1	1-0	5-1	2-3	0-2	1-0	0-0
QPR	2-0	3-2	3-0	2-1	0-2	1-0	2-1	2-1	1-2	2-0	1-2	3-1	0-1	0-2	2-2	*	3-1	0-0	0-0	0-3	0-3	2-3	1-1	0-2
Scunthorpe	2-2	1-1	0-1	2-4	3-2	3-3	3-3	2-1	0-0	1-2	3-1	0-2	2-0	1-0	2-1	2-2	*	3-2	1-1	1-1	2-3	1-0	1-3	3-1
Sheff Utd	1-0	1-1	2-1	2-0	3-3	1-0	2-2	2-1	0-1	2-0	1-2	3-0	4-1	0-1	2-1	2-1	3-2	*	2-2	1-2	2-0	0-1	1-1	1-3
Sheff Wed	1-0	2-1	0-1	0-0	1-0	0-2	1-2	0-0	2-2	1-0	1-0	0-2	0-1	1-1	2-1	2-1	0-0	2-0	*	5-0	2-3	3-2	0-1	0-0
Southampton	2-3	1-0	2-0	0-1	1-0	0-0	1-1	1-3	0-1	1-2	4-0	1-0	2-0	0-2	0-1	2-3	1-2	3-2	2-4	*	3-2	3-1	0-3	0-0
Stoke	0-0	1-1	1-1	1-1	2-1	2-1	2-1	2-4	0-2	1-0	2-0	0-1	2-0	3-2	3-1	3-1	3-2	0-1	0-0	3-2	*	3-1	0-0	1-0
WBA	2-0	2-1	4-1	1-2	3-3	4-2	4-3	2-1	1-1	2-0	1-1	1-0	1-1	3-0	0-0	5-1	5-0	1-0	2-1	1-1	1-1	*	1-1	3-0
Watford	0-3	1-1	1-2	1-2	2-2	1-1	2-2	2-1	0-2	1-0	2-0	1-0	1-1	1-0	0-0	2-4	2-1	0-0	2-1	3-2	0-0	0-3	*	1-2
Wolves	1-0	2-1	1-1	2-3	3-0	2-0	1-0	1-0	0-3	0-1	1-1	1-1	2-0	1-0	1-0	3-3	2-1	2-1	1-1	2-2	2-4	0-1	1-2	*

LEAGUE 1 2007/08 RESULTS

	B'mouth	Brighton	Bristol R	Carlisle	Cheltenham	Crewe	Doncaster	Gillingham	Hartlepool	H'dersfield	Leeds	Leyton O	Luton	Millwall	North'mpton	Nott'ham F	Oldham	Port Vale	Southend	Swansea	Swindon	Tranmere	Walsall	Yeovil
Bournemouth	*	0-2	2-1	1-3	2-2	1-0	0-2	1-0	2-0	0-1	1-3	3-1	4-3	2-0	1-1	2-0	0-3	0-1	1-4	1-4	2-2	2-1	1-1	2-0
Brighton	3-2	*	0-0	2-2	2-1	3-0	1-0	4-2	2-1	1-2	0-1	1-1	3-1	3-0	2-1	0-2	1-0	2-3	3-2	0-1	2-1	0-0	1-1	1-2
Bristol R	0-2	0-2	*	3-0	2-0	1-1	0-1	1-1	0-0	2-3	0-3	2-3	1-1	2-1	2-2	2-2	1-0	3-2	1-1	0-2	0-1	1-1	1-1	1-1
Carlisle	1-1	2-0	1-1	*	2-0	1-1	0-1	1-1	4-2	2-1	3-1	1-0	2-1	4-0	2-0	0-2	1-1	3-2	1-2	0-0	3-0	0-1	2-1	2-1
Cheltenham	1-0	2-1	1-0	1-0	*	2-2	2-1	2-0	1-1	0-2	3-1	1-0	2-1	4-0	2-0	0-3	1-1	3-2	0-1	1-2	3-0	0-1	2-1	2-1
Crewe	1-4	2-1	1-1	0-1	2-2	*	0-4	2-3	3-1	2-0	0-1	1-1	1-0	0-1	1-0	0-3	1-4	0-2	1-3	0-4	0-0	4-3	0-0	2-0
Doncaster	1-2	0-0	2-0	1-0	2-1	2-0	*	2-1	2-0	2-0	0-1	4-2	2-0	0-0	0-1	1-0	1-1	1-2	3-1	0-4	2-0	0-2	2-1	1-2
Gillingham	2-1	1-0	3-2	0-0	0-0	2-0	2-1	*	2-1	1-0	1-1	3-1	2-1	2-0	0-1	3-0	0-0	1-2	1-1	1-2	2-1	0-2	2-1	0-0
Hartlepool	1-1	1-2	1-0	2-2	0-2	3-0	4-0	4-0	*	2-1	1-1	3-1	4-0	1-1	0-1	3-0	4-1	3-2	4-3	1-2	2-1	3-1	2-1	1-2
Huddersfield	1-0	2-1	2-1	0-2	2-3	1-1	1-0	4-0	2-0	*	1-0	0-1	1-0	4-2	1-2	1-1	1-3	3-0	1-2	1-3	1-0	1-0	2-0	1-0
Leeds	2-0	0-0	1-0	3-2	1-2	2-0	0-1	2-1	2-0	4-0	*	1-1	1-0	4-2	3-0	2-1	1-3	3-0	4-1	2-0	2-1	0-2	2-0	1-0
Leyton O	1-0	2-2	3-1	0-3	2-0	3-1	1-1	0-0	2-4	0-1	0-2	*	2-1	0-1	2-2	0-1	1-0	3-1	2-2	0-5	3-0	0-2	1-0	1-1
Luton	1-4	1-2	1-2	0-0	1-1	1-1	1-1	4-0	2-1	1-0	1-1	0-1	*	0-1	4-1	2-1	3-0	2-1	1-0	1-3	0-1	1-0	0-1	1-0
Millwall	2-1	3-0	0-1	3-0	1-1	1-1	0-3	1-1	0-1	4-0	1-0	1-1	0-0	*	2-0	2-2	2-3	3-0	4-1	2-2	1-2	0-1	0-1	1-0
Northampton	4-1	0-1	2-2	2-2	2-1	2-1	0-0	4-0	2-1	2-1	1-2	4-0	2-0	1-2	*	1-2	2-3	2-1	0-1	4-2	1-1	2-1	0-2	1-1
Nottm F	0-0	0-0	1-1	0-1	3-1	2-0	0-0	4-0	0-1	2-1	1-2	4-0	2-0	2-2	2-2	*	0-0	2-1	0-1	0-0	1-0	3-1	1-1	3-2
Oldham	2-0	1-1	0-1	2-0	2-1	3-2	1-3	2-1	0-1	4-1	0-1	2-0	1-1	1-1	0-1	0-0	*	1-1	4-1	2-1	1-0	3-1	2-2	3-0
Port Vale	1-3	0-1	1-1	1-1	3-0	0-1	1-3	2-1	0-2	0-0	3-3	1-1	1-2	1-1	2-2	0-2	0-3	*	1-2	2-1	2-0	0-0	0-1	1-1
Southend	2-1	2-0	0-1	2-1	3-0	2-2	4-1	3-0	2-1	1-0	3-2	4-1	1-0	2-0	1-1	1-1	3-0	1-1	*	3-0	2-1	0-1	1-0	1-1
Swansea	1-2	0-0	2-2	2-1	3-0	1-1	1-2	1-1	0-1	3-2	0-1	2-1	2-0	1-2	3-0	0-0	2-1	2-0	3-0	*	2-1	1-0	1-0	1-1
Swindon	4-1	0-3	1-0	2-2	3-0	1-1	5-0	1-1	3-1	2-1	0-1	1-1	2-1	2-1	1-1	2-1	3-0	6-0	0-1	1-1	*	1-0	0-0	1-0
Tranmere	3-1	2-0	0-2	2-0	1-0	1-1	2-0	1-0	2-2	1-0	1-1	2-1	2-1	2-0	1-1	2-1	0-1	2-0	0-1	0-1	2-1	*	0-0	2-0
Walsall	1-3	1-2	0-1	2-0	2-0	1-1	2-2	2-0	4-0	3-0	1-1	0-0	0-0	3-0	0-2	0-1	0-3	0-0	0-2	1-3	2-2	1-1	*	2-0
Yeovil	2-1	0-1	0-0	2-1	0-3	2-1	2-1	2-1	3-1	2-1	0-0	0-1	0-0	1-0	1-0	0-3	0-0	0-3	0-3	1-3	1-1	1-1	0-2	*

LEAGUE 2 2007/08 RESULTS

	Wycombe	Wrexham	Stockport	Shrewsbury	Rotherham	Rochdale	Peterboro	Notts Co	Morecambe	MK Dons	Mansfield	Macclesf'ld	Lincoln	Hereford	Grimsby	Darlington	Dagenham	Chesterfield	Chester	Bury	Brentford	Bradford	Barnet	Accrington
Accrington	0-2	0-2	0-2	1-2	0-1	1-2	0-2	0-2	3-2	0-1	1-0	3-2	0-3	0-2	4-1	0-3	1-0	2-1	3-3	0-2	1-0	0-2	0-2	*
Barnet	2-1	3-2	2-1	4-1	2-0	0-0	0-2	1-1	0-1	0-2	1-1	2-2	5-2	1-2	0-3	0-0	3-1	0-2	3-1	3-0	1-2	2-1	*	2-2
Bradford	0-1	2-1	1-1	4-2	3-2	0-2	1-2	3-0	1-0	0-0	1-2	1-1	2-1	1-2	2-1	0-0	0-2	1-0	2-1	1-2	1-2	*	0-1	2-1
Brentford	1-3	2-0	1-1	1-1	1-1	0-2	1-0	0-0	0-1	0-3	1-2	1-0	1-0	0-3	2-1	0-2	0-2	1-3	2-1	1-4	*	2-2	2-2	3-1
Bury	2-2	0-1	2-3	1-1	3-0	1-1	2-0	2-1	2-1	1-5	2-0	1-0	1-2	0-1	1-1	1-2	0-2	0-1	0-2	*	1-2	2-2	3-0	2-1
Chester	2-0	0-2	0-0	3-1	0-1	0-4	1-2	0-1	0-1	0-2	0-1	0-0	1-2	1-1	0-2	2-1	4-0	0-0	*	2-1	3-1	0-1	3-0	2-3
Chesterfield	2-2	2-1	0-0	4-1	0-2	3-4	1-2	1-1	2-2	1-2	2-0	2-2	4-1	4-0	0-2	1-1	1-1	*	0-0	3-1	1-0	1-1	0-1	4-2
Dagenham	2-2	3-0	0-1	1-1	3-1	3-1	2-3	1-1	2-0	1-2	2-0	0-1	1-0	4-0	3-2	0-3	*	3-1	6-2	2-1	4-0	1-4	1-1	1-3
Darlington	1-0	3-0	4-0	1-2	0-3	1-1	2-3	2-2	1-2	0-1	1-2	1-0	1-0	2-1	3-2	*	2-3	0-3	1-0	2-1	3-0	1-3	1-0	1-0
Grimsby	0-1	4-1	2-1	3-1	2-1	1-2	1-4	2-2	1-2	0-1	2-1	1-1	1-0	2-1	*	0-4	4-1	4-2	0-0	0-0	1-1	4-2	1-1	1-2
Hereford	0-0	2-0	0-1	3-1	0-1	2-1	0-1	0-0	0-3	2-1	2-1	0-1	3-1	*	2-0	5-1	1-4	0-1	2-2	0-1	3-1	1-1	1-0	0-0
Lincoln	1-0	2-4	0-1	0-4	1-3	2-1	1-1	2-1	1-1	1-2	1-2	3-1	*	2-1	1-2	0-4	2-0	2-4	2-1	0-1	3-1	4-2	1-2	2-0
Macclesfield	1-2	3-2	0-2	2-1	1-1	2-2	0-3	2-1	1-2	3-3	0-0	*	3-1	0-1	1-2	0-0	3-0	0-3	1-2	2-2	1-0	0-1	2-0	2-1
Mansfield	0-4	2-1	4-2	3-1	0-1	0-4	2-0	2-0	1-2	1-2	*	5-0	1-3	0-0	2-0	0-1	2-0	1-3	0-4	1-1	2-3	0-0	2-1	5-0
MK Dons	2-2	4-1	0-2	3-0	1-1	0-1	3-0	0-0	1-2	*	1-0	1-1	4-0	0-0	2-0	0-2	0-1	0-3	1-1	1-1	1-1	0-0	2-3	5-0
Morecambe	0-1	2-2	2-0	3-0	5-1	1-1	3-2	1-1	*	0-1	3-1	0-1	1-2	0-3	0-4	0-3	0-1	1-1	1-1	1-1	3-1	2-1	0-0	0-1
Notts Co	1-0	2-2	2-0	2-1	0-1	1-0	0-1	*	1-1	0-1	0-0	0-1	0-1	2-3	1-1	0-1	1-0	0-2	3-1	1-0	1-3	0-1	0-0	1-0
Peterboro	2-1	0-0	0-1	2-1	3-1	3-0	*	0-0	1-1	1-2	2-1	0-1	4-0	1-1	2-1	0-2	1-0	0-2	2-3	0-2	7-0	2-1	1-0	8-2
Rochdale	1-0	0-0	1-2	1-1	4-1	*	0-2	4-2	1-0	3-2	1-0	0-1	0-2	2-4	3-1	3-1	0-0	2-1	1-0	0-1	3-0	2-1	3-0	4-1
Rotherham	0-1	3-0	1-4	2-0	*	2-4	3-1	4-2	3-1	3-2	3-2	3-0	3-2	2-3	2-1	0-2	1-1	3-1	1-1	2-1	1-0	1-0	3-0	0-1
Shrewsbury	1-1	3-0	3-1	*	1-1	2-4	3-1	0-0	2-0	3-3	0-0	2-0	1-2	2-3	2-1	1-0	4-0	2-3	1-1	0-1	0-1	1-0	2-0	2-0
Stockport	2-1	2-1	*	1-1	2-2	3-4	1-2	1-1	2-1	2-3	0-0	2-0	1-3	2-3	1-1	1-0	1-0	0-4	2-2	1-2	0-1	2-1	3-0	2-0
Wrexham	0-0	*	0-1	1-1	0-1	0-2	1-2	1-0	0-2	1-0	1-1	1-1	1-0	2-2	0-0	0-2	0-0	2-2	0-2	2-1	1-0	1-1	2-1	1-3
Wycombe	*	2-1	0-0	1-1	1-0	0-1	2-2	3-1	2-0	1-1	1-1	2-1	2-0	1-0	3-0	2-0	0-1	0-1	0-2	1-0	1-0	2-1	0-1	0-1

CONFERENCE 2007/08 RESULTS

	Aldershot	Altrincham	Burton	Cambridge	Crawley	Droylsden	Ebbsfleet	Exeter	Farsley C	Forest G	Grays	Halifax	Histon	K'minster	Northwich	Oxford	Rushden	Salisbury	Stafford	Stevenage	Torquay	Weymouth	Woking	York
Aldershot	*	2-1	1-0	0-0	0-1	3-1	2-0	2-0	0-1	2-1	3-2	1-0	3-1	2-1	5-0	1-0	2-1	2-1	4-3	3-1	0-3	0-0	2-1	2-0
Altrincham	1-2	*	0-0	0-3	2-3	3-2	1-3	1-4	0-0	3-1	0-1	3-3	1-2	2-1	1-2	1-3	1-2	3-1	2-0	1-5	1-1	3-2	2-2	2-2
Burton	2-0	2-1	*	1-2	1-0	3-0	1-1	4-4	1-0	3-1	2-3	2-1	1-3	0-2	4-1	1-2	1-0	4-3	2-1	3-0	3-1	2-1	2-0	4-3
Cambridge U	1-1	2-1	0-0	*	2-1	5-0	1-1	0-1	5-1	1-1	1-0	2-2	1-0	0-3	2-1	2-1	1-0	1-1	1-2	2-1	2-0	0-0	1-0	2-0
Crawley	0-1	0-1	1-1	2-1	*	5-0	1-2	2-2	4-1	3-0	1-0	0-4	0-1	0-4	1-3	2-0	4-1	1-1	1-2	2-1	2-3	1-1	5-3	6-1
Droylsden	2-2	0-2	0-2	0-2	5-0	*	1-1	2-3	0-3	5-3	1-2	2-0	0-1	0-4	1-3	3-1	1-4	0-3	2-1	0-3	1-2	1-3	5-3	3-4
Ebbsfleet U	2-2	2-0	2-1	2-1	1-0	1-1	*	1-1	3-1	3-3	4-1	1-0	5-4	1-0	2-1	1-3	1-4	4-2	2-1	4-0	2-1	4-1	1-1	1-1
Exeter	1-1	2-1	1-4	1-1	2-0	2-3	1-1	*	1-1	0-2	2-2	0-3	2-2	4-0	0-0	2-2	0-2	2-0	1-5	3-0	1-3	3-2	0-1	3-2
Farsley C	1-3	3-1	0-1	2-1	1-5	1-2	3-1	1-1	*	0-2	1-2	3-0	1-1	1-0	0-1	0-1	1-0	2-2	1-0	0-0	4-3	0-0	3-0	0-1
Forest G	2-3	3-1	3-1	3-1	1-0	3-2	3-3	0-2	0-2	*	1-2	2-0	3-1	2-2	2-1	0-1	0-1	0-3	1-2	4-2	2-2	3-2	3-0	1-2
Grays	2-1	1-0	0-0	2-1	2-1	3-1	4-1	2-2	0-1	1-2	*	3-3	3-1	5-1	3-1	0-2	3-0	1-1	5-1	0-2	2-0	0-2	1-0	0-2
Halifax	0-0	2-2	2-2	1-2	3-0	3-0	1-0	0-3	2-0	2-0	0-0	*	0-1	1-6	3-1	0-3	3-0	1-1	0-0	1-2	3-2	2-1	1-0	2-2
Histon	1-2	1-0	2-2	1-0	3-0	3-0	1-3	2-2	3-1	3-1	1-2	0-1	*	2-1	1-1	0-1	2-1	2-0	3-3	1-4	4-5	2-1	0-1	3-1
Kidderminstr	1-2	1-1	4-1	1-0	3-1	3-1	1-0	4-0	2-1	2-2	1-0	1-1	1-1	*	0-0	1-0	2-1	1-2	6-0	0-2	2-5	0-2	0-1	3-0
Northwich	1-2	1-1	0-3	0-2	2-0	3-3	2-1	0-0	4-0	2-1	0-0	1-1	3-0	0-0	*	1-0	1-0	0-1	4-3	0-2	1-3	2-2	2-3	3-0
Oxford	2-3	4-0	0-3	1-2	1-0	1-0	2-2	2-2	5-1	0-1	0-0	1-1	3-0	0-1	0-1	*	1-0	2-1	2-1	2-1	3-3	2-2	1-1	0-1
Rushden & D	1-1	1-1	0-0	1-2	1-1	0-0	0-2	0-2	1-2	0-1	0-1	3-0	3-0	0-0	0-1	5-0	*	2-1	4-3	0-0	3-3	1-3	0-0	1-1
Salisbury	0-4	3-3	2-0	0-2	4-1	1-0	2-3	2-0	2-1	0-1	0-1	1-0	3-3	3-1	2-0	3-1	1-1	*	1-0	1-0	2-1	3-2	2-1	3-0
Stafford	1-2	1-1	0-3	2-1	1-5	0-1	2-0	1-5	2-1	1-3	0-2	2-3	0-1	1-3	2-0	0-1	0-1	1-5	*	1-2	0-2	2-1	0-1	0-4
Stevenage	3-1	2-1	3-3	1-2	3-1	5-0	3-1	3-0	5-0	2-1	2-1	3-2	2-1	1-0	1-2	0-0	2-1	3-1	3-0	*	1-3	3-0	1-1	3-2
Torquay	1-2	1-1	3-3	1-2	1-2	1-2	2-1	1-3	2-1	2-1	1-1	4-2	0-1	1-0	1-0	3-2	3-2	4-0	2-0	4-2	*	3-2	0-0	1-3
Weymouth	0-2	2-2	1-2	2-2	2-1	3-1	2-0	3-1	2-1	1-2	1-1	1-3	0-1	2-1	0-1	0-1	1-2	0-3	1-3	1-0	0-0	*	0-1	1-1
Woking	0-1	2-0	2-1	0-0	1-1	1-1	1-0	0-1	2-1	1-1	0-1	3-0	3-3	3-0	2-3	1-2	1-1	3-2	2-2	2-0	0-2	1-1	*	1-1
York	2-0	2-2	0-0	1-2	1-1	0-1	0-1	3-2	4-1	0-2	0-0	3-2	1-4	1-1	1-0	2-3	2-3	1-3	0-2	0-2	0-1	2-0	2-3	*

Sponsored by Stan James

	Alfreton	Barrow	Blythe Sp	Boston	Burscough	Gainsboro	Harrogate	Hinckley	Hucknall	Hyde	Kettering	Leigh RMI	Nuneaton	Redditch	Solihull M	Southport	Stalybridge	Tamworth	Telford	Vauxhall M	Worcester	Workington
Alfreton	*	0-0	1-1	2-1	1-2	3-1	1-2	0-0	2-1	0-3	1-2	1-0	1-3	0-0	0-0	1-2	3-4	1-2	0-1	4-0	3-1	2-0
Barrow	2-1	*	1-1	1-0	4-1	4-1	2-2	0-1	2-1	1-0	1-1	1-2	0-1	2-0	5-1	1-0	1-3	2-0	4-0	4-1	1-0	1-1
Blyth Sp	2-0	2-3	*	2-1	1-4	1-1	0-1	1-3	1-2	0-2	2-0	2-0	1-0	2-4	1-2	1-0	0-1	1-1	1-2	0-2	6-0	0-2
Boston	2-1	2-1	3-2	*	0-1	0-1	0-1	1-1	2-3	2-1	0-1	5-1	1-1	3-0	2-0	1-2	3-1	1-0	2-1	5-1	2-2	2-0
Burscough	1-1	2-1	2-2	2-1	*	2-2	2-1	1-1	2-1	3-2	1-1	5-2	2-0	0-2	2-2	1-1	0-2	2-3	1-3	0-0	2-1	0-1
Gainsborough	2-2	1-1	4-0	1-3	0-1	*	0-1	2-2	4-1	3-3	3-1	2-1	1-1	3-0	0-2	0-3	2-1	1-0	1-1	3-0	1-1	1-1
Harrogate	0-1	2-2	0-1	3-2	1-0	3-1	*	1-1	0-0	2-1	0-0	0-0	1-2	2-0	1-0	1-0	2-0	3-2	1-0	2-0	0-1	1-1
Hinckley	1-0	1-2	1-1	0-1	0-2	1-2	2-3	*	2-1	2-1	0-0	3-1	0-0	1-2	0-1	2-3	0-3	2-0	1-1	0-1	2-4	1-1
Hucknall T	2-2	0-1	0-3	1-2	1-0	0-1	0-1	1-1	*	1-4	0-2	3-0	2-2	1-2	2-2	1-2	0-3	3-1	0-2	2-0	5-0	1-2
Hyde	0-2	2-1	2-4	2-1	1-0	3-0	2-2	5-2	4-2	*	0-3	1-1	2-0	4-0	3-0	1-3	1-3	1-2	1-0	6-3	3-1	2-1
Kettering	1-1	3-1	1-0	3-0	0-1	2-1	3-1	5-2	3-2	0-2	*	3-0	3-2	2-0	6-1	5-2	0-1	2-1	3-0	6-0	3-0	0-1
Leigh RMI	1-0	1-2	0-2	2-2	2-1	1-3	0-2	2-2	2-0	1-5	1-4	*	1-3	0-1	1-1	0-1	1-3	0-0	0-3	3-1	0-1	2-1
Nuneaton	1-0	0-0	1-1	2-2	2-3	2-2	1-2	4-0	2-1	1-0	1-1	1-0	*	1-0	2-1	0-2	2-1	1-0	2-0	2-0	1-1	3-0
Redditch	1-1	0-5	1-0	3-1	3-1	1-0	1-3	3-2	0-1	3-1	0-2	1-1	0-0	*	1-0	1-1	0-2	3-1	0-1	2-0	3-0	2-0
Solihull M	0-3	1-1	0-1	1-3	1-3	3-1	3-1	0-2	2-2	1-4	1-3	1-0	3-1	0-0	*	4-1	0-4	1-0	2-0	1-1	2-3	2-2
Southport	1-0	1-0	2-1	2-2	1-0	3-0	0-0	4-0	5-0	2-1	0-1	2-0	2-2	1-1	3-2	*	2-3	2-2	1-1	3-2	0-1	1-1
Stalybridge	3-1	2-2	0-0	3-0	2-4	5-1	3-2	2-1	0-3	3-1	0-1	3-1	0-2	6-0	4-0	2-2	*	0-0	1-2	4-1	1-0	3-0
Tamworth	0-1	0-0	3-0	1-1	4-2	2-2	1-1	3-0	4-0	2-1	1-2	2-0	1-2	1-0	4-0	0-0	2-0	*	0-0	1-1	0-2	1-1
Telford	3-0	0-2	3-1	1-1	1-0	2-1	3-1	3-0	1-0	2-1	0-1	6-1	0-0	1-0	4-0	1-5	3-0	4-1	*	3-2	1-1	3-3
Vauxhall M	3-2	0-2	2-2	1-0	2-0	0-3	0-1	0-1	0-3	3-4	0-6	2-2	0-4	2-0	3-2	1-2	2-5	1-3	1-3	*	1-1	2-5
Worcester	1-1	1-1	2-2	2-1	2-1	0-1	1-1	2-1	0-1	0-2	2-3	3-1	2-0	1-0	0-0	2-1	2-1	3-3	1-3	1-0	*	2-2
Workington	1-2	0-1	2-0	0-1	0-1	1-2	0-1	1-1	1-3	2-0	1-1	2-1	2-0	1-1	1-1	2-3	1-0	5-0	0-1	1-0	1-0	*

	B Stortford	Basingstoke	Bath	Bognor	Braintree	Bromley	Cambridge C	Dorchester	Eastbourne	Eastleigh	Fisher	Hampton	Havant & W	Hayes	Lewes	Maidenhead	Newport Co	St Albans	Sutton Utd	Thurrock	Welling	Weston -SM
B Stortford	*	0-0	1-1	5-3	3-4	2-0	4-0	0-0	2-1	2-2	1-2	6-2	4-1	0-1	1-1	2-1	0-0	3-4	3-1	1-0	1-2	2-2
Basingstoke	1-2	*	0-4	3-2	2-2	1-1	2-1	1-0	2-3	3-4	1-5	1-2	2-3	1-1	1-1	0-0	3-1	3-1	1-0	3-0	2-1	0-0
Bath	4-0	0-1	*	0-0	0-0	1-1	2-0	1-0	0-0	2-0	0-1	2-0	1-1	2-2	1-1	2-0	1-1	3-0	2-3	3-1	2-0	1-0
Bognor	0-2	1-1	1-3	*	2-1	1-2	2-0	0-0	0-2	0-3	0-1	2-4	1-0	3-0	0-5	1-2	0-2	1-0	1-1	3-1	0-0	2-0
Braintree	2-1	2-1	2-0	3-2	*	2-1	0-1	1-0	1-0	0-2	2-3	3-0	1-0	0-1	3-0	1-1	0-0	0-0	1-0	0-0	2-1	4-0
Bromley	3-1	3-2	1-1	2-1	4-0	*	3-1	0-1	1-0	1-2	2-3	3-0	2-1	2-1	3-0	1-1	2-2	3-4	1-0	8-1	2-0	3-1
Cambridge C	2-4	3-0	2-2	2-2	4-0	1-2	*	2-2	1-1	1-2	3-2	0-2	2-0	2-1	1-2	1-1	2-2	4-0	4-1	2-2	3-1	3-1
Dorchester	0-4	2-2	0-0	1-1	0-0	2-3	3-2	*	0-4	0-1	2-1	0-1	1-0	1-0	1-3	3-0	2-3	0-3	0-0	0-1	0-0	5-1
Eastbourne	1-1	6-0	0-0	3-0	2-0	1-2	0-1	4-1	*	3-2	2-1	0-1	2-2	1-0	0-2	2-1	2-3	0-0	0-0	0-1	1-0	1-2
Eastleigh	0-0	1-1	4-4	1-0	2-1	1-4	1-0	3-1	1-2	*	3-0	1-1	1-1	3-1	3-0	3-2	0-2	1-1	1-2	2-0	3-1	3-2
Fisher	0-1	4-1	2-1	3-1	2-0	0-3	1-1	1-1	0-4	1-4	*	0-3	4-2	4-2	0-3	0-1	1-3	0-0	4-2	2-0	3-2	3-1
Hampton	1-1	2-2	0-0	1-1	3-0	3-2	2-2	4-0	0-2	3-1	0-2	*	1-1	4-1	6-0	1-1	1-0	4-1	2-2	2-3	4-0	5-1
Havant &W	1-2	1-1	1-0	2-0	0-0	1-0	2-1	4-0	2-1	1-0	1-1	0-3	*	4-1	1-2	0-3	2-0	3-1	2-0	3-0	1-0	1-1
Hayes & Y	2-2	1-1	3-0	0-2	3-3	6-1	3-1	2-2	1-1	2-4	2-1	0-0	3-1	*	2-1	1-4	1-3	2-1	3-3	1-1	0-1	2-2
Lewes	1-0	4-0	1-0	0-1	0-0	2-2	3-1	2-0	1-1	3-2	1-0	1-2	4-0	2-1	*	0-0	1-0	0-2	4-0	1-0	2-0	3-0
Maidenhead	5-0	1-2	0-1	1-2	0-1	2-3	1-1	3-1	1-2	0-5	2-3	1-2	3-3	0-1	0-0	*	2-3	0-0	1-1	3-0	0-1	0-0
Newport Co	1-0	2-0	2-3	2-2	2-0	3-1	4-1	3-2	1-1	1-2	1-2	2-2	0-1	1-1	1-3	2-0	*	2-0	1-4	1-2	0-1	5-0
St Albans	1-2	4-1	1-2	1-1	1-1	1-0	0-2	0-3	2-3	3-2	0-1	1-0	1-0	2-0	1-3	1-1	0-0	*	1-2	0-5	1-2	0-3
Sutton Utd	0-1	1-2	0-4	0-2	0-3	2-2	0-3	1-3	1-5	0-0	0-2	2-1	1-3	2-0	0-3	2-3	0-0	0-0	*	2-1	1-2	0-3
Thurrock	1-0	1-1	1-0	1-0	1-1	2-1	5-2	3-1	3-2	4-1	0-0	0-5	0-2	2-0	2-3	2-3	3-0	2-1	2-1	*	2-0	3-0
Welling	2-1	0-1	1-0	2-3	0-2	3-1	2-6	1-1	1-0	3-1	0-1	1-3	0-2	1-2	0-4	2-3	0-0	1-1	0-0	2-0 3-2	*	2-1
Weston SM	0-4	3-3	0-2	3-2	1-2	0-1	0-1	1-0	1-2	3-1	3-1	0-3	3-1	3-1	3-1	1-2	2-2	2-0	3-0	3-1	0-3	*

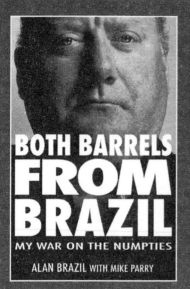

SCOTTISH PREMIER LEAGUE 2007/08 RESULTS

	Aberdeen	Celtic	Dundee U	Falkirk	Gretna	Hearts	Hibs	Inverness	K'marnock	Motherwell	Rangers	St Mirren
Aberdeen	*	1-3 1-5	2-0 2-1	1-1 2-1	3-0 2-0	0-1 1-1	3-1 2-1	1-0	2-1	1-1 1-2	1-1 2-0	1-1 4-0
Celtic	3-0 1-0	*	3-0 0-0	4-0	3-0	5-0 3-0	1-1 2-0	2-1 5-0	1-0 0-0	0-1 3-0	2-1 3-2	1-1 2-0
Dundee Utd	1-0 3-0	0-2 0-1	*	0-0 2-0	1-2	4-1	0-1 1-1	1-1 0-1	2-0	2-0 1-0	2-1 3-3	1-1 2-0
Falkirk	0-0	1-4 0-1	3-0	*	2-0 0-0	2-1 2-1	0-2 1-1	1-0 2-1	0-0 1-1	0-0 1-0	1-3	0-1 4-0
Gretna	1-1	1-2 0-3	3-2 0-3	0-4 2-0	*	*	0-1	1-2 0-4	4-2 1-2	1-2 1-3	1-2	0-0
Hearts	4-1	1-1	1-0 1-3	0-4 2-0	*	*	0-1	2-3 1-0	1-1 0-2	1-2 1-3	0-4 4-2	0-1 3-2
Hibernian	3-3 3-1	0-2 3-2	2-2	0-3 1-1	2-0	2-0	*	4-1 2-2	2-0 1-0	1-0 0-2	1-2 0-0	2-0 0-1
Inv CT	3-4 1-2	3-2	0-3 1-1	1-2 2-1	2-1	2-1	*	*	3-1 3-0	0-1	0-3 0-1	1-0 0-0
Kilmarnock	0-1 3-1	1-2	1-2 2-1	0-1 2-1	3-0 3-1	0-3 2-1	2-1	4-1 2-2	*	0-1	1-2 0-2	1-0 0-0
Motherwell	3-0 2-1	1-4 1-2	5-3 2-2	0-3	3-0	0-1 0-2	1-0 2-1	2-1 3-1	3-1 3-0	*	1-1 1-1	2-0 4-0
Rangers	3-1 3-0	1-3 3-0	2-0 3-1	7-2 2-0	4-0 4-2	2-1	2-1 0-1	2-0	2-0	3-1 1-0	*	0-3
St Mirren	0-1	1-5 0-1	0-3	1-5 1-0	2-0 1-0	2-1	2-1 1-1	2-1 1-1	0-0 1-0	0-1 3-1	0-3	*

SCOTTISH DIVISION ONE 2007/08 RESULTS

	Clyde	Dundee	Dunfermline	Hamilton	Livingston	Morton	Partick	Queen of S	St J'stone	Stirling
Clyde	*	1-1 1-2	1-2 2-1	0-2 2-3	3-2 2-1	1-1 0-1	1-4 1-2	0-0 1-4	1-0 1-3	3-0 1-3
Dundee	2-0 0-1	*	0-0 1-1	1-1 1-0	2-0 4-1	2-0 2-1	3-0 1-0	2-1 2-3	3-2 2-1	3-0 3-1
Dunfermline	2-1 1-1	0-1 0-1	*	0-5 1-1	1-1 0-4	0-1 2-0	1-1 1-0	4-0 2-0	0-1 0-0	2-1 2-1
Hamilton	2-0 0-0	1-0 2-0	2-1 3-0	*	3-1 1-1	3-0 1-0	1-1 1-0	1-0 2-0	2-0 1-0	0-0 4-0
Livingston	4-2 1-1	0-2 1-1	0-2 1-1	1-3 2-0	*	6-1 4-0	1-0 0-4	2-2 1-0	0-2 0-2	2-1 4-3
Morton	1-2 3-2	1-2 0-2	3-0 0-1	0-2 1-3	2-2 1-1	*	0-0 4-2	0-3 0-1	1-2 2-2	2-1 1-1
Partick	4-0 1-1	1-1 1-0	0-1 1-1	3-0 0-3	3-0 2-1	0-3 1-1	*	0-0 2-0	2-2 0-0	1-1 1-0
Queen of Sth	3-1 1-1	1-0 2-1	1-1 0-1	2-2 2-1	1-0 1-0	0-0 1-3	1-2 2-0	*	3-3 3-1	3-1 2-2
St Johnstone	1-1 1-2	1-1 1-1	1-1 0-0	2-1 4-1	5-2 5-2	3-2 2-2	2-0 2-1	2-1 2-0	*	2-2 2-1
Stirling	1-1 0-2	1-6 2-2	3-0 2-3	2-4 0-1	1-4 3-3	0-0 1-2	2-0 1-1	0-0 1-3	0-0 3-1	*

SCOTTISH DIVISION TWO 2007/08 RESULTS

	Airdrie U	Alloa	Ayr	Berwick	Brechin	Cow'beath	Peterhead	Queen's P	Raith	Ross Co
Airdrie Utd	*	1-1 2-0	0-0 0-2	4-0 3-0	1-2 2-1	3-1 4-0	2-0 1-1	1-0 3-2	3-0 0-1	0-1 2-0
Alloa	0-6 1-2	*	1-2 2-1	2-1 2-1	2-2 0-4	3-2 3-2	0-2 2-0	1-2 2-0	2-0 2-1	2-0 3-1
Ayr	1-2 1-1	3-1 2-0	*	4-0 4-0	0-3 2-1	1-4 1-1	0-3 1-2	2-3 3-1	0-1 0-3	0-2 1-4
Berwick	2-0 2-4	1-2 0-3	0-1 1-1	*	2-2 3-3	1-1 4-5	2-2 1-2	1-1 1-4	2-5 2-1	0-4 0-1
Brechin	2-1 4-2	0-0 0-0	2-2 5-1	2-2 5-0	*	0-1 1-1	2-2 3-1	0-1 2-1	3-2 0-1	3-3 1-2
Cowdenbeath	0-1 1-1	1-1 1-4	2-0 1-1	1-2 3-1	0-2 1-0	*	0-4 0-2	1-0 2-4	1-0 1-4	2-2 2-4
Peterhead	0-1 1-4	1-4 2-2	4-1 3-0	9-2 4-3	2-0 1-2	4-2 1-0	*	1-0 1-0	1-0 0-1	1-1 1-2
Queen's Park	0-2 0-1	1-0 1-1	1-3 1-1	3-1 1-0	2-3 3-0	0-1 2-3	2-0 1-1	*	0-1 2-5	3-2 0-1
Raith	1-0 2-1	2-1 3-2	1-2 2-3	3-1 3-0	1-1 1-1	3-2 2-0	2-5 2-2	0-1 0-2	*	0-1 0-2
Ross County	3-2 1-1	6-1 2-2	2-0 2-4	4-0 2-1	2-1 0-0	3-0 4-1	1-0 5-1	3-2 1-1	2-3 2-3	*

SCOTTISH DIVISION THREE 2007/08 RESULTS

	Albion	Arbroath	Dumbarton	East Fife	Elgin	E Stirling	Forfar	Montrose	Stnhsmuir	Stranraer
Albion	*	0-2 5-2	0-1 2-0	2-2 1-4	3-4 1-1	2-2 2-3	0-0 2-1	0-3 1-3	1-1 3-3	3-2 1-1
Arbroath	1-4 1-0	*	1-1 0-0	2-3 0-1	2-0 4-0	0-1 2-0	3-4 1-1	2-1 0-0	1-0 2-2	0-0 2-2
Dumbarton	2-0 2-0	2-1 1-1	*	0-3 1-1	1-0 1-4	1-0 3-1	0-0 0-0	0-0 1-3	1-2 1-0	0-2 0-1
East Fife	0-0 4-0	2-1 0-2	2-1 2-0	*	2-0 4-0	3-1 1-0	3-0 3-0	2-0 0-0	0-1 7-0	3-1 2-1
Elgin	3-2 1-1	1-3 2-1	2-1 2-1	2-3 1-2	*	6-0 3-0	3-1 2-2	0-2 2-1	1-5 2-0	2-3 0-5
E Stirling	4-5 3-0	0-1 2-3	3-2 1-1	0-3 0-2	0-0 3-1	*	3-1 4-1	3-1 0-3	3-4 1-1	2-3 1-3
Forfar	1-4 1-0	1-3 1-0	1-1 3-1	0-2 2-3	4-0 0-1	1-0 0-2	*	1-1 1-4	0-1 1-2	1-0 1-1
Montrose	0-1 2-1	3-3 5-0	3-1 0-1	0-1 3-1	3-2 0-0	2-0 3-1	2-2 0-1	*	1-0 2-1	0-2 2-4
Stenhsmuir	2-2 0-1	1-0 0-3	2-1 1-1	0-1 2-1	2-2 2-3	0-3 3-0	2-0 4-0	0-0 0-4	*	1-1 1-4
Stranraer	3-0 3-1	0-3 1-1	2-0 2-0	0-2 0-2	0-0 3-3	2-1 2-1	2-1 3-0	1-0 0-2	3-1 2-3	*

9-1 Diamonds are the 24 carat each-way value

LAST season, which was highlighted by terrific television coverage on Setanta Sports, ended with Aldershot finishing runaway winners of the Conference. They are joined in League 2 by Exeter City, who beat Cambridge United in the Play-Off final.

Wrexham and Mansfield were the two teams to make the move in the opposite direction and it is interesting that, at the time of writing, both clubs' futures are of some concern with the possibility of both being put up for sale.

On that basis alone, neither team makes any great appeal at best prices of 9-1 and 14-1 respectively, as managers Brian Little and Paul Holland have not been able to be as active in the transfer market as I'm sure they would have liked to be.

Ante-post favourites this time around are Stevenage Borough but the fact that 13-2 is available is an indication of the likely openness of the league.

Graham Westley has retuned to Broadhall Way and has wasted no time in making some significant signings, most notably strikers Lee Boylan from Cambridge and Iyesden Christie from Kidderminster, as well as persuading leading scorer Steve Morison to come off the transfer list.

With experienced defender Mark Albrighton also coming in from Cambridge, the Hertfordshire side look sure to be thereabouts.

The aforementioned Cambridge have endured an awful summer with eight of the 11 players that started the Play-Off final having left the club as well as manager Jimmy Quinn. Gary Brabin, formerly manager at Southport, has taken over the reins but, in the circumstances, they make no great betting appeal at a best-priced 12-1.

It remains to be seen how Torquay will recover from the Play-Off semi-final defeat by West Country rivals Exeter last season and being beaten by Ebbsfleet in the FA Trophy final.

Paul Buckle's side were always in the van last term and a similar scenario is likely this time around. However, they were a bigger price this time last year than the 7-1 available now and the league looks stronger this time around.

The losses of goalkeeper Simon Rayner to Crawley and Lee Phillips to Rushden are blows.

One club who have made some notable signings during the close season are **Rushden & Diamonds**.

They are better than their finishing position suggests, as their FA Cup and Trophy runs meant they had to play eight games in the last 16 days of the season. They didn't really recover from the sale of star striker Simeon Jackson to Gillingham but Garry Hill has acquired proven goalscorer Daryl Clare from Burton and very useful front man Lee Phillips, as well as ex-Chelsea midfielder Rob Wolleaston from Cambridge.

At 9-1 – as short as 13-2 in places – they look worth an each-way bet.

The promoted clubs – Kettering Town, Eastbourne Borough, Barrow and **Lewes** – will be looking to maintain their Conference status in their first year, as Histon and Salisbury did last term.

However, the other two promoted clubs, Farsley Celtic and Droylsden, returned from whence they came and, on recent evidence, the jump from Con-

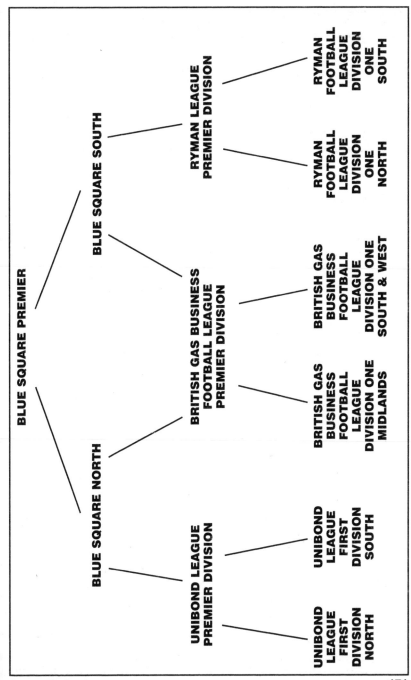

BLUE SQUARE PREMIER

BLUE SQUARE NORTH

BLUE SQUARE SOUTH

UNIBOND LEAGUE PREMIER DIVISION

BRITISH GAS BUSINESS FOOTBALL LEAGUE PREMIER DIVISION

RYMAN LEAGUE PREMIER DIVISION

UNIBOND LEAGUE FIRST DIVISION NORTH

UNIBOND LEAGUE FIRST DIVISION SOUTH

BRITISH GAS BUSINESS FOOTBALL LEAGUE DIVISION ONE MIDLANDS

BRITISH GAS BUSINESS FOOTBALL LEAGUE DIVISION ONE SOUTH & WEST

RYMAN FOOTBALL LEAGUE DIVISION ONE NORTH

RYMAN FOOTBALL LEAGUE DIVISION ONE SOUTH

ference North to Conference in particular is a particularly steep one.

Lewes will not have been helped by a curious change of management in the close season. Steve King, who won them two promotions, has left the club to be replaced by Kevin Keehan and a large percentage of last season's successful squad have gone too.

Backing teams for relegation is not my cup of tea, but it looks like it is going to be a long hard season at The Dripping Pan and I suspect The Rooks will find the Conference a bridge too far.

Burton, under Nigel Clough, always appear to be in the upper reaches of the table without entirely convincing that they can win the title. The Brewers have not been particularly active thus far in the transfer market and they will find it hard to replace Daryl Clare's goals.

Oxford, under manager Darren Patterson, finished last season quite well, as did Grays but both still look like works in progress. That comment could also apply to York City and it is hard to envisage The Minstermen making a title charge.

Kidderminster and Forest Green both finished in mid-table respectability but Christie's summer move is likely to affect the former while the latter have a huge hole to fill with Conference leading scorer Stuart Fleetwood going to Charlton.

Histon, under Steve Fallon, and Salisbury, under Nick Holmes, will both be looking to consolidate on their promising debut seasons while Ebbsfleet will look to push on following their Trophy success.

Of the bigger-priced clubs, it is **Crawley** who catch the eye. The Sussex side, managed by Steve Evans, have made some interesting signings, notably veteran striker Steve Fletcher, former Weymouth captain Simon Weatherstone, goalkeeper Simon Rayner and wide man Danny Forrest.

The Red Devils look more settled off the pitch this time around and, at 40-1, make some each-way appeal.

Woking, who have not pulled up any trees in a while, have a new manager in the shape of Kim Grant while Weymouth, who only narrowly avoided relegation last term, should enjoy a better campaign this time.

John Hollins has been wheeling and dealing in the transfer market and the fitness coach who inspired Cambridge to their long unbeaten start to last season's campaign has been acquired.

Havant & Waterlooville head the market in the Conference South.

The Hawks, who did so well in defeat at Liverpool in the memorable third-round FA Cup tie, must go well but may be put under pressure by promoted sides Chelmsford and AFC Wimbledon amongst others.

The former, under ex-Canvey Island supremo Jeff King, won what looked a hot Ryman Premiership last term, and, having kept nearly all of that squad together, they have strengthened, most notably, with the additions of Danny Webb from AFC Wimbledon, Kevin James from Eastleigh and Dave Rainford from Dagenham & Redbridge.

They are likely to make a bold bid for back-to-back promotions, as will The Dons.

Terry Brown is another who has been busy in the transfer market, bringing in strikers Chris Sullivan from Braintree and Belal Aiteouakrim from Hendon. With their significant fan base behind them, they look sure to be thereabouts.

Others worth consideration are Newport County, under new boss Dean Holdsworth, who were beaten by Eastbourne in last term's Play-Off final, and **Eastleigh**, with the latter getting the nod at 14-1.

Managed by ex-Havant boss Ian Baird, The Spitfires finished sixth in the table last term. They have made a couple of useful signings, in particular Trevor Challis from Weymouth and Terry Jordan, who was wanted by several clubs, from Havant.

In the Conference North, I make no apology for once again suggesting **Southport**.

The Sandgrounders, who lost in the Play-Off semi-finals via a penalty shootout last season, have once again acquired the services of Liam Watson as their manager.

He was in charge when they were last promoted and has done really well at Burscough in the interim. He has signed ten of his old players already, including the League's leading scorer Ciaran Kilheeney, and at odds of 8-1, they look well worth an each-way investment.

The three relegated teams, Farsley Celtic, Droylsden and Stafford must all enter calculations but, at a bigger price, promoted **Kings Lynn**, for whom Julian Joachim is a significant signing, are worth consideration.

FINAL BRITISH DRAWS CHART 2007/08

X = Score draw
V = Void match

0 = 0-0 draw
*= Pools panel

Pools No	Aug 11	Aug 18	Aug 25	Sep 1	Sep 8	Sep 15	Sep 22	Sep 29	Oct 6	Oct 13	Oct 20	Oct 27	Nov 3	Nov 10	Nov 17	Nov 24	Dec 1	Dec 8	Dec 15	Dec 22	Dec 29	Jan 5	Jan 12	Jan 19	Jan 26	Feb 2	Feb 9	Feb 16	Feb 23	Mar 1	Mar 8	Mar 15	Mar 22	Mar 29	Apr 5	Apr 12	Apr 19	Apr 26	May 3	May 10	0	X
1	-	-	-	-	X	-	-	0	-	0	-	-	0	-	-	-	-	-	X	-	X	-	X	X	-	X	-	-	-	X	0*	X	-	-	-	-	-	X	-	-	4	9
2	-	-	-	-	0	0	-	X	-	-	-	-	-	0	-	-	-	-	-	X	-	-	-	-	-	0	-	-	-	-	-	-	-	-	-	-	-	-	-	X	4	3
3	X	-	-	X	X	-	X	-	-	0	-	-	-	X	-	-	-	-	-	-	-	-	-	-	-	-	-	-	-	-	-	-	0	0*	-	-	-	-	-	-	3	5
4	-	0	-	-	0	0	0	-	-	-	0	-	-	-	-	-	-	-	-	-	-	-	-	0	-	-	-	-	-	0	0	-	-	X	-	0	-	-	-	-	9	1
5	-	-	-	-	-	-	X	-	-	-	-	-	X	-	-	-	-	-	-	X	0	-	-	-	-	-	-	-	-	-	-	-	X	-	-	-	-	X	-	-	1	5
6	-	-	X	-	-	-	-	-	X	-	-	X	-	-	-	-	0	-	X	-	-	-	X	-	-	-	-	-	-	-	-	-	0*	-	-	-	-	0	-	-	3	5
7	-	-	-	-	X	-	X	X	-	-	-	X*	-	0	-	-	X	0	-	-	-	X	-	-	-	-	-	-	-	0	0	-	-	0	-	0	X	-	-	-	6	7
8	X	-	-	-	-	X	X	X	-	-	X	-	-	X	-	-	-	-	-	-		-	-	X	V	-	X	0*	-	-	-	0	-	-	X	-	-	X	-	-	2	10
9	-	X	X	-	-	-	X	-	-	-	X	X	-	-	-	0	-	-	-	-	-	-	X	0	-	X	-	X	-	-	-	-	-	-	-	-	-	-	-	X	2	9
10	-	X	-	-	X	X	-	X	-	X	-	-	-	-	-	-	X	-	-	-	-	-	-	-	-	-	-	X	-	-	-	-	-	-	-	X	-	X	-	-	-	9
11	X	X	-	0	-	X	-	-	0	-	-	-	-	-	-	-	-	-	-	-	X	-	-	-	X	X	X	-	-	0	-	X	-	-	-	-	-	-	X	-	3	9
12	-	X	-	-	-	-	-	X	-	0	-	X	0	X	X	0	-	X	X	-	-	-	-	0	-	-	V	-	X	-	-	0	-	-	-	-	X	-	-	0	6	9
13	-	-	-	-	-	X	X	X	-	-	X	-	0	-	-	-	-	-	X	X	-	-	-	X	-	-	X	X	X	X	-	-	-	-	-	X	-	-	-	-	1	12
14	-	X	-	-	-	X	-	0	X	-	X	-	-	-	-	-	X	X	-	-	X	-	X	-	X	-	-	-	-	-	V	-	-	0	X	X	-	-	-	-	2	11
15	0	-	-	0	X	-	-	-	X	-	-	-	-	-	-	-	X	0	-	0	X	X	-	-	-	-	-	-	-	-	-	-	X	-	-	-	-	X	-	-	4	7
16	X	-	-	-	-	X	-	X	-	-	-	-	-	-	-	X	0	-	-	-	X	-	-	-	-	-	0	-	0	-	-	-	-	0	-	0*	-	-	-	-	5	5
17	-	-	-	-	0	-	-	-	-	-	-	-	X	-	-	-	-	0*	0	-	-	-	-	X	-	-	-	-	-	-	-	-	-	-	-	X	-	-	-	-	3	3
18	-	-	-	-	-	-	-	-	-	-	-	X	-	-	-	-	-	-	-	-	-	-	-	X	X	-	-	-	X	0*	-	0	X	-	-	-	-	-	X	0	3	6
19	-	-	-	-	-	-	-	-	-	-	X	X	-	X	-	-	-	-	-	-	-	-	-	-	X	-	-	-	-	-	-	-	0	X	-	-	X	-	-	-	1	6
20	-	-	-	X	-	X	X	X	-	0	-	-	-	-	-	-	-	0	-	-	-	X	-	X	0	-	X	-	X	-	V	-	X	-	-	-	-	-	-	X	3	10
21	0	-	X	-	-	-	X	-	-	-	-	-	-	0	-	-	-	-	-	X*	X	X	-	X	-	-	-	-	-	X	-	-	X	-	-	-	X	-	0	-	3	9
22	-	-	-	-	-	X	0	-	0	-	X	-	-	-	-	-	-	-	-	-	-	-	-	-	-	-	-	-	-	-	V	-	-	X	-	-	-	X	-	-	2	4

23	-	X	-	-	-	-	-	-	-	-	-	-	-	-	-	-	-	-	-	-	-	0	-	-	X	-	-	-	X	-	-	-	-	0	X	-	-	-	-	X	2	5
24	X	-	-	-	-	-	-	-	X	X	-	-	-	-	0	-	X	-	-	-	-	-	-	-	-	0	X	-	-	X	0	-	-	0	X	-	-	-	X	X	4	9
25	0	-	-	X	-	-	-	-	-	X	-	-	-	-	-	-	-	X	-	0	X	X	X	-	-	-	-	-	-	0	X	-	-	-	-	0	X	-	-	-	4	8
26	-	-	-	-	-	-	-	X	-	-	0	-	-	-	-	-	-	X	X	-	-	-	-	-	-	-	-	-	-	-	-	-	-	-	-	X	-	-	-	-	1	4
27	X	-	-	-	X	-	-	-	-	-	-	-	V	-	X	X	-	-	0	-	-	-	X	-	X	X	X	-	-	-	-	-	-	-	-	-	-	X	-	-	1	9
28	-	-	-	X	-	0	-	-	X	-	-	X	-	-	X	-	-	-	-	-	-	-	-	-	-	-	-	-	-	-	-	X	X	-	X	-	-	-	-	-	1	7
29	-	-	-	X	-	-	-	-	-	V	-	-	-	-	X	0	-	-	-	-	-	0	X	0	-	-	X	-	-	0	-	X	X	0	X	-	-	-	-	-	5	7
30	X	0	-	-	-	-	-	-	-	-	V	X	-	-	0	-	-	X	X	-	-	X	X	X	-	X	-	-	-	-	-	X	V	-	-	X	-	V	-	-	2	10
31	X	-	-	-	X	-	-	-	-	X	0	-	-	-	-	X	X	-	-	-	-	-	-	-	-	-	-	-	-	-	-	-	-	-	-	-	-	-	-	-	1	5
32	X	-	-	-	-	-	-	X	-	-	X	0	-	-	-	-	-	-	-	-	-	-	-	-	-	-	X	-	-	-	-	-	-	0	-	X	-	-	X	0	3	6
33	0	-	-	-	0*	X	-	-	-	-	X	X	X	-	-	-	-	X	-	X	-	-	-	0	-	-	-	X	-	-	0	-	-	-	-	-	-	-	-	-	4	7
34	-	-	-	-	-	-	X	-	V	-	-	X	-	-	-	-	-	-	-	-	-	-	-	-	-	-	-	-	-	-	0	-	-	-	0	-	-	X	X	-	2	4
35	X	X	-	0	-	-	-	-	X	-	X	-	-	-	0*	-	0	-	-	-	-	0	-	-	-	X	-	-	-	-	-	-	X	-	-	0	X	-	-	-	5	7
36	0	X	X	-	X	-	-	-	-	-	-	X	-	-	-	-	-	0	-	-	-	0	-	-	-	-	-	X	-	-	X	-	0	0	-	X	-	-	0	-	6	7
37	-	X	X	X	-	-	-	-	-	-	X	-	-	-	-	-	X	-	-	0*	-	-	-	-	-	-	-	-	-	-	-	-	-	-	-	X	-	-	X	X	1	8
38	-	X	X	-	-	-	X	-	X	-	-	X	-	-	-	X	X	0	-	-	-	-	-	X	-	-	X	-	-	-	-	-	-	-	-	-	-	-	-	-	1	9
39	0	-	-	X	-	-	X	-	-	-	-	0	X	-	-	-	-	-	-	X	X	-	-	-	-	X	-	-	0	-	-	-	-	0	0	-	-	-	-	-	5	6
40	X	0	-	-	-	-	X	-	-	-	X	-	-	-	-	-	-	X	X	X	-	-	-	-	-	-	X	-	-	0	X	0*	X	-	-	-	-	-	-	-	3	9
41	-	X	-	-	X	-	-	-	-	-	-	-	-	-	-	V	X	-	-	-	-	-	-	-	-	-	-	-	-	-	-	-	-	-	-	-	-	X	X	X	-	6
42	-	-	-	-	-	X	-	-	-	-	-	-	-	-	-	V	-	-	X	-	-	X	0	-	-	-	-	-	-	-	-	-	-	-	X	-	-	-	-	-	1	4
43	-	-	X	-	X	-	-	-	-	0	-	-	X	-	-	-	-	-	-	-	-	-	X	-	-	-	-	-	-	-	-	X	0	-	-	-	-	-	X	-	2	6
44	-	-	-	-	0	X	0	X	X	X	-	-	-	-	-	-	-	-	-	0	-	-	-	-	-	-	X	-	-	-	-	-	-	-	-	X	-	-	-	-	3	6
45	-	-	-	-	-	-	-	-	-	X	-	-	-	-	-	-	-	-	-	0*	-	X	X	X	-	-	-	-	-	-	X	-	-	0	-	-	X	-	-	-	2	6
46	-	-	-	-	X	-	X	-	-	-	-	X	-	0	-	X	-	X	-	-	-	X	-	-	-	-	X	-	-	-	0	0	-	-	-	0	-	-	-	-	4	7
47	-	-	-	-	-	X	X	-	-	-	-	X	-	X	X	X	-	-	-	X	-	-	0	-	-	-	-	X*	-	X	-	X	-	0	0	-	-	X	-	-	3	11
48	-	X	-	X	X	-	-	-	-	X	X	X	X	X	-	-	-	-	-	-	-	-	-	-	-	0	-	X	0	-	-	X	X	X	X	-	-	-	X	-	2	14
49	X	0	-	-	-	X	X	X	-	-	-	-	-	-	-	-	-	X	X	-	-	-	-	-	-	-	-	X	-	X	X	-	0	0	-	-	-	-	0	-	4	9
0	6	4	0	3	5	3	3	2	2	5	3	2	3	4	3	3	3	6	2	5	1	4	2	5	1	3	1	1	3	7	7	5	6	4	3	6	0	1	3	3	133-	
X	12	12	7	8	12	13	15	12	8	7	12	15	6	6	5	6	9	9	9	8	8	9	10	10	6	7	12	8	5	6	5	8	10	13	8	10	7	10	9	7	-	359

SATURDAY 2ND AUGUST 2008

SCOTTISH DIVISION ONE

Clyde v Morton	-	-	-	-	-	0-1/1-1	02-05-06
Partick v Dunfermline	4-0	4-1	-	-	-	1-1/0-1	02-02-02
Queen of Sth v Airdrie Utd	-	-	1-0/0-0	1-0/2-0	1-1/0-3	-	03-02-02
Ross County v Dundee	-	-	-	3-0/0-0	1-0/0-0	-	02-02-00
St Johnstone v Livingston	-	-	-	-	1-2/1-2	5-2/5-2	04-02-03

SCOTTISH DIVISION TWO

Arbroath v Alloa	0-1/0-1	3-1/2-1	0-3/2-1	-	-	-	07-08-10
Ayr v Raith	-	1-0/1-0	-	2-1/0-0	1-0/0-2	0-3/0-1	13-09-07
Brechin v Stirling	-	-	0-3/5-3	-	0-1/1-4	-	06-00-07
East Fife v Peterhead	3-3/0-2	-	0-2/1-2	-	-	-	01-02-05
Queen's Park v Stranraer	-	0-4/0-2	-	-	-	-	05-03-05

SCOTTISH DIVISION THREE

Albion v Forfar	-	-	-	-	-	2-1/0-0	03-02-08
Berwick v E Stirling	-	-	-	3-2/1-0	2-2/2-0	-	10-04-05
Cowdenbeath v Annan Ath	-	-	-	-	-	-	00-00-00
Dumbarton v Montrose	-	-	-	-	2-0/2-1	1-3/0-0	08-04-07
Stenhsmuir v Elgin	-	-	0-2/4-0	3-1/1-2	2-0/3-2	2-3/2-2	04-01-03

FRIDAY 8TH AUGUST 2008
CONFERENCE

Barrow v Oxford Utd	-	-	-	-	-	-	00-00-00

SATURDAY 9TH AUGUST 2008
CHAMPIONSHIP

Birmingham v Sheff Utd	-	-	-	-	-	-	04-01-02
Blackpool v Bristol C	0-0	1-0	1-1	1-1	0-1	1-1	04-06-03
Cardiff v Southampton	-	-	-	2-1	1-0	1-0	03-00-00
Charlton v Swansea	-	-	-	-	-	-	00-00-00
Coventry v Norwich	1-1	0-2	-	1-1/2-2	3-0	1-0	08-04-01
Crystal Pal v Watford	0-1	1-0	-	3-1	-	0-2	04-01-05
Derby v Doncaster	-	-	-	-	-	-	00-00-00
Ipswich v Preston	3-0	2-0	3-0	0-4	2-3	2-1	04-00-02
Plymouth v Wolves	-	-	1-2	2-0	1-1	1-1	03-02-02
QPR v Barnsley	1-0	4-0	-	-	1-0	2-0	07-01-00
Sheff Weds v Burnley	1-3	-	-	0-0	1-1	0-2	01-02-03

LEAGUE 1

Bristol R v Carlisle	1-2	1-0	-	1-1	-	3-0	03-03-01
Crewe v Brighton	-	-	3-1	2-1	1-1	2-1	05-01-00
Hartlepool v Colchester	-	0-0	2-1	0-1	-	-	06-01-02
Huddersfield v Stockport	2-1	-	5-3	-	-	-	06-02-02
Leicester v MK Dons	4-0	-	-	-	-	-	03-01-02
Leyton O v Hereford	-	-	-	-	-	-	01-00-02
Northampton v Cheltenham	1-2	1-0	1-1	1-2	2-0	2-1	04-01-02
Oldham v Millwall	-	-	-	-	1-2	1-1	01-04-04
Scunthorpe v Leeds	-	-	-	-	-	-	00-00-00
Southend v Peterboro	-	-	-	-	-	-	02-01-02
Swindon v Tranmere	1-1	2-0	2-1	1-2	-	1-0	08-03-02
Yeovil v Walsall	-	-	-	2-1	-	0-2	01-00-01

LEAGUE 2

Accrington v Aldershot	-	4-2	3-3	3-2	-	-	02-01-00
Barnet v Chesterfield	-	-	-	-	-	0-2	02-01-02
Bournemouth v Gillingham	-	-	-	2-1	1-1	1-0	03-03-01
Bradford v Notts Co	-	-	-	-	-	3-0	02-00-00
Bury v Brentford	-	-	-	-	-	1-2	02-03-04
Dagenham & R v Chester	1-0	0-0	-	-	-	6-2	03-02-00
Darlington v Exeter	2-2	-	-	-	-	-	07-03-01
Grimsby v Rochdale	-	-	0-1	4-1	0-4	1-2	01-00-05
Luton v Port Vale	0-0	2-0	1-0	-	-	2-1	05-02-00
Rotherham v Lincoln	-	-	-	-	-	3-2	03-02-00
Shrewsbury v Macclesfield	2-3	-	0-1	1-1	2-1	2-0	03-03-03
Wycombe v Morecambe	-	-	-	-	-	2-0	01-00-00

SCOTTISH PREMIER LEAGUE

Aberdeen v Inv CT	-	-	0-0	0-0	1-1/1-1	1-0	01-04-00
Falkirk v Rangers	-	-	-	1-1/1-2	1-0	1-3	01-01-10
Hearts v Motherwell	4-2/2-1	0-0/3-2	0-1/0-0	2-1/3-0	4-1	1-2	21-11-05
Kilmarnock v Hibernian	2-1/6-2	0-2/2-0	3-1	2-2/3-1	2-1/0-2	2-1	12-07-07

SCOTTISH DIVISION ONE

Airdrie Utd v Partick	-	-	4-2/0-1	-	1-2/1-1	-	05-09-02
Dundee v Clyde	-	-	-	3-3/0-1	3-0/1-4	0-1/2-0	03-01-03
Dunfermline v Queen of Sth	-	-	-	-	-	2-0/4-0	03-00-00
Morton v St Johnstone	-	-	-	-	-	2-2/1-2	02-03-04
Livingston v Ross County	-	-	-	-	0-0/1-1	-	02-04-00

SCOTTISH DIVISION TWO

Alloa v Ayr	0-1/2-3	-	1-3/5-1	0-4/1-1	0-1/1-1	2-1/1-2	02-05-07
Peterhead v Arbroath	-	-	-	-	-	-	00-00-00
Raith v Queen's Park	-	-	-	-	-	0-2/0-1	00-00-02
Stirling v East Fife	0-0/1-2	-	-	-	-	-	08-02-06
Stranraer v Brechin	3-1/2-3	-	4-2/0-1	1-1/2-0	3-1/0-2	-	06-03-09

SCOTTISH DIVISION THREE

Annan Ath v Stenhsmuir	-	-	-	-	-	-	00-00-00
E Stirling v Albion	0-3/0-4	3-4/1-8	1-1/0-2	3-1/1-0	0-1/0-0	4-5/3-0	13-06-17
Elgin v Dumbarton	-	-	-	-	0-2/0-1	2-1/2-1	04-00-04
Forfar v Cowdenbeath	2-1/1-1	-	-	-	1-1/2-0	-	07-06-01
Montrose v Berwick	-	-	-	0-0/1-2	0-1/1-2	-	03-03-13

CONFERENCE

Crawley v York	-	-	1-0	0-1	3-0	6-1	03-00-01
Eastbourne v Rushden & D	-	-	-	-	-	-	00-00-00
Ebbsfleet U v Mansfield	-	-	-	-	-	-	00-00-00
Histon v Torquay	-	-	-	-	-	4-5	00-00-01
Kettering v Forest G	2-3	-	-	-	-	-	02-00-02
Kidderminstr v Lewes	-	-	-	-	-	-	00-00-00
Northwich v Cambridge U	-	-	-	-	0-4	0-2	00-00-02
Salisbury v Burton	-	-	-	-	-	2-0	03-01-03
Weymouth v Grays	-	-	1-1	-	3-2	1-1	01-02-00
Woking v Altrincham	-	-	-	3-1	2-0	2-0	06-01-02
Wrexham v Stevenage	-	-	-	-	-	-	00-00-00

SUNDAY 10TH AUGUST 2008
CHAMPIONSHIP

Nottm Forest v Reading	2-0	0-1	1-0	-	-	-	03-00-01

SCOTTISH PREMIER LEAGUE

Celtic v St Mirren	-	-	-	-	2-0/5-1	1-1	09-03-01

MONDAY 11TH AUGUST 2008
SCOTTISH PREMIER LEAGUE

Hamilton v Dundee Utd	-	-	-	-	-	-	00-00-04

TUESDAY 12TH AUGUST 2008
CONFERENCE

Altrincham v Barrow	1-2	1-1	2-0	-	-	-	02-06-01
Burton v Northwich	1-1	0-1	1-0	-	2-0	4-1	03-01-01
Cambridge U v Kidderminster	0-2	0-0	1-3	0-2	1-1	0-3	00-02-04
Forest G v Salisbury	-	-	-	-	-	0-3	01-00-01
Grays v Kettering	-	1-1	-	-	-	-	00-01-00
Lewes v Crawley	-	-	-	-	-	-	00-00-00
Mansfield v Histon	-	-	-	-	-	-	00-00-00
Oxford Utd v Weymouth	-	-	-	-	4-1	0-1	01-00-01
Rushden & D v Ebbsfleet U	-	-	-	-	0-0	0-1	01-01-02
Stevenage v Eastbourne	-	-	-	-	-	-	00-00-00
Torquay v Woking	-	-	-	-	-	2-0	01-00-00

THURSDAY 14TH AUGUST 2008
CONFERENCE

York v Wrexham	1-1	-	-	-	-	-	06-05-01

SATURDAY 16TH AUGUST 2008

PREMIER LEAGUE

Arsenal v WBA	5-2	-	1-1	3-1	-	-	02-01-00
Aston Villa v Man City	1-0	1-1	1-2	0-1	1-3	1-1	03-05-06
Bolton v Stoke	-	-	-	-	-	-	03-02-01
Everton v Blackburn	2-1	0-1	0-1	1-0	1-0	1-1	06-02-06
Hull v Fulham	-	-	-	-	-	-	00-03-01
Middlesboro v Tottenham	5-1	1-0	1-0	3-3	2-3	1-1	05-06-03
Sunderland v Liverpool	2-1	-	-	0-2	-	0-2	01-01-06
West Ham v Wigan	-	4-0	1-3	0-2	0-2	1-1	01-01-03

CHAMPIONSHIP

Barnsley v Coventry	-	-	-	-	0-1	1-4	01-01-02
Bristol C v Derby	-	-	-	-	-	-	00-02-02
Burnley v Ipswich	1-1	4-2	0-2	3-0	1-0	2-2	03-02-01
Doncaster v Cardiff	-	-	-	-	-	-	00-04-02
Norwich v Blackpool	-	-	-	-	-	1-2	00-00-01
Preston v C Palace	1-2	4-1	-	2-0	0-0	0-1	04-01-02
Reading v Plymouth	-	-	0-0	1-2	-	-	02-01-01
Sheff Utd v QPR	-	-	3-2	2-3	-	2-1	04-06-02
Southampton v Birmingham	2-0	0-0	0-0	-	4-3	-	02-02-00
Swansea v Nottm Forest	-	-	-	1-1	0-0	0-0	00-03-00
Watford v Charlton	-	-	-	-	2-2	1-1	03-04-01
Wolves v Sheff Weds	2-2	-	-	1-3	2-2	2-1	02-04-01

LEAGUE 1

Brighton v Bristol R	-	-	-	-	-	0-0	02-01-03
Carlisle v Crewe	-	-	-	-	0-2	1-0	03-00-04
Cheltenham v Swindon	2-0	-	-	-	-	1-1	01-01-00
Colchester v Huddersfield	2-0	-	0-0	1-1	-	-	01-03-00
Hereford v Yeovil	0-0	-	-	-	-	-	00-03-03
Leeds v Oldham	-	-	-	-	-	1-3	03-02-01
Millwall v Southend	-	-	-	-	-	2-1	04-02-01
Milton K v Northampton	-	-	-	-	-	-	00-00-00
Peterboro v Leyton O	-	-	-	1-1	-	-	03-02-02
Stockport v Leicester	-	-	-	-	-	-	00-00-00
Tranmere v Hartlepool	-	0-0	2-1	0-0	-	3-1	03-02-00
Walsall v Scunthorpe	-	-	-	2-2	-	-	04-02-00

LEAGUE 2

Aldershot v Bournemouth	-	-	-	-	-	-	00-00-00
Brentford v Grimsby	-	1-3	-	-	-	0-1	02-00-03
Chester v Wycombe	-	-	0-2	1-0	0-1	2-2	02-01-03
Chesterfield v Bury	-	-	-	-	-	3-1	03-02-03
Exeter v Shrewsbury	1-1	3-2	-	-	-	-	04-03-02
Gillingham v Luton	-	-	-	-	-	2-1	04-00-01
Lincoln v Dagenham & R	-	-	-	-	-	2-0	01-00-00
Macclesfield v Bradford	-	-	-	-	-	0-1	00-00-01
Morecambe v Rotherham	-	-	-	-	-	5-1	01-00-00
Notts Co v Darlington	-	-	1-1	3-2	0-1	0-1	01-02-02
Port Vale v Accrington	-	-	-	-	-	-	00-00-00
Rochdale v Barnet	-	-	-	1-1	0-2	3-0	03-06-03

SCOTTISH PREMIER LEAGUE

Hibernian v Falkirk	-	-	-	2-3	0-1/2-0	1-1	06-04-04
Inv CT v Hamilton	-	-	-	-	-	-	00-00-00

Motherwell v Aberdeen	1-2/0-1/2-3	1-0	0-0/0-1	3-1	0-2/0-2	3-0/2-1	10-13-16
Rangers v Hearts	2-0/1-0	2-1/0-1	3-2/2-1	1-0/2-0	2-0/0-0/2-1	2-1	31-07-02
St Mirren v Kilmarnock	-	-	-	-	0-1/0-2	0-0/1-0	02-01-05

SCOTTISH DIVISION ONE

Airdrie Utd v Dundee	-	-	-	4-0/7-0	0-1/0-3	-	04-05-07
Clyde v Ross County	2-1/1-0	2-2/1-0	1-0/1-0	1-0/2-0	3-0/2-4	-	11-04-01
Morton v Livingston	-	-	-	-	-	2-2/1-1	08-05-04
St Johnstone v Dunfermline	-	-	-	-	-	0-0/1-1	05-07-06

SCOTTISH DIVISION TWO

Alloa v Raith	-	-	-	1-2/1-1	1-2/2-3	2-1/2-0	03-01-06
Ayr v Arbroath	1-0/4-0	-	1-1/2-2	-	-	-	02-03-01
Brechin v Peterhead	-	-	-	-	1-0/3-1	2-2/3-1	05-03-00
East Fife v Queen's Park	1-1/1-0	-	1-4/0-1	1-0/0-1	1-0/1-0	-	09-07-05
Stranraer v Stirling	-	0-1/1-1	0-0/0-3	-	2-1/3-1	-	04-07-06

SCOTTISH DIVISION THREE

Annan Ath v E Stirling	-	-	-	-	-	-	00-00-00
Berwick v Dumbarton	1-2/0-1	1-4/1-2	0-4/0-3	-	3-0/2-1	-	09-03-12
Cowdenbeath v Albion	-	1-4/1-1	2-0/1-2	2-1/2-1	-	-	11-08-06
Forfar v Elgin	-	-	-	-	-	4-0/0-1	01-00-01
Stenhsmuir v Montrose	-	-	1-1/0-1	6-2/5-1	5-0/2-5	0-4/0-0	10-02-08

CONFERENCE

Altrincham v Kettering	-	-	3-3	-	-	-	03-05-03
Burton v Woking 0-2	2-0	0-1	1-1	2-1	2-0	03-01-02	
Cambridge U v Barrow	-	-	-	-	-	-	00-00-00
Forest G v Crawley	-	-	1-1	2-2	1-0	1-0	03-02-00
Grays v Northwich	-	-	-	-	1-0	3-1	02-00-00
Lewes v Salisbury -	-	-	-	1-0	-	01-00-00	
Mansfield v Kidderminster	-	1-0	2-1	-	-	-	03-01-00
Oxford Utd v Eastbourne	-	-	-	-	-	-	00-00-00
Rushden & D v Wrexham	2-2	2-3	-	0-2	-	-	00-01-02
Stevenage v Weymouth	-	-	-	-	1-0	3-0	02-00-00
York v Histon -	-	-	-	1-4	00-00-01		

SUNDAY 17TH AUGUST 2008
PREMIER LEAGUE

| Chelsea v Portsmouth | - | 3-0 | 3-0 | 2-0 | 2-1 | 1-0 | 05-01-00 |
| Man Utd v Newcastle | 5-3 | 0-0 | 2-1 | 2-0 | 2-0 | 6-0 | 11-05-00 |

SCOTTISH PREMIER LEAGUE

| Dundee Utd v Celtic | 0-2 | 1-5 | 0-3/2-3 | 2-4 | 1-4/1-1 | 0-2/0-2 | 08-06-20 |

SCOTTISH DIVISION ONE

| Queen of Sth v Partick | - | - | 1-0/3-1 | - | 0-2/4-3 | 1-2/2-0 | 04-03-07 |

MONDAY 18TH AUGUST 2008
CONFERENCE

| Torquay v Ebbsfleet U | - | - | - | - | - | 3-1 | 01-00-00 |

THURSDAY 21ST AUGUST 2008
CONFERENCE

| Wrexham v Oxford Utd | 1-0 | - | - | 1-1 | - | - | 05-01-00 |

FRIDAY 22ND AUGUST 2008
LEAGUE 1

Southend v Brighton	-	-	-	-	-	2-0	05-00-00

SATURDAY 23RD AUGUST 2008
PREMIER LEAGUE

Blackburn v Hull	-	-	-	-	-	-	02-01-00
Fulham v Arsenal	0-1	0-1	0-3	0-4	2-1	0-3	01-00-06
Liverpool v Middlesboro	1-1	2-0	1-1	2-0	2-0	3-2	10-04-00
Newcastle v Bolton	1-0	0-0	2-1	3-1	1-2	0-0	06-02-01
Stoke v Aston Villa	-	-	-	-	-	-	00-00-00
Tottenham v Sunderland	4-1	-	-	3-2	-	2-0	07-01-00
WBA v Everton	1-2	-	1-0	4-0	-	-	02-00-01

CHAMPIONSHIP

Birmingham v Barnsley	-	-	-	-	2-0	-	05-03-02
Blackpool v Sheff Utd	-	-	-	-	-	2-2	00-01-01
Cardiff v Norwich	-	2-1	-	0-1	1-0	1-2	02-00-02
Charlton v Reading	-	-	-	-	0-0	-	03-01-01
Coventry v Bristol C	-	-	-	-	-	0-3	00-00-01
Crystal Pal v Burnley	1-1	0-0	-	2-0	2-2	5-0	02-03-02
Derby v Southampton	-	-	-	2-2	2-2	-	05-05-01
Ipswich v Wolves	2-4	-	2-1	1-1	0-1	3-0	06-03-04
Nottm Forest v Watford	0-1	1-1	1-2	-	-	-	01-02-03
Plymouth v Swansea	-	-	-	-	-	-	04-00-02
QPR v Doncaster	-	-	-	-	-	-	00-00-00
Sheff Weds v Preston	0-1	-	-	2-0	1-3	2-1	02-00-04

LEAGUE 1

Bristol R v Hereford	-	-	-	-	2-1	-	01-00-00
Crewe v Walsall	-	1-0	-	-	-	0-0	05-01-04
Hartlepool v Stockport	-	2-2	3-1	-	1-1	-	05-03-01
Huddersfield v MK Dons	-	-	3-1	5-0	-	-	02-00-01
Leicester v Tranmere	-	-	-	-	-	-	01-01-02
Leyton O v Carlisle	2-1	1-1	-	0-0	1-1	0-3	05-04-02
Northampton v Millwall	-	-	-	-	3-0	1-1	02-02-01
Oldham v Cheltenham	0-0	-	-	-	0-2	2-1	01-01-01
Scunthorpe v Peterboro	-	-	-	-	-	-	01-03-01
Swindon v Colchester	2-2	2-0	0-3	1-0	-	-	03-02-01
Yeovil v Leeds	-	-	-	-	-	0-1	00-00-01

LEAGUE 2

Accrington v Macclesfield	-	-	-	-	3-2	3-2	02-00-00
Barnet v Brentford	-	-	-	-	-	1-2	00-01-02
Bournemouth v Exeter	2-0	-	-	-	-	-	03-01-01
Bradford v Rochdale	-	-	-	-	-	1-2	00-00-01
Bury v Morecambe	-	-	-	-	-	2-1	01-00-00
Dagenham & R v Port Vale	-	-	-	-	-	-	00-00-00
Darlington v Gillingham	-	-	-	-	-	-	03-02-00
Grimsby v Chesterfield	-	4-0	-	-	-	4-2	02-01-01
Luton v Notts Co	2-2	2-0	-	-	-	-	04-04-02
Rotherham v Chester	-	-	-	-	-	1-1	05-02-01
Shrewsbury v Aldershot	-	1-2	-	-	-	-	00-00-01
Wycombe v Lincoln	-	-	1-0	0-3	1-3	1-0	03-00-03

SCOTTISH PREMIER LEAGUE

Aberdeen v Rangers	2-2	2-3/1-1	0-0/1-2/1-3	3-2/2-0	1-2/2-0	1-1/2-0	11-12-17
Celtic v Falkirk	-	-	-	3-1/2-1	1-0	4-0	11-00-01
Hearts v St Mirren	-	-	-	-	0-1/1-1	0-1/3-2	06-05-03
Inv CT v Hibernian	-	-	1-2/3-0	2-0	0-0/3-0	2-0	04-01-01
Kilmarnock v Hamilton	-	-	-	-	-	-	03-01-02
Motherwell v Dundee Utd	1-2/2-2	3-1/0-1	4-2/2-0	4-5/2-0/1-1	2-3	5-3/2-2	16-08-13

SCOTTISH DIVISION ONE

Dundee v Morton	-	-	-	-	-	2-1/2-0	07-03-02
Dunfermline v Airdrie Utd	-	-	-	-	-	-	05-06-01
Livingston v Clyde	-	-	-	-	1-1/0-0	4-2/0-0	08-07-04
Partick v St Johnstone	-	-	0-4/0-4	-	1-5/2-0	2-2/0-0	04-04-07
Ross County v Queen of Sth	2-0/0-3	1-0/1-2	1-0/1-1	1-1/3-1	1-0/1-0	-	07-03-02

SCOTTISH DIVISION TWO

Arbroath v East Fife	-	0-1/0-0	-	1-0/2-1	1-1/1-3	2-3/0-1	06-04-09
Peterhead v Alloa	-	-	-	3-1/3-0	1-2/0-0	1-4/2-2	02-02-02
Queen's Park v Brechin	-	-	-	-	-	3-0/2-3	04-04-08
Raith v Stranraer	1-1/3-0	-	-	-	1-1/0-0	-	04-04-00
Stirling v Ayr	-	-	1-1/2-0	3-3/1-0	1-3/4-2	-	06-07-03

SCOTTISH DIVISION THREE

Albion v Berwick	-	-	-	0-2/0-1	0-1/0-1	-	05-04-09
Dumbarton v Stenhsmuir	0-0/3-1	0-1/4-0	-	-	4-0/1-1	1-2/1-0	09-04-07
E Stirling v Forfar	-	-	-	-	-	2-1/4-1	05-00-06
Elgin v Cowdenbeath	-	0-4/0-0	0-4/2-0	0-3/0-4	-	-	01-01-06
Montrose v Annan Ath	-	-	-	-	-	-	00-00-00

CONFERENCE

Barrow v Mansfield	-	-	-	-	-	-	00-00-00
Crawley v Torquay	-	-	-	-	-	2-3	00-00-01
Eastbourne v Cambridge U	-	-	-	-	-	-	00-00-00
Ebbsfleet U v Stevenage	2-1	2-3	2-1	0-2	1-1	0-1	02-01-03
Histon v Burton	-	-	-	-	-	2-2	00-01-00
Kettering v Rushden & D	-	-	-	-	-	-	00-02-03
Kidderminstr v Altrincham	-	-	-	1-1	3-2	1-1	02-06-05
Northwich v York	-	-	3-0	-	1-2	0-1	01-00-02
Salisbury v Grays	-	-	-	-	-	0-1	00-00-01
Weymouth v Lewes	-	-	3-3	2-0	-	-	01-01-00
Woking v Forest G	1-0	1-1	0-1	2-1	3-3	1-1	04-04-02

SUNDAY 24TH AUGUST 2008
PREMIER LEAGUE

Man City v West Ham	0-1	-	-	2-1	2-0	1-1	06-02-01
Wigan v Chelsea	-	-	-	0-1	2-3	0-2	00-00-03

MONDAY 25TH AUGUST 2008
PREMIER LEAGUE

Portsmouth v Man Utd	-	1-0	2-0	1-3	2-1	1-1	03-01-01

CONFERENCE

Altrincham v Wrexham	-	-	-	-	-	-	00-00-00
Burton v Kidderminster	-	-	-	1-0	1-1	0-2	01-01-01

Sponsored by Stan James

Cambridge U v Kettering	-	-	-	-	-	-	00-00-00
Forest G v Weymouth	-	-	-	-	3-2	3-2	02-00-00
Grays v Eastbourne	-	-	1-1	-	-	-	00-01-00
Lewes v Ebbsfleet U	-	-	-	-	-	-	00-00-00
Mansfield v Northwich	-	-	-	-	-	-	00-00-00
Oxford Utd v Woking	-	-	-	-	0-0	0-0	00-02-00
Rushden & D v Histon	-	-	-	-	-	2-3	00-00-01
Stevenage v Crawley	-	-	1-0	2-1	2-3	3-1	03-00-01
Torquay v Salisbury	-	-	-	-	-	4-0	01-00-00
York v Barrow	-	-	-	-	-	-	00-00-00

THURSDAY 28TH AUGUST 2008
CONFERENCE

Torquay v York	3-1	1-1	-	-	-	0-0	04-05-01

SATURDAY 30TH AUGUST 2008
PREMIER LEAGUE

Arsenal v Newcastle	1-0	3-2	1-0	2-0	1-1	3-0	11-02-03
Bolton v WBA	1-1	-	1-1	2-0	-	-	05-04-02
Everton v Portsmouth	-	1-0	2-1	0-1	3-0	3-1	04-00-01
Hull v Wigan	-	-	-	-	-	-	00-03-00
Man Utd v Fulham	3-0	1-3	1-0	4-2	5-1	2-0	06-00-01
Middlesboro v Stoke	-	-	-	-	-	-	01-00-03
Sunderland v Man City	0-3	-	-	1-2	-	1-2	02-01-04
West Ham v Blackburn	2-1	-	-	3-1	2-1	2-1	10-02-01

CHAMPIONSHIP

Barnsley v Derby	-	-	-	-	1-2	-	03-01-03
Bristol C v QPR	1-3	1-0	-	-	-	2-2	02-02-01
Burnley v Plymouth	-	-	2-0	1-0	4-0	1-0	07-01-00
Doncaster v Coventry	-	-	-	-	-	-	00-00-00
Norwich v Birmingham	-	-	1-0	-	1-0	-	04-02-03
Preston v Charlton	-	-	-	-	-	0-2	00-00-01
Reading v C Palace	2-1	0-3	-	3-2	-	-	02 00-03
Sheff Utd v Cardiff	-	5-3	2-1	0-0	-	3-3	02-02-01
Southampton v Blackpool	-	-	-	-	-	1-0	01-00-00
Swansea v Sheff Weds	-	-	-	-	-	-	00-00-00
Watford v Ipswich	0-2	1-2	2-2	2-1	-	2-0	04-03-04
Wolves v Nottm Forest	2-1	-	2-1	-	-	-	06-01-00

LEAGUE 1

Brighton v Leyton O	-	-	-	-	4-1	1-1	04-02-04
Carlisle v Yeovil	-	2-0	-	-	1-4	2-1	02-00-01
Cheltenham v Leicester	-	-	-	-	-	-	00-00-00
Colchester v Oldham	0-1	2-1	0-0	0-0	-	-	02-04-02
Hereford v Crewe	-	-	-	-	-	-	00-00-04
Leeds v Bristol R	-	-	-	-	-	1-0	01-00-00
Millwall v Huddersfield	-	-	-	-	0-0	1-2	00-02-01
Milton K v Swindon	-	-	1-1	3-1	0-1	-	02-01-01
Peterboro v Hartlepool	-	3-4	3-0	-	3-5	-	03-03-04
Stockport v Scunthorpe	-	-	-	-	-	-	02-00-01
Tranmere v Northampton	4-0	-	-	-	1-1	2-2	02-03-00
Walsall v Southend	-	-	-	2-2	-	0-2	01-01-01

LEAGUE 2

Aldershot v Bradford	-	-		-	-	-	00-00-00
Brentford v Rotherham	-	-	-	2-1	0-1	1-1	04-03-04
Chester v Barnet	1-1	1-0	-	0-0	2-0	3-0	06-02-03
Chesterfield v Wycombe	4-0	2-2	-	-	-	2-0	06-01-03
Exeter v Luton	-	-	-	-	-	-	00-01-00
Gillingham v Accrington	-	-	-	-	-	-	00-00-00
Lincoln v Grimsby	-	-	0-0	5-0	2-0	1-2	02-03-01
Macclesfield v Darlington	1-0	0-1	1-0	1-0	1-1	0-0	05-05-01
Morecambe v Dagenham & R	2-1	3-2	1-0	2-0	1-1	1-0	05-03-01
Notts Co v Shrewsbury	-	-	3-0	2-1	1-1	2-1	04-03-01
Port Vale v Bournemouth	-	2-1	2-1	0-0	2-1	1-3	06-03-01
Rochdale v Bury	1-2	0-0	0-3	1-1	1-3	1-2	01-03-06

SCOTTISH PREMIER LEAGUE

Dundee Utd v Kilmarnock	1-2/2-2	1-1/4-1	3-0/1-1	0-0/2-2	1-0	2-0	05-12-08
Falkirk v Inv CT	1-1/2-3	2-1/2-1	-	0-2/1-4	3-1/1-0	1-0/2-1	07-04-05
Hamilton v Hearts	-	-	-	-	-	-	00-00-02
Hibernian v Motherwell	3-1/1-0	0-2/3-3	1-0	2-1	3-1/2-0	1-0/0-2	19-13-04
St Mirren v Aberdeen	-	-	-	-	1-1/0-2	0-1	03-02-08

SCOTTISH DIVISION ONE

Airdrie Utd v Morton	-	1-6/2-0	-	-	-	-	10-05-06
Dunfermline v Livingston	2-1/2-0	2-2	0-0	0-1/3-2	-	0-4/1-1	08-04-04
Partick v Ross County	-	-	4-0/0-0	-	3-2/1-1	-	03-04-01
St Johnstone v Clyde	0-1/1-2	3-0/1-3	3-0/0-0	0-0/1-0	0-0/2-1	1-1/1-2	05-06-04

SCOTTISH DIVISION TWO

Alloa v Stranraer	-	-	1-2/3-0	-	1-1/1-0	-	05-07-03
Arbroath v Stirling	-	-	2-1/3-2	-	-	-	07-01-05
Ayr v Queen's Park	-	-	-	-	-	2-3/3-1	01-00-01
East Fife v Brechin	-	-	-	-	-	-	10-03-03
Peterhead v Raith	-	-	-	0-1/0-0	0-1/0-0	0-1/1-0	01-02-03

SCOTTISH DIVISION THREE

Annan Ath v Albion	-	-	-	-	-	-	00-00-00
Berwick v Forfar	2-1/0-0	0-4/3-1	1-0/1-1	-	-	-	08-06-03
Dumbarton v E Stirling	-	-	-	-	2-0/2-1	3-1/1-0	13-03-04
Montrose v Elgin	1-0/2-0	3-3/4-3	2-0/2-0	2-0/1-3	2-0/0-1	0-0/3-2	10-03-03
Stenhsmuir v Cowdenbeath	4-1/1-1	-	2-2/1-1	2-0/1-2	-	-	05-06-06

CONFERENCE

Barrow v Stevenage	-	-	-	-	-	-	00-00-01
Burton v Lewes	-	-	-	-	-	-	00-00-00
Crawley v Northwich	-	-	0-0	-	0-2	2-1	01-01-01
Eastbourne v Altrincham	-	-	-	-	-	-	00-00-00
Ebbsfleet U v Oxford Utd	-	-	-	-	1-0	1-3	01-00-01
Histon v Forest G	-	-	-	-	-	2-2	00-01-00
Kettering v Woking	0-3	-	-	-	-	-	04-02-04
Kidderminstr v Rushden & D	0-2	-	0-0	-	0-0	2-0	04-03-02
Mansfield v Grays	-	-	-	-	-	-	00-00-00
Salisbury v Wrexham	-	-	-	-	-	-	00-00-00
Weymouth v Cambridge U	-	-	-	-	2-1	2-2	01-01-00

SUNDAY 31ST AUGUST 2008
PREMIER LEAGUE

Aston Villa v Liverpool	0-1	0-0	1-1	0-2	0-0	1-2	06-07-07
Chelsea v Tottenham	1-1	4-2	0-0	2-1	1-0	2-0	13-05-01

SCOTTISH PREMIER LEAGUE

Celtic v Rangers	3-3/1-0	3-0/1-0	1-0/0-2	3-0/0-0	2-0/0-1	2-1/3-2	17-08-15

SCOTTISH DIVISION ONE

Queen of Sth v Dundee	-	-	-	0-0/1-3	2-0/2-2	2-1/1-0	03-02-01

TUESDAY 2ND SEPTEMBER 2008
CONFERENCE

Barrow v Rushden & D	-	-	-	-	-	-	00-00-01
Crawley v Grays	-	-	-	1-3	0-1	2-1	01-00-02
Eastbourne v Forest G	-	-	-	-	-	-	00-00-00
Ebbsfleet U v Cambridge U	-	-	-	0-0	2-0	2-1	02-01-00
Histon v Altrincham	-	-	-	-	-	1-0	01-00-00
Kettering v Stevenage	1-0	-	-	-	-	-	03-00-05
Kidderminstr v Torquay	2-0	1-2	-	-	-	2-5	03-00-02
Northwich v Oxford Utd	-	-	-	-	1-0	1-0	02-00-00
Salisbury v Weymouth	-	-	-	-	-	1-1	02-02-01
Woking v Lewes	-	-	-	-	-	-	00-00-00
Wrexham v Burton	-	-	-	-	-	-	00-00-00
York v Mansfield	-	1-2	-	-	-	-	02-00-03

FRIDAY 5TH SEPTEMBER 2008
LEAGUE 1

Hereford v Swindon	-	-	-	-	0-0	-	00-01-00

SATURDAY 6TH SEPTEMBER 2008
LEAGUE 1

Brighton v Scunthorpe	-	-	-	-	1-1	-	01-03-01
Carlisle v Southend	1-0	1-2	-	-	-	1-2	05-02-02
Cheltenham v Huddersfield	1-0	1-1	-	-	2-1	0-2	02-01-01
Colchester v Leicester	-	-	-	-	1-1	1-1	00-02-00
Leeds v Crewe	-	-	0-2	1-0	-	1-1	01-01-01
Millwall v Hartlepool	-	-	-	-	-	0-1	00-00-01
Milton K v Yeovil	-	-	-	1-1	-	-	00-01-00
Peterboro v Bristol R	-	-	-	1-2	4-1	-	01-04-02
Stockport v Northampton	4-0	-	-	4-2	-	-	03-00-00
Tranmere v Oldham	1-2	2-1	2-0	4-0	1-0	0-1	06-02-02
Walsall v Leyton O	-	-	-	-	-	0-0	00-01-01

LEAGUE 2

Aldershot v Darlington	-	-	-	-	-	-	00-00-00
Brentford v Dagenham & R	-	-	-	-	-	2-3	00-00-01
Chester v Bury	-	-	2-1	1-1	1-0	2-1	07-02-01
Chesterfield v Rotherham	-	-	-	0-1	2-1	0-2	02-02-02
Exeter v Accrington	-	3-2	1-2	1-3	-	-	01-00-02
Gillingham v Grimsby	3-0	-	-	-	-	-	03-00-02
Lincoln v Barnet	-	-	-	4-1	1-0	4-1	07-01-03
Macclesfield v Luton	-	-	-	-	-	-	01-01-00

Morecambe v Shrewsbury	-	3-3	-	-	-	1-1	00-02-00
Notts Co v Bournemouth	-	0-1	-	-	-	-	03-00-04
Port Vale v Bradford	-	-	0-1	0-1	0-1	-	01-04-04
Rochdale v Wycombe	-	-	1-1	1-2	0-2	0-1	00-02-03

CONFERENCE

Altrincham v Salisbury	-	-	-	-	-	3-1	01-00-00
Cambridge U v Wrexham	2-2	-	-	-	-	-	01-03-04
Forest G v Ebbsfleet U	2-1	1-2	1-5	0-0	0-1	2-2	01-02-03
Grays v Kidderminster	-	-	-	2-2	3-0	5-1	02-01-00
Lewes v Barrow	-	-	-	-	-	-	00-00-00
Mansfield v Eastbourne	-	-	-	-	-	-	00-00-00
Oxford Utd v Kettering	-	-	-	-	-	-	00-00-00
Rushden & D v Crawley	-	-	-	-	1-1	1-1	03-02-00
Stevenage v Burton	0-1	1-0	0-1	2-3	2-1	3-3	02-01-03
Torquay v Northwich	-	-	-	-	-	1-0	01-00-00
Weymouth v Histon	-	-	-	1-0	-	0-1	01-00-01
York v Woking	-	-	0-2	2-1	0-1	2-3	01-00-03

FRIDAY 12TH SEPTEMBER 2008
LEAGUE 1

Hartlepool v Cheltenham	-	-	-	-	-	0-2	00-01-03

SATURDAY 13TH SEPTEMBER 2008
PREMIER LEAGUE

Blackburn v Arsenal	2-0	0-2	0-1	1-0	0-2	1-1	04-03-07
Fulham v Bolton	4-1	2-1	2-0	2-1	1-1	2-1	06-06-02
Liverpool v Man Utd	1-2	1-2	0-1	0-0	0-1	0-1	07-04-09
Man City v Chelsea	0-3	0-1	1-0	0-1	0-1	0-2	02-03-10
Newcastle v Hull	-	-	-	-	-	-	01-00-01
Portsmouth v Middlesboro	-	5-1	2-1	1-0	0-0	0-1	06-03-02
WBA v West Ham	1-2	1-1	-	0-1	-	-	00-02-03
Wigan v Sunderland	-	0-0	0-1	1-0	-	3-0	02-01-01

CHAMPIONSHIP

Birmingham v Doncaster	-	-	-	-	-	-	00-00-00
Blackpool v Barnsley	1-2	0-2	0-2	1-1	-	1-1	00-02-03
Cardiff v Bristol C	0-2	-	-	-	-	2-1	01-02-03
Charlton v Wolves	-	2-0	-	-	-	2-3	05-02-04
Coventry v Preston	1-2	4-1	1-1	0-1	0-4	2-1	02-02-03
Crystal Pal v Swansea	-	-	-	-	-	-	00-00-00
Derby v Sheff Utd	2-1	2-0	0-1	0-1	-	-	03-01-03
Ipswich v Reading	3-1	1-1	1-1	0-3	-	-	03-02-02
Nottm Forest v Burnley	2-0	1-1	1-0	-	-	-	04-01-00
Plymouth v Norwich	-	-	-	1-1	3-1	3-0	02-01-00
QPR v Southampton	-	-	-	1-0	0-2	0-3	05-02-04
Sheff Weds v Watford	2-2	-	-	1-1	-	0-1	02-03-02

LEAGUE 1

Bristol R v Walsall	-	-	-	-	1-2	1-1	03-02-03
Crewe v Colchester	2-0	-	-	-	-	-	04-00-00
Huddersfield v Tranmere	1-2	-	1-3	1-0	2-2	1-0	09-02-03
Leicester v Millwall	4-1	-	3-1	1-1	-	-	05-02-01
Leyton O v Stockport	-	-	-	2-2	-	-	01-03-02
Northampton v Peterboro	0-1	-	-	0-1	-	-	01-01-04

186   *Sponsored by Stan James*

Oldham v MK Dons	-	-	3-0	1-2	-	-	02-01-02
Scunthorpe v Carlisle	3-1	2-3	-	-	3-0	-	08-03-03
Southend v Hereford	-	-	-	-	-	-	01-00-00
Swindon v Leeds	-	-	-	-	-	0-1	01-01-02
Yeovil v Brighton	-	-	-	-	2-0	2-1	02-00-00

LEAGUE 2

Accrington v Notts Co	-	-	-	-	1-2	0-2	00-00-02
Barnet v Morecambe	1-1	2-1	5-1	-	-	0-1	03-01-01
Bournemouth v Macclesfield	2-2	-	-	-	-	-	01-01-00
Bradford v Exeter	-	-	-	-	-	-	03-01-00
Bury v Lincoln	2-0	2-1	0-1	1-1	2-2	1-1	05-03-02
Dagenham & R v Chesterfield	-	-	-	-	-	0-3	00-00-01
Darlington v Port Vale	-	-	-	-	-	-	00-00-00
Grimsby v Chester	-	-	1-0	1-0	0-2	1-2	03-00-02
Luton v Aldershot	-	-	-	-	-	-	00-00-00
Rotherham v Rochdale	-	-	-	-	-	2-4	02-02-02
Shrewsbury v Gillingham	-	-	-	-	-	-	01-01-01
Wycombe v Brentford	4-0	1-2	-	-	-	1-0	06-02-02

SCOTTISH PREMIER LEAGUE

Aberdeen v Hamilton	-	-	-	-	-	-	01-01-00
Falkirk v Hearts	-	-	-	2-2/1-2	1-1	2-1/2-1	07-02-04
Hibernian v Dundee Utd	2-1/1-1	2-2	2-0/3-2	2-1/3-1	2-1	2-2	20-07-05
Inv CT v St Mirren	4-1/3-1	2-0/1-1	-	-	1-2/2-1	1-0/0-0	07-03-02
Motherwell v Celtic	2-1/0-4	0-2/1-1	2-3/2-1	4-4/1-3	1-1	1-4/1-2	08-14-16
Rangers v Kilmarnock	6-1/4-0	4-0/2-0	2-0/2-1	3-0/4-0	3-0/0-1	2-0	23-01-05

SCOTTISH DIVISION ONE

Clyde v Partick	-	-	2-1/1-1	-	0-0/2-0	1-2/1-4	08-04-05
Dundee v Dunfermline	2-3/2-2	0-2/0-1	1-2/2-1	-	-	1-1/0-0	05-06-08
Morton v Queen of Sth	-	-	-	-	-	0-1/0-3	01-03-03
Livingston v Airdrie Utd	-	-	-	-	3-0/1-3	-	06-01-04
Ross County v St Johnstone	0-0/2-3	0-3/2-0	0-1/4-0	2-1/2-2	2-2/1-1	-	03-04-03

SCOTTISH DIVISION TWO

Brechin v Arbroath	-	-	4-1/4-3	-	-	-	05-03-02
Queen's Park v Peterhead	2-0/1-2	0-2/1-0	1-2/1-1	-	-	1-1/2-0	04-02-04
Raith v East Fife	-	-	-	-	-	-	00-00-00
Stirling v Alloa	-	-	2-0/0-4	1-2/0-0	5-0/4-0	-	06-03-04
Stranraer v Ayr	-	-	2-1/1-3	-	1-3/0-3	-	04-01-07

SCOTTISH DIVISION THREE

Albion v Dumbarton	-	-	-	-	2-1/0-1	2-0/0-1	07-03-09
Cowdenbeath v Berwick	1-2/0-1	-	-	0-1/1-1	-	3-1/1-2	07-05-10
E Stirling v Stenhsmuir	-	-	3-2/1-4	0-0/0-7	5-0/0-1	1-1/3-4	04-06-09
Elgin v Annan Ath	-	-	-	-	-	-	00-00-00
Forfar v Montrose	-	-	-	-	-	1-4/1-1	06-04-05

CONFERENCE

Burton v Weymouth	-	-	-	-	1-1	2-1	06-01-01
Cambridge U v Torquay	0-1	1-1	-	-	-	2-0	05-03-01
Crawley v Mansfield	-	-	-	-	-	-	00-00-00
Eastbourne v Histon	-	-	-	1-1	1-1	-	00-02-00
Kettering v York	-	-	-	-	-	-	00-00-00
Kidderminstr v Oxford Utd	1-3	1-1	1-3	-	0-0	0-2	00-03-03

Lewes v Rushden & D	-	-	-	-	-	-	00-00-00
Northwich v Forest G	2-1	0-4	2-1	-	2-0	1-1	04-04-01
Salisbury v Barrow	-	-	-	-	-	-	00-00-00
Stevenage v Altrincham	-	-	-	3-0	0-1	2-1	04-02-01
Woking v Grays	-	-	-	1-1	1-0	0-1	02-02-01
Wrexham v Ebbsfleet U	-	-	-	-	-	-	00-00-00

SUNDAY 14TH SEPTEMBER 2008
PREMIER LEAGUE

Stoke v Everton	-	-	-	-	-	-	00-00-00

MONDAY 15TH SEPTEMBER 2008
PREMIER LEAGUE

Tottenham v Aston Villa	1-0	2-1	5-1	0-0	2-1	4-4	09-06-05

TUESDAY 16TH SEPTEMBER 2008
CHAMPIONSHIP

Barnsley v Cardiff	3-2	-	-	-	1-2	1-1	01-01-01
Bristol C v Birmingham	-	-	-	-	-	-	03-00-01
Burnley v Blackpool	-	-	-	-	-	2-2	05-03-02
Doncaster v Charlton	-	-	-	-	-	-	00-00-00
Norwich v QPR	-	-	-	3-2	1-0	3-0	10-03-02
Preston v Nottm Forest	1-1	2-2	3-2	-	-	-	02-03-00
Reading v Sheff Weds	2-1	-	-	2-0	-	-	02-00-00
Sheff Utd v Coventry	0-0	2-1	1-1	2-1	-	2-1	03-04-03
Southampton v Ipswich	-	-	-	0-2	1-0	1-1	03-02-03
Swansea v Derby	-	-	-	-	-	-	00-00-00
Watford v Plymouth	-	-	3-1	1-1	-	0-1	04-02-03
Wolves v C Palace	4-0	-	-	2-1	1-1	0-3	04-02-05

SATURDAY 20TH SEPTEMBER 2008
PREMIER LEAGUE

Blackburn v Fulham	2-1	0-2	1-3	2-1	2-0	1-1	05-01-03
Bolton v Arsenal	2-2	1-1	1-0	2-0	3-1	2-3	04-02-03
Hull v Everton	-	-	-	-	-	-	00-00-00
Liverpool v Stoke	-	-	-	-	-	-	00-00-00
Man City v Portsmouth	-	1-1	2-0	2-1	0-0	3-1	06-04-00
Sunderland v Middlesboro	1-3	-	-	0-3	-	3-2	05-02-05
West Ham v Newcastle	2-2	-	-	2-4	0-2	2-2	06-06-05

CHAMPIONSHIP

Birmingham v Blackpool	-	-	-	-	-	-	02-00-00
Bristol C v Doncaster	-	-	2-2	0-0	1-0	-	01-02-00
Coventry v QPR	-	-	1-2	3-0	0-1	0-0	03-03-06
Crystal Pal v Plymouth	-	-	-	1-0	0-1	2-1	03-00-01
Derby v Cardiff	-	2-2	0-1	2-1	3-1	-	02-01-01
Norwich v Sheff Utd	2-3	1-0	-	2-1	-	1-0	09-04-02
Nottm Forest v Charlton	-	-	-	-	-	-	03-02-01
Preston v Wolves	0-2	-	2-2	2-0	0-1	2-1	03-02-03
Sheff Weds v Ipswich	0-1	-	-	0-1	2-0	1-2	03-02-03
Southampton v Barnsley	-	-	-	-	5-2	2-3	02-00-01
Swansea v Burnley	-	-	-	-	-	-	01-01-01
Watford v Reading	0-3	1-0	0-1	0-0	0-0	-	02-03-02

LEAGUE 1

Brighton v Walsall	0-2	-	-	-	-	1-1	00-02-02
Carlisle v Leeds	-	-	-	-	-	3-1	01 00 00
Colchester v MK Dons	-	-	0-1	2-0	-	-	01-00-01
Crewe v Southend	-	-	-	-	-	1-3	00-00-02
Hartlepool v Oldham	-	0-0	2-1	1-1	-	4-1	02-02-00
Hereford v Scunthorpe	-	-	-	-	-	-	04-01-04
Huddersfield v Northampton	2-0	3-0	-	-	1-1	1-2	03-02-02
Leyton O v Leicester	-	-	-	-	-	-	00-00-00
Millwall v Cheltenham	-	-	-	-	2-0	1-0	02-00-00
Peterboro v Tranmere	0-0	0-0	1-0	-	-	-	02-05-00
Stockport v Swindon	2-5	2-4	3-3	-	3-0	-	04-02-02
Yeovil v Bristol R	-	4-0	4-2	-	-	0-0	02-01-00

LEAGUE 2

Aldershot v Gillingham	-	-	-	-	-	-	00-00-00
Barnet v Bury	-	-	-	1-1	2-1	3-0	03-03-00
Bradford v Bournemouth	-	-	4-2	1-2	0-0	-	05-02-04
Brentford v Lincoln	-	-	-	-	-	1-0	01-00-00
Darlington v Accrington	-	-	-	-	2-1	1-0	02-00-00
Exeter v Notts Co	-	-	-	-	-	-	00-00-01
Morecambe v Grimsby	-	-	-	-	-	0-4	00-00-01
Port Vale v Macclesfield	-	-	-	-	-	-	00-00-00
Rochdale v Chesterfield	-	-	-	-	-	0-1	05-02-01
Rotherham v Luton	-	-	-	-	-	-	00-01-01
Wycombe v Dagenham & R	-	-	-	-	-	0-1	01-00-01

SCOTTISH PREMIER LEAGUE

Aberdeen v Dundee Utd	1-2/3-0	0-1/3-0	1-0	2-0	3-1/2-4	2-0/2-1	19-06-11
Hamilton v Hibernian	-	-	-	-	-	-	00-01-03
Hearts v Inv CT	-	-	1-0/0-2	0-0	4-1/1-0	2-3/1-0	04-01-02
Kilmarnock v Celtic	1-1/0-4	0-5/0-1	2-4/0-1	0-1/1-4	1-2/1-2	1-2	04-08-17
St Mirren v Falkirk	4-4/1-2	0-0/1-1	2-0/0-1	-	1-0	1-5/1-0	08-05-10

SCOTTISH DIVISION ONE

Airdrie Utd v Clyde	-	-	3-1/2-4	1-3/1-1	2-1/1-0	-	07-06-04
Dundee v Livingston	2-1/0-0	2-1/1-0/2-0	0-0/0-1	-	0-1/2-0	4-1/2-0	12-02-03
Dunfermline v Ross County	-	-	-	-	-	-	00-00-00
Partick v Morton	-	-	-	2-0/1-1	-	1-1/0-3	03-05-06
Queen of Sth v St Johnstone	0-0/1-2	1-1/1-1	0-1/2-0	1-3/3-2	0-1/1-0	3-3/3-1	04-05-04

SCOTTISH DIVISION TWO

Alloa v East Fife	-	2-0/1-1	-	-	-	-	04-04-03
Arbroath v Queen's Park	-	-	-	1-1/1-0	1-2/1-0	-	10-12-01
Peterhead v Stranraer	-	1-2/2-0	-	-	5-2/5-0	-	03-00-01
Raith v Stirling	-	-	-	5-2/2-3	1-3/0-1	-	04-01-05

SCOTTISH DIVISION THREE

Annan Ath v Forfar	-	-	-	-	-	-	00-00-00
Dumbarton v Cowdenbeath	1-1/3-1	-	-	-	-	-	08-05-05
Elgin v Albion	0-1/1-2	1-5/1-2	1-0/1-1	2-2/2-1	0-3/3-0	3-2/1-1	06-04-06
Montrose v E Stirling	2-2/5-4	5-1/1-0	4-1/4-1	3-0/2-0	1-0/4-0	3-1/2-0	22-07-05
Stenhsmuir v Berwick	2-0/1-0	0-3/3-1	-	0-1/1-0	2-3/2-0	-	11-08-10

CONFERENCE

Altrincham v Lewes	-	-	-	-	-	-	00-00-00

Barrow v Kettering	-	-	2-1	0-1	0-1	1-1	02-03-03
Ebbsfleet U v Woking	4-2	2-2	1-1	2-0	1-0	1-1	03-03-00
Forest G v Stevenage	0-3	3-1	1-1	2-0	4-4	4-2	04-03-03
Grays v Wrexham	-	-	-	-	-	-	00-00-00
Histon v Northwich	-	-	-	-	-	1-1	00-01-00
Mansfield v Cambridge U	-	1-1	0-0	-	-	-	03-03-01
Oxford Utd v Crawley	-	-	-	-	1-1	1-0	01-01-00
Rushden & D v Burton	-	-	-	-	1-2	0-0	01-03-01
Torquay v Eastbourne	-	-	-	-	-	-	00-00-00
Weymouth v Kidderminster	-	-	-	-	1-1	2-1	02-01-00
York v Salisbury	-	-	-	-	-	1-3	00-00-01

SUNDAY 21ST SEPTEMBER 2008
PREMIER LEAGUE

Chelsea v Man Utd	2-2	1-0	1-0	3-0	0-0	2-1	08-06-05
Tottenham v Wigan	-	-	-	2-2	3-1	4-0	02-01-00
WBA v Aston Villa	0-0	-	1-1	1-2	-	-	00-02-01

LEAGUE 2

Chester v Shrewsbury	-	2-1	1-1	0-1	0-0	3-1	06-04-03

SCOTTISH PREMIER LEAGUE

Rangers v Motherwell	3-0/2-0	1-0/4-0	4-1/4-1	2-0/1-0	1-1	3-1/1-0	33-02-03

SCOTTISH DIVISION TWO

Ayr v Brechin	-	3-2/1-2	0-1/0-1	-	1-2/1-1	2-1/0-3	06-02-05

TUESDAY 23RD SEPTEMBER 2008
CONFERENCE

Altrincham v Mansfield	-	-	-	-	-	-	00-00-00
Ebbsfleet U v Eastbourne	-	-	-	-	-	-	00-00-00
Forest G v Torquay	-	-	-	-	-	2-2	00-01-00
Grays v Stevenage	-	-	-	2-2	0-2	0-2	01-01-03
Histon v Lewes	-	-	-	1-1	3-2	-	01-01-00
Kettering v Burton	1-2	-	-	-	-	-	00-00-01
Kidderminstr v York	1-2	4-1	-	0-0	2-1	3-0	05-01-01
Northwich v Barrow	-	-	-	2-0	-	-	04-01-00
Oxford Utd v Cambridge U	1-1	2-2	2-1	-	1-1	1-2	05-04-01
Weymouth v Crawley	2-0	0-1	-	-	3-2	1-2	05-02-04
Woking v Salisbury	-	-	-	-	-	3-2	01-00-00
Wrexham v Rushden & D	3-0	1-1	-	2-0	-	-	02-01-00

FRIDAY 26TH SEPTEMBER 2008
LEAGUE 1

Southend v Leyton O	1-0	1-2	0-1	-	-	1-2	01-03-05
Tranmere v Colchester	1-1	1-1	1-1	0-0	-	-	00-06-00

SATURDAY 27TH SEPTEMBER 2008
PREMIER LEAGUE

Arsenal v Hull	-	-	-	-	-	-	00-00-00
Aston Villa v Sunderland	1-0	-	-	2-1	-	0-1	04-03-01
Everton v Liverpool	1-2	0-3	1-0	1-3	3-0	1-2	06-06-08
Fulham v West Ham	0-1	-	-	1-2	0-0	0-1	00-01-04
Man Utd v Bolton	0-1	4-0	2-0	4-1	4-1	2-0	06-01-02

190

Middlesboro v WBA	3-0	-	4-0	2-2	-	-	06-02-00
Newcastle v Blackburn	5-1	0-1	3-0	0-1	0-2	0-1	07-05-04
Stoke v Chelsea	-	-	-	-	-	-	00-00-01

CHAMPIONSHIP

Barnsley v Norwich	-	-	-	-	1-3	1-3	03-01-04
Blackpool v Coventry	-	-	-	-	-	4-0	01-00-00
Burnley v Preston	2-0	1-1	2-0	0-2	3-2	2-3	06-02-05
Cardiff v Birmingham	-	-	-	-	2-0	-	01-00-02
Charlton v Sheff Weds	-	-	-	-	-	3-2	02-00-03
Doncaster v Southampton	-	-	-	-	-	-	00-00-00
Ipswich v C Palace	1-2	1-3	-	0-2	1-2	1-0	05-01-06
Plymouth v Nottm Forest	-	-	3-2	-	-	-	01-00-00
QPR v Derby	-	-	0-2	1-1	1-2	-	00-02-04
Reading v Swansea	-	-	-	-	-	-	05-02-00
Sheff Utd v Watford	1-2	2-2	1-1	1-4	1-0	1-1	04-04-04
Wolves v Bristol C	-	-	-	-	-	1-1	05-03-00

LEAGUE 1

Bristol R v Crewe	-	-	-	-	-	1-1	01-03-01
Cheltenham v Stockport	0-2	-	-	3-3	-	-	00-01-01
Leeds v Hereford	-	-	-	-	-	-	00-00-00
Leicester v Hartlepool	-	-	-	-	-	-	00-00-00
Milton K v Peterboro	-	-	1-1	-	0-2	1-1	00-02-01
Northampton v Brighton	-	-	-	-	0-2	1-0	04-00-01
Oldham v Huddersfield	4-0	-	2-1	0-3	1-1	4-1	04-02-02
Scunthorpe v Yeovil	-	3-0	1-0	3-4	1-0	-	03-00-01
Swindon v Millwall	-	-	-	-	-	2-1	03-01-02
Walsall v Carlisle	-	-	-	-	-	1-1	03-03-02

LEAGUE 2

Bournemouth v Darlington	2-0	-	-	-	-	-	01-00-01
Bury v Wycombe	-	-	2-2	2-1	0-4	2-2	03-04-02
Chesterfield v Brentford	0-2	1-2	3-1	1-3	3-1	1-0	04-03-05
Dagenham & R v Rotherham	-	-	-	-	-	0-2	00-00-01
Gillingham v Port Vale	-	-	-	3-0	3-2	1-2	03-00-01
Grimsby v Barnet	-	-	-	3-0	5-0	4-1	03-00-00
Lincoln v Morecambe	-	-	-	-	-	1-1	00-01-00
Luton v Chester	-	-	-	-	-	-	00-00-00
Macclesfield v Exeter	1-1	-	-	-	-	-	01-02-02
Notts Co v Aldershot	-	-	-	-	-	-	00-00-00
Shrewsbury v Bradford	-	-	-	-	-	1-0	03-01-02

SCOTTISH PREMIER LEAGUE

Celtic v Aberdeen	7-0	4-0/1-2	2-3/3-2/2-0	2-0/3-0	1-0/2-1	3-0/1-0	29-04-06
Dundee Utd v Hearts	0-3	2-1/0-2	1-1/2-1	0-3/1-1	0-1	4-1	10-12-12
Falkirk v Hamilton	-	-	1-1/1-1	-	-	-	05-04-02
Hibernian v Rangers	2-4/0-2	0-1	0-1/0-1	2-1/1-2	2-1/0-2/3-3	1-2/0-0	07-08-22
Inv CT v Kilmarnock	-	-	0-2/1-2	2-2/3-3	3-4	3-1/3-0	02-02-03
Motherwell v St Mirren	-	-	-	-	0-0/2-3	1-1	07-04-02

SCOTTISH DIVISION ONE

Clyde v Queen of Sth	2-1/2-2	3-1/2-0	2-0/0-1	1-0/3-0	4-0/0-1	0-0/1-4	18-05-06
Morton v Dunfermline	-	-	-	-	-	0-1/3-0	04-03-04
Livingston v Partick	3-0/3-1	2-0/2-2	-	-	2-2/0-1	0-4/1-0	05-07-04
Ross County v Airdrie Utd	-	-	1-2/3-1	2-2/0-1	2-1/1-1	1-1/3-2	04-04-04
St Johnstone v Dundee	-	-	-	1-1/0-0	2-1/2-0	1-1/1-1	07-10-07

SCOTTISH DIVISION TWO

Brechin v Raith	1-2/1-0	0-3/1-1	-	-	1-0/1-2	0-1/3-2	03-01-05
East Fife v Ayr	-	-	-	-	-	-	01-01-00
Queen's Park v Alloa	-	-	-	-	-	1-0/1-1	08-05-05
Stirling v Peterhead	1-0/2-1	3-1/0-2	-	1-3/2-1	2-0/2-1	-	07-00-03
Stranraer v Arbroath	-	-	2-1/3-3	-	-	1-1/0-3	09-03-05

SCOTTISH DIVISION THREE

Albion v Stenhsmuir	-	-	1-0/1-1	0-2/1-2	2-5/2-1	1-1/3-3	03-06-08
Berwick v Annan Ath	-	-	-	-	-	-	00-00-00
Cowdenbeath v Montrose	-	3-3/0-0	0-0/0-0	2-0/2-0	-	-	09-07-07
E Stirling v Elgin	1-2/2-2	3-1/2-1	0-1/0-3	0-2/0-2	2-1/0-2	3-1/0-0	06-02-08
Forfar v Dumbarton	2-0/0-1	3-1/1-0	0-2/6-0	2-0/2-3	-	3-1/1-1	08-01-03

CONFERENCE

Barrow v Ebbsfleet U	-	-	-	-	-	-	00-00-00
Burton v Forest G	2-3	2-3	4-1	1-0	1-0	1-1	04-01-02
Cambridge U v Grays	-	-	-	1-1	2-0	1-0	02-01-00
Crawley v Kettering	-	-	-	-	-	-	00-00-01
Eastbourne v Kidderminster	-	-	-	-	-	-	00-00-00
Lewes v Oxford Utd	-	-	-	-	-	-	00-00-00
Northwich v Weymouth	-	-	-	-	0-1	2-2	01-01-01
Rushden & D v Altrincham	-	-	-	-	3-0	1-0	04-00-00
Salisbury v Mansfield	-	-	-	-	-	-	00-00-00
Stevenage v York	-	-	2-2	1-1	1-2	3-2	01-02-01
Woking v Histon	-	-	-	-	-	3-3	00-01-00
Wrexham v Torquay	2-1	-	1-1	4-2	1-0	-	06-02-00

SUNDAY 28TH SEPTEMBER 2008
PREMIER LEAGUE

Portsmouth v Tottenham	-	2-0	1-0	0-2	1-1	0-1	02-01-02
Wigan v Man City	-	-	-	4-3	4-0	1-1	02-01-01

LEAGUE 1

Accrington v Rochdale	-	-	-	-	1-1	1-2	00-01-01

TUESDAY 30TH SEPTEMBER 2008
CHAMPIONSHIP

Bristol C v Plymouth	0-0	1-0	-	-	-	1-2	04-02-01
Burnley v Watford	4-7	2-3	3-1	4-1	-	2-2	06-02-02
Cardiff v Coventry	-	0-1	2-1	0-0	1-0	0-1	02-01-02
Crystal Pal v Charlton	-	-	0-1	-	-	0-1	03-01-03
Derby v Birmingham	-	-	-	-	0-1	1-2	01-02-02
Doncaster v Sheff Utd	-	-	-	-	-	-	00-00-00
Ipswich v Barnsley	-	-	-	-	5-1	0-0	06-03-01
Preston v Swansea	-	-	-	-	-	-	02-02-01
QPR v Blackpool	2-1	5-0	-	-	-	3-2	04-00-00
Sheff Weds v Nottm Forest	2-0	-	-	-	-	-	05-00-06
Southampton v Norwich	-	-	4-3	1-0	2-1	0-1	06-03-02
Wolves v Reading	0-1	-	4-1	0-2	-	-	04-01-03

FRIDAY 3RD OCTOBER 2008
LEAGUE 1

Hartlepool v Swindon	-	2-0	3-0	1-1	0-1	1-1	02-02-01

Sponsored by Stan James

SATURDAY 4TH OCTOBER 2008

PREMIER LEAGUE

Blackburn v Man Utd	1-0	1-0	1-1	4-3	0-1	1-1	04-05-05
Chelsea v Aston Villa	2-0	1-0	1-0	2-1	1-1	4-4	10-04-05
Man City v Liverpool	0-3	2-2	1-0	0-1	0-0	0-0	03-07-04
Portsmouth v Stoke	3-0	-	-	-	-	-	03-04-01
Sunderland v Arsenal	0-4	-	-	0-3	-	0-1	02-03-03
Tottenham v Hull	-	-	-	-	-	-	00-00-00
WBA v Fulham	1-0	-	1-1	0-0	-	-	02-03-02
Wigan v Middlesboro	-	-	-	1-1	0-1	1-0	01-01-01

CHAMPIONSHIP

Barnsley v Doncaster	-	-	1-3	0-2	-	-	00-00-02
Birmingham v QPR	-	-	-	-	2-1	-	04-02-00
Blackpool v Cardiff	1-0	-	-	-	-	0-1	07-03-01
Charlton v Ipswich	-	-	-	-	-	3-1	04-03-02
Coventry v Southampton	-	-	-	1-1	2-1	1-1	07-06-03
Norwich v Derby	1-0	2-1	-	2-0	1-2	-	07-00-01
Nottm Forest v C Palace	2-1	3-2	-	-	-	-	07-02-02
Plymouth v Sheff Weds	-	2-0	-	1-1	1-2	1-2	01-02-02
Reading v Burnley	3-0	2-2	0-0	2-1	-	-	04-05-00
Sheff Utd v Bristol C	-	-	-	-	-	2-1	04-00-00
Swansea v Wolves	-	-	-	-	-	-	00-00-01
Watford v Preston	0-1	2-0	0-2	1-2	-	0-0	03-02-04

LEAGUE 1

Brighton v Cheltenham	-	-	-	-	2-1	2-1	04-00-00
Carlisle v Tranmere	-	-	-	-	1-0	0-1	01-01-01
Colchester v Bristol R	-	-	-	-	-	-	02-00-01
Crewe v Northampton	3-3	-	-	-	2-2	1-0	04-03-00
Hereford v Walsall	-	-	-	-	0-1	-	00-02-04
Huddersfield v Leicester	-	-	-	-	-	-	01-00-00
Leyton O v Scunthorpe	2-0	1-1	1-1	-	2-2	-	04-06-01
Millwall v MK Dons	1-1	2-0	-	-	-	-	01-02-02
Peterboro v Leeds	-	-	-	-	-	-	00-00-00
Stockport v Oldham	1-2	1-1	1-2	-	-	-	00-01-02
Yeovil v Southend	-	4-0	3-1	0-2	-	0-3	02-00-02

LEAGUE 2

Aldershot v Bury	-	-	-	-	-	-	00-00-00
Barnet v Accrington	-	0-0	3-0	-	1-2	2-2	01-02-01
Bradford v Luton	-	-	0-1	-	-	-	00-00-01
Brentford v Macclesfield	-	-	-	-	-	1-0	01-00-00
Chester v Lincoln	-	-	0-1	2-2	4-1	1-2	04-02-03
Darlington v Shrewsbury	5-1	-	3-0	0-1	1-2	2-0	06-03-04
Exeter v Gillingham	-	-	-	-	-	-	02-01-00
Morecambe v Chesterfield	-	-	-	-	-	1-1	00-01-00
Port Vale v Notts Co	3-2	1-0	-	-	-	-	04-01-02
Rochdale v Dagenham & R	-	-	-	-	-	1-0	01-00-00
Rotherham v Grimsby	0-1	-	-	-	-	2-1	02-01-02
Wycombe v Bournemouth	-	2-0	-	-	-	-	02-04-03

SCOTTISH PREMIER LEAGUE

Aberdeen v Hibernian	0-1	3-1/0-1	0-1/3-0	0-1/1-0/4-0	2-1/2-2	3-1/2-1	20-07-10
Celtic v Hamilton	-	-	-	-	-	-	02-00-00
Dundee Utd v Inv CT	-	-	2-1/1-1	1-1/2-4	3-1/1-1	0-1	02-03-02
Hearts v Kilmarnock	1-1/3-0	2-1	3-0/3-0	1-0/2-0	0-2/1-0	1-1/0-2	16-08-04
St Mirren v Rangers	-	-	-	-	2-3/0-1	0-3	00-02-11

SCOTTISH DIVISION ONE

Clyde v Dunfermline	-	-	-	-	-	2-1/1-2	01-01-03
Partick v Dundee	1-1/1-3	1-2/0-1	-	-	3-1/2-1	1-1/1-0	09-04-07
Queen of Sth v Livingston	-	-	-	-	2-0/1-1	1-0/1-0	05-04-06
Ross County v Morton	-	-	-	-	-	-	01-00-01
St Johnstone v Airdrie Utd	-	-	1-1/1-2	1-0/2-2	1-0/4-3	-	11-06-02

SCOTTISH DIVISION TWO

Arbroath v Raith	-	-	-	-	-	-	00-02-00
Ayr v Peterhead	-	-	-	1-1/1-2	1-2/0-0	1-2/0-3	00-02-04
Brechin v Alloa	-	-	4-0/2-3	-	2-0/2-3	0-0/0-0	06-02-06
East Fife v Stranraer	-	-	-	-	-	3-1/2-1	05-04-06
Queen's Park v Stirling	0-1/3-3	0-2/1-4	-	-	-	-	04-05-03

SCOTTISH DIVISION THREE

Albion v Montrose	1-1/3-0	0-1/3-0	1-2/1-2	1-1/1-1	3-1/2-2	1-3/0-3	10-09-13
Berwick v Elgin	-	-	-	3-1/1-1	3-1/0-0	-	02-02-00
Cowdenbeath v E Stirling	-	2-1/2-0	2-1/3-2	5-1/5-0	-	-	18-03-06
Dumbarton v Annan Ath	-	-	-	-	-	-	00-00-00
Stenhsmuir v Forfar	2-1/1-4	2-0/0-2	-	-	-	4-0/2-0	08-03-06

CONFERENCE

Altrincham v Ebbsfleet U	-	-	-	2-2	0-2	1-3	00-01-02
Burton v Crawley	-	-	1-0	3-1	2-1	1-0	13-02-02
Forest G v Wrexham	-	-	-	-	-	-	00-00-00
Grays v Lewes	-	-	4-0	-	-	-	01-00-00
Histon v Salisbury	-	-	-	-	4-2	2-0	02-00-00
Kettering v Northwich	2-2	-	-	2-0	-	-	07-06-02
Kidderminstr v Barrow	-	-	-	-	-	-	01-01-02
Mansfield v Woking	-	-	-	-	-	-	00-00-00
Oxford Utd v Rushden & D	3-0	-	0-0	2-2	0-1	1-0	03-02-01
Torquay v Stevenage	-	-	-	-	-	4-2	01-00-00
Weymouth v Eastbourne	-	1-0	0-1	2-1	-	-	02-00-01
York v Cambridge U	3-1	2-0	-	1-0	1-2	1-2	06-00-03

SUNDAY 5TH OCTOBER 2008
PREMIER LEAGUE

Everton v Newcastle	2-1	2-2	2-0	1-0	3-0	3-1	09-03-04
West Ham v Bolton	1-1	-	-	1-2	3-1	1-1	04-02-01

SCOTTISH PREMIER LEAGUE

Motherwell v Falkirk	-	-	-	5-0/3-1	4-2/3-3	0-3	08-03-02

TUESDAY 7TH OCTOBER 2008
CONFERENCE

Barrow v Burton	-	-	-	-	-	-	00-00-01
Cambridge U v Lewes	-	-	-	-	-	-	00-00-00
Crawley v Forest G	-	-	4-2	1-0	3-1	3-0	04-01-00
Eastbourne v Kettering	-	-	-	-	-	-	00-00-00
Ebbsfleet U v Histon	-	-	-	-	-	0-1	00-00-01
Northwich v Kidderminster	-	-	-	-	0-1	1-1	04-05-05
Rushden & D v Grays	-	-	-	-	1-3	1-1	00-01-01
Salisbury v Altrincham	-	-	-	-	-	3-3	00-01-00
Stevenage v Mansfield	-	-	-	-	-	-	00-00-00
Torquay v Oxford Utd	2-3	3-0	-	3-3	-	3-2	02-02-01
Woking v Weymouth	-	-	-	-	4-0	1-1	01-01-00
Wrexham v York	1-1	-	-	-	-	-	04-05-03

Sponsored by Stan James

FRIDAY 10TH OCTOBER 2008
LEAGUE 1

Northampton v Hartlepool	-	-	-	-	-	1-1	03-03-00

LEAGUE 2

Dagenham & R v Barnet	5-1	5-2	2-0	-	-	1-1	03-02-00
Lincoln v Rochdale	2-0	1-1	1-1	1-1	7-1	2-1	05-08-06

SATURDAY 11TH OCTOBER 2008
LEAGUE 1

Bristol R v Leyton O	1-2	1-1	1-1	3-3	-	2-3	02-05-02
Cheltenham v Colchester	1-1	-	-	-	-	-	00-02-01
Leeds v Brighton	-	-	1-1	3-3	-	0-0	02-03-00
Leicester v Yeovil	-	-	-	-	-	-	00-00-00
Milton K v Carlisle	-	-	-	-	-	-	00-00-00
Scunthorpe v Crewe	-	-	-	-	2-2	-	02-03-00
Southend v Stockport	-	-	-	-	-	-	01-00-00
Swindon v Huddersfield	0-1	-	1-2	0-0	-	3-2	04-02-03
Tranmere v Millwall	-	-	-	-	3-1	2-0	05-02-00
Walsall v Peterboro	-	-	2-1	-	5-0	-	03-02-01

LEAGUE 2

Accrington v Bradford	-	-	-	-	-	0-2	00-00-01
Bournemouth v Rotherham	-	-	-	2-0	1-3	-	03-04-02
Bury v Exeter 1-0	-	-	-	-	-	-	04-01-00
Chesterfield v Chester	-	-	-	-	-	1-1	00-01-02
Gillingham v Morecambe	-	-	-	-	-	-	00-00-00
Grimsby v Wycombe	-	3-1	0-0	0-1	2-2	0-1	01-03-02
Luton v Darlington	-	-	-	-	-	-	01-00-00
Macclesfield v Aldershot	-	-	-	-	-	-	00-00-00
Shrewsbury v Port Vale	-	-	-	-	-	-	00-00-00

CONFERENCE

Altrincham v Oxford Utd	-	-	-	-	0-3	1-3	00-00-02
Burton v Mansfield	-	-	-	-	-	-	00-00-00
Cambridge U v Weymouth	-	-	-	-	7-0	0-0	01-01-00
Crawley v Barrow	-	-	-	-	-	-	00-00-00
Eastbourne v Stevenage	-	-	-	-	-	-	00-00-00
Kidderminstr v Ebbsfleet U	-	-	-	0-2	1-2	2-1	01-00-02
Lewes v Forest G	-	-	-	-	-	-	00-00-00
Northwich v Grays	-	-	-	-	0-3	1-0	01-00-01
Rushden & D v Torquay	3-0	-	-	1-0	-	2-1	03-01-00
Salisbury v Kettering	-	-	-	-	-	-	00-00-01
Woking v York	-	-	1-0	2-0	1-2	0-3	02-00-02
Wrexham v Histon	-	-	-	-	-	-	00-00-00

SUNDAY 12TH OCTOBER 2008
LEAGUE 1

Oldham v Hereford	-	-	-	-	-	-	00-00-00

MONDAY 13TH OCTOBER 2008
LEAGUE 2

Notts Co v Brentford	2-2	2-0	-	-	-	1-1	04-06-01

SATURDAY 18TH OCTOBER 2008

PREMIER LEAGUE

Arsenal v Everton	2-1	2-1	7-0	2-0	1-1	1-0	17-02-01
Aston Villa v Portsmouth	-	2-1	3-0	1-0	0-0	1-3	03-01-01
Bolton v Blackburn	1-1	2-2	0-1	0-0	1-2	1-2	03-04-04
Fulham v Sunderland	1-0	-	-	2-1	-	1-3	03-00-01
Hull v West Ham	-	-	-	-	-	-	00-02-00
Liverpool v Wigan	-	-	-	3-0	2-0	1-1	02-01-00
Man Utd v WBA	1-0	-	1-1	3-0	-	-	02-01-00
Middlesboro v Chelsea	1-1	1-2	0-1	3-0	2-1	0-2	05-03-05

CHAMPIONSHIP

Bristol C v Norwich	-	-	-	-	-	2-1	02-00-00
Burnley v Birmingham	-	-	-	-	1-2	-	00-01-02
Cardiff v Charlton	-	-	-	-	-	0-2	00-00-01
Crystal Pal v Barnsley	-	-	-	-	2-0	2-0	07-02-02
Derby v Plymouth	-	-	1-0	1-0	1-0	-	04-00-00
Doncaster v Blackpool	-	-	2-0	0-1	0-0	-	02-01-02
Ipswich v Swansea	-	-	-	-	-.	-	00-00-00
Preston v Reading	1-0	2-1	3-0	0-3	-	-	07-02-02
QPR v Nottm Forest	-	-	2-1	-	-	-	04-03-04
Southampton v Watford	-	-	-	1-3	-	0-3	01-00-02
Wolves v Coventry	0-2	-	0-1	2-2	1-0	1-0	03-01-02

LEAGUE 1

Brighton v Hereford	-	-	-	-	-	-	00-00-01
Carlisle v Peterboro	-	-	-	1-0	-	-	02-05-00
Cheltenham v Scunthorpe	-	2-1	0-2	-	1-1	-	02-02-01
Crewe v MK Dons	-	1-0	-	-	-	-	01-00-02
Huddersfield v Bristol R	-	2-1	-	-	-	2-1	03-02-01
Leyton O v Tranmere	-	-	-	-	3-1	3-0	04-00-01
Millwall v Leeds	-	-	1-1	0-1	-	0-2	00-01-02
Northampton v Yeovil	-	2-0	1-1	-	1-1	1-2	01-02-01
Oldham v Leicester	-	-	-	-	-	-	03-01-00
Southend v Swindon	-	-	-	2-0	-	2-1	04-01-01
Stockport v Colchester	1-1	1-3	1-2	-	-	-	01-02-02
Walsall v Hartlepool	-	-	2-1	1-0	2-0	2-2	04-01-01

LEAGUE 2

Aldershot v Brentford	-	-	-	-	-	-	00-00-00
Bradford v Gillingham	1-3	0-1	-	1-0	4-2	-	03-00-02
Dagenham & R v Bury	-	-	-	-	-	1-1	00-01-00
Exeter v Grimsby	-	-	-	-	-	-	02-01-00
Lincoln v Chesterfield	-	-	-	-	-	2-4	01-04-04
Luton v Accrington	-	-	-	-	-	-	00-00-00
Morecambe v Rochdale	-	-	-	-	-	1-1	00-01-00
Notts Co v Macclesfield	-	-	0-5	1-1	1-2	0-1	00-03-03
Rotherham v Barnet	-	-	-	-	-	1-0	03-02-01
Shrewsbury v Bournemouth	0-0	-	-	-	-	-	03-02-02
Wycombe v Darlington	-	-	1-1	0-1	1-0	2-0	03-01-02

SCOTTISH PREMIER LEAGUE

Falkirk v Aberdeen	-	-	-	1-2	0-2/1-2	0-0	01-03-08
Hamilton v St Mirren	-	-	2-2/0-0	3-1/0-0	-	-	05-12-01

Sponsored by Stan James

Hibernian v Hearts	1-2	1-0/1-1	1-1/2-2	2-0/2-1	2-2/0-1	1-1	11-14-11
Inv CT v Celtic	-	-	1-3/0-2	1-1	1-1/1-2	3-2	01-02-03
Kilmarnock v Motherwell	0-3/1-0	2-0	2-0	4-1/2-0	1-2	0-1	11 03 12
Rangers v Dundee Utd	3-0	2-1	1-1/0-1	3-0	2-2/5-0	2-0/3-1	23-04-07

SCOTTISH DIVISION ONE

Airdrie Utd v Queen of Sth	-	-	0-1/2-0	4-0/1-1	2-2/0-3	-	04-02-02
Dundee v Ross County	-	-	-	0-0/0-0	3-1/3-2	-	02-02-00
Dunfermline v Partick	4-1/0-0	2-1/1-0	-	-	-	1-0/1-1	05-02-00
Morton v Clyde	-	-	-	-	-	3-2/1-2	03-03-06
Livingston v St Johnstone	-	-	-	-	1-1/3-2	0-2/0-2	03-02-03

SCOTTISH DIVISION TWO

Alloa v Arbroath	0-3/3-2	2-2/4-0	4-2/2-2	-	-	-	10-08-08
Peterhead v East Fife	0-2/2-2	-	2-0/0-0	-	-	-	02-04-02
Raith v Ayr	-	1-1/2-1	-	3-3/1-1	1-0/0-1	2-3/1-2	10-10-08
Stirling v Brechin	-	-	1-5/1-2	-	2-1/0-1	-	05-02-06
Stranraer v Queen's Park	-	1-0/3-1	-	-	-	-	08-02-03

SCOTTISH DIVISION THREE

Annan Ath v Cowdenbeath	-	-	-	-	-	-	00-00-00
E Stirling v Berwick	-	-	-	1-2/0-1	0-1/0-3	-	07-03-09
Elgin v Stenhsmuir	-	-	1-1/4-2	1-2/0-2	2-0/2-1	2-0/1-5	04-01-03
Forfar v Albion	-	-	-	-	-	1-0/1-4	09-02-01
Montrose v Dumbarton	-	-	-	-	1-1/0-5	0-1/3-1	04-07-07

CONFERENCE

Barrow v Eastbourne	-	-	-	-	-	-	00-00-00
Ebbsfleet U v Torquay	-	-	-	-	-	2-1	01-00-00
Forest G v Cambridge U	-	-	-	1-0	1-1	3-1	02-01-00
Grays v Woking	-	-	-	2-2	3-0	1-1	01-03-01
Histon v Crawley	-	-	-	-	-	3-0	01-00-00
Kettering v Kidderminster	-	-	-	-	-	-	06-04-02
Lewes v Northwich	-	-	-	-	-	-	00-00-00
Mansfield v Wrexham	-	-	-	2-2	3-0	2-1	03-01-00
Oxford Utd v Burton	-	-	-	-	0-0	0-3	00-01-01
Stevenage v Salisbury	-	-	-	-	-	3-1	01-00-00
Weymouth v Altrincham	-	-	-	-	1-2	2-2	00-01-02
York v Rushden & D	0-0	-	-	-	3-1	2-3	01-01-02

SUNDAY 19TH OCTOBER 2008
PREMIER LEAGUE

Stoke v Tottenham	-	-	-	-	-	-	00-00-00

CHAMPIONSHIP

Sheff Weds v Sheff Utd	2-0	-	-	1-2	-	2-0	03-02-03

LEAGUE 2

Chester v Port Vale	-	-	-	-	-	-	00-00-02

MONDAY 20TH OCTOBER 2008
PREMIER LEAGUE

Newcastle v Man City	2-0	3-0	4-3	1-0	0-1	0-2	06-01-03

TUESDAY 21ST OCTOBER 2008
CHAMPIONSHIP

Barnsley v Sheff Weds	-	1-1	0-0	-	0-3	0-0	03-04-01
Birmingham v C Palace	-	-	0-1	-	2-1	-	06-01-03
Blackpool v Derby	-	-	-	-	-	-	00-00-00
Charlton v Bristol C	-	-	-	-	-	1-1	05-01-00
Coventry v Burnley	0-1	4-0	0-2	1-0	1-0	1-2	03-00-04
Norwich v Wolves	0-3	-	-	1-2	0-1	1-1	04-02-05
Nottm Forest v Ipswich	2-1	1-1	1-1	-	-	-	03-02-02
Plymouth v Preston	-	-	0-2	0-0	2-0	2-2	04-02-02
Reading v Doncaster	-	-	-	-	-	-	00-00-00
Sheff Utd v Southampton	-	-	-	3-0	-	1-2	03-01-02
Swansea v QPR	-	-	-	-	-	-	00-00-00
Watford v Cardiff	-	2-1	0-0	2-1	-	2-2	02-02-00

LEAGUE 1

Bristol R v Oldham	-	-	-	-	-	1-0	04-01-01
Colchester v Millwall	-	-	-	-	-	-	00-01-02
Hartlepool v Huddersfield	-	-	0-1	3-1	-	2-1	03-01-02
Hereford v Carlisle	-	-	0-0	-	-	-	04-03-02
Leeds v Leyton O	-	-	-	-	-	1-1	00-01-00
Leicester v Walsall	2-0	-	-	-	-	-	02-00-00
Milton K v Stockport	-	-	2-1	-	2-0	0-2	04-00-01
Peterboro v Brighton	-	2-2	-	-	-	-	02-02-03
Scunthorpe v Southend	4-1	1-1	3-2	1-0	-	-	04-04-00
Swindon v Northampton	2-0	-	-	-	-	1-1	02-02-00
Tranmere v Cheltenham	1-0	-	-	-	2-2	1-0	02-01-00
Yeovil v Crewe	-	-	-	-	2-0	0-3	01-00-01

LEAGUE 2

Accrington v Shrewsbury	-	0-1	-	-	3-3	1-2	00-01-02
Barnet v Wycombe	-	-	-	0-0	2-1	2-1	05-01-00
Bournemouth v Dagenham & R	-	-	-	-	-	-	00-00-00
Brentford v Morecambe	-	-	-	-	-	0-1	00-00-01
Bury v Rotherham	-	-	-	-	-	3-0	03-02-00
Darlington v Bradford	-	-	-	-	-	1-3	00-00-02
Gillingham v Notts Co	-	-	-	-	-	-	03-00-01
Grimsby v Luton	-	3-2	-	-	-	-	04-01-01
Macclesfield v Lincoln	0-1	0-0	2-1	1-1	2-1	1-2	04-04-03
Port Vale v Exeter	-	-	-	-	-	-	01-01-00
Rochdale v Chester	-	-	2-2	2-2	0-0	1-2	03-04-03

WEDNESDAY 22ND OCTOBER 2008
LEAGUE 2

Chesterfield v Aldershot	-	-	-	-	-	-	00-00-00

FRIDAY 24TH OCTOBER 2008
LEAGUE 1

Tranmere v Crewe	2-1	-	-	-	1-0	1-1	05-03-02

LEAGUE 2

Grimsby v Bradford	1-2	-	-	-	-	1-1	01-03-02

SATURDAY 25TH OCTOBER 2008
PREMIER LEAGUE

Blackburn v Middlesboro	1-0	2-2	0-4	3-2	2-1	1-1	06-05-03

Sponsored by Stan James

Everton v Man Utd	1-2	3-4	1-0	0-2	2-4	0-1	03-03-14
Man City v Stoke	-	-	-	-	-	-	03-00-01
Portsmouth v Fulham	-	1-1	4-3	1-0	1-1	0-1	02-03-02
Sunderland v Newcastle	0-1	-	-	1-4	-	1-1	00-05-05
Tottenham v Bolton	3-1	0-1	1-2	1-0	4-1	1-1	05-02-02
WBA v Hull	-	-	-	-	2-0	1-2	04-02-01
Wigan v Aston Villa	-	-	-	3-2	0-0	1-2	01-01-01

CHAMPIONSHIP

Barnsley v Bristol C	1-4	0-1	2-1	2-0	-	3-0	07-01-03
Birmingham v Sheff Weds	-	-	-	-	2-0	-	02-00-01
Blackpool v C Palace	-	-	-	-	-	1-1	00-01-00
Charlton v Burnley	-	-	-	-	-	1-3	00-00-02
Coventry v Derby	3-0	2-0	6-2	6-1	1-2	-	09-01-03
Norwich v Doncaster	-	-	-	-	-	-	00-00-00
Nottm Forest v Cardiff	-	1-2	0-0	-	-	-	00-01-01
Plymouth v Ipswich	-	-	1-2	2-1	1-1	1-1	03-03-02
Reading v QPR	-	-	1-0	2-1	-	-	04-00-01
Sheff Utd v Preston	1-0	2-0	1-1	2-1	-	1-1	05-03-00
Swansea v Southampton	-	-	-	-	-	-	00-00-00
Watford v Wolves	1-1	-	1-1	3-1	-	3-0	08-04-02

LEAGUE 1

Bristol R v Southend	0-1	1-1	2-1	-	-	1-1	04-03-02
Colchester v Carlisle	-	-	-	-	-	-	03-02-01
Hartlepool v Brighton	-	0-0	-	-	-	1-2	01-06-02
Hereford v Stockport	-	-	-	-	0-2	0-1	01-01-03
Leeds v Walsall	-	-	-	-	-	2-0	02-00-00
Leicester v Northampton	-	-	-	-	-	-	00-00-00
Milton K v Cheltenham	-	-	-	-	-	-	00-00-00
Peterboro v Huddersfield	0-1	-	1-2	-	-	-	01-01-03
Scunthorpe v Millwall	-	-	-	-	3-0	-	01-00-01
Swindon v Oldham	0-1	1-2	1-0	2-3	-	3-0	06-02-05
Yeovil v Leyton O	-	1-2	1-0	-	2-1	0-1	02-00-02

LEAGUE 2

Accrington v Wycombe	-	-	-	-	2-1	0-2	01-00-01
Barnet v Exeter	-	2-3	1-0	-	-	-	04-03-03
Bournemouth v Lincoln	0-1	-	-	-	-	-	01-00-01
Brentford v Shrewsbury	-	-	-	-	-	1-1	03-04-01
Bury v Luton	-	-	-	-	-	-	01-02-00
Chesterfield v Notts Co	0-0	0-1	-	-	-	1-1	06-02-01
Darlington v Dagenham & R	-	-	-	-	-	2-3	00-00-01
Gillingham v Chester	-	-	-	-	-	-	01-01-01
Macclesfield v Rotherham	-	-	-	-	-	1-1	00-03-00
Port Vale v Morecambe	-	-	-	-	-	-	00-00-00
Rochdale v Aldershot	-	-	-	-	-	-	00-00-00

SCOTTISH PREMIER LEAGUE

Celtic v Hibernian	1-0/3-2	6-0	2-1/1-3	3-2/1-1	2-1/1-0	1-1/2-0	22-11-03
Dundee Utd v St Mirren	-	-	-	-	1-0/0-2	2-0/1-1	09-03-04
Hamilton v Rangers	-	-	-	-	-	-	00-00-02
Hearts v Aberdeen	0-0	2-0/1-0	0-0/1-0	2-0/1-2/1-0	0-1/1-1	4-1	20-08-10
Inv CT v Motherwell	-	-	1-1/1-0	1-2/0-1	0-1/2-0	0-3	02-01-04
Kilmarnock v Falkirk	-	-	-	1-1/2-1	2-1	0-1/2-1	06-05-02

SCOTTISH DIVISION ONE

Airdrie Utd v Dunfermline	-	-	-	-	-	-	03-04-04
Clyde v Livingston	-	-	-	-	1-1/0-1	2-1/3-2	07-04-07
Morton v Dundee	-	-	-	-	-	0-2/1-2	02-05-04
Queen of Sth v Ross County	2-0/1-0	1-0/1-1	0-1/1-0	2-3/0-0	2-0/2-0	-	06-02-04
St Johnstone v Partick	-	-	2-1/1-1	-	2-0/2-0	2-1/2-0	09-05-01

SCOTTISH DIVISION TWO

Alloa v Peterhead	-	-	-	4-1/0-2	1-1/2-4	2-0/2-0	03-01-02
Ayr v Stirling	-	-	3-2/0-3	2-5/3-0	0-0/3-2	-	08-03-05
Brechin v Queen's Park	-	-	-	-	-	2-1/0-1	12-02-02
East Fife v Arbroath	-	0-1/1-2	-	1-1/0-3	2-1/1-2	0-2/2-1	06-03-10
Stranraer v Raith	2-2/1-0	-	-	-	1-4/0-2	-	02-03-03

SUNDAY 26TH OCTOBER 2008
PREMIER LEAGUE

Chelsea v Liverpool	2-1	0-1	1-0	2-0	1-0	0-0	12-05-02
West Ham v Arsenal	2-2	-	-	0-0	1-0	0-1	02-05-08

TUESDAY 28TH OCTOBER 2008
PREMIER LEAGUE

Bolton v Everton	1-2	2-0	3-2	0-1	1-1	1-2	02-04-03
Hull v Chelsea	-	-	-	-	-	-	01-00-00
Man Utd v West Ham	3-0	-	-	1-0	0-1	4-1	13-00-02
Middlesboro v Man City	3-1	2-1	3-2	0-0	0-2	8-1	07-02-01
Stoke v Sunderland	-	3-1	0-1	-	2-1	-	05-00-04

CHAMPIONSHIP

Bristol C v Sheff Utd	-	-	-	-	-	2-0	04-00-00
Burnley v Reading	2-5	3-0	0-0	0-3	-	-	02-03-04
Cardiff v Blackpool	2-1	-	-	-	-	3-1	02-07-02
Crystal Pal v Nottm Forest	0-0	1-0	-	-	-	-	04-05-02
Derby v Norwich	2-1	0-4	-	2-0	0-0	-	03-02-03
Doncaster v Barnsley	-	-	4-0	2-0	-	-	02-00-00
Ipswich v Charlton	-	-	-	-	-	2-0	06-01-02
Preston v Watford	1-1	2-1	2-1	1-1	-	1-0	05-04-00
QPR v Birmingham	-	-	-	-	0-2	-	00-04-02
Sheff Weds v Plymouth	-	1-3	-	0-0	1-1	1-1	01-03-01
Southampton v Coventry	-	-	-	1-1	2-0	0-0	06-08-02
Wolves v Swansea	-	-	-	-	-	-	00-01-00

LEAGUE 1

Brighton v Leicester	0-1	-	1-1	1-2	-	-	02-02-03
Carlisle v Hartlepool	1-3	-	-	-	-	4-2	06-00-05
Cheltenham v Bristol R	-	1-2	1-1	2-3	-	1-0	01-02-02
Crewe v Peterboro	0-1	-	-	-	-	-	01-02-02
Huddersfield v Yeovil	-	3-1	-	1-2	2-3	1-0	02-00-02
Leyton O v MK Dons	-	-	-	-	-	-	00-00-00
Millwall v Hereford	-	-	-	-	-	-	00-00-00
Northampton v Colchester	4-1	-	-	-	-	-	05-03-01
Oldham v Scunthorpe	-	-	-	1-1	1-0	-	01-02-00
Southend v Leeds	-	-	-	-	1-1	1-0	01-01-00
Stockport v Tranmere	2-3	1-1	1-1	-	-	-	02-05-01
Walsall v Swindon	-	-	3-2	1-0	0-2	2-2	03-04-01

200

LEAGUE 2

Aldershot v Port Vale	-	-	-	-	-	-	00-00-00
Bradford v Bury	-	-	-	-	-	1-2	03-01-01
Chester v Brentford	-	-	-	-	-	0-2	01-02-04
Dagenham & R v Grimsby	-	-	-	-	-	0-0	00-01-00
Exeter v Chesterfield	-	-	-	-	-	-	01-01-01
Lincoln v Gillingham	-	-	-	-	-	-	02-03-03
Luton v Bournemouth	-	1-1	1-0	-	-	1-4	03-02-03
Morecambe v Accrington	-	1-0	1-2	3-2	-	0-1	06-00-02
Notts Co v Rochdale	-	-	0-0	1-1	1-2	1-0	02-02-01
Rotherham v Darlington	-	-	-	-	-	0-2	03-00-02
Shrewsbury v Barnet	-	0-1	-	2-2	0-1	1-0	04-02-03
Wycombe v Macclesfield	-	-	1-1	4-5	3-0	2-1	03-04-03

WEDNESDAY 29TH OCTOBER 2008
PREMIER LEAGUE

Arsenal v Tottenham	3-0	2-1	1-0	1-1	3-0	2-1	12-07-01
Aston Villa v Blackburn	3-0	0-2	1-0	1-0	2-0	1-1	07-02-05
Fulham v Wigan	-	-	-	1-0	0-1	1-1	07-04-02
Liverpool v Portsmouth	-	3-0	1-1	3-0	0-0	4-1	03-02-00
Newcastle v WBA	2-1	-	3-1	3-0	-	-	04-01-00

SATURDAY 1ST NOVEMBER 2008
PREMIER LEAGUE

Chelsea v Sunderland	3-0	-	-	2-0	-	2-0	07-01-01
Everton v Fulham	2-0	3-1	1-0	3-1	4-1	3-0	07-00-00
Man Utd v Hull	-	-	-	-	-	-	00-00-00
Middlesboro v West Ham	2-2	-	-	2-0	1-0	1-2	09-02-02
Portsmouth v Wigan	-	-	-	0-2	1-0	2-0	02-00-01
Stoke v Arsenal	-	-	-	-	-	-	00-00-00
Tottenham v Liverpool	2-3	2-1	1-1	0-0	0-1	0-2	07-05-08
WBA v Blackburn	0-2	-	1-1	2-0	-	-	04-03-01

CHAMPIONSHIP

Birmingham v Coventry	-	-	-	-	3 0	-	02-00-00
Bristol C v Reading	-	-	-	-	-	-	03-01-02
Burnley v Norwich	2-0	3-5	-	2-0	3-0	2-1	05-01-01
Cardiff v Wolves	-	-	1-1	2-2	4-0	2-3	01-03-01
Charlton v Barnsley	-	-	-	-	-	1-1	03-06-00
Crystal Pal v Sheff Weds	0-0	-	-	2-0	1-2	2-1	06-04-01
Doncaster v Swansea	-	3-1	-	2-1	2-2	0-4	02-01-03
Ipswich v QPR	-	-	0-2	2-2	2-1	0-0	03-04-04
Preston v Southampton	-	-	-	1-1	3-1	5-1	02-01-00
Sheff Utd v Plymouth	-	-	2-1	2-0	-	0-1	03-00-01
Watford v Blackpool	-	-	-	-	-	1-1	01-02-00

LEAGUE 1

Brighton v Millwall	1-0	-	1-0	1-2	0-1	3-0	03-01-03
Cheltenham v Leeds	-	-	-	-	-	1-0	01-00-00
Huddersfield v Crewe	1-1	-	-	-	1-2	1-1	04-03-03
Leicester v Bristol R	-	-	-	-	-	-	01-01-01
Leyton O v Hartlepool	1-2	-	-	-	-	2-4	08-02-03
Milton K v Tranmere	-	-	2-1	1-2	-	-	01-01-01
Oldham v Yeovil	-	-	-	2-0	1-0	3-0	03-00-00
Peterboro v Hereford	-	-	-	-	3-0	1-1	03-02-00

Scunthorpe v Swindon	-	-	-	1-2	-	-	00-00-01
Southend v Colchester	-	-	-	3-1	0-3	-	01-00-02
Stockport v Carlisle	-	-	-	0-0	-	-	03-02-00
Walsall v Northampton	-	-	-	-	-	0-2	03-03-04

LEAGUE 2

Bournemouth v Chesterfield	-	2-2	0-0	1-2	0-3	-	04-04-02
Bradford v Barnet	-	-	-	-	-	1-1	01-01-00
Brentford v Rochdale	-	-	-	-	-	0-2	01-00-01
Dagenham & R v Accrington	-	0-1	0-5	1-2	-	1-3	00-00-04
Exeter v Chester	-	2-1	-	-	-	-	03-02-04
Grimsby v Darlington	-	-	0-1	0-1	0-1	0-4	00-01-04
Lincoln v Port Vale	-	-	-	-	-	-	00-00-00
Macclesfield v Gillingham	-	-	-	-	-	-	01-00-00
Morecambe v Aldershot	-	2-0	0-0	5-2	2-1	-	03-01-00
Notts Co v Bury	-	-	0-1	2-2	0-1	1-3	02-02-06
Rotherham v Wycombe	-	-	-	-	-	1-1	03-02-00
Shrewsbury v Luton	-	-	-	-	-	-	00-00-02

SCOTTISH PREMIER LEAGUE

Aberdeen v Kilmarnock	0-1	3-1	3-2	1-2/2-2/0-0	3-1/3-0	2-1	14-07-06
Falkirk v Dundee Utd	-	-	-	1-3/1-0	5-1/2-0	3-0	05-01-05
Hearts v Celtic	1-4/2-1	0-1/1-1	0-2/1-2	2-3/3-0	2-1/1-2	1-1	10-06-24
Motherwell v Hamilton	-	-	-	-	-	-	01-01-00
Rangers v Inv CT	-	-	1-0/1-1	1-1	0-1/1-1	2-0	02-03-01
St Mirren v Hibernian	-	-	-	-	1-0/1-1	2-1	06-03-05

SCOTTISH DIVISION ONE

Dundee v Airdrie Utd	-	-	-	0-2/2-3	1-0/2-1	-	07-03-05
Dunfermline v St Johnstone	-	-	-	-	-	0-0/0-1	08-08-04
Livingston v Morton	-	-	-	-	-	4-0/6-1	09-03-04
Partick v Queen of Sth	-	-	1-2/3-1	-	1-1/0-0	2-0/0-0	06-04-03
Ross County v Clyde	1-1/1-1	0-1/0-0	0-1/1-1	3-1/0-1	1-1/2-2	-	05-07-04

SCOTTISH DIVISION TWO

Arbroath v Ayr	1-1/1-2	-	0-0/2-0	-	-	-	02-02-02
Peterhead v Brechin	-	-	-	-	1-1/1-4	1-2/2-0	02-01-05
Queen's Park v East Fife	0-0/1-2	-	1-2/2-1	2-0/1-1	3-0/1-1	-	10-04-07
Raith v Alloa	-	-	-	4-2/0-1	0-0/3-0	2-1/3-2	05-02-02
Stirling v Stranraer	-	1-0/2-2	1-1/1-1	-	3-3/0-2	-	06-06-04

SCOTTISH DIVISION THREE

Albion v Cowdenbeath	-	1-2/2-4	2-3/1-4	0-3/1-3	-	-	09-02-16
Dumbarton v Berwick	1-2/2-2	1-1/4-1	3-1/1-1	-	2-0/1-2	-	08-09-07
E Stirling v Annan Ath	-	-	-	-	-	-	00-00-00
Elgin v Forfar	-	-	-	-	-	2-2/3-1	01-01-00
Montrose v Stenhsmuir	-	-	0-2/0-3	0-3/0-2	0-1/3-2	1-0/2-1	05-02-12

CONFERENCE

Altrincham v Histon	-	-	-	-	-	1-2	00-00-01
Barrow v Forest G	-	-	-	-	-	-	01-00-00
Burton v Ebbsfleet U	1-1	3-0	3-2	0-0	0-1	1-1	05-04-03
Cambridge U v Rushden & D	4-1	-	3-1	-	0-1	1-0	03-00-01
Kettering v Weymouth	-	-	-	-	-	-	02-00-00
Kidderminstr v Grays	-	-	-	0-5	2-1	1-0	02-00-01
Northwich v Eastbourne	-	-	-	-	-	-	00-00-00

Sponsored by Stan James

Oxford Utd v York	2-0	0-0	-	-	2-0	1-1	03-03-01
Salisbury v Crawley	-	-	-	-	-	4-1	04-01-03
Torquay v Mansfield	-	1-0	-	0-2	1-0	-	06-04-02
Woking v Stevenage	1-5	1-1	1-2	3-2	0-1	0-2	05-03-06
Wrexham v Lewe s	-	-	-	-	-	-	00-00-00

SUNDAY 2ND NOVEMBER 2008
PREMIER LEAGUE

Bolton v Man City	2-0	1-3	0-1	2-0	0-0	0-0	03-03-03

CHAMPIONSHIP

Derby v Nottm Forest	0-0	4-2	3-0	-	-	-	04-02-03

MONDAY 3RD NOVEMBER 2008
PREMIER LEAGUE

Newcastle v Aston Villa	1-1	1-1	0-3	1-1	3-1	0-0	09-04-03

SATURDAY 8TH NOVEMBER 2008
PREMIER LEAGUE

Arsenal v Man Utd	2-2	1-1	2-4	0-0	2-1	2-2	09-07-04
Aston Villa v Middlesboro	1-0	0-2	2-0	2-3	1-1	1-1	06-06-02
Hull v Bolton	-	-	-	-	-	-	01-00-01
Liverpool v WBA	2-0	-	3-0	1-0	-	-	03-00-00
Man City v Tottenham	2-3	0-0	0-1	0-2	1-2	2-1	04-03-07
Sunderland v Portsmouth	-	-	-	1-4	-	2-0	06-03-02
West Ham v Everton	0-1	-	-	2-2	1-0	0-2	04-04-07
Wigan v Stoke	-	2-1	0-1	-	-	-	04-02-03

CHAMPIONSHIP

Barnsley v Sheff Utd	-	-	-	-	-	0-1	04-03-02
Blackpool v Ipswich	-	-	-	-	-	1-1	00-01-00
Coventry v C Palace	1-0	2-1	-	1-4	2-4	0-2	05-02-05
Norwich v Preston	2-0	3-2	-	0-3	2-0	1-0	05-00-02
Nottm Forest v Birmingham	-	-	-	-	-	-	03-01-01
Plymouth v Charlton	-	-	-	-	-	1-2	01 00 02
QPR v Cardiff	0-4	-	1-0	1-0	1-0	0-2	04-00-02
Reading v Derby	2-1	3-1	0-1	5-0	-	1-0	06-00-01
Sheff Weds v Doncaster	-	-	2-0	-	-	-	01-00-00
Southampton v Bristol C	-	-	-	-	-	2-0	01-00-00
Wolves v Burnley	3-0	-	2-0	0-1	2-1	2-3	06-00-02

SCOTTISH PREMIER LEAGUE

Celtic v Motherwell	3-1	3-0/1-1	2-0/2-0	5-0	2-1/1-0	3-0/0-1	22-08-07
Dundee Utd v Aberdeen	1-1/0-2	3-2	1-1/1-2	1-1/1-1	3-1	1-0/3-0	13-16-07
Hamilton v Falkirk	-	-	0-1/1-0	-	-	-	03-04-04
Hibernian v Inv CT	-	-	2-1	1-2/0-2	2-0	1-0/2-0	04-00-02
Kilmarnock v Rangers	1-1/0-1	2-3	0-1	2-3/1-3	2-2/1-3	1-2/0-2	01-06-20
St Mirren v Hearts	-	-	-	-	2-2	1-3/1-1	02-05-05

SCOTTISH DIVISION ONE

Airdrie Utd v Livingston	-	-	-	-	0-1/3-1	-	03-03-04
Dunfermline v Dundee	4-2/0-1	2-0	3-1/5-0	-	-	0-1/0-1	11-02-05
Partick v Clyde	-	-	0-0/1-0	-	1-1/0-4	4-0/1-1	05-06-05
Queen of Sth v Morton	-	-	-	-	-	1-3/0-0	04-02-02
St Johnstone v Ross County	1-1/2-0	1-1/1-1	1-1/0-2	1-1/1-1	3-1/2-1	-	03-06-01

SCOTTISH DIVISION TWO

Alloa v Stirling	-	-	1-1/3-0	2-4/0-0	1-2/1-1	-	05-05-03
Arbroath v Brechin	-	-	2-2/1-4	-	-	-	02-03-05
Ayr v Stranraer	-	-	0-1/0-0	-	0-2/1-0	-	07-03-02
East Fife v Raith	-	-	-	-	-	-	00-00-00
Peterhead v Queen's Park	3-0/3-1	4-1/1-1	2-2/1-1	-	-	1-0/1-0	06-03-01

SCOTTISH DIVISION THREE

Annan Ath v Montrose	-	-	-	-	-	-	00-00-00
Berwick v Albion	-	-	-	0-1/2-1	1-1/3-0	-	09-07-01
Cowdenbeath v Elgin	-	3-2/2-0	3-1/1-1	5-2/2-1	-	-	07-01-00
Forfar v E Stirling	-	-	-	-	-	0-2/1-0	07-02-02
Stenhsmuir v Dumbarton	2-2/2-1	1-1/1-2	-	-	1-0/5-1	2-1/1-1	08-05-07

SUNDAY 9TH NOVEMBER 2008
PREMIER LEAGUE

Blackburn v Chelsea	2-3	2-3	0-1	1-0	0-2	0-1	06-03-06
Fulham v Newcastle	2-1	2-3	1-3	1-0	2-1	0-1	04-00-03

CHAMPIONSHIP

Swansea v Watford	-	-	-	-	-	-	00-00-00

WEDNESDAY 12TH NOVEMBER 2008
SCOTTISH PREMIER LEAGUE

Aberdeen v St Mirren	-	-	-	-	2-0	4-0/1-1	10-03-00
Celtic v Kilmarnock	5-0/2-0	5-1	2-1	4-2/2-0	4-1/2-0	0-0/1-0	22-06-00
Dundee Utd v Hibernian	1-1/1-2	1-2/0-0	1-4	1-0	0-3/0-0	0-0/1-1/1-1	11-15-09
Hearts v Hamilton	-	-	-	-	-	-	02-00-00
Inv CT v Falkirk	1-2/3-4	1-2/0-0	-	0-3/2-0	3-2/1-1	4-2/0-1	04-03-09
Motherwell v Rangers	1-0	1-1/0-1	0-2/2-3	0-1	1-2/0-1	1-1/1-1	09-07-21

FRIDAY 14TH NOVEMBER 2008
LEAGUE 1

Bristol R v Scunthorpe	2-1	1-0	0-3	-	-	-	02-02-01

LEAGUE 2

Chesterfield v Shrewsbury	-	-	-	-	-	4-1	04-00-02

SATURDAY 15TH NOVEMBER 2008
PREMIER LEAGUE

Arsenal v Aston Villa	3-1	2-0	3-1	5-0	1-1	1-1	10-06-04
Blackburn v Sunderland	0-0	-	-	2-0	-	1-0	03-04-01
Bolton v Liverpool	2-3	2-2	1-0	2-2	2-0	1-3	03-03-03
Fulham v Tottenham	3-2	2-1	2-0	1-0	1-1	3-3	04-02-01
Man Utd v Stoke	-	-	-	-	-	-	00-00-00
Newcastle v Wigan	-	-	-	3-1	2-1	1-0	03-00-00
WBA v Chelsea	0-2	-	1-4	1-2	-	-	00-00-04
West Ham v Portsmouth	-	-	-	2-4	1-2	0-1	02-01-03

CHAMPIONSHIP

Barnsley v Watford	-	-	-	-	-	3-2	04-03-05
Birmingham v Charlton	1-1	1-2	1-1	0-1	-	-	03-04-03
Blackpool v Preston	-	-	-	-	-	0-0	03-04-01
Bristol C v Nottm Forest	-	-	-	1-1	1-1	-	00-02-01

Sponsored by Stan James

Cardiff v C Palace	-	0-2	-	1-0	0-0	1-1	01-02-01
Coventry v Plymouth	-	-	2-1	3-1	0-1	3-1	03-00-01
Derby v Sheff Weds	2-2	-	-	0-2	1-0	-	05-03-01
Doncaster v Ipswich	-	-	-	-	-	-	00-00-00
Norwich v Swansea	-	-	-	-	-	-	00-00-00
QPR v Burnley	-	-	3-0	1-1	3-1	2-4	02-01-02
Sheff Utd v Reading	1-3	1-2	0-1	1-1	1-2	-	03-03-04
Southampton v Wolves	-	2-0	-	0-0	2-0	0-0	02-02-00

LEAGUE 1

Carlisle v Brighton	-	-	-	-	3-1	2-0	05-01-01
Colchester v Walsall	-	-	5-0	0-0	-	-	04-01-02
Crewe v Leyton O	-	-	-	-	0-4	0-2	02-01-03
Hartlepool v MK Dons	-	-	5-0	2-1	1-0	-	03-00-00
Hereford v Cheltenham	-	-	-	-	-	-	01-00-01
Leeds v Huddersfield	-	-	-	-	-	4-0	01-00-00
Millwall v Stockport	-	-	-	-	-	-	01-00-01
Northampton v Oldham	0-2	-	-	-	2-3	2-0	02-02-03
Swindon v Leicester	-	-	-	-	-	-	02-03-00
Tranmere v Southend	-	-	-	0-0	-	1-0	05-03-01
Yeovil v Peterboro	-	-	-	-	-	-	00-00-00

LEAGUE 2

Accrington v Bournemouth	-	-	-	-	-	-	00-00-00
Aldershot v Exete r	-	2-1	2-1	1-0	3-2	2-0	05-00-00
Barnet v Notts Co	-	-	-	2-1	2-3	1-1	01-01-02
Bury v Grimsby	-	-	3-1	1-2	3-0	1-1	04-01-01
Chester v Morecambe	2-1	2-1	-	-	-	0-1	03-01-01
Darlington v Lincoln	0-0	0-0	0-3	4-2	1-1	2-0	09-06-02
Gillingham v Rotherham	1-1	2-0	3-1	1-1	1-0	-	06-02-00
Luton v Dagenham & R	-	-	-	-	-	-	00-00-00
Port Vale v Brentford	1-0	1-0	0-1	1-0	1-0	-	07-01-01
Rochdale v Macclesfield	3-1	1-2	3-0	3-1	5-0	1-1	05-03-02
Wycombe v Bradford	-	-	-	-	-	2-1	03-00-00

SCOTTISH PREMIER LEAGUE

Falkirk v Motherwell	-	-	-	0-1/1-1	0-1/1-2	1-0/0-0	03-04-07
Hamilton v Celtic	-	-	-	-	-	-	01-00-01
Hibernian v Aberdeen	1-2/2-0/3-1	1-1/0-1	2-1/1-2	1-2	1-1/0-0	3-3/3-1	13-10-14
Inv CT v Hearts	-	-	1-1	0-1/0-0	0-0	2-1/0-3	01-03-02
Kilmarnock v Dundee Utd	1-2	0-2	5-2/3-0	2-1	0-0/1-0	2-1/1-2	12-06-07
Rangers v St Mirren	-	-	-	-	1-1	2-0/4-0	09-01-02

SCOTTISH DIVISION ONE

Clyde v St Johnstone	1-2/2-1	2-0/2-3	1-0/1-1	0-1/2-3	1-0/0-1	1-0/1-3	06-01-08
Dundee v Queen of Sth	-	-	-	3-1/2-3	2-1/1-0	2-1/2-3	04-00-02
Morton v Airdrie Utd	-	3-1/1-1	-	-	-	-	05-07-08
Livingston v Dunfermline	1-1	0-0/0-0	2-0/1-1/2-0	1-1/0-1	-	1-1/0-2	05-07-05
Ross County v Partick	-	-	0-1/2-1	-	2-5/2-1	-	04-00-04

SCOTTISH DIVISION TWO

Brechin v East Fife	-	-	-	-	-	-	10-04-02
Queen's Park v Ayr	-	-	-	-	-	1-1/1-3	00-01-01
Raith v Peterhead	-	-	-	0-2/1-0	5-2/2-0	2-2/2-5	03-01-02
Stirling v Arbroath	-	-	5-2/0-3	-	-	-	04-04-04
Stranraer v Alloa	-	-	3-0/0-1	-	2-2/3-4	-	03-08-05

SCOTTISH DIVISION THREE

Albion v Annan Ath	-	-	-	-	-	-	00-00-00
Cowdenbeath v Stenhsmuir	1-0/3-3	-	0-6/0-2	4-1/1-1	-	-	05-06-07
E Stirling v Dumbarton	-	-	-	-	0-2/1-5	3-2/1-1	08-03-09
Elgin v Montrose	0-0/0-2	2-3/2-1	1-3/2-2	0-0/1-0	3-2/0-2	0-2/2-1	05-04-07
Forfar v Berwick	0-2/2-2	1-5/0-2	1-1/0-2	-	-	-	03-05-09

CONFERENCE

Crawley v Cambridge U	-	-	-	1-0	1-1	2-1	02-01-00
Eastbourne v Woking	-	-	-	-	-	-	00-00-00
Ebbsfleet U v Barrow	-	-	-	-	-	-	00-00-00
Forest G v Altrincham	-	-	-	5-0	2-2	3-1	02-02-00
Grays v Oxford Utd	-	-	-	-	2-2	0-0	00-02-00
Histon v Kettering	-	-	-	-	-	-	00-00-00
Lewes v Burton	-	-	-	-	-	-	00-00-00
Mansfield v Salisbury	-	-	-	-	-	-	00-00-00
Rushden & D v Kidderminster	3-1	-	0-0	-	0-1	0-1	03-03-03
Stevenage v Northwich	2-2	1-0	4-1	-	0-2	1-2	07-02-04
Weymouth v Wrexham	-	-	-	-	-	-	00-00-00
York v Torquay	4-3	0-0	-	-	-	0-1	03-06-01

SUNDAY 16TH NOVEMBER 2008
PREMIER LEAGUE

Everton v Middlesboro	2-1	1-1	1-0	1-0	0-0	2-0	08-04-02
Hull v Man City	-	-	-	-	-	-	01-00-00

TUESDAY 18TH NOVEMBER 2008
CONFERENCE

Cambridge U v York	3-0	2-0	-	2-0	0-5	2-0	05-02-02
Crawley v Ebbsfleet U	-	-	1-1	1-2	1-1	1-2	02-03-05
Eastbourne v Salisbury	-	-	-	-	1-0	-	01-00-00
Grays v Rushden & D	-	-	-	-	3-1	3-0	02-00-00
Kettering v Barrow	-	-	2-0	1-3	3-2	3-1	07-00-01
Mansfield v Altrincham	-	-	-	-	-	-	00-00-00
Northwich v Burton	1-3	1-2	4-0	-	0-3	0-2	01-00-04
Oxford Utd v Kidderminster	2-1	2-1	0-2	-	0-1	0-0	02-02-02
Stevenage v Histon	-	-	-	-	-	2-1	01-00-00
Torquay v Lewes	-	-	-	-	-	-	00-00-00
Weymouth v Woking	-	-	-	-	2-3	0-1	00-00-02
Wrexham v Forest G	-	-	-	-	-	-	00-00-00

FRIDAY 21ST NOVEMBER 2008
CHAMPIONSHIP

Swansea v Birmingham	-	-	-	-	-	-	01-01-02

LEAGUE 2

Grimsby v Bournemouth	-	1-1	-	-	-	-	02-01-00

SATURDAY 22ND NOVEMBER 2008
PREMIER LEAGUE

Aston Villa v Man Utd	0-1	0-2	0-1	0-2	0-3	1-4	03-05-12
Chelsea v Newcastle	3-0	5-0	4-0	3-0	1-0	2-1	11-04-00
Liverpool v Fulham	2-0	0-0	3-1	5-1	4-0	2-0	05-02-00
Man City v Arsenal	1-5	1-2	0-1	1-3	1-0	1-3	02-02-10
Middlesboro v Bolton	2-0	2-0	1-1	4-3	5-1	0-1	05-02-03

Sponsored by Stan James

Portsmouth v Hull	-	-	-	-	-	-	01-01-01
Stoke v WBA	-	4-1	-	-	1-0	3-1	10-02-00

CHAMPIONSHIP

Burnley v Doncaster	-	-	-	-	-	-	03-00-01
Charlton v Sheff Utd	-	-	-	-	1-1	0-3	02-04-01
Crystal Pal v Bristol C	-	-	-	-	-	2-0	03-00-00
Ipswich v Derby	0-1	2-1	3-2	2-0	2-1	-	07-00-02
Nottm Forest v Norwich	4-0	2-0	-	-	-	-	08-02-02
Plymouth v Cardiff	2-2	-	1-1	0-1	3-3	2-2	01-07-02
Preston v Barnsley	-	-	-	-	1-0	1-2	01-01-02
Reading v Southampton	-	-	-	2-0	-	-	01-00-00
Sheff Weds v Coventry	5-1	-	-	3-2	2-1	1-1	06-07-03
Watford v QPR	-	-	3-0	3-1	-	2-4	04-00-01
Wolves v Blackpool	-	-	-	-	-	2-1	02-00-00

LEAGUE 1

Brighton v Huddersfield	-	-	-	-	0-0	1-1	02-04-00
Bristol R v Swindon	-	-	-	-	1-0	0-1	02-02-03
Carlisle v Cheltenham	-	1-1	-	1-1	2-0	1-0	02-05-00
Crewe v Stockport	1-0	-	-	-	-	-	04-02-04
Hereford v Northampton	-	-	-	-	-	-	03-01-03
Leeds v Hartlepool	-	-	-	-	-	2-0	01-00-00
Leyton O v Millwall	-	-	-	-	2-0	0-1	01-00-01
Peterboro v Colchester	0-1	1-2	0-3	-	-	-	05-00-03
Scunthorpe v Leicester	-	-	-	-	-	0-0	00-01-00
Southend v Oldham	-	-	-	2-1	-	0-1	02-03-01
Walsall v MK Dons	2-0	1-0	0-0	1-1	0-0	-	03-03-00
Yeovil v Tranmere	-	-	-	2-2	0-2	1-1	00-02-01

LEAGUE 2

Barnet v Macclesfield	-	-	-	1-0	1-0	2-2	05-02-02
Brentford v Darlington	-	-	-	-	-	0-2	02-00-01
Bury v Gillingham	-	-	-	-	-	-	06-01-00
Chester v Aldershot	-	4-2	-	-	-	-	01-00-00
Chesterfield v Accrington	-	-	-	-	-	4-2	01-00-00
Dagenham & R v Notts Co	-	-	-	-	-	1-1	00-01-00
Lincoln v Shrewsbury	1-1	-	2-0	1-1	1-1	0-4	02-04-05
Morecambe v Exeter	-	0-3	2-2	2-2	2-2	-	00-03-01
Rochdale v Luton	-	-	-	-	-	-	01-00-00
Rotherham v Bradford	3-2	1-2	-	1-1	4-1	1-1	06-03-02
Wycombe v Port Vale	3-1	2-1	-	-	-	-	03-00-01

SCOTTISH PREMIER LEAGUE

Dundee Utd v Hamilton	-	-	-	-	-	-	02-01-01
Hearts v Falkirk	-	-	-	5-0	0-0/1-0	4-2/0-0	08-04-01
Kilmarnock v Inv CT	-	-	2-2/0-1	2-2	1-1/3-2	2-2/4-1	02-04-01
Motherwell v Hibernian	0-2/2-1	0-1	1-2/1-1/2-2	1-3/2-2	1-6	2-1/1-0	11-14-11
Rangers v Aberdeen	2-0/2-1	3-0	5-0	0-0/1-1	1-0/3-0	3-0/3-1	28-08-02
St Mirren v Celtic	-	-	-	-	1-3	1-5/0-1	01-01-10

SCOTTISH DIVISION ONE

Airdrie Utd v Ross County	-	-	1-2/2-1	0-1/2-3	0-2/0-1	0-1/2-0	03-02-07
Dunfermline v Morton	-	-	-	-	-	0-1/2-0	07-02-03
Partick v Livingston	2-2/1-3	1-1/5-2	-	-	2-3/0-0	3-0/2-1	05-06-06
Queen of Sth v Clyde	2-1/1-1	4-1/1-2	0-1/0-1	1-2/2-1	0-2/0-0	1-1/3-1	11-06-11

SCOTTISH DIVISION TWO

Alloa v Queen's Park	-	-	-	-	-	2-0/1-2	06-06-05
Arbroath v Stranraer	-	-	0-1/0-4	-	-	2-2/0-0	07-05-05
Ayr v East Fife	-	-	-	-	-	-	01-00-01
Peterhead v Stirling	1-0/6-0	2-2/0-0	-	1-3/2-0	2-3/2-1	-	05-03-02
Raith v Brechin	3-1/1-2	2-1/1-1	-	-	1-1/1-0	1-1/1-1	04-04-02

SCOTTISH DIVISION THREE

Annan Ath v Elgin	-	-	-	-	-	-	00-00-00
Berwick v Cowdenbeath	2-1/1-2	-	-	1-0/1-0	-	1-1/4-5	09-04-08
Dumbarton v Albion	-	-	-	-	3-1/3-1	2-0/2-0	09-06-03
Montrose v Forfar	-	-	-	-	-	0-1/2-2	07-03-05
Stenhsmuir v E Stirling	-	-	6-0/3-2	6-1/5-0	2-0/1-1	0-3/3-0	13-04-02

CONFERENCE

Altrincham v Cambridge U	-	-	-	2-1	5-0	0-3	02-00-01
Barrow v Weymouth	-	-	-	-	-	-	00-00-00
Burton v Stevenage	1-2	1-1	0-3	3-1	2-1	3-0	03-01-02
Ebbsfleet U v Kettering	0-2	-	-	-	-	-	00-00-01
Forest G v Mansfield	-	-	-	-	-	-	00-00-00
Histon v Oxford Utd	-	-	-	-	-	1-0	01-00-00
Kidderminstr v Wrexham	0-2	-	-	-	-	-	00-00-01
Lewes v Grays	-	-	3-2	-	-	-	01-00-00
Rushden & D v Eastbourne	-	-	-	-	-	-	00-00-00
Salisbury v Northwich	-	-	-	-	-	2-0	01-00-00
Woking v Torquay	-	-	-	-	-	0-1	00-00-01
York v Crawley	-	-	3-1	0-0	5-0	1-1	02-02-00

SUNDAY 23RD NOVEMBER 2008
PREMIER LEAGUE

Sunderland v West Ham	0-1	2-0	0-2	1-1	-	2-1	05-04-02
Tottenham v Blackburn	0-4	1-0	0-0	3-2	1-1	1-2	06-03-05

MONDAY 24TH NOVEMBER 2008
PREMIER LEAGUE

Wigan v Everton	-	-	-	1-1	0-2	1-2	00-01-02

CHAMPIONSHIP

Barnsley v Burnley	-	-	-	-	1-0	1-1	03-02-00

TUESDAY 25TH NOVEMBER 2008
CHAMPIONSHIP

Birmingham v Ipswich	-	-	-	-	2-2	-	04-03-00
Blackpool v Sheff Weds	-	4-1	1-2	-	-	2-1	02-00-01
Bristol C v Watford	-	-	-	-	-	0-0	03-05-01
Cardiff v Reading	-	2-3	2-0	2-5	-	-	04-01-03
Coventry v Swansea	-	-	-	-	-	-	00-00-00
Derby v Preston	0-2	5-1	3-1	1-1	1-1	-	02-02-01
Doncaster v Nottm Forest	-	-	-	1-2	1-0	1-0	02-00-01
Norwich v C Palace	2-0	2-1	1-1	1-1	0-1	1-0	07-06-04
QPR v Charlton	-	-	-	-	-	1-0	02-01-03
Sheff Utd v Wolves	3-3	-	3-3	1-0	-	3-1	08-05-01
Southampton v Plymouth	-	-	-	0-0	1-0	0-2	01-01-01

Sponsored by Stan James

LEAGUE 1

Cheltenham v Southend	-	1-1	0-3	-	-	1-1	02-03-01
Colchester v Yeovil	-	-	-	3-2	-	-	02-00-01
Hartlepool v Bristol R	2-0	-	-	-	1-2	1-0	03-01-01
Huddersfield v Leyton O	-	3-0	-	-	3-1	0-1	07-01-01
Leicester v Crewe	-	-	1-1	1-1	-	-	00-02-00
Millwall v Carlisle	-	-	-	-	2-0	3-0	02-01-00
Milton K v Hereford	-	-	-	-	1-3	0-0	00-01-01
Northampton v Leeds	-	-	-	-	-	1-1	00-01-00
Oldham v Walsall	-	-	5-3	2-1	-	0-2	03-02-02
Stockport v Brighton	-	1-1	-	-	-	-	03-02-00
Swindon v Peterboro	1-1	2-0	0-1	-	0-1	-	04-02-02
Tranmere v Scunthorpe	-	-	-	0-2	0-2	-	01-00-02

LEAGUE 2

Accrington v Bury	-	-	-	-	1-1	0-2	00-01-01
Aldershot v Lincoln	-	-	-	-	-	-	00-00-00
Bournemouth v Morecambe	-	-	-	-	-	-	00-00-00
Bradford v Chesterfield	-	-	2-3	2-0	1-0	1-0	04-00-01
Darlington v Chester	-	-	1-0	1-0	1-0	1-0	07-02-02
Exeter v Rotherham	-	-	-	-	-	-	04-02-01
Gillingham v Rochdale	-	-	-	-	-	-	03-03-01
Luton v Brentford	0-1	4-1	4-2	-	-	-	05-01-02
Macclesfield v Grimsby	-	-	3-1	1-1	2-1	1-2	02-01-01
Notts Co v Wycombe	1-1	1-1	0-1	1-2	1-0	1-0	05-02-05
Port Vale v Barnet	-	-	-	-	-	-	01-00-00
Shrewsbury v Dagenham & R	-	2-1	-	-	-	4-0	02-00-00

SATURDAY 29TH NOVEMBER 2008
PREMIER LEAGUE

Aston Villa v Fulham	3-1	3-0	2-0	0-0	1-1	2-1	05-02-00
Middlesboro v Newcastle	1-0	0-1	2-2	1-2	1-0	2-2	05-05-06
Portsmouth v Blackburn	-	1-2	0-1	2-2	3-0	0-1	02-04-05
Stoke v Hull	-	-	-	0-3	1-1	1-1	02-03-02
Sunderland v Bolton	0-2	-	-	0-0	-	3-1	04-02-01
Tottenham v Everton	4-3	3-0	5-2	2-0	0-2	1-3	12-06-02
Wigan v WBA -		1-0	-	0-1	-	-	02-00-02

CHAMPIONSHIP

Burnley v Derby	2-0	1-0	0-2	2-2	0-0	-	03-02-01
Charlton v Southampton	2-1	2-1	0-0	-	-	1-1	03-05-01
Crystal Pal v QPR	-	-	-	2-1	3-0	1-1	04-07-01
Ipswich v Sheff Utd	3-2	3-0	5-1	1-1	-	1-1	06-07-00
Nottm Forest v Barnsley	-	-	-	0-2	-	-	03-01-01
Plymouth v Blackpool	1-3	1-0	-	-	-	3-0	06-00-03
Preston v Bristol C	-	-	-	-	-	0-0	03-02-01
Reading v Coventry	1-2	1-2	1-2	2-0	-	-	01-00-03
Sheff Weds v Norwich	2-2	-	-	1-0	3-2	4-1	06-04-02
Watford v Doncaster	-	-	-	-	-	-	00-00-00
Wolves v Birmingham	-	1-1	-	-	2-3	-	06-01-04

SCOTTISH PREMIER LEAGUE

Aberdeen v Motherwell	1-1	0-3/0-2	2-1/1-3	2-2/2-2	2-1	1-2/1-1	16-14-07
Celtic v Inv CT	-	-	3-0	2-1/2-1	3-0	5-0/2-1	06-00-00
Falkirk v Hibernian	-	-	-	0-2/0-0	2-1	1-1/0-2	05-06-04
Hamilton v Kilmarnock	-	-	-	-	-	-	01-02-02

Hearts v Rangers	0-4/0-2	0-4/1-1	0-0/1-2	1-0/1-1	0-1	4-2/0-4	08-08-23
St Mirren v Dundee Utd	-	-	-	-	1-3/0-1	0-3	02-05-08

SCOTTISH DIVISION ONE

Dundee v St Johnstone	-	-	-	2-1/0-1	1-1/2-1	2-1/3-2	08-07-08

CONFERENCE

Altrincham v Rushden & D	-	-	-	-	2-1	1-2	02-00-02
Barrow v Histon	-	-	-	-	-	-	00-00-00
Burton v Eastbourne	-	-	-	-	-	-	00-00-00
Cambridge U v Ebbsfleet U	-	-	-	1-1	3-0	1-1	01-02-00
Grays v Torquay	-	-	-	-	-	2-0	01-00-00
Kettering v Lewes	-	-	-	-	-	-	00-00-00
Northwich v Crawley	-	-	1-0	-	2-1	2-0	03-00-00
Oxford Utd v Forest G	-	-	-	-	0-2	1-0	01-00-01
Salisbury v York	-	-	-	-	-	3-0	01-00-00
Stevenage v Wrexham	-	-	-	-	-	-	00-00-00
Weymouth v Mansfield	-	-	-	-	-	-	00-00-00
Woking v Kidderminster	-	-	-	0-1	3-0	3-0	06-02-03

SUNDAY 30TH NOVEMBER 2008
PREMIER LEAGUE

Chelsea v Arsenal	1-1	1-2	0-0	1-0	1-1	2-1	06-08-05
Man City v Man Utd	3-1	4-1	0-2	3-1	0-1	1-0	05-03-06

CHAMPIONSHIP

Swansea v Cardiff	-	-	-	-	-	-	03-02-02

MONDAY 1ST DECEMBER 2008
PREMIER LEAGUE

Liverpool v West Ham	2-0	-	-	2-0	2-1	4-0	12-03-00

SATURDAY 6TH DECEMBER 2008
PREMIER LEAGUE

Arsenal v Wigan	-	-	-	4-2	2-1	2-0	03-00-00
Blackburn v Liverpool	2-2	1-3	2-2	0-1	1-0	0-0	05-05-04
Bolton v Chelsea	1-1	0-2	0-2	0-2	0-1	0-1	02-02-05
Everton v Aston Villa	2-1	2-0	1-1	4-1	0-1	2-2	07-07-06
Fulham v Man City	0-1	2-2	1-1	2-1	1-3	3-3	02-04-02
Hull v Middlesboro	-	-	-	-	-	-	00-02-00
Man Utd v Sunderland	2-1	-	-	0-0	-	1-0	07-01-00
Newcastle v Stoke	-	-	-	-	-	-	01-00-00
WBA v Portsmouth	-	-	2-0	2-1	-	-	08-03-03
West Ham v Tottenham	2-0	-	-	2-1	3-4	1-1	07-03-05

CHAMPIONSHIP

Barnsley v Reading	-	-	-	-	-	-	01-00-02
Birmingham v Watford	-	-	-	-	-	-	04-01-02
Blackpool v Charlton	-	-	-	-	-	5-3	01-00-00
Bristol C v Swansea	-	-	-	1-0	0-0	-	04-01-01
Cardiff v Preston	-	2-2	0-1	2-2	4-1	2-2	02-04-03
Coventry v Nottm Forest	0-1	1-3	2-0	-	-	-	02-05-06
Derby v C Palace	0-1	2-1	-	2-1	1-0	-	06-01-02
Doncaster v Plymouth	-	-	-	-	-	-	00-01-00
QPR v Wolves	-	-	1-1	0-0	0-1	0-0	00-07-02

Sponsored by Stan James

Sheff Utd v Burnley	4-2	1-0	2-1	3-0	-	0-0	07-01-00
Southampton v Sheff Weds	-	-	-	3-0	2-1	0-0	04-04-06

LEAGUE 1

Cheltenham v Crewe	0-4	-	-	-	1-1	2-2	00-02-01
Colchester v Hereford	-	-	-	-	-	-	03-04-00
Hartlepool v Yeovil	-	-	-	0-1	-	2-0	01-00-01
Huddersfield v Walsall	-	-	3-1	3-1	-	2-0	04-01-00
Leicester v Southend	-	-	-	-	1-0	-	04-00-01
Millwall v Bristol R	-	-	-	-	-	0-1	03-03-03
Milton K v Scunthorpe	-	-	-	1-0	-	-	01-00-00
Northampton v Leyton O	-	1-0	2-2	1-1	0-1	2-0	03-02-04
Oldham v Brighton	-	1-3	-	-	1-1	1-1	03-03-01
Stockport v Peterboro	2-1	2-2	1-0	1-1	0-1	1-2	04-05-04
Swindon v Carlisle	-	-	-	-	-	2-2	01-01-00
Tranmere v Leeds	-	-	-	-	-	1-2	00-00-01

LEAGUE 2

Accrington v Brentford	-	-	-	-	-	1-0	01-00-00
Aldershot v Wycombe	-	-	-	-	-	-	00-00-00
Bournemouth v Chester	-	-	-	-	-	-	02-02-00
Bradford v Dagenham & R	-	-	-	-	-	0-2	00-00-01
Darlington v Rochdale	0-1	1-0	0-3	2-1	0-5	1-1	08-03-07
Exeter v Lincoln	2-0	-	-	-	-	-	04-04-02
Gillingham v Chesterfield	-	-	-	1-0	2-1	-	06-02-05
Luton v Barnet	-	-	-	-	-	-	00-00-00
Macclesfield v Bury	0-0	1-0	2-1	1-0	2-3	2-2	03-02-01
Notts Co v Morecambe	-	-	-	-	-	1-1	00-01-00
Port Vale v Grimsby	-	5-1	-	-	-	-	03-01-03
Shrewsbury v Rotherham	-	-	-	-	-	1-1	03-04-02

SCOTTISH PREMIER LEAGUE

Falkirk v St Mirren	2-0/3-1	0-0/1-0	0-0/1-2	-	1-1/2-0/0-2	0-1/4-0	14-08-03
Hibernian v Celtic	0-1	1-2/0-4	2-2/1-3	0-1/1-2	2-2/2-1	3-2/0-2	07-09-21
Inv CT v Dundee Utd	-	-	1-1/0-1	1-1/1-0	0-0/1-0	0-3/1-1	02-04-02
Kilmarnock v Aberdeen	2-2/2-0	1-3/3-1/4-0	0-1/0-1	4-2	1-0/1-2	0-1/3-1	17-05-07
Motherwell v Hearts	6-1	1-1/1-1	2-0/2-0	1-1	0-1/0-2	0-2/0-1	10-09-18
Rangers v Hamilton	-	-	-	-	-	-	02-00-00

SCOTTISH DIVISION ONE

Clyde v Airdrie Utd	-	-	1-2/1-0	1-0/3-1	0-0/0-1	-	05-03-08
Morton v Partick	-	-	-	2-1/1-0	-	4-2/0-0	09-04-02
Livingston v Dundee	1-1	1-1	1-0/1-1	-	2-3/1-3	0-2/1-1	02-05-05
Ross County v Dunfermline	-	-	-	-	-	-	00-00-00
St Johnstone v Queen of Sth	2-2/0-1	4-1/2-2	1-3/0-0	4-0/2-1	5-0/3-0	2-0/2-1	09-03-02

SCOTTISH DIVISION TWO

Brechin v Ayr -		3-1/0-3	5-0/3-0	-	0-2/2-0	2-2/5-1	05-04-05
East Fife v Alloa	-	0-1/0-1	-	-	-	-	04-04-04
Queen's Park v Arbroath	-	-	-	2-2/0-0	0-3/1-0	-	10-07-06
Stirling v Raith	-	-	-	1-0/2-2	1-1/0-1	-	03-03-04
Stranraer v Peterhead	-	0-2/1-1	-	-	2-1/1-1	-	01-02-01

SCOTTISH DIVISION THREE

Albion v Elgin	1-1/1-1	1-2/1-2	2-2/2-0	0-2/1-2	3-1/6-2	3-4/1-1	03-07-06
Berwick v Stenhsmuir	2-2/0-0	2-1/3-0	-	0-2/3-0	0-1/2-1	-	15-06-08

Cowdenbeath v Dumbarton	3-1/2-0	-	-	-	-	-	07-03-08
E Stirling v Montrose	1-1/0-3	1-1/1-4	1-1/1-2	1-1/1-0	0-3/0-2	0-3/3-1	11-06-16
Forfar v Annan Ath	-	-	-	-	-	-	00-00-00

CONFERENCE

Crawley v Altrincham	-	-	-	2-0	1-1	0-1	01-01-01
Eastbourne v Northwich	-	-	-	-	-	-	00-00-00
Ebbsfleet U v Weymouth	-	-	-	-	1-3	4-1	03-00-01
Forest G v Burton	2-0	1-1	3-2	1-0	1-0	3-1	05-01-01
Histon v Woking	-	-	-	-	-	0-1	00-00-01
Kidderminstr v Salisbury	-	-	-	-	-	1-2	00-00-01
Lewes v Stevenage	-	-	-	-	-	-	00-00-00
Mansfield v Oxford Utd	-	3-1	1-3	1-0	-	-	03-00-01
Rushden & D v Barrow	-	-	-	-	-	-	01-00-00
Torquay v Cambridge U	3-2	3-0	-	-	-	1-2	04-00-05
Wrexham v Kettering	-	-	-	-	-	-	00-00-00
York v Grays - -	-	1-2	2-2	2-0	01-01-01		

SUNDAY 7TH DECEMBER 2008
CHAMPIONSHIP

Norwich v Ipswich	0-2	3-1	-	1-2	1-1	2-2	06-04-03

TUESDAY 9TH DECEMBER 2008
CHAMPIONSHIP

Burnley v Cardiff	-	1-1	1-0	3-3	2-0	3-3	06-03-00
Charlton v Coventry	-	-	-	-	-	4-1	01-04-00
Crystal Pal v Southampton	-	-	2-2	2-1	0-2	1-1	04-04-02
Nottm Forest v Sheff Utd	3-0	3-1	1-1	-	-	-	05-03-02
Plymouth v Birmingham	-	-	-	-	0-1	-	00-00-03
Preston v Doncaster	-	-	-	-	-	-	02-01-00
Reading v Blackpool	-	-	-	-	-	-	02-05-00
Sheff Weds v QPR	-	1-3	-	1-1	3-2	2-1	07-01-04
Swansea v Barnsley	-	-	-	3-1	-	-	01-00-00
Wolves v Derby	1-1	-	2-0	1-1	0-1	-	02-03-04

CONFERENCE

Barrow v Altrincham	4-0	2-1	2-0	-	-	-	04-03-02
Burton v Cambridge U	-	-	-	2-0	2-1	1-2	02-00-01
Eastbourne v Torquay	-	-	-	-	-	-	00-00-00
Ebbsfleet U v Forest G	1-1	1-1	0-0	2-0	1-1	0-2	01-04-01
Histon v York	-	-	-	-	-	3-1	01-00-00
Kettering v Crawley	-	-	-	-	-	-	00-00-01
Kidderminstr v Mansfield	-	2-1	1-3	-	-	-	02-01-01
Northwich v Wrexham	-	-	-	-	-	-	00-00-00
Salisbury v Lewes	-	-	-	-	1-1	-	00-01-00
Stevenage v Grays	-	-	-	0-1	1-0	0-0	03-01-01
Weymouth v Oxford Utd	-	-	-	-	1-1	0-1	00-01-01
Woking v Rushden & D	-	-	-	-	3-0	1-1	02-02-03

WEDNESDAY 10TH DECEMBER 2008
CHAMPIONSHIP

Ipswich v Bristol C	-	-	-	-	-	6-0	03-01-00
Watford v Norwich	2-1	1-2	-	2-1	-	1-1	04-02-02

Sponsored by Stan James

FRIDAY 12TH DECEMBER 2008
LEAGUE 1

Brighton v MK Dons	2-3	-	-	-	-	-	00-00-01

LEAGUE 2

Chesterfield v Macclesfield	-	-	-	-	-	2-2	02-01-00
Lincoln v Accrington	-	-	-	-	3-1	2-0	02-00-00

SATURDAY 13TH DECEMBER 2008
PREMIER LEAGUE

Aston Villa v Bolton	2-0	1-1	1-1	2-2	0-1	4-0	04-03-02
Chelsea v West Ham	2-3	-	-	4-1	1-0	1-0	09-01-04
Liverpool v Hull	-	-	-	-	-	-	00-00-00
Man City v Everton	3-1	5-1	0-1	2-0	2-1	0-2	09-00-05
Middlesboro v Arsenal	0-2	0-4	0-1	2-1	1-1	2-1	04-01-09
Portsmouth v Newcastle	-	1-1	1-1	0-0	2-1	0-0	03-05-01
Stoke v Fulham	-	-	-	-	-	-	02-01-01
Sunderland v WBA	1-2	0-1	-	1-1	2-0	-	04-05-02
Tottenham v Man Utd	0-2	1-2	0-1	1-2	0-4	1-1	04-04-12
Wigan v Blackburn	-	-	-	0-3	0-3	5-3	01-00-02

CHAMPIONSHIP

Burnley v Southampton	-	-	-	1-1	2-3	2-3	00-01-02
Charlton v Derby	-	-	-	-	-	-	04-02-04
Crystal Pal v Doncaster	-	-	-	-	-	-	00-00-00
Ipswich v Cardiff	-	1-1	3-1	1-0	3-1	1-1	03-02-00
Nottm Forest v Blackpool	-	-	-	1-1	1-1	-	00-02-00
Plymouth v QPR	0-1	2-0	2-1	3-1	1-1	2-1	04-01-01
Preston v Birmingham	-	-	-	-	1-0	-	04-01-01
Reading v Norwich	0-2	0-1	-	4-0	-	-	02-00-04
Sheff Weds v Bristol C	-	1-0	2-3	-	-	0-1	02-00-02
Swansea v Sheff Utd	-	-	-	-	-	-	00-01-00
Watford v Coventry	5-2	1-1	2-3	4-0	-	2-1	05-01-01
Wolves v Barnsley	-	-	-	-	2-0	1-0	06-06-02

LEAGUE 1

Bristol R v Tranmere	-	-	-	-	-	1-1	03-01-00
Carlisle v Leicester	-	-	-	-	-	-	00-00-00
Crewe v Swindon	0-1	-	-	-	-	0-0	02-01-03
Hereford v Hartlepool	-	-	-	-	3-1	-	05-00-02
Leeds v Colchester	-	-	-	-	3-0	-	01-00-02
Leyton O v Cheltenham	-	1-4	2-3	1-0	2-0	2-0	04-01-03
Peterboro v Oldham	0-1	2-2	1-2	-	-	-	00-03-02
Scunthorpe v Northampton	-	1-0	2-0	-	1-0	-	08-02-00
Southend v Huddersfield	-	1-2	-	1-1	-	4-1	01-02-04
Walsall v Millwall	1-2	1-1	-	-	-	3-0	04-03-01
Yeovil v Stockport	-	-	-	-	-	-	00-00-00

LEAGUE 2

Barnet v Gillingham	-	-	-	-	-	-	03-00-01
Brentford v Bradford	-	-	1-2	1-1	2-1	2-2	05-02-02
Bury v Port Vale	-	-	-	-	-	-	02-03-00
Chester v Notts Co	-	-	3-2	0-2	0-0	0-1	02-02-03
Dagenham & R v Exeter	-	0-2	2-3	2-2	4-1	-	01-01-02
Grimsby v Shrewsbury	-	-	0-1	1-1	2-1	1-1	02-02-01

Morecambe v Darlington	-	-	-	-	-	0-3	00-00-01
Rochdale v Bournemouth	1-1	-	-	-	-	-	00-01-00
Rotherham v Aldershot	-	-	-	-	-	-	00-00-00
Wycombe v Luton	1-2	0-0	-	-	-	-	00-03-04

SCOTTISH PREMIER LEAGUE

Aberdeen v Falkirk	-	-	-	3-0/1-0	2-1	1-1/2-1	07-06-00
Celtic v Hearts	4-2/1-0	5-0/2-2	3-0/0-2	1-1/1-0	2-1/1-3	5-0/3-0	24-11-05
Dundee Utd v Rangers	0-3/1-4	1-3/2-0/3-3	1-1	0-0/1-4	2-1	2-1/3-3	07-10-19
Hibernian v Hamilton	-	-	-	-	-	-	03-01-00
Motherwell v Kilmarnock	0-1	2-1/1-0	0-1/1-1	2-2	5-0/0-1	1-2/1-0	12-06-09
St Mirren v Inv CT	0-4/1-4	0-4/0-0	-	-	1-1/0-1	2-1/1-1	03-05-04

SCOTTISH DIVISION ONE

Clyde v Dundee -	-	-	1-1/3-3	2-1/1-1	1-2/1-1	02-04-02	
Partick v Airdrie Utd	-	-	3-2/1-1	-	4-2/0-1	-	06-06-05
Queen of Sth v Dunfermline	-	-	-	-	-	0-1/1-1	00-02-02
Ross County v Livingston	-	-	-	-	0-3/0-2	-	00-02-04
St Johnstone v Morton	-	-	-	-	-	2-2/3-2	05-02-02

SCOTTISH DIVISION TWO

Arbroath v Peterhead	-	-	-	-	-	-	00-00-00
Ayr v Alloa	3-1/0-1	-	4-3/1-1	1-1/0-1	0-1/4-3	2-0/3-1	08-02-03
Brechin v Stranraer	3-1/3-1	-	4-1/2-1	2-3/0-0	3-0/1-1	-	07-07-04
East Fife v Stirling	1-1/2-1	-	-	-	-	-	06-06-05
Queen's Park v Raith	-	-	-	-	-	2-5/0-1	00-00-02

SCOTTISH DIVISION THREE

Annan Ath v Berwick	-	-	-	-	-	-	00-00-00
Dumbarton v Forfar	1-2/1-2	2-1/1-1	0-1/1-1	2-0/0-0	-	0-0/0-0	02-07-03
Elgin v E Stirling	3-1/3-0	3-1/3-0	1-3/0-0	1-1/3-0	5-0/2-1	6-0/3-0	11-03-02
Montrose v Cowdenbeath	-	1-3/1-1	3-1/1-2	0-1/0-3	-	-	08-04-13
Stenhsmuir v Albion	-	-	3-0/1-1	1-0/4-2	3-2/0-4	0-1/2-2	09-04-05

FRIDAY 19TH DECEMBER 2008
LEAGUE 1

Hartlepool v Southend	2-1	-	-	1-2	-	4-3	04-01-03

SATURDAY 20TH DECEMBER 2008
PREMIER LEAGUE

Arsenal v Liverpool	1-1	4-2	3-1	2-1	3-0	1-1	08-07-05
Blackburn v Stoke	-	-	-	-	-	-	02-00-00
Bolton v Portsmouth	-	1-0	0-1	1-0	3-2	0-1	07-02-02
Everton v Chelsea	1-3	0-1	0-1	1-1	2-3	0-1	04-07-08
Fulham v Middlesboro	1-0	3-2	0-2	1-0	2-1	1-2	05-00-02
Hull v Sunderland	-	-	-	-	0-1	-	01-01-01
Man Utd v Wigan	-	-	-	4-0	3-1	4-0	03-00-00
Newcastle v Tottenham	2-1	4-0	0-1	3-1	3-1	3-1	09-04-03
WBA v Man City	1-2	-	2-0	2-0	-	-	04-00-04
West Ham v Aston Villa	2-2	-	-	4-0	1-1	2-2	04-09-02

CHAMPIONSHIP

Barnsley v Plymouth	1-1	1-0	-	-	2-2	3-2	04-03-01
Birmingham v Reading	-	-	-	-	-	1-1	03-02-02
Blackpool v Swansea	-	-	-	1-0	1-1	-	03-05-00

214

Match							
Bristol C v Burnley	-	-	-	-	-	2-2	02-03-01
Cardiff v Sheff Weds	-	-	-	1-0	1-2	1-0	02-00-01
Coventry v Ipswich	2-4	1-1	1-2	1-1	1-2	2-1	03-03-04
Derby v Watford	3-0	3-2	2-2	1-2	-	-	04-03-03
Doncaster v Wolves	-	-	-	-	-	-	00-00-00
Norwich v Charlton	-	-	1-0	-	-	1-1	01-02-05
QPR v Preston	-	-	1-2	0-2	1-0	2-2	01-02-02
Sheff Utd v C Palace	2-1	0-3	-	1-0	-	0-1	05-02-06
Southampton v Nottm Forest	-	-	-	-	-	-	01-04-04

LEAGUE 1

Match							
Cheltenham v Walsall	-	-	-	-	-	1-2	00-00-01
Colchester v Scunthorpe	-	-	-	1-0	-	0-1	06-02-03
Huddersfield v Hereford	-	-	-	-	-	-	00-00-00
Leicester v Peterboro	-	-	-	-	-	-	01-00-01
Millwall v Crewe	-	1-1	4-3	1-3	2-2	2-0	04-02-01
Milton K v Leeds	-	-	-	-	-	-	05-03-02
Northampton v Carlisle	-	2-0	-	0-3	3-2	2-2	05-06-01
Oldham v Leyton O	-	-	-	-	3-3	2-0	01-01-00
Stockport v Bristol R	-	-	-	0-1	2-1	-	04-00-02
Swindon v Yeovil	-	-	-	4-2	-	0-1	01-00-01
Tranmere v Brighton	-	1-0	-	-	2-1	2-0	03-02-00

LEAGUE 2

Match							
Accrington v Rotherham	-	-	-	-	-	0-1	00-00-01
Aldershot v Grimsby	-	-	-	-	-	-	00-00-00
Bournemouth v Bury	1-2	-	-	-	-	-	03-03-01
Bradford v Chester	-	-	-	-	-	2-1	03-02-00
Darlington v Barnet	-	-	-	2-1	2-0	1-0	06-01-05
Exeter v Rochdale	1-1	-	-	-	-	-	06-04-01
Gillingham v Brentford	-	-	-	3-2	2-1	-	04-01-01
Luton v Morecambe	-	-	-	-	-	-	00-00-00
Macclesfield v Dagenham & R	-	-	-	-	-	1-1	03-02-00
Notts Co v Lincoln	-	-	1-0	2-1	3-1	0-1	03-00-03
Port Vale v Chesterfield	5-2	1-1	1-0	3-1	3-2	-	06-01-00
Shrewsbury v Wycombe	-	-	0-1	1-1	0-0	0-1	01-05-02

SCOTTISH PREMIER LEAGUE

Match							
Falkirk v Celtic	-	-	-	0-3	0-1/1-0	1-4/0-1	02-02-09
Hamilton v Motherwell	-	-	-	-	-	-	01-00-01
Hearts v Dundee Utd	2-0/2-1	3-0/3-1	3-2	3-0	4-0/0-4	1-3/1-0	23-05-07
Inv CT v Aberdeen	-	-	1-3/0-1	1-1/0-1	1-1	1-2/3-4	00-02-05
Kilmarnock v St Mirren	-	-	-	-	1-1	0-0/1-0	03-02-01
Rangers v Hibernian	2-1	5-2/3-0	4-1/3-0	0-3/2-0	3-0	0-1/2-1	28-04-04

SCOTTISH DIVISION ONE

Match							
Airdrie Utd v St Johnstone	-	-	1-0/0-0	3-1/2-1	2-1/1-2	-	05-06-08
Dundee v Partick	4-1	1-0/2-1	-	-	0-1/3-1	3-0/1-0	08-04-06
Dunfermline v Clyde	-	-	-	-	-	1-1/2-1	04-02-00
Morton v Ross County	-	-	-	-	-	-	00-00-02
Livingston v Queen of Sth	-	-	-	-	2-0/0-1	2-2/1-0	07-03-05

SCOTTISH DIVISION TWO

Match							
Alloa v Brechin	-	-	2-2/1-1	-	2-2/2-3	2-2/0-4	04-05-03
Peterhead v Ayr	-	-	-	3-3/1-2	3-1/2-2	3-0/4-1	03-02-01
Raith v Arbroath	-	-	-	-	-	-	01-01-00

Stirling v Queen's Park	1-0/1-0	1-0/0-0	-	-	-	-	07-03-03
Stranraer v East Fife	-	-	-	-	-	0-2/0-2	05-04-06

SCOTTISH DIVISION THREE

Annan Ath v Dumbarton	-	-	-	-	-	-	00-00-00
E Stirling v Cowdenbeath	-	1-1/0-1	0-2/2-1	0-1/1-1	-	-	09-08-11
Elgin v Berwick	-	-	-	2-2/1-3	1-2/2-1	-	01-01-02
Forfar v Stenhsmuir	1-0/3-3	2-0/1-1	-	-	-	0-1/1-2	08-05-04
Montrose v Albion	0-1/1-1	1-0/3-1	1-1/0-1	0-2/2-2	2-1/2-3	0-1/2-1	14-04-14

CONFERENCE

Altrincham v Burton	-	-	-	1-2	2-3	0-0	00-01-03
Cambridge U v Salisbury	-	-	-	-	-	1-1	00-01-00
Crawley v Kidderminster	-	-	-	2-0	0-0	0-4	01-01-01
Forest G v Kettering	1-0	-	-	-	-	-	04-00-00
Grays v Barrow	-	-	-	-	-	-	00-00-00
Lewes v Woking	-	-	-	-	-	-	00-00-00
Mansfield v Weymouth	-	-	-	-	-	-	00-00-00
Oxford Utd v Stevenage	-	-	-	-	2-0	2-1	02-00-00
Rushden & D v Northwich	-	-	-	-	1-0	1-0	04-01-02
Torquay v Histon	-	-	-	-	-	1-0	01-00-00
Wrexham v Eastbourne	-	-	-	-	-	-	00-00-00
York v Ebbsfleet U	-	-	0-0	1-0	0-2	0-1	01-01-02

FRIDAY 26TH DECEMBER 2008
PREMIER LEAGUE

Aston Villa v Arsenal	1-1	0-2	1-3	0-0	0-1	1-2	05-07-08
Chelsea v WBA	2-0	-	1-0	4-0	-	-	03-01-00
Liverpool v Bolton	2-0	3-1	1-0	1-0	3-0	4-0	08-01-00
Man City v Hull	-	-	-	-	-	-	01-00-00
Middlesboro v Everton	1-1	1-0	1-1	0-1	2-1	0-2	05-04-05
Portsmouth v West Ham	-	-	-	1-1	2-0	0-0	01-02-03
Stoke v Man Utd	-	-	-	-	-	-	00-00-00
Sunderland v Blackburn	0-0	-	-	0-1	-	1-2	02-03-03
Tottenham v Fulham	1-1	0-3	2-0	1-0	0-0	5-1	04-02-01
Wigan v Newcastle	-	-	-	1-0	1-0	1-0	03-00-00

CHAMPIONSHIP

Burnley v Barnsley	-	-	-	-	4-2	2-1	03-01-01
Charlton v QPR	-	-	-	-	-	0-1	03-02-01
Crystal Pal v Norwich	2-0	1-0	3-3	4-1	3-1	1-1	09-03-05
Ipswich v Birmingham	-	-	-	-	1-0	-	04-01-02
Nottm Forest v Doncaster	-	-	-	4-0	0-1	0-0	01-01-01
Plymouth v Southampton	-	-	-	2-1	1-1	1-1	01-02-00
Preston v Derby	4-2	3-0	3-0	1-1	1-2	-	03-01-01
Reading v Cardiff	-	2-1	2-1	5-1	-	-	04-01-03
Sheff Weds v Blackpool	-	0-1	3-2	-	-	2-1	02-00-01
Swansea v Coventry	-	-	-	-	-	-	00-00-00
Watford v Bristol C	-	-	-	-	-	1-2	04-03-02
Wolves v Sheff Utd	1-3	-	4-2	0-0	-	0-0	05-06-03

LEAGUE 1

Brighton v Colchester	-	2-1	-	-	-	-	02-02-00
Bristol R v MK Dons	-	-	-	-	1-1	-	00-01-00
Carlisle v Huddersfield	-	1-0	-	-	1-1	2-1	02-01-00
Crewe v Oldham	1-2	-	-	-	2-1	1-4	01-00-02

216

Hereford v Tranmere	-	-	-	-	-	-	01-00-00
Leeds v Leicester	-	3-2	0-2	2-1	1-2	-	07-02-04
Leyton O v Swindon	-	-	-	-	-	2-1	01-00-00
Peterboro v Millwall	-	-	-	-	-	-	00-03-01
Scunthorpe v Hartlepool	4-0	-	-	2-0	-	-	08-03-01
Southend v Northampton	-	0-1	2-1	-	-	1-1	02-03-01
Walsall v Stockport	-	-	3-0	-	2-0	-	03-01-03
Yeovil v Cheltenham	-	0-0	4-1	-	0-1	2-1	04-04-02

LEAGUE 2

Barnet v Aldershot	-	2-1	2-1	-	-	-	02-00-00
Brentford v Bournemouth	-	1-0	2-1	0-2	0-0	-	07-04-03
Bury v Darlington	2-2	1-1	0-1	1-0	1-1	1-2	04-05-02
Chester v Accrington	-	3-3	-	-	2-0	2-3	01-01-01
Chesterfield v Luton	2-1	1-0	0-1	-	-	-	03-02-02
Dagenham & R v Gillingham	-	-	-	-	-	-	00-00-00
Grimsby v Notts Co	-	2-0	3-2	4-0	0-2	1-1	04-03-01
Lincoln v Bradford	-	-	-	-	-	1-2	00-00-01
Morecambe v Macclesfield	-	-	-	-	-	0-1	01-00-02
Rochdale v Shrewsbury	1-1	-	1-1	4-3	1-1	1-1	06-04-02
Rotherham v Port Vale	-	-	-	1-1	1-5	-	02-01-02
Wycombe v Exeter	-	-	-	-	-	-	00-00-00

CONFERENCE

Barrow v Wrexham	-	-	-	-	-	-	00-00-00
Burton v York - -	0-2	0-0	1-2	4-3	01-01-02		
Eastbourne v Lewes	-	-	1-2	3-1	2-1	0-2	02-00-02
Ebbsfleet U v Grays	-	-	-	1-3	2-0	4-1	03-00-02
Histon v Cambridge U	-	-	-	-	-	1-0	01-00-00
Kettering v Mansfield	-	-	-	-	-	-	00-00-00
Kidderminstr v Forest G	-	-	-	1-3	2-2	1-0	01-03-01
Northwich v Altrincham	-	-	-	-	1-1	1-2	03-05-04
Salisbury v Oxford Utd	-	-	-	-	-	3-1	01-00-00
Stevenage v Rushden & D	-	-	-	-	1-0	2-1	04-02-01
Weymouth v Torquay	-	-	-	-	-	0-0	00-01-00
Woking v Crawley	-	-	2-0	0-0	1-2	1-1	01-02-01

SATURDAY 27TH DECEMBER 2008
SCOTTISH PREMIER LEAGUE

Aberdeen v Hearts	1-1/0-1	0-1	0-1/2-0	1-1	1-3/1-0	1-1/0-1	16-09-13
Dundee Utd v Falkirk	-	-	-	2-1/0-2	1-2/1-5	2-0/0-0	08-01-03
Hibernian v Kilmarnock	2-0	3-1/3-0	0-1/3-0	4-2/2-1	2-2/0-1	4-1/2-0	12-09-06
Motherwell v Inv CT	-	-	1-2	0-2/0-1	1-4/1-0	2-1/3-1	03-00-04
Rangers v Celtic	3-2/1-2	0-1/1-2	2-0/1-2	3-1/0-1	1-1/2-0	3-0/1-0	19-11-10
St Mirren v Hamilton	-	-	1-0/0-1	2-1/0-2	-	-	10-01-07

SCOTTISH DIVISION ONE

Airdrie Utd v Morton	-	1-6/2-0	-	-	-	-	10-05-06
Dunfermline v Livingston	2-1/2-0	2-2	0-0	0-1/3-2	-	0-4/1-1	08-04-04
Partick v Ross County	-	-	4-0/0-0	-	3-2/1-1	-	03-04-01
Queen of Sth v Dundee	-	-	-	0-0/1-3	2-0/2-2	2-1/1-0	03-02-01
St Johnstone v Clyde	0-1/1-2	3-0/1-3	3-0/0-0	0-0/1-0	0-0/2-1	1-1/1-2	05-06-04

SCOTTISH DIVISION TWO

Alloa v Stranraer	-	-	1-2/3-0	-	1-1/1-0	-	05-07-03
Arbroath v Stirling	-	-	2-1/3-2	-	-	-	07-01-05

Ayr v Queen's Park	-	-	-	-	-	2-3/3-1	01-00-01
East Fife v Brechin	-	-	-	-	-	-	10-03-03
Peterhead v Raith	-	-	-	0-1/0-0	0-1/0-0	0-1/1-0	01-02-03

SCOTTISH DIVISION THREE

Albion v E Stirling	6-0/3-1	5-0/5-1	3-3/1-1	4-2/2-0	4-0/2-1	2-3/2-2	18-09-08
Berwick v Montrose	-	-	-	1-1/1-1	1-2/1-0	-	08-08-04
Cowdenbeath v Forfar	1-1/2-2	-	-	-	3-2/2-1	-	05-02-06
Dumbarton v Elgin	-	-	-	-	3-1/1-0	1-0/1-4	06-01-01
Stenhsmuir v Annan Ath	-	-	-	-	-	-	00-00-00

SUNDAY 28TH DECEMBER 2008
PREMIER LEAGUE

Arsenal v Portsmouth	-	1-1	3-0	4-0	2-2	3-1	03-02-00
Blackburn v Man City	1-0	2-3	0-0	2-0	4-2	1-0	08-01-03
Bolton v Wigan	-	-	-	1-1	0-1	4-1	04-03-01
Everton v Sunderland	2-1	-	-	2-2	-	7-1	05-02-01
Fulham v Chelsea	0-0	0-1	1-4	1-0	0-2	1-2	01-02-04
Hull v Aston Villa	-	-	-	-	-	-	00-00-00
Man Utd v Middlesboro	1-0	2-3	1-1	0-0	1-1	4-1	07-04-03
Newcastle v Liverpool	1-0	1-1	1-0	1-3	2-1	0-3	06-05-05
WBA v Tottenham	2-3	-	1-1	2-0	-	-	01-01-01
West Ham v Stoke	-	0-1	2-0	-	-	-	01-01-01

CHAMPIONSHIP

Barnsley v Preston	-	-	-	-	0-1	1-0	02-00-02
Birmingham v Swansea	-	-	-	-	-	-	02-01-01
Blackpool v Wolves	-	-	-	-	-	0-0	00-01-01
Bristol C v C Palace	-	-	-	-	-	1-1	01-02-00
Cardiff v Plymouth	1-1	-	0-1	0-2	2-2	1-0	03-02-05
Coventry v Sheff Weds	1-1	-	-	2-1	3-1	0-0	09-05-02
Derby v Ipswich	1-4	2-2	3-2	3-3	2-1	-	03-04-02
Doncaster v Burnley	-	-	-	-	-	-	02-00-02
Norwich v Nottm Forest	0-0	1-0	-	-	-	-	06-04-02
QPR v Watford	-	-	3-1	1-2	-	1-1	01-02-02
Sheff Utd v Charlton	-	-	-	-	2-1	0-2	05-00-02
Southampton v Reading	-	-	-	0-0	-	-	00-01-00

LEAGUE 1

Cheltenham v Peterboro	1-1	-	-	2-1	-	-	02-01-00
Colchester v Leyton O	-	-	-	-	-	-	02-02-00
Hartlepool v Crewe	-	-	-	-	-	3-0	01-00-01
Huddersfield v Scunthorpe	-	3-2	-	1-4	1-1	-	01-01-01
Leicester v Hereford	-	-	-	-	-	-	00-00-00
Millwall v Yeovil	-	-	-	-	1-1	2-1	01-01-00
Milton K v Southend	-	-	-	2-1	-	-	01-00-00
Northampton v Bristol R	-	2-0	2-1	4-0	-	0-1	05-01-03
Oldham v Carlisle	-	-	-	-	0-0	2-0	02-01-00
Stockport v Leeds	-	-	-	-	-	-	00-00-00
Swindon v Brighton	-	2-1	-	-	-	0-3	04-01-03
Tranmere v Walsall	-	-	2-1	1-2	-	0-0	02-02-01

LEAGUE 2

Accrington v Grimsby	-	-	-	-	4-1	4-1	02-00-00
Aldershot v Dagenham & R	-	2-1	4-0	3-1	1-1	-	05-01-00

Sponsored by Stan James

Bournemouth v Barnet	-	-	-	-	-	-	00-01-00
Bradford v Morecambe	-	-	-	-	-	1-0	01-00-00
Darlington v Chesterfield	-	-	-	-	-	0-0	01-03-02
Exeter v Brentford	-	-	-	-	-	-	00-02-02
Gillingham v Wycombe	-	-	-	-	-	-	03-01-01
Luton v Lincoln	-	-	-	-	-	-	00-01-01
Macclesfield v Chester	-	-	1-2	1-0	1-1	1-2	02-02-02
Notts Co v Rotherham	-	-	-	-	-	0-1	04-01-01
Port Vale v Rochdale	-	-	-	-	-	-	00-00-00
Shrewsbury v Bury	4-1	-	2-2	0-1	1-3	0-1	04-04-03

CONFERENCE

Cambridge U v Stevenage	-	-	-	1-0	1-0	2-1	03-00-00
Crawley v Eastbourne	-	3-1	-	-	-	-	01-00-00
Forest G v Barrow	-	-	-	-	-	-	00-01-00
Grays v Histon	-	-	-	-	-	0-1	00-00-01
Lewes v Kettering	-	-	-	-	-	-	00-00-00
Mansfield v Burton	-	-	-	-	-	-	00-00-00
Northwich v Salisbury	-	-	-	-	-	0-1	00-00-01
Oxford Utd v Ebbsfleet U	-	-	-	-	1-0	0-0	01-01-00
Rushden & D v Weymouth	-	-	-	-	4-1	3-2	02-01-00
Torquay v Kidderminster	2-2	1-1	-	-	-	1-0	01-03-01
Wrexham v Woking	-	-	-	-	-	-	00-00-00
York v Altrincham	-	-	-	5-0	1-0	2-2	02-01-00

THURSDAY 1ST JANUARY 2009
CONFERENCE

Altrincham v Northwich	-	-	-	-	3-0	1-2	02-03-07
Cambridge U v Histon	-	-	-	-	-	1-0	01-00-00
Crawley v Woking	-	-	2-1	2-2	0-0	5-3	02-02-00
Forest G v Kidderminster	-	-	-	0-0	2-1	2-2	03-02-00
Grays v Ebbsfleet U	-	-	-	6-1	0-2	1-1	03-01-01
Lewes v Eastbourne	-	-	1-0	1-0	1-1	2-2	02-02-00
Mansfield v Kettering	-	-	-	-	-	-	00-00-00
Oxford Utd v Salisbury	-	-	-	-	-	2-1	01-00-00
Rushden & D v Stevenage	-	-	-	-	2-2	0-0	03-03-01
Torquay v Weymouth	-	-	-	-	-	3-2	01-00-00
Wrexham v Barrow	-	-	-	-	-	-	00-00-00
York v Burton	-	-	1-2	0-1	3-2	0-0	01-01-02

SATURDAY 3RD JANUARY 2009
LEAGUE 1

Brighton v Northampton	-	-	-	-	1-1	2-1	03-01-01
Carlisle v Walsall	-	-	-	-	-	2-1	03-03-02
Colchester v Tranmere	2-2	1-1	1-2	1-0	-	-	02-02-02
Crewe v Bristol R	-	-	-	-	-	1-1	03-01-01
Hartlepool v Leicester	-	-	-	-	-	-	00-00-00
Hereford v Leeds	-	-	-	-	-	-	00-00-00
Huddersfield v Oldham	1-1	-	2-1	3-2	0-3	1-1	03-04-01
Leyton O v Southend	2-1	2-1	2-2	-	-	2-2	04-02-03
Millwall v Swindon	-	-	-	-	-	1-2	04-01-01
Peterboro v MK Dons	-	-	0-3	-	4-0	1-2	01-00-02
Stockport v Cheltenham	1-1	-	-	2-2	-	-	00-02-00
Yeovil v Scunthorpe	-	2-1	4-3	0-1	0-2	-	02-00-02

LEAGUE 2

Match							
Aldershot v Notts Co	-	-	-	-	-	-	00-00-00
Barnet v Grimsby	-	-	-	0-1	0-1	0-3	00-00-03
Bradford v Shrewsbury	-	-	-	-	-	4-2	04-01-01
Brentford v Chesterfield	2-1	1-1	2-2	1-1	2-1	2-1	05-06-01
Chester v Luton	-	-	-	-	-	-	00-00-00
Darlington v Bournemouth	2-2	-	-	-	-	-	00-02-00
Exeter v Macclesfield	1-1	-	-	-	-	-	00-03-02
Morecambe v Lincoln	-	-	-	-	-	1-2	00-00-01
Port Vale v Gillingham	-	-	-	0-0	2-0	2-1	03-01-00
Rochdale v Accrington	-	-	-	-	4-2	4-1	02-00-00
Rotherham v Dagenham & R	-	-	-	-	-	2-1	01-00-00
Wycombe v Bury	-	-	1-2	4-0	3-0	1-0	06-00-03

SCOTTISH PREMIER LEAGUE

Match							
Celtic v Dundee Utd	5-0/2-0	5-0/2-1/2-1	1-0	2-0/3-3	2-2	3-0/0-0	26-08-02
Falkirk v Kilmarnock	-	-	-	1-2	1-2/0-2	1-1/0-0	03-04-04
Hamilton v Aberdeen	-	-	-	-	-	-	00-00-02
Hearts v Hibernian	5-1/4-4	2-0	2-1/1-2	4-0/4-1	3-2/2-0	0-1/1-0	20-11-05
Inv CT v Rangers	-	-	1-1	0-1/2-3	2-1	0-3/0-1	01-01-04
St Mirren v Motherwell	-	-	-	-	2-0/0-0	0-1/3-1	05-04-05

SCOTTISH DIVISION ONE

Match							
Clyde v Partick	-	-	2-1/1-1	-	0-0/2-0	1-2/1-4	08-04-05
Dundee v Dunfermline	2-3/2-2	0-2/0-1	1-2/2-1	-	-	1-1/0-0	05-06-08
Morton v Queen of Sth	-	-	-	-	-	0-1/0-3	01-03-03
Livingston v Airdrie Utd	-	-	-	-	3-0/1-3	-	06-01-04
Ross County v St Johnstone	0-0/2-3	0-3/2-0	0-1/4-0	2-1/2-2	2-2/1-1	-	03-04-03

SCOTTISH DIVISION TWO

Match							
Brechin v Arbroath	-	-	4-1/4-3	-	-	-	05-03-02
Queen's Park v Peterhead	2-0/1-2	0-2/1-0	1-2/1-1	-	-	1-1/2-0	04-02-04
Raith v East Fife	-	-	-	-	-	-	00-00-00
Stirling v Alloa	-	-	2-0/0-4	1-2/0-0	5-0/4-0	-	06-03-04
Stranraer v Ayr	-	-	2-1/1-3	-	1-3/0-3	-	04-01-07

SCOTTISH DIVISION THREE

Match							
Albion v Dumbarton	-	-	-	-	2-1/0-1	2-0/0-1	07-03-09
Cowdenbeath v Berwick	1-2/0-1	-	-	0-1/1-1	-	3-1/1-2	07-05-10
E Stirling v Stenhsmuir	-	-	3-2/1-4	0-0/0-7	5-0/0-1	1-1/3-4	04-06-09
Elgin v Annan Ath	-	-	-	-	-	-	00-00-00
Forfar v Montrose	-	-	-	-	-	1-4/1-1	06-04-05

CONFERENCE

Match							
Altrincham v Forest G	-	-	-	2-1	2-2	1-0	02-02-00
Barrow v Cambridge U	-	-	-	-	-	-	00-00-00
Burton v Torquay	-	-	-	-	-	3-1	01-00-00
Eastbourne v Oxford Utd	-	-	-	-	-	-	00-00-00
Ebbsfleet U v Wrexham	-	-	-	-	-	-	00-00-00
Histon v Mansfield	-	-	-	-	-	-	00-00-00
Kettering v Grays	-	0-0	-	-	-	-	00-01-00
Kidderminstr v Crawley	-	-	-	1-0	0-1	1-1	01-01-01
Salisbury v Rushden & D	-	-	-	-	-	1-1	00-01-01
Stevenage v Lewes	-	-	-	-	-	-	00-00-00
Weymouth v York	-	-	-	-	1-2	1-2	00-00-02
Woking v Northwich	2-3	3-0	2-0	-	3-2	2-3	09-04-02

SATURDAY 10TH JANUARY 2009
PREMIER LEAGUE

Arsenal v Bolton	2-1	2-1	2-2	1-1	2-1	2-0	06-03-00
Aston Villa v WBA	2-1	-	1-1	0-0	-	-	01-02-00
Everton v Hull	-	-	-	-	-	-	00-00-00
Fulham v Blackburn	0-4	3-4	0-2	2-1	1-1	2-2	03-03-03
Man Utd v Chelsea	2-1	1-1	1-3	1-0	1-1	2-0	05-09-05
Middlesboro v Sunderland	3-0	-	-	0-2	-	2-2	06-04-02
Newcastle v West Ham	4-0	-	-	0-0	2-2	3-1	09-05-03
Portsmouth v Man City	-	4-2	1-3	2-1	2-1	0-0	05-02-03
Stoke v Liverpool	-	-	-	-	-	-	00-00-00
Wigan v Tottenham	-	-	-	1-2	3-3	1-1	00-02-01

CHAMPIONSHIP

Barnsley v Southampton	-	-	-	-	2-2	2-2	01-02-00
Blackpool v Birmingham	-	-	-	-	-	-	01-01-00
Burnley v Swansea	-	-	-	-	-	-	02-01-00
Cardiff v Derby	-	4-1	0-2	0-0	2-2	-	01-02-01
Charlton v Nottm Forest	-	-	-	-	-	-	02-02-02
Doncaster v Bristol C	-	-	1-1	2-0	0-1	-	01-01-01
Ipswich v Sheff Weds	2-1	-	-	2-1	0-2	4-1	03-00-05
Plymouth v C Palace	-	-	-	2-0	1-0	1-0	03-00-01
QPR v Coventry	-	-	4-1	0-1	0 1	1-2	05-04-03
Reading v Watford	1-0	2-1	3-0	0-0	0-2	-	04-02-01
Sheff Utd v Norwich	0-1	1-0	-	1-3	-	2-0	07-03-05
Wolves v Preston	4-0	-	2-2	1-1	1-3	1-0	03-02-03

LEAGUE 1

Bristol R v Yeovil	-	0-1	2-2	-	-	1-1	00-02-01
Cheltenham v Millwall	-	-	-	-	3-2	0-1	01-00-01
Leeds v Carlisle	-	-	-	-	-	3-2	01-00-00
Leicester v Leyton O	-	-	-	-	-	-	00-00-00
Milton K v Colchester	-	-	2-0	1-1	-	-	01-01-00
Northampton v Huddersfield	0-0	0-1	-	-	1-1	3-0	02-02-03
Oldham v Hartlepool	-	0-2	3-2	2-1	-	0-1	02-00-02
Scunthorpe v Hereford	-	-	-	-	-	-	05-02-02
Southend v Crewe	-	-	-	-	-	3-0	02-00-00
Swindon v Stockport	0-1	1-2	3-0	-	2-0	-	02-03-03
Tranmere v Peterboro	1-1	0-0	5-0	-	-	-	04-03-00
Walsall v Brighton	1-0	-	-	-	-	1-2	03-00-01

LEAGUE 2

Accrington v Darlington	-	-	-	-	0-2	0-3	00-00-02
Bournemouth v Bradford	-	-	2-0	0-1	1-1	-	05-03-03
Bury v Barnet	-	-	-	0-0	2-2	3-0	02-04-00
Chesterfield v Rochdale	-	-	-	-	-	3-4	01-04-03
Dagenham & R v Wycombe	-	-	-	-	-	2-2	00-01-01
Gillingham v Aldershot	-	-	-	-	-	-	00-00-00
Grimsby v Morecambe	-	-	-	-	-	1-2	00-00-01
Lincoln v Brentford	-	-	-	-	-	3-1	01-00-00
Luton v Rotherham	-	-	-	-	-	-	01-00-01
Macclesfield v Port Vale	-	-	-	-	-	-	00-00-00
Notts Co v Exeter	-	-	-	-	-	-	00-01-00
Shrewsbury v Chester	-	0-0	5-0	3-1	2-1	0-0	08-04-01

SCOTTISH DIVISION THREE

Annan Ath v Albion	-	-	-	-	-	-	00-00-00
Berwick v Forfar	2-1/0-0	0-4/3-1	1-0/1-1	-	-	-	08-06-03
Dumbarton v E Stirling	-	-	-	-	2-0/2-1	3-1/1-0	13-03-04
Montrose v Elgin	1-0/2-0	3-3/4-3	2-0/2-0	2-0/1-3	2-0/0-1	0-0/3-2	10-03-03
Stenhsmuir v Cowdenbeath	4-1/1-1	-	2-2/1-1	2-0/1-2	-	-	05-06-06

FRIDAY 16TH JANUARY 2009
LEAGUE 1

Hartlepool v Northampton	-	-	-	-	-	0-1	03-01-02

SATURDAY 17TH JANUARY 2009
PREMIER LEAGUE

Blackburn v Newcastle	5-2	1-1	2-2	0-3	1-3	3-1	09-04-03
Bolton v Man Utd	1-1	1-2	2-2	1-2	0-4	1-0	01-03-05
Chelsea v Stoke	-	-	-	-	-	-	01-00-00
Hull v Arsenal	-	-	-	-	-	-	00-00-00
Liverpool v Everton	0-0	0-0	2-1	3-1	0-0	1-0	10-08-02
Man City v Wigan	-	-	-	0-1	0-1	0-0	01-01-02
Sunderland v Aston Villa	1-0	-	-	1-3	-	1-1	03-03-02
Tottenham v Portsmouth	-	4-3	3-1	3-1	2-1	2-0	05-00-00
WBA v Middlesboro	1-0	-	1-2	0-2	-	-	02-02-04
West Ham v Fulham	1-1	-	-	2-1	3-3	2-1	02-02-01

CHAMPIONSHIP

Birmingham v Cardiff	-	-	-	-	1-0	-	02-01-00
Bristol C v Wolves	-	-	-	-	-	0-0	03-02-03
Coventry v Blackpool	-	-	-	-	-	3-1	01-00-00
Crystal Pal v Ipswich	1-1	3-4	-	2-2	2-0	0-1	05-05-02
Derby v QPR	-	-	0-0	1-2	1-1	-	01-03-02
Norwich v Barnsley	-	-	-	-	5-1	1-0	04-04-00
Nottm Forest v Plymouth	-	-	0-3	-	-	-	00-00-01
Preston v Burnley	3-1	5-3	1-0	0-0	2-0	2-1	08-03-02
Sheff Weds v Charlton	-	-	-	-	-	0-0	03-02-00
Southampton v Doncaster	-	-	-	-	-	-	00-00-00
Swansea v Reading	-	-	-	-	-	-	03-01-03
Watford v Sheff Utd	2-0	0-2	0-0	2-3	0-1	1-0	04-03-05

LEAGUE 1

Brighton v Leeds	-	-	1-0	2-1	-	0-1	03-01-01
Carlisle v MK Dons	-	-	-	-	-	-	00-00-00
Colchester v Cheltenham	1-1	-	-	-	-	-	02-01-00
Crewe v Scunthorpe	-	-	-	-	1-3	-	02-02-01
Hereford v Oldham	-	-	-	-	-	-	00-00-00
Huddersfield v Swindon	2-3	-	4-0	1-1	-	1-0	04-03-02
Leyton O v Bristol R	1-2	1-1	4-2	2-3	-	3-1	04-01-04
Millwall v Tranmere	-	-	-	-	2-2	0-1	02-03-02
Peterboro v Walsall	-	-	0-2	-	0-2	-	01-01-04
Stockport v Southend	-	-	-	-	-	-	01-00-00
Yeovil v Leicester	-	-	-	-	-	-	00-00-00

LEAGUE 2

Aldershot v Macclesfield	-	-	-	-	-	-	00-00-00
Barnet v Dagenham & R	2-1	2-4	5-0	-	-	3-1	04-00-01
Bradford v Accrington	-	-	-	-	-	0-3	00-00-01

Brentford v Notts Co	1-1	2-3	-	-	-	0-0	04-04-03
Chester v Chesterfield	-	-	-	-	-	0-0	02-01-00
Darlington v Luton	-	-	-	-	*	-	01 00 00
Exeter v Bury	1-2	-	-	-	-	-	02-01-02
Morecambe v Gillingham	-	-	-	-	-	-	00-00-00
Port Vale v Shrewsbury	-	-	-	-	-	-	00-00-00
Rochdale v Lincoln	0-1	0-3	3-1	1-2	2-0	0-2	08-06-05
Rotherham v Bournemouth	-	-	-	2-0	0-2	-	05-01-03
Wycombe v Grimsby	-	4-1	2-0	3-1	1-1	3-0	04-02-00

SCOTTISH PREMIER LEAGUE

Aberdeen v Celtic	0-4/1-1	1-3	0-1	1-3/2-2	0-1/1-2	1-3/1-5	06-14-18
Dundee Utd v Motherwell	1-1/2-1	0-2/1-0	0-1	1-1	1-1/1-1/0-0	1-0/2-0	13-19-06
Hamilton v Inv CT	-	-	-	-	-	-	00-00-00
Hibernian v St Mirren	-	-	-	-	5-1	0-1/2-0	12-01-02
Kilmarnock v Hearts	0-1/1-0	0-2/1-1	1-1	2-4/1-0	0-0/1-0	3-1/0-0	12-09-08
Rangers v Falkirk	-	-	-	2-2	4-0/2-1	7-2/2-0	09-04-00

SCOTTISH DIVISION ONE

Dundee v Morton	-	-	-	-	-	2-1/2-0	07-03-02
Dunfermline v Airdrie Utd	-	-	-	-	-	-	05-06-01
Livingston v Clyde	-	-	-	-	1-1/0-0	4-2/0-0	08-07-04
Partick v St Johnstone	-	-	0-4/0-4	-	1-5/2-0	2-2/0-0	04-04-07
Ross County v Queen of Sth	2-0/0-3	1-0/1-2	1-0/1-1	1-1/3-1	1-0/1-0	-	07-03-02

SCOTTISH DIVISION TWO

Arbroath v East Fife	-	0-1/0-0	-	1-0/2-1	1-1/1-3	2-3/0-1	06-04-09
Peterhead v Alloa	-	-	-	3-1/3-0	1-2/0-0	1-4/2-2	02-02-02
Queen's Park v Brechin	-	-	-	-	-	3-0/2-3	04-04-08
Raith v Stranraer	1-1/3-0	-	-	-	1-1/0-0	-	04-04-00
Stirling v Ayr	-	-	1-1/2-0	3-3/1-0	1-3/4-2	-	06-07-03

SCOTTISH DIVISION THREE

Albion v Berwick	-	-	-	0-2/0-1	0-1/0-1	-	05-04-09
Dumbarton v Stenhsmuir	0-0/3-1	0-1/4-0	-	-	4-0/1-1	1-2/1-0	09-04-07
E Stirling v Forfar	-	-	-	-	-	2-1/4-1	05-00-06
Elgin v Cowdenbeath	-	0-4/0-0	0-4/2-0	0-3/0-4	-	-	01-01-06
Montrose v Annan Ath	-	-	-	-	-	-	00-00-00

CONFERENCE

Cambridge U v Woking	-	-	-	0-2	3-0	1-0	02-00-01
Ebbsfleet U v Rushden & D	-	-	-	-	1-0	0-3	01-01-03
Forest G v Eastbourne	-	-	-	-	-	-	00-00-00
Grays v Burton	-	-	-	2-3	0-1	0-0	00-01-02
Kettering v Salisbury	-	-	-	-	-	-	01-00-00
Kidderminstr v Weymouth	-	-	-	-	0-1	0-2	01-00-02
Mansfield v Crawley	-	-	-	-	-	-	00-00-00
Northwich v Histon	-	-	-	-	-	1-3	00-00-01
Oxford Utd v Altrincham	-	-	-	-	1-1	4-0	01-01-00
Stevenage v Barrow	-	-	-	-	-	-	00-00-01
Torquay v Wrexham	2-1	-	1-0	1-0	1-1	-	04-03-01
York v Lewes	-	-	-	-	-	-	00-00-00

SATURDAY 24TH JANUARY 2009
LEAGUE 1

Bristol R v Colchester	-	-	-	-	-	-	02-01-00

Match							
Cheltenham v Brighton	-	-	-	-	1-1	2-1	02-02-00
Leeds v Peterboro	-	-	-	-	-	-	00-00-00
Leicester v Huddersfield	-	-	-	-	-	-	01-00-00
Milton K v Millwall	2-0	0-1	-	-	-	-	02-02-01
Northampton v Crewe	1-1	-	-	-	1-2	0-0	01-03-03
Oldham v Stockport	2-0	2-0	1-2	-	-	-	02-00-01
Scunthorpe v Leyton O	2-1	1-1	1-0	-	3-1	-	07-03-01
Southend v Yeovil	-	0-2	0-1	4-1	-	1-1	01-01-02
Swindon v Hartlepool	-	1-1	3-0	1-1	0-1	2-1	02-02-01
Tranmere v Carlisle	-	-	-	-	0-2	2-0	01-01-01
Walsall v Hereford	-	-	-	-	1-0	-	03-03-00

LEAGUE 2

Match							
Accrington v Barnet	-	2-0	4-1	-	2-1	0-2	03-00-01
Bournemouth v Wycombe	-	1-0	-	-	-	-	06-01-02
Bury v Aldershot	-	-	-	-	-	-	00-00-00
Chesterfield v Morecambe	-	-	-	-	-	2-2	00-01-00
Dagenham & R v Rochdale	-	-	-	-	-	1-1	00-01-00
Gillingham v Exeter	-	-	-	-	-	-	02-01-00
Grimsby v Rotherham	0-0	-	-	-	-	0-1	01-01-03
Lincoln v Chester	-	-	1-1	3-1	2-0	0-1	03-03-03
Luton v Bradford	-	-	4-0	-	-	-	01-00-00
Macclesfield v Brentford	-	-	-	-	-	1-0	01-00-00
Notts Co v Port Vale	1-0	1-2	-	-	-	-	01-02-04
Shrewsbury v Darlington	2-2	-	4-0	3-1	2-2	0-0	06-04-03

SCOTTISH PREMIER LEAGUE

Match							
Aberdeen v Rangers	2-2	2-3/1-1	0-0/1-2/1-3	3-2/2-0	1-2/2-0	1-1/2-0	11-12-17
Celtic v Hibernian	1-0/3-2	6-0	2-1/1-3	3-2/1-1	2-1/1-0	1-1/2-0	22-11-03
Dundee Utd v St Mirren	-	-	-	-	1-0/0-2	2-0/1-1	09-03-04
Hearts v Inv CT	-	-	1-0/0-2	0-0	4-1/1-0	2-3/1-0	04-01-02
Kilmarnock v Hamilton	-	-	-	-	-	-	03-01-02
Motherwell v Falkirk	-	-	-	5-0/3-1	4-2/3-3	0-3	08-03-02

SCOTTISH DIVISION ONE

Match							
Airdrie Utd v Dundee	-	-	-	4-0/7-0	0-1/0-3	-	04-05-07
Clyde v Ross County	2-1/1-0	2-2/1-0	1-0/1-0	1-0/2-0	3-0/2-4	-	11-04-01
Morton v Livingston	-	-	-	-	-	2-2/1-1	08-05-04
Queen of Sth v Partick	-	-	1-0/3-1	-	0-2/4-3	1-2/2-0	04-03-07
St Johnstone v Dunfermline	-	-	-	-	-	0-0/1-1	05-07-06

SCOTTISH DIVISION TWO

Match							
Alloa v Raith	-	-	-	1-2/1-1	1-2/2-3	2-1/2-0	03-01-06
Ayr v Arbroath	1-0/4-0	-	1-1/2-2	-	-	-	02-03-01
Brechin v Peterhead	-	-	-	-	1-0/3-1	2-2/3-1	05-03-00
East Fife v Queen's Park	1-1/1-0	-	1-4/0-1	1-0/0-1	1-0/1-0	-	09-07-05
Stranraer v Stirling	-	0-1/1-1	0-0/0-3	-	2-1/3-1	-	04-07-06

SCOTTISH DIVISION THREE

Match							
Annan Ath v E Stirling	-	-	-	-	-	-	00-00-00
Berwick v Dumbarton	1-2/0-1	1-4/1-2	0-4/0-3	-	3-0/2-1	-	09-03-12
Cowdenbeath v Albion	-	1-4/1-1	2-0/1-2	2-1/2-1	-	-	11-08-06
Forfar v Elgin	-	-	-	-	-	4-0/0-1	01-00-01
Stenhsmuir v Montrose	-	-	1-1/0-1	6-2/5-1	5-0/2-5	0-4/0-0	10-02-08

Sponsored by Stan James

CONFERENCE

Altrincham v Torquay	-	-	-	-	-	1-1	00-01-00
Barrow v Kidderminster	-	-	-	-	-	•	02-00-02
Burton v Kettering	2-0	-	-	-	-	-	01-00-00
Crawley v Oxford Utd	-	-	-	-	0-1	2-0	01-00-01
Eastbourne v York	-	-	-	-	-	-	00-00-00
Histon v Grays	-	-	-	-	-	2-2	00-01-00
Lewes v Mansfield	-	-	-	-	-	-	00-00-00
Rushden & D v Forest G	-	-	-	-	2-0	1-2	03-01-01
Salisbury v Stevenage	-	-	-	-	-	1-0	01-00-00
Weymouth v Northwich	-	-	-	-	1-1	2-0	01-02-00
Woking v Ebbsfleet U	2-3	3-2	2-0	1-3	2-2	1-0	03-01-02
Wrexham v Cambridge U	5-0	-	-	-	-	-	03-03-02

TUESDAY 27TH JANUARY 2009
PREMIER LEAGUE

Portsmouth v Aston Villa	-	2-1	1-2	1-1	2-2	2-0	02-02-01
Sunderland v Fulham	0-3	-	-	2-1	-	1-1	01-02-01
Tottenham v Stoke	-	-	-	-	-	-	00-00-00
WBA v Man Utd	1-3	-	0-3	1-2	-	-	00-00-03
West Ham v Hull	-	-	-	-	-	-	01-00-01
Wigan v Liverpool	-	-	-	0-1	0-4	0-1	00-00-03

CHAMPIONSHIP

Barnsley v Ipswich	-	-	-	-	1-0	4-1	05-01-04
Birmingham v Derby	-	-	-	-	1-0	1-1	02-02-01
Blackpool v QPR	1-3	0-1	-	-	-	1-0	01-01-02
Charlton v C Palace	-	-	2-2	-	-	2-0	03-03-01
Coventry v Cardiff	-	1-3	1-1	3-1	2-2	0-0	01-03-01
Norwich v Southampton	-	-	2-1	3-1	0-1	2-1	06-03-02
Nottm Forest v Sheff Weds	4-0	-	-	-	-	-	04-01-06
Plymouth v Bristol C	2-0	0-1	-	-	-	1-1	04-02-01
Reading v Wolves	0-1	-	1-2	1-1	-	-	03-02-03
Sheff Utd v Doncaster	-	-	-	-	-	-	00-00-00
Swansea v Preston	-	-	-	-	-	-	03-02-00
Watford v Burnley	2-1	1-1	0-1	3-1	-	1 2	04-02-04

LEAGUE 1

Bristol R v Cheltenham	-	2-0	1-1	0-1	-	2-0	02-01-02
Colchester v Northampton	2-0	-	-	-	-	-	06-01-02
Hartlepool v Carlisle	2-1	-	-	-	-	2-2	05-03-03
Hereford v Millwall	-	-	-	-	-	-	00-00-00
Leeds v Southend	-	-	-	-	2-0	4-1	02-00-00
Leicester v Brighton	2-0	-	0-1	0-0	-	-	05-01-01
Milton K v Leyton O	-	-	-	-	-	-	00-00-00
Peterboro v Crewe	0-0	-	-	-	-	-	02-02-01
Scunthorpe v Oldham	-	-	-	4-2	1-1	-	01-01-01
Swindon v Walsall	-	-	1-2	1-0	1-1	0-3	02-03-03
Tranmere v Stockport	1-0	3-2	1-0	-	-	-	06-02-00
Yeovil v Huddersfield	-	2-1	-	1-2	3-1	0-2	02-00-02

LEAGUE 2

Accrington v Morecambe	-	1-0	2-1	2-0	-	3-2	06-01-01
Barnet v Shrewsbury	-	0-1	-	1-0	0-0	4-1	03-05-01
Bournemouth v Luton	-	6-3	0-1	-	-	4-3	06-01-01
Brentford v Aldershot	-	-	-	-	-	-	00-00-00

Bury v Bradford	-	-	-	-	-	2-2	01-02-02
Darlington v Rotherham	-	-	-	-	-	1-1	00-04-01
Gillingham v Lincoln	-	-	-	-	-	-	03-04-01
Grimsby v Dagenham & R	-	-	-	-	-	1-4	00-00-01
Macclesfield v Wycombe	-	-	2-1	2-1	0-2	1-2	04-02-04
Port Vale v Chester	-	-	-	-	-	-	01-00-01
Rochdale v Notts Co	-	-	0-3	3-0	0-1	4-2	02-00-03

CONFERENCE

Altrincham v York	-	-	-	0-3	0-4	2-2	00-01-02
Burton v Barrow	-	-	-	-	-	-	01-00-00
Cambridge U v Oxford Utd	1-1	1-1	2-1	-	0-3	2-1	04-04-02
Ebbsfleet U v Crawley	-	-	0-0	1-1	1-0	1-0	04-03-03
Grays v Weymouth	-	-	2-0	-	2-2	0-2	01-01-01
Kidderminstr v Histon	-	-	-	-	-	1-1	00-01-00
Lewes v Torquay	-	-	-	-	-	-	00-00-00
Mansfield v Rushden & D	-	-	0-0	0-1	-	-	00-01-02
Salisbury v Forest G	-	-	-	-	-	0-0	00-01-01
Stevenage v Kettering	2-0	-	-	-	-	-	04-04-00
Woking v Eastbourne	-	-	-	-	-	-	00-00-00
Wrexham v Northwich	-	-	-	-	-	-	00-00-00

WEDNESDAY 28TH JANUARY 2009
PREMIER LEAGUE

Blackburn v Bolton	0-0	3-4	0-1	0-0	0-1	4-1	04-04-03
Chelsea v Middlesboro	1-0	0-0	2-0	1-0	3-0	1-0	10-03-00
Everton v Arsenal	2-1	1-1	1-4	1-0	1-0	1-4	06-06-08
Man City v Newcastle	1-0	1-0	1-1	3-0	0-0	3-1	05-04-01

LEAGUE 2

| Chesterfield v Exeter | - | - | - | - | - | - | 03-00-00 |

FRIDAY 30TH JANUARY 2009
CHAMPIONSHIP

| Doncaster v Norwich | - | - | - | - | - | - | 00-00-00 |

SATURDAY 31ST JANUARY 2009
PREMIER LEAGUE

Arsenal v West Ham	3-1	-	-	2-3	0-1	2-0	10-00-05
Aston Villa v Wigan	-	-	-	0-2	1-1	0-2	00-01-02
Bolton v Tottenham	1-0	2-0	3-1	1-0	2-0	1-1	05-03-01
Fulham v Portsmouth	-	2-0	3-1	1-3	1-1	0-2	04-01-02
Hull v WBA	-	-	-	-	0-1	1-3	01-01-05
Liverpool v Chelsea	1-0	1-2	0-1	1-4	2-0	1-1	12-03-04
Man Utd v Everton	3-0	3-2	0-0	1-1	3-0	2-1	13-04-03
Middlesboro v Blackburn	1-0	0-1	1-0	0-2	0-1	1-2	06-01-07
Newcastle v Sunderland	2-0	-	-	3-2	-	2-0	05-03-02
Stoke v Man City	-	-	-	-	-	-	02-00-02

CHAMPIONSHIP

Bristol C v Barnsley	2-0	2-1	0-0	3-0	-	3-2	07-02-02
Burnley v Charlton	-	-	-	-	-	1-0	02-00-00
Cardiff v Nottm Forest	-	0-0	3-0	-	-	-	01-01-00
Crystal Pal v Blackpool	-	-	-	-	-	0-0	00-01-00
Derby v Coventry	1-0	1-3	2-2	1-1	1-1	-	06-06-01

Sponsored by Stan James

Ipswich v Plymouth	-	-	3-2	3-1	3-0	0-0	06-02-00
Preston v Sheff Utd	2-0	3-3	0-1	0-0	-	3-1	05-02-01
QPR v Reading	-	-	0-0	1-2	-	-	00-03-02
Sheff Weds v Birmingham	-	-	-	-	0-3	-	01-00-02
Southampton v Swansea	-	-	-	-	-	-	00-00-00
Wolves v Watford	0-0	-	0-0	1-1	-	1-2	04-09-01

LEAGUE 1

Brighton v Hartlepool	-	2-0	-	-	-	2-1	06-03-00
Carlisle v Colchester	-	-	-	-	-	-	03-01-02
Cheltenham v MK Dons	-	-	-	-	-	-	00-00-00
Crewe v Tranmere	2-0	-	-	-	1-1	4-3	05-02-03
Huddersfield v Peterboro	0-1	-	2-1	-	-	-	02-01-02
Leyton O v Yeovil	-	2-0	2-3	-	0-0	0-0	01-02-01
Millwall v Scunthorpe	-	-	-	-	0-1	-	00-00-02
Northampton v Leicester	-	-	-	-	-	-	00-00-00
Oldham v Swindon	4-0	0-1	1-2	2-2	-	2-2	06-05-02
Southend v Bristol R	2-2	0-1	2-0	-	-	0-1	04-03-02
Stockport v Hereford	-	-	-	-	0-2	2-3	02-00-03
Walsall v Leeds	-	-	-	-	-	1-1	00-01-01

LEAGUE 2

Aldershot v Rochdale	-	-	-	-	-	-	00-00-00
Bradford v Grimsby	0-0	-	-	-	-	2-1	03-01-02
Chester v Gillingham	-	-	-	-	-	-	02-01-00
Dagenham & R v Darlington	-	-	-	-	-	0-3	00-00-01
Exeter v Barnet	-	1-1	0-3	-	-	-	03-05-02
Lincoln v Bournemouth	1-2	-	-	-	-	-	01-00-01
Luton v Bury	-	-	-	-	-	-	00-02-01
Morecambe v Port Vale	-	-	-	-	-	-	00-00-00
Notts Co v Chesterfield	1-1	1-1	-	-	-	1-0	05-04-00
Rotherham v Macclesfield	-	-	-	-	-	3-0	03-00-00
Shrewsbury v Brentford	-	-	-	-	-	0-1	05-01-02
Wycombe v Accrington	-	-	-	-	1-1	0-1	00-01-01

SCOTTISH PREMIER LEAGUE

Falkirk v Aberdeen	-	-	-	1-2	0-2/1-2	0-0	01-03-08
Hamilton v Hearts	-	-	-	-	-	-	00-00-02
Hibernian v Motherwell	3-1/1-0	0-2/3-3	1-0	2-1	3-1/2-0	1-0/0-2	19-13-04
Inv CT v Celtic	-	-	1-3/0-2	1-1	1-1/1-2	3-2	01-02-03
Rangers v Dundee Utd	3-0	2-1	1-1/0-1	3-0	2-2/5-0	2-0/3-1	23-04-07
St Mirren v Kilmarnock	-	-	-	-	0-1/0-2	0-0/1-0	02-01-05

SCOTTISH DIVISION ONE

Airdrie Utd v Partick	-	-	4-2/0-1	-	1-2/1-1	-	05-09-02
Dundee v Clyde	-	-	-	3-3/0-1	3-0/1-4	0-1/2-0	03-01-03
Dunfermline v Queen of Sth	-	-	-	-	-	2-0/4-0	03-00-00
Morton v St Johnstone	-	-	-	-	-	2-2/1-2	02-03-04
Livingston v Ross County	-	-	-	-	0-0/1-1	-	02-04-00

SCOTTISH DIVISION TWO

Arbroath v Alloa	0-1/0-1	3-1/2-1	0-3/2-1	-	-	-	07-08-10
Ayr v Raith	-	1-0/1-0	-	2-1/0-0	1-0/0-2	0-3/0-1	13-09-07
Brechin v Stirling	-	-	0-3/5-3	-	0-1/1-4	-	06-00-07
East Fife v Peterhead	3-3/0-2	-	0-2/1-2	-	-	-	01-02-05
Queen's Park v Stranraer	-	0-4/0-2	-	-	-	-	05-03-05

SCOTTISH DIVISION THREE

Albion v Forfar	-	-	-	-	-	2-1/0-0	03-02-08
Berwick v E Stirling	-	-	-	3-2/1-0	2-2/2-0	-	10-04-05
Cowdenbeath v Annan Ath	-	-	-	-	-	-	00-00-00
Dumbarton v Montrose	-	-	-	-	2-0/2-1	1-3/0-0	08-04-07
Stenhsmuir v Elgin	-	-	0-2/4-0	3-1/1-2	2-0/3-2	2-3/2-2	04-01-03

CONFERENCE

Barrow v Salisbury	-	-	-	-	-	-	00-00-00
Crawley v Wrexham	-	-	-	-	-	-	00-00-00
Eastbourne v Mansfield	-	-	-	-	-	-	00-00-00
Ebbsfleet U v Kidderminster	-	-	-	1-2	1-3	5-4	01-00-02
Forest G v Histon	-	-	-	-	-	3-1	01-00-00
Kettering v Altrincham	-	-	0-1	-	-	-	05-04-02
Northwich v Woking	1-3	1-4	1-3	-	0-2	1-3	04-02-09
Oxford Utd v Lewes	-	-	-	-	-	-	00-00-00
Rushden & D v Cambridge U	4-1	-	0-1	-	3-1	1-2	02-00-02
Torquay v Grays	-	-	-	-	-	0-0	00-01-00
Weymouth v Burton	-	-	-	-	1-1	1-2	00-05-03
York v Stevenage	-	-	3-1	0-1	0-1	0-2	01-00-03

TUESDAY 3RD FEBRUARY 2009
CHAMPIONSHIP

Bristol C v Charlton	-	-	-	-	-	0-1	02-01-03
Burnley v Coventry	3-1	1-2	2-2	4-0	1-2	2-0	04-01-02
Cardiff v Watford	-	3-0	0-3	1-3	-	1-2	01-00-03
Crystal Pal v Birmingham	-	-	2-0	-	0-1	-	04-02-04
Derby v Blackpool	-	-	-	-	-	-	00-00-00
Doncaster v Reading	-	-	-	-	-	-	00-00-00
Ipswich v Nottm Forest	3-4	1-2	6-0	-	-	-	03-00-04
Preston v Plymouth	-	-	1-1	0-0	3-0	2-0	03-03-02
QPR v Swansea	-	-	-	-	-	-	00-00-00
Sheff Weds v Barnsley	-	2-1	1-0	-	2-1	1-0	08-00-00
Southampton v Sheff Utd	-	-	-	0-1	-	3-2	03-01-02
Wolves v Norwich	1-0	-	-	2-0	2-2	2-0	07-03-01

LEAGUE 1

Brighton v Peterboro	-	1-0	-	-	-	-	02-03-02
Carlisle v Hereford	-	-	3-1	-	-	-	05-01-03
Cheltenham v Tranmere	3-1	-	-	-	1-0	1-1	02-01-00
Crewe v Yeovil	-	-	-	-	2-3	2-0	01-00-01
Huddersfield v Hartlepool	-	-	0-2	2-1	-	2-0	04-01-01
Leyton O v Leeds	-	-	-	-	-	0-2	00-00-01
Millwall v Colchester	-	-	-	-	-	-	03-00-00
Northampton v Swindon	1-0	-	-	-	-	1-1	01-02-01
Oldham v Bristol R	-	-	-	-	-	0-1	03-01-02
Southend v Scunthorpe	1-2	4-2	0-0	3-0	-	-	04-02-02
Stockport v MK Dons	-	-	3-1	-	1-2	2-3	01-01-03
Walsall v Leicester	1-4	-	-	-	-	-	00-00-02

LEAGUE 2

Aldershot v Chesterfield	-	-	-	-	-	-	00-00-00
Bradford v Darlington	-	-	-	-	-	0-0	00-01-01
Chester v Rochdale	-	-	0-0	2-3	0-1	0-4	02-03-05
Dagenham & R v Bournemouth	-	-	-	-	-	-	00-00-00
Exeter v Port Vale	-	-	-	-	-	-	00-02-00

228

Lincoln v Macclesfield	3-0	3-2	2-0	2-2	2-1	3-1	07-03-01
Luton v Grimsby	-	1-2	-	-	-	-	02-01-03
Morecambe v Brentford	-	-	-	-	-	3 1	01-00-00
Notts Co v Gillingham	-	-	-	-	-	-	00-02-02
Rotherham v Bury	-	-	-	-	-	2-1	01-01-03
Shrewsbury v Accrington	-	0-0	-	-	2-1	2-0	02-01-00
Wycombe v Barnet	-	-	-	1-0	1-1	0-0	02-02-02

SATURDAY 7TH FEBRUARY 2009
PREMIER LEAGUE

Blackburn v Aston Villa	0-0	0-2	2-2	2-0	1-2	0-4	07-03-04
Chelsea v Hull	-	-	-	-	-	-	01-00-00
Everton v Bolton	0-0	1-2	3-2	0-4	1-0	2-0	06-01-02
Man City v Middlesboro	0-0	0-1	1-1	0-1	1-0	3-1	03-03-04
Portsmouth v Liverpool	-	1-0	1-2	1-3	2-1	0-0	02-01-02
Sunderland v Stoke	-	1-1	1-0	-	2-2	-	04-04-01
Tottenham v Arsenal	1-1	2-2	4-5	1-1	2-2	1-3	05-10-05
WBA v Newcastle	2-2	-	0-0	0-3	-	-	00-03-02
West Ham v Man Utd	1-1	-	-	1-2	1-0	2-1	03-07-05
Wigan v Fulham	-	-	-	1-0	0-0	1-1	05-05-03

CHAMPIONSHIP

Barnsley v C Palace	-	-	-	-	2-0	0-0	04-04-03
Birmingham v Burnley	-	-	-	-	0-1	-	01 00 02
Blackpool v Doncaster	-	-	1-1	4-2	3-1	-	04-01-00
Charlton v Cardiff	-	-	-	-	-	3-0	01-00-00
Coventry v Wolves	0-2	-	2-2	2-0	2-1	1-1	02-02-02
Norwich v Bristol C	-	-	-	-	-	1-3	01-00-01
Nottm Forest v QPR	-	-	2-1	-	-	-	05-06-00
Plymouth v Derby	-	-	0-2	0-2	3-1	-	01-01-02
Reading v Preston	5-1	3-2	3-1	2-1	-	-	07-04-00
Sheff Utd v Sheff Weds	3-1	-	-	1-0	-	2-2	03-05-00
Swansea v Ipswich	-	-	-	-	-	-	00-00-00
Watford v Southampton	-	-	-	3-0	-	3-2	03-00-00

LEAGUE 1

Bristol R v Huddersfield	-	1-1	-	-	-	2-3	01-04-01
Colchester v Stockport	1-0	2-1	3-2	-	-	-	03-01-01
Hartlepool v Walsall	-	-	1-3	1-1	3-1	0-1	02-02-02
Hereford v Brighton	-	-	-	-	-	-	00-01-00
Leeds v Millwall	-	-	1-1	2-1	-	4-2	02-01-00
Leicester v Oldham	-	-	-	-	-	-	02-01-01
Milton K v Crewe	-	3-1	-	-	-	-	02-01-00
Peterboro v Carlisle	-	-	-	1-1	-	-	02-02-03
Scunthorpe v Cheltenham	-	5-2	4-1	-	1-0	-	03-01-01
Swindon v Southend	-	-	-	1-2	-	0-1	02-02-02
Tranmere v Leyton O	-	-	-	-	3-0	1-1	04-01-00
Yeovil v Northampton	-	0-2	1-1	-	0-0	1-0	01-02-01

LEAGUE 2

Accrington v Luton	-	-	-	-	-	-	00-00-00
Barnet v Rotherham	-	-	-	-	-	2-0	04-01-01
Bournemouth v Shrewsbury	2-1	-	-	-	-	-	04-01-02
Brentford v Chester	-	-	-	-	-	3-0	03-02-02
Bury v Dagenham & R	-	-	-	-	-	0-2	00-00-01
Chesterfield v Lincoln	-	-	-	-	-	4-1	04-03-02

Darlington v Wycombe	-	-	1-0	1-1	3-2	1-0	03-02-01
Gillingham v Bradford	1-0	1-0	-	2-1	1-0	-	04-00-01
Grimsby v Exeter	-	-	-	-	-	-	03-00-00
Macclesfield v Notts Co	-	-	1-2	0-0	1-1	1-1	01-03-02
Port Vale v Aldershot	-	-	-	-	-	-	00-00-00
Rochdale v Morecambe	-	-	-	-	-	1-0	01-00-00

SCOTTISH DIVISION TWO

Alloa v Ayr	0-1/2-3	-	1-3/5-1	0-4/1-1	0-1/1-1	2-1/1-2	02-05-07
Peterhead v Arbroath	-	-	-	-	-	-	00-00-00
Raith v Queen's Park	-	-	-	-	-	0-2/0-1	00-00-02
Stirling v East Fife	0-0/1-2	-	-	-	-	-	08-02-06
Stranraer v Brechin	3-1/2-3	-	4-2/0-1	1-1/2-0	3-1/0-2	-	06-03-09

SCOTTISH DIVISION THREE

Annan Ath v Stenhsmuir	-	-	-	-	-	-	00-00-00
E Stirling v Albion	0-3/0-4	3-4/1-8	1-1/0-2	3-1/1-0	0-1/0-0	4-5/3-0	13-06-17
Elgin v Dumbarton	-	-	-	-	0-2/0-1	2-1/2-1	04-00-04
Forfar v Cowdenbeath	2-1/1-1	-	-	-	1-1/2-0	-	07-06-01
Montrose v Berwick	-	-	-	0-0/1-2	0-1/1-2	-	03-03-13

CONFERENCE

Altrincham v Eastbourne	-	-	-	-	-	-	00-00-00
Barrow v Torquay	-	-	-	-	-	-	00-00-00
Burton v Rushden & D	-	-	-	-	1-2	2-1	02-01-02
Grays v Crawley	-	-	-	1-0	0-0	2-1	02-01-00
Histon v Weymouth	-	-	-	2-1	-	2-2	01-01-00
Kettering v Oxford Utd	-	-	-	-	-	-	00-00-00
Kidderminstr v Cambridge U	2-1	2-2	1-1	1-0	1-0	1-0	04-02-00
Lewes v Wrexham	-	-	-	-	-	-	00-00-00
Mansfield v York	-	2-0	-	-	-	-	03-01-01
Northwich v Ebbsfleet U	1-2	0-0	1-2	-	1-2	3-3	00-02-03
Salisbury v Woking	-	-	-	-	-	2-1	01-00-00
Stevenage v Forest G	0-0	2-1	2-2	2-1	3-3	0-0	04-06-00

SATURDAY 14TH FEBRUARY 2009
CHAMPIONSHIP

Birmingham v Nottm Forest	-	-	-	-	-	-	00-01-04
Bristol C v Southampton	-	-	-	-	-	2-1	01-00-00
Burnley v Wolves	2-1	-	1-1	0-1	0-1	1-3	01-01-06
Charlton v Plymouth	-	-	-	-	-	1-2	00-01-02
Crystal Pal v Coventry	1-1	1-1	-	2-0	1-0	1-1	03-04-05
Derby v Reading	3-0	2-3	2-1	2-2	-	0-4	03-01-03
Doncaster v Sheff Weds	-	-	0-4	-	-	-	00-00-01
Ipswich v Blackpool	-	-	-	-	-	2-1	01-00-00
Preston v Norwich	1-2	0-0	-	2-0	2-1	0-0	04-02-01
Sheff Utd v Barnsley	-	-	-	-	-	1-0	02-04-03
Watford v Swansea	-	-	-	-	-	-	00-00-00

LEAGUE 1

Brighton v Carlisle	-	-	-	-	1-2	2-2	03-01-03
Cheltenham v Hereford	-	-	-	-	-	-	00-01-01
Huddersfield v Leeds	-	-	-	-	-	1-0	01-00-00
Leicester v Swindon	-	-	-	-	-	-	03-02-00
Leyton O v Crewe	-	-	-	-	1-1	0-1	02-02-02
Milton K v Hartlepool	-	-	4-2	2-1	0-0	-	02-01-00

Oldham v Northampton	4-0	-	-	-	3-0	0-1	04-01-02
Peterboro v Yeovil	-	-	-	-	-	-	00-00-00
Scunthorpe v Bristol R	2-2	1-2	4-0	-	-	-	01-01-03
Southend v Tranmere	-	-	-	3-1	-	1-2	03-03-03
Stockport v Millwall	-	-	-	-	-	-	01-00-01
Walsall v Colchester	-	-	2-1	0-2	-	-	02-01-04

LEAGUE 2

Bournemouth v Accrington	-	-	-	-	-	-	00-00-00
Bradford v Wycombe	-	-	-	-	-	0-1	01-00-02
Brentford v Port Vale	1-1	3-2	1-0	0-1	4-3	-	05-02-02
Dagenham & R v Luton	-	-	-	-	-	-	00-00-00
Exeter v Aldershot-	2-1	3-1	4-0	0-0	1-1	03-02-00	
Grimsby v Bury -	-	5-1	2-1	2-0	1-0	04-01-01	
Lincoln v Darlington	1-1	1-1	0-0	2-2	1-3	0-4	06-07-04
Macclesfield v Rochdale	3-2	2-1	3-0	1-3	1-0	2-2	05-02-03
Morecambe v Chester	1-1	0-1	-	-	-	5-3	01-01-03
Notts Co v Barnet	-	-	-	1-0	1-1	0-0	02-02-00
Rotherham v Gillingham	1-1	1-1	1-3	3-0	3-2	-	03-03-02
Shrewsbury v Chesterfield	-	-	-	-	-	2-3	01-04-01

SCOTTISH PREMIER LEAGUE

Celtic v Rangers	3-3/1-0	3-0/1-0	1-0/0-2	3-0/0-0	2-0/0-1	2-1/3-2	17-08-15
Dundee Utd v Inv CT	-	-	2-1/1-1	1-1/2-4	3-1/1-1	0-1	02-03-02
Hearts v Aberdeen	0-0	2-0/1-0	0-0/1-0	2-0/1-2/1-0	0-1/1-1	4-1	20-08-10
Kilmarnock v Hibernian	2-1/6-2	0-2/2-0	3-1	2-2/3-1	2-1/0-2	2-1	12-07-07
Motherwell v Hamilton	-	-	-	-	-	-	01-01-00
St Mirren v Falkirk	4-4/1-2	0-0/1-1	2-0/0-1	-	1-0	1-5/1-0	08-05-10

SCOTTISH DIVISION ONE

Clyde v Morton	-	-	-	-	-	0-1/1-1	02-05-06
Partick v Dunfermline	4-0	4-1	-	-	-	1-1/0-1	02-02-02
Queen of Sth v Airdrie Utd	-	-	1-0/0-0	1-0/2-0	1-1/0-3	-	03-02-02
Ross County v Dundee	-	-	-	3-0/0-0	1-0/0-0	-	02-02-00
St Johnstone v Livingston	-	-	-	-	1-2/1-2	5-2/5-2	04-02-03

SCOTTISH DIVISION TWO

Brechin v Raith	1-2/1-0	0-3/1-1	-	-	1-0/1-2	0-1/3-2	03-01-05
East Fife v Ayr	-	-	-	-	-	-	01-01-00
Queen's Park v Alloa	-	-	-	-	-	1-0/1-1	08-05-05
Stirling v Peterhead	1-0/2-1	3-1/0-2	-	1-3/2-1	2-0/2-1	-	07-00-03
Stranraer v Arbroath	-	-	2-1/3-3	-	-	1-1/0-3	09-03-05

SCOTTISH DIVISION THREE

Albion v Stenhsmuir	-	-	1-0/1-1	0-2/1-2	2-5/2-1	1-1/3-3	03-06-08
Berwick v Annan Ath	-	-	-	-	-	-	00-00-00
Cowdenbeath v Montrose	-	3-3/0-0	0-0/0-0	2-0/2-0	-	-	09-07-07
E Stirling v Elgin	1-2/2-2	3-1/2-1	0-1/0-3	0-2/0-2	2-1/0-2	3-1/0-0	06-02-08
Forfar v Dumbarton	2-0/0-1	3-1/1-0	0-2/6-0	2-0/2-3	-	3-1/1-1	08-01-03

CONFERENCE

Cambridge U v Mansfield	-	1-2	2-2	-	-	-	04-01-02
Eastbourne v Crawley	-	1-1	-	-	-	-	00-01-00
Ebbsfleet U v Burton	3-2	1-2	0-2	0-1	0-0	2-1	03-02-07
Kidderminstr v Northwich	-	-	-	-	0-1	0-0	09-03-02
Oxford Utd v Barrow	-	-	-	-	-	-	00-00-00

Rushden & D v Lewes	-	-	-	-	-	-	00-00-00
Salisbury v Histon	-	-	-	-	0-3	3-3	00-01-01
Torquay v Altrincham	-	-	-	-	-	1-1	00-01-00
Weymouth v Stevenage	-	-	-	-	0-1	1-0	01-00-01
Woking v Kettering	2-1	-	-	-	-	-	04-05-01
Wrexham v Grays	-	-	-	-	-	-	00-00-00
York v Forest G	-	-	1-3	5-1	0-0	0-2	01-01-02

SUNDAY 15TH FEBRUARY 2009
CHAMPIONSHIP

Cardiff v QPR	1-2	-	1-0	0-0	0-1	3-1	02-02-02

FRIDAY 20TH FEBRUARY 2009
LEAGUE 2

Chesterfield v Bournemouth	-	1-1	2-3	3-0	0-1	-	04-03-03
Port Vale v Lincoln	-	-	-	-	-	-	00-00-00

SATURDAY 21ST FEBRUARY 2009
PREMIER LEAGUE

Arsenal v Sunderland	3-1	-	-	3-1	-	3-2	07-01-00
Aston Villa v Chelsea	2-1	3-2	0-0	1-1	0-0	2-0	07-07-05
Bolton v West Ham	1-0	-	-	4-1	4-0	1-0	05-01-01
Fulham v WBA	3-0	-	1-0	6-1	-	-	04-03-00
Hull v Tottenham	-	-	-	-	-	-	00-00-00
Liverpool v Man City	1-2	2-1	2-1	1-0	1-0	1-0	10-03-01
Man Utd v Blackburn	3-1	2-1	0-0	1-2	4-1	2-0	10-03-01
Middlesboro v Wigan	-	-	-	2-3	1-1	1-0	01-01-01
Newcastle v Everton	2-1	4-2	1-1	2-0	1-1	3-2	11-03-02
Stoke v Portsmouth	1-1	-	-	-	-	-	04-02-02

CHAMPIONSHIP

Barnsley v Charlton	-	-	-	-	-	3-0	05-02-02
Blackpool v Watford	-	-	-	-	-	1-1	00-03-00
Coventry v Birmingham	-	-	-	-	0-1	-	00-01-01
Norwich v Burnley	2-0	2-0	-	2-1	1-4	2-0	05-00-02
Nottm Forest v Derby	3-0	1-1	2-2	-	-	-	03-06-00
Plymouth v Sheff Utd	-	-	3-0	0-0	-	0-1	01-02-01
QPR v Ipswich	-	-	2-4	2-1	1-3	1-1	03-04-04
Reading v Bristol C	-	-	-	-	-	-	03-01-02
Sheff Weds v C Palace	0-0	-	-	0-0	3-2	2-2	05-04-02
Southampton v Preston	-	-	-	0-0	1-1	0-1	00-02-01
Swansea v Doncaster	-	1-1	-	1-2	2-0	1-2	02-02-02
Wolves v Cardiff	-	-	2-3	2-0	1-2	3-0	03-00-02

LEAGUE 1

Bristol R v Leicester	-	-	-	-	-	-	00-03-00
Carlisle v Stockport	-	-	-	6-0	-	-	03-01-01
Colchester v Southend	-	-	-	0-3	3-0	-	01-00-00
Crewe v Huddersfield	1-0	-	-	-	2-0	2-0	05-03-02
Hartlepool v Leyton O	4-1	-	-	-	-	1-1	08-03-02
Hereford v Peterboro	-	-	-	-	0-0	0-1	01-02-02
Leeds v Cheltenham	-	-	-	-	-	1-2	00-00-01
Millwall v Brighton	1-0	-	2-0	0-2	0-1	3-0	04-00-03
Northampton v Walsall	-	-	-	-	-	0-2	02-03-05
Swindon v Scunthorpe	-	-	-	1-1	-	-	00-01-00

Tranmere v MK Dons	-	-	2-0	1-2	-	-	01-00-02
Yeovil v Oldham	-	-	-	0-2	1-0	0-0	01-01-01

LEAGUE 2

Accrington v Dagenham & R	-	2-3	0-3	1-0	-	1-0	02-00-02
Aldershot v Morecambe	-	2-2	3-3	2-0	0-1	-	01-02-01
Barnet v Bradford	-	-	-	-	-	2-1	01-00-01
Bury v Notts Co	-	-	1-0	2-3	0-1	2-1	04-02-04
Chester v Exeter	-	3-2	-	-	-	-	03-04-02
Darlington v Grimsby	-	-	1-0	0-0	2-2	3-2	02-03-00
Gillingham v Macclesfield	-	-	-	-	-	-	00-01-00
Luton v Shrewsbury	-	-	-	-	-	-	02-00-00
Rochdale v Brentford	-	-	-	-	-	1-1	01-01-00
Wycombe v Rotherham	-	-	-	-	-	1-0	03-01-01

SCOTTISH PREMIER LEAGUE

Aberdeen v Dundee Utd	1-2/3-0	0-1/3-0	1-0	2-0	3-1/2-4	2-0/2-1	19-06-11
Falkirk v Hamilton	-	-	1-1/1-1	-	-	-	05-04-02
Hearts v St Mirren	-	-	-	-	0-1/1-1	0-1/3-2	06-05-03
Inv CT v Hibernian	-	-	1-2/3-0	2-0	0-0/3-0	2-0	04-01-01
Motherwell v Celtic	2-1/0-4	0-2/1-1	2-3/2-1	4-4/1-3	1-1	1-4/1-2	08-14-16
Rangers v Kilmarnock	6-1/4-0	4-0/2-0	2-0/2-1	3-0/4-0	3-0/0-1	2-0	23-01-05

SCOTTISH DIVISION ONE

Airdrie Utd v Clyde	-	-	3-1/2-4	1-3/1-1	2-1/1-0	-	07-06-04
Dundee v Livingston	2-1/0-0	2-1/1-0/2-0	0-0/0-1	-	0-1/2-0	4-1/2-0	12-02-03
Dunfermline v Ross County	-	-	-	-	-	-	00-00-00
Partick v Morton	-	-	-	2-0/1-1	-	1-1/0-3	03-05-06
Queen of Sth v St Johnstone	0-0/1-2	1-1/1-1	0-1/2-0	1-3/3-2	0-1/1-0	3-3/3-1	04-05-04

SCOTTISH DIVISION TWO

Alloa v East Fife	-	2-0/1-1	-	-	-	-	04-04-03
Arbroath v Queen's Park	-	-	-	1-1/1-0	1-2/1-0	-	10-12-01
Ayr v Brechin	-	3-2/1-2	0-1/0-1	-	1-2/1-1	2-1/0-3	06-02-05
Peterhead v Stranraer	-	1-2/2-0	-	-	5-2/5-0	-	03-00-01
Raith v Stirling	-	-	-	5-2/2-3	1-3/0-1	-	04-01-05

SCOTTISH DIVISION THREE

Annan Ath v Forfar	-	-	-	-	-	-	00-00-00
Dumbarton v Cowdenbeath	1-1/3-1	-	-	-	-	-	08-05-05
Elgin v Albion	0-1/1-2	1-5/1-2	1-0/1-1	2-2/2-1	0-3/3-0	3-2/1-1	06-04-06
Montrose v E Stirling	2-2/5-4	5-1/1-0	4-1/4-1	3-0/2-0	1-0/4-0	3-1/2-0	22-07-05
Stenhsmuir v Berwick	2-0/1-0	0-3/3-1	-	0-1/1-0	2-3/2-0	-	11-08-10

CONFERENCE

Altrincham v Woking	-	-	-	0-4	2-3	2-2	02-03-04
Barrow v Grays	-	-	-	-	-	-	00-00-00
Burton v Wrexham	-	-	-	-	-	-	00-00-00
Crawley v Salisbury	-	-	-	-	-	1-1	05-03-00
Forest G v Northwich	1-0	0-0	1-3	-	2-1	4-1	07-01-01
Histon v Eastbourne	-	-	-	3-1	1-2	-	01-00-01
Kettering v Torquay	-	-	-	-	-	-	00-00-00
Lewes v Cambridge U	-	-	-	-	-	-	00-00-00
Mansfield v Ebbsfleet U	-	-	-	-	-	-	00-00-00
Stevenage v Kidderminster	-	-	-	3-1	1-2	2-1	05-01-03
Weymouth v Rushden & D	-	-	-	-	1-1	1-2	01-01-01
York v Oxford Utd	0-1	2-2	-	-	1-0	0-1	03-01-03

TUESDAY 24TH FEBRUARY 2009
CONFERENCE

Burton v Altrincham	-	-	-	1-0	2-1	2-1	03-01-00
Crawley v Lewes	-	-	-	-	-	-	00-00-00
Eastbourne v Ebbsfleet U	-	-	-	-	-	-	00-00-00
Grays v Cambridge U	-	-	-	5-3	1-1	2-1	02-01-00
Histon v Barrow	-	-	-	-	-	-	00-00-00
Northwich v Kettering	1-2	-	-	4-1	-	-	06-05-04
Oxford Utd v Mansfield	-	1-1	1-0	1-2	-	-	02-01-01
Rushden & D v York	2-1	-	-	-	0-1	1-1	02-01-01
Stevenage v Woking	1-1	1-1	0-2	1-1	3-2	1-1	03-05-06
Torquay v Forest G	-	-	-	-	-	1-0	01-00-00
Wrexham v Kidderminster	0-2	-	-	-	-	-	00-00-01

FRIDAY 27TH FEBRUARY 2009
CHAMPIONSHIP

Doncaster v Derby	-	-	-	-	-	-	00-00-00

SATURDAY 28TH FEBRUARY 2009
PREMIER LEAGUE

Arsenal v Fulham	2-1	0-0	2-0	4-1	3-1	2-1	06-01-00
Aston Villa v Stoke	-	-	-	-	-	-	00-00-00
Bolton v Newcastle	4-3	1-0	2-1	2-0	2-1	1-3	06-00-03
Chelsea v Wigan	-	-	-	1-0	4-0	1-1	02-01-00
Everton v WBA	1-0	-	2-1	2-2	-	-	02-01-00
Hull v Blackburn	-	-	-	-	-	-	02-00-01
Man Utd v Portsmouth	-	3-0	2-1	3-0	3-0	2-0	05-00-00
Middlesboro v Liverpool	1-0	0-0	2-0	0-0	0-0	1-1	05-05-04
Sunderland v Tottenham	2-0	-	-	1-1	-	1-0	03-02-03
West Ham v Man City	0-0	-	-	1-0	0-1	0-2	05-01-03

CHAMPIONSHIP

Barnsley v QPR	1-0	3-3	-	-	2-0	0-0	04-03-01
Bristol C v Blackpool	2-0	2-1	1-1	1-1	2-4	1-0	07-03-03
Burnley v Sheff Weds	2-7	-	-	1-2	1-1	1-1	01-02-03
Norwich v Coventry	2-0	1-1	-	-	1-1	2-0	05-06-01
Preston v Ipswich	0-0	1-1	1-1	3-1	1-0	2-2	02-04-00
Reading v Nottm Forest	1-0	3-0	1-0	-	-	-	03-01-00
Sheff Utd v Birmingham	-	-	-	-	-	-	02-03-02
Southampton v Cardiff	-	-	-	3-2	2-2	1-0	02-01-00
Swansea v Charlton	-	-	-	-	-	-	00-00-00
Watford v C Palace	3-3	1-5	-	1-2	-	0-2	02-03-05
Wolves v Plymouth	-	-	1-1	1-1	2-2	1-0	04-03-00

LEAGUE 1

Brighton v Crewe	-	-	1-3	2-2	1-4	3-0	01-02-03
Carlisle v Bristol R	0-0	0-2	-	1-3	-	1-1	02-02-03
Cheltenham v Northampton	1-1	4-3	1-0	3-1	0-2	1-1	04-02-01
Colchester v Hartlepool	-	1-2	1-1	2-0	-	-	04-01-04
Hereford v Leyton O	-	-	-	-	-	-	02-01-00
Leeds v Scunthorpe	-	-	-	-	-	-	00-00-00
Millwall v Oldham	-	-	-	-	1-0	2-3	04-03-02
Milton K v Leicester	2-3	-	-	-	-	-	03-00-03
Peterboro v Southend	-	-	-	-	-	-	03-01-01
Stockport v Huddersfield	2-1	-	2-3	-	-	-	04-04-02

Tranmere v Swindon	0-1	1-0	2-1	1-0	-	2-1	09-03-01
Walsall v Yeovil	-	-	-	0-2	-	2-0	01-00-01

LEAGUE 2

Aldershot v Accrington	-	2-1	0-0	1-4	-	-	01-01-01
Brentford v Bury	-	-	-	-	-	1-4	03-02-04
Chester v Dagenham & R	5-2	2-1	-	-	-	4-0	03-01-01
Chesterfield v Barnet	-	-	-	-	-	0-1	02-00-03
Exeter v Darlington	0-4	-	-	-	-	-	05-02-04
Gillingham v Bournemouth	-	-	-	1-0	1-1	2-1	05-02-00
Lincoln v Rotherham	-	-	-	-	-	1-3	01-00-04
Macclesfield v Shrewsbury	1-2	-	2-1	2-0	2-2	2-1	07-01-01
Morecambe v Wycombe	-	-	-	-	-	0-1	00-00-01
Notts Co v Bradford	-	-	-	-	-	1-3	00-00-02
Port Vale v Luton	1-2	1-0	3-1	-	-	1-2	04-00-03
Rochdale v Grimsby	-	-	2-0	2-2	1-0	3-1	03-01-02

SCOTTISH PREMIER LEAGUE

Aberdeen v Kilmarnock	0-1	3-1	3-2	1-2/2-2/0-0	3-1/3-0	2-1	14-07-06
Celtic v St Mirren	-	-	-	-	2-0/5-1	1-1	09-03-01
Dundee Utd v Hearts	0-3	2-1/0-2	1-1/2-1	0-3/1-1	0-1	4-1	10-12-12
Hamilton v Rangers	-	-	-	-	-	-	00-00-02
Hibernian v Falkirk	-	-	-	2-3	0-1/2-0	1-1	06-04-04
Inv CT v Motherwell	-	-	1-1/1-0	1-2/0-1	0-1/2-0	0-3	02-01-04

SCOTTISH DIVISION ONE

Clyde v Queen of Sth	2-1/2-2	3-1/2-0	2-0/0-1	1-0/3-0	4-0/0-1	0-0/1-4	18-05-06
Morton v Dunfermline	-	-	-	-	-	0-1/3-0	04-03-04
Livingston v Partick	3-0/3-1	2-0/2-2	-	-	2-2/0-1	0-4/1-0	05-07-04
Ross County v Airdrie Utd	-	-	1-2/3-1	2-2/0-1	2-1/1-1	1-1/3-2	04-04-04
St Johnstone v Dundee	-	-	-	1-1/0-0	2-1/2-0	1-1/1-1	07-10-07

SCOTTISH DIVISION TWO

Brechin v East Fife	-	-	-	-	-	-	10-04-02
Queen's Park v Ayr	-	-	-	-	-	1-1/1-3	00-01-01
Raith v Peterhead	-	-	-	0-2/1-0	5-2/2-0	2-2/2-5	03-01-02
Stirling v Arbroath	-	-	5-2/0-3	-	-	-	04-04-04
Stranraer v Alloa	-	-	3-0/0-1	-	2-2/3-4	-	03-08-05

SCOTTISH DIVISION THREE

Albion v Annan Ath	-	-	-	-	-	-	00-00-00
Cowdenbeath v Stenhsmuir	1-0/3-3	-	0-6/0-2	4-1/1-1	-	-	05-06-07
E Stirling v Dumbarton	-	-	-	-	0-2/1-5	3-2/1-1	08-03-09
Elgin v Montrose	0-0/0-2	2-3/2-1	1-3/2-2	0-0/1-0	3-2/0-2	0-2/2-1	05-04-07
Forfar v Berwick	0-2/2-2	1-5/0-2	1-1/0-2	-	-	-	03-05-09

CONFERENCE

Altrincham v Stevenage	-	-	-	1-1	2-1	1-5	01-01-05
Barrow v Northwich	-	-	-	1-1	-	-	01-02-02
Cambridge U v Crawley	-	-	-	2-1	1-2	2-1	02-00-01
Forest G v Grays	-	-	-	1-2	0-0	1-2	00-01-02
Kidderminstr v Eastbourne	-	-	-	-	-	-	00-00-00
Lewes v Histon	-	-	-	0-3	3-1	-	01-00-01
Oxford Utd v Torquay	2-2	1-0	-	1-0	-	3-3	02-03-00
Rushden & D v Mansfield	-	-	0-0	1-2	-	-	01-01-01
Woking v Burton	2-2	1-0	1-0	2-2	0-0	2-1	03-03-00

Wrexham v Salisbury	-	-	-	-	-	-	00-00-00
York v Weymouth	-	-	-	-	1-0	2-0	02-00-00

TUESDAY 3RD MARCH 2009
PREMIER LEAGUE

Portsmouth v Chelsea	-	0-2	0-2	0-2	0-2	1-1	00-01-05
Stoke v Bolton	-	-	-	-	-	-	02-03-01
Tottenham v Middlesboro	0-3	0-0	2-0	2-0	2-1	1-1	06-05-03
WBA v Arsenal	1-2	-	0-2	2-1	-	-	01-00-02
Wigan v West Ham	-	1-1	1-2	1-2	0-3	1-0	01-01-03

CHAMPIONSHIP

Birmingham v Bristol C	-	-	-	-	-	-	01-01-02
Blackpool v Burnley	-	-	-	-	-	3-0	04-01-05
Cardiff v Barnsley	1-1	-	-	-	2-0	3-0	02-01-00
Charlton v Doncaster	-	-	-	-	-	-	00-00-00
Coventry v Sheff Utd	2-1	0-1	1-2	2-0	-	0-1	04-02-04
Crystal Pal v Wolves	4-2	-	-	1-1	2-2	0-2	03-04-04
Derby v Swansea	-	-	-	-	-	-	00-00-00
Ipswich v Southampton	-	-	-	2-2	2-1	2-0	05-02-01
Nottm Forest v Preston	2-2	0-1	2-0	-	-	-	02-02-01
Plymouth v Watford	-	-	1-0	3-3	-	1-1	02-05-02
QPR v Norwich	-	-	-	3-0	3-3	1-0	07-05-03
Sheff Weds v Reading	3-2	-	-	1-1	-	-	01-01-00

LEAGUE 1

Bristol R v Brighton	-	-	-	-	-	0-2	04-00-02
Crewe v Carlisle	-	-	-	-	5-1	0-1	05-00-00
Hartlepool v Tranmere	-	0-0	0-1	0-0	-	3-1	01-03-01
Huddersfield v Colchester	1-1	-	2-2	2-0	-	-	02-02-00
Leicester v Stockport	-	-	-	-	-	-	00-00-00
Leyton O v Peterboro	-	-	-	2-1	-	-	03-01-03
Northampton v MK Dons	-	-	-	-	-	-	00-00-00
Oldham v Leeds	-	-	-	-	-	0-1	02-03-01
Scunthorpe v Walsall	-	-	-	1-3	-	-	03-01-02
Southend v Millwall	-	-	-	-	-	1-0	02-03-02
Swindon v Cheltenham	0-3	-	-	-	-	3-0	01-00-01
Yeovil v Hereford	4-0	-	-	-	-	-	05-00-01

LEAGUE 2

Accrington v Port Vale	-	-	-	-	-	-	00-00-00
Barnet v Rochdale	-	-	-	1-1	3-2	0-0	08-02-06
Bournemouth v Aldershot	-	-	-	-	-	-	00-00-00
Bradford v Macclesfield	-	-	-	-	-	1-1	00-01-00
Bury v Chesterfield	-	-	-	-	-	0-1	06-01-01
Dagenham & R v Lincoln	-	-	-	-	-	1-0	01-00-00
Darlington v Notts Co	-	-	1-2	1-1	0-1	2-2	00-02-03
Grimsby v Brentford	-	1-0	-	-	-	1-2	03-00-02
Luton v Gillingham	-	-	-	-	-	3-1	04-01-00
Rotherham v Morecambe	-	-	-	-	-	3-1	01-00-00
Shrewsbury v Exeter	1-0	2-2	-	-	-	-	03-04-02
Wycombe v Chester	-	-	4-2	3-3	1-0	1-0	05-01-00

Sponsored by Stan James

WEDNESDAY 4TH MARCH 2009
PREMIER LEAGUE

Blackburn v Everton	0-1	2-1	0-0	0-2	1-1	0-0	05-04-05
Fulham v Hull	-	-	-	-	-	-	01-02-01
Liverpool v Sunderland	0-0	-	-	1-0	-	3-0	04-04-00
Man City v Aston Villa	3-1	4-1	2-0	3-1	0-2	1-0	09-02-03
Newcastle v Man Utd	2-6	1-2	1-3	0-2	2-2	1-5	03-05-08

SCOTTISH PREMIER LEAGUE

Falkirk v Dundee Utd	-	-	-	1-3/1-0	5-1/2-0	3-0	05-01-05
Hamilton v Hibernian	-	-	-	-	-	-	00-01-03
Hearts v Motherwell	4-2/2-1	0-0/3-2	0-1/0-0	2-1/3-0	4-1	1-2	21-11-05
Kilmarnock v Celtic	1-1/0-4	0-5/0-1	2-4/0-1	0-1/1-4	1-2/1-2	1-2	04-08-17
Rangers v Inv CT			1-0/1-1	1-1	0-1/1-1	2-0	02-03-01
St Mirren v Aberdeen	-	-	-	-	1-1/0-2	0-1	03-02-08

SATURDAY 7TH MARCH 2009
CHAMPIONSHIP

Birmingham v Southampton	3-2	2-1	2-1	-	2-1	-	04-00-00
Blackpool v Norwich	-	-	-	-	-	1-3	00-00-01
Cardiff v Doncaster	-	-	-	-	-	-	03-01-02
Charlton v Watford	-	-	-	-	0-0	2-2	04-03-01
Coventry v Barnsley	-	-	-	-	4-1	4-0	04-00-00
Crystal Pal v Preston	2-0	1-1	-	1-1	3-0	2-1	04-02-01
Derby v Bristol C	-	-	-	-	-	-	03-00-01
Ipswich v Burnley	2-2	6-1	1-1	2-1	1-1	0-0	02-04-00
Nottm Forest v Swansea	-	-	-	1-2	3-1	0-0	01-01-01
Plymouth v Reading	-	-	2-2	0-2	-	-	01-02-01
QPR v Sheff Utd	-	-	0-1	2-1	-	1-1	06-02-04
Sheff Weds v Wolves	0-4	-	-	0-2	2-2	1-3	00-03-04

LEAGUE 1

Bristol R v Leeds	-	-	-	-	-	0-3	00-00-01
Crewe v Hereford	-	-	-	-	-	-	03-01-00
Hartlepool v Peterboro	-	1-0	2-2	-	1-0	-	06-02 02
Huddersfield v Millwall	-	-	-	-	4-2	1-0	03-00-00
Leicester v Cheltenham	-	-	-	-	-	-	00-00-00
Leyton O v Brighton	-	-	-	-	1-4	2-2	04-01-05
Northampton v Tranmere	0-4	-	-	-	1-3	2-1	02-00-03
Oldham v Colchester	2-0	0-0	1-1	1-0	-	-	04-03-01
Scunthorpe v Stockport	-	-	-	-	-	-	02-01-00
Southend v Walsall	-	-	-	0-0	-	1-0	01-01-01
Swindon v MK Dons	-	-	2-1	0-1	2-1	-	02-00-02
Yeovil v Carlisle	-	3-0	-	-	2-1	2-1	03-00-00

LEAGUE 2

Accrington v Gillingham	-	-	-	-	-	-	00-00-00
Barnet v Chester	0-3	0-0	-	1-3	1-0	3-1	05-03-03
Bournemouth v Port Vale	-	2-1	4-0	1-2	0-4	0-1	05-02-03
Bradford v Aldershot	-	-	-	-	-	-	00-00-00
Bury v Rochdale	1-1	1-2	0-0	2-1	0-1	1-1	01-05-04
Dagenham & R v Morecambe	1-1	1-3	2-1	3-1	2-1	2-0	06-02-01
Darlington v Macclesfield	0-0	0-1	3-1	1-0	4-0	2-2	05-04-02
Grimsby v Lincoln	-	-	2-4	3-0	0-0	1-0	04-01-01
Luton v Exeter	-	-	-	-	-	-	01-00-00

Rotherham v Brentford	-	-	-	2-2	2-0	1-2	05-02-04
Shrewsbury v Notts Co	-	-	1-1	2-0	2-0	0-0	03-03-02
Wycombe v Chesterfield	2-0	3-3	-	-	-	1-0	06-03-01

SCOTTISH DIVISION ONE

Airdrie Utd v Livingston	-	-	-	-	0-1/3-1	-	03-03-04
Dunfermline v Dundee	4-2/0-1	2-0	3-1/5-0	-	-	0-1/0-1	11-02-05
Partick v Clyde	-	-	0-0/1-0	-	1-1/0-4	4-0/1-1	05-06-05
Queen of Sth v Morton	-	-	-	-	-	1-3/0-0	04-02-02
St Johnstone v Ross County	1-1/2-0	1-1/1-1	1-1/0-2	1-1/1-1	3-1/2-1	-	03-06-01

SCOTTISH DIVISION TWO

Alloa v Stirling	-	-	1-1/3-0	2-4/0-0	1-2/1-1	-	05-05-03
Arbroath v Brechin	-	-	2-2/1-4	-	-	-	02-03-05
Ayr v Stranraer	-	-	0-1/0-0	-	0-2/1-0	-	07-03-02
East Fife v Raith	-	-	-	-	-	-	00-00-00
Peterhead v Queen's Park	3-0/3-1	4-1/1-1	2-2/1-1	-	-	1-0/1-0	06-03-01

SCOTTISH DIVISION THREE

Annan Ath v Elgin -	-	-	-	-	-	00-00-00	
Berwick v Cowdenbeath	2-1/1-2	-	-	1-0/1-0	-	1-1/4-5	09-04-08
Dumbarton v Albion	-	-	-	-	3-1/3-1	2-0/2-0	09-06-03
Montrose v Forfar	-	-	-	-	-	0-1/2-2	07-03-05
Stenhsmuir v E Stirling	-	-	6-0/3-2	6-1/5-0	2-0/1-1	0-3/3-0	13-04-02

CONFERENCE

Cambridge U v Burton	-	-	-	2-2	1-2	0-0	00-02-01
Crawley v Weymouth	5-0	2-1	-	-	0-3	1-1	04-06-01
Eastbourne v Wrexham	-	-	-	-	-	-	00-00-00
Ebbsfleet U v York	-	-	4-0	2-2	0-1	1-2	01-01-02
Forest G v Oxford Utd	-	-	-	-	1-5	0-0	00-01-01
Grays v Altrincham	-	-	-	1-1	1-1	1-0	01-02-00
Kettering v Histon	-	-	-	-	-	-	00-00-00
Mansfield v Lewes	-	-	-	-	-	-	00-00-00
Northwich v Stevenage	1-1	1-2	1-1	-	0-0	0-2	02-05-06
Salisbury v Kidderminster	-	-	-	-	-	0-1	00-00-01
Torquay v Rushden & D	1-1	-	-	2-1	-	3-2	02-02-00
Woking v Barrow	-	-	-	-	-	-	00-00-01

TUESDAY 10TH MARCH 2009
CHAMPIONSHIP

Barnsley v Birmingham	-	-	--	-	1-0	-	03-02-05
Bristol C v Coventry	-	-	-	-	-	2-1	01-00-00
Burnley v C Palace	0-0	2-3	-	0-0	1-1	1-1	01-04-02
Doncaster v QPR	-	-	-	-	-	-	00-00-00
Norwich v Cardiff	-	4-1	-	1-0	1-0	1-2	03-00-01
Preston v Sheff Weds	2-2	-	-	0-0	0-0	1-0	03-03-00
Reading v Charlton	-	-	-	-	2-0	-	03-02-00
Sheff Utd v Blackpool	-	-	-	-	-	1-1	01-01-00
Southampton v Derby	-	-	-	0-0	0-1	-	04-03-04
Swansea v Plymouth	-	-	-	-	-	-	02-01-03
Watford v Nottm Forest	1-1	1-1	0-2	-	-	-	01-02-03
Wolves v Ipswich	1-1	-	2-0	1-0	1-0	1-1	06-06-01

Sponsored by Stan James

LEAGUE 1

Brighton v Southend	-	-	-	-	-	3-2	03-00-02
Carlisle v Leyton O	3-0	0-1	-	2-3	3-1	1-0	08-01-02
Colchester v Swindon	1-0	0-1	0-1	1-0	-	-	02-00-04
Hereford v Bristol R	-	-	-	-	0-0	-	00-01-00
Leeds v Yeovil	-	-	-	-	-	1-0	01-00-00
Millwall v Northampton	-	-	-	-	0-1	2-0	02-01-02
Milton K v Huddersfield	-	-	2-1	2-2	-	-	01-02-00
Peterboro v Scunthorpe	-	-	-	-	-	-	01-02-02
Stockport v Hartlepool	-	1-2	1-0	-	3-3	-	05-01-03
Tranmere v Leicester	-	-	-	-	-	-	01-01-02
Walsall v Crewe	-	1-1	-	-	-	1-1	04-04-02

LEAGUE 2

Aldershot v Shrewsbury	-	1-1	-	-	-	-	00-01-00
Brentford v Barnet		-	-	-	-	2-1	03-00-00
Chester v Rotherham	-	-	-	-	-	0-1	02-02-04
Exeter v Bournemouth	1-3	-	-	-	-	-	01-01-03
Gillingham v Darlington	-	-	-	-	-	-	04-01-00
Lincoln v Wycombe	-	-	2-3	1-2	1-0	1-0	02-00-04
Macclesfield v Accrington	-	-	-	-	3-3	2-1	01-01-00
Morecambe v Bury	-	-	-	-	-	2-1	01-00-00
Notts Co v Luton	2-1	1-1	-	-	-	-	02-03-05
Port Vale v Dagenham & R	-	-	-	-	-	-	00-00-00
Rochdale v Bradford	-	-	-	-	-	2-1	01-00-00

SCOTTISH DIVISION ONE

Clyde v St Johnstone	1-2/2-1	2-0/2-3	1-0/1-1	0-1/2-3	1-0/0-1	1-0/1-3	06-01-08
Dundee v Queen of Sth	-	-	-	3-1/2-3	2-1/1-0	2-1/2-3	04-00-02
Morton v Airdrie Utd	-	3-1/1-1	-	-	-	-	05-07-08
Livingston v Dunfermline	1-1	0-0/0-0	2-0/1-1/2-0	1-1/0-1	-	1-1/0-2	05-07-05
Ross County v Partick	-	-	0-1/2-1	-	2-5/2-1	-	04-00-04

CONFERENCE

Weymouth v Salisbury	-	-	-	-	-	0-3	03-01-01

WEDNESDAY 11TH MARCH 2009
LEAGUE 2

Chesterfield v Grimsby	-	4-4	-	-	-	1-2	02-01-01

SATURDAY 14TH MARCH 2009
PREMIER LEAGUE

Arsenal v Blackburn	1-2	1-0	3-0	3-0	6-2	2-0	07-04-03
Aston Villa v Tottenham	0-1	1-0	1-0	1-1	1-1	2-1	12-07-01
Bolton v Fulham	0-0	0-2	3-1	2-1	2-1	0-0	07-04-03
Chelsea v Man City	5-0	1-0	0-0	2-0	3-0	6-0	07-06-02
Everton v Stoke	-	-	-	-	-	-	00-00-00
Hull v Newcastle	-	-	-	-	-	-	01-00-01
Man Utd v Liverpool	4-0	0-1	2-1	1-0	2-0	3-0	10-06-04
Middlesboro v Portsmouth	-	0-0	1-1	1-1	0-4	2-0	04-04-03
Sunderland v Wigan	-	1-1	1-1	0-1	-	2-0	01-02-01
West Ham v WBA	0-1	3-4	-	1-0	-	-	02-00-03

CHAMPIONSHIP

Barnsley v Blackpool	2-1	3-0	1-0	2-2	-	2-1	04-01-00
Bristol C v Cardiff	2-0	-	-	-	-	1-0	04-02-00
Burnley v Nottm Forest	1-0	0-3	1-0	-	-	-	03-01-01
Doncaster v Birmingham	-	-	-	-	-	-	00-00-00
Norwich v Plymouth	-	-	-	2-0	1-3	2-1	02-00-01
Preston v Coventry	2-2	4-2	3-2	3-1	1-1	1-0	05-02-00
Reading v Ipswich	3-1	1-1	1-1	2-0	-	-	03-02-02
Sheff Utd v Derby	2-0	1-1	0-1	2-1	-	-	04-01-02
Southampton v QPR	-	-	-	1-1	1-2	2-3	04-01-06
Swansea v C Palace	-	-	-	-	-	-	00-00-00
Watford v Sheff Weds	1-0	-	-	2-1	-	2-1	05-01-01
Wolves v Charlton	-	0-4	-	-	-	2-0	06-03-02

LEAGUE 1

Brighton v Yeovil	-	-	-	-	1-3	1-2	00-00-02
Carlisle v Scunthorpe	1-2	1-4	-	-	0-2	-	04-01-09
Cheltenham v Hartlepool	-	-	-	-	-	1-1	02-01-01
Colchester v Crewe	1-2	-	-	-	-	-	02-00-02
Hereford v Southend	-	-	-	-	-	-	00-00-01
Leeds v Swindon	-	-	-	-	-	2-1	03-01-00
Millwall v Leicester	2-2	-	2-0	0-1	-	-	04-03-01
Milton K v Oldham	-	-	1-1	0-1	-	-	03-01-01
Peterboro v Northampton	0-0	-	-	0-1	-	-	03-01-02
Stockport v Leyton O	-	-	-	1-1	-	-	03-03-00
Tranmere v Huddersfield	2-1	-	3-0	2-1	2-2	3-0	11-02-01
Walsall v Bristol R	-	-	-	-	2-2	0-1	02-03-03

LEAGUE 2

Aldershot v Luton	-	-	-	-	-	-	00-00-00
Brentford v Wycombe	1-0	1-1	-	-	-	1-3	03-06-01
Chester v Grimsby	-	-	2-1	1-2	0-2	0-2	01-00-04
Chesterfield v Dagenham & R	-	-	-	-	-	1-1	00-01-00
Exeter v Bradford	-	-	-	-	-	-	01-02-01
Gillingham v Shrewsbury	-	-	-	-	-	-	02-00-01
Lincoln v Bury	1-1	2-1	1-0	1-1	0-2	1-1	02-05-03
Macclesfield v Bournemouth	0-1	-	-	-	-	-	00-00-01
Morecambe v Barnet	1-1	1-3	1-1	-	-	0-0	01-03-01
Notts Co v Accrington	-	-	-	-	3-2	1-0	02-00-00
Port Vale v Darlington	-	-	-	-	-	-	00-00-00
Rochdale v Rotherham	-	-	-	-	-	4-1	01-02-03

SCOTTISH PREMIER LEAGUE

Aberdeen v Hamilton	-	-	-	-	-	-	01-01-00
Celtic v Falkirk	-	-	-	3-1/2-1	1-0	4-0	11-00-01
Hibernian v Hearts	1-2	1-0/1-1	1-1/2-2	2-0/2-1	2-2/0-1	1-1	11-14-11
Inv CT v Kilmarnock	-	-	0-2/1-2	2-2/3-3	3-4	3-1/3-0	02-02-03
Motherwell v Dundee Utd	1-2/2-2	3-1/0-1	4-2/2-0	4-5/2-0/1-1	2-3	5-3/2-2	16-08-13
St Mirren v Rangers	-	-	-	-	2-3/0-1	0-3	00-02-11

SCOTTISH DIVISION ONE

Airdrie Utd v Queen of Sth	-	-	0-1/2-0	4-0/1-1	2-2/0-3	-	04-02-02
Dundee v Ross County	-	-	-	0-0/0-0	3-1/3-2	-	02-02-00
Dunfermline v Partick	4-1/0-0	2-1/1-0	-	-	-	1-0/1-1	03-03-06
Morton v Clyde	-	-	-	-	-	3-2/1-2	03-03-06
Livingston v St Johnstone	-	-	-	-	1-1/3-2	0-2/0-2	03-02-03

Sponsored by Stan James

SCOTTISH DIVISION TWO

Alloa v Arbroath	0-3/3-2	2-2/4-0	4-2/2-2	-	-	-	10-08-08
Peterhead v East Fife	0-2/2-2	-	2-0/0-0	-	-	-	02-04-02
Raith v Ayr	-	1-1/2-1	-	3-3/1-1	1-0/0-1	2-3/1-2	10-10-08
Stirling v Brechin	-	-	1-5/1-2	-	2-1/0-1	-	05-02-06
Stranraer v Queen's Park	-	1-0/3-1	-	-	-	-	08-02-03

SCOTTISH DIVISION THREE

Annan Ath v Cowdenbeath	-	-	-	-	-	-	00-00-00
E Stirling v Berwick	-	-	-	1-2/0-1	0-1/0-3	-	07-03-09
Elgin v Stenhsmuir	-	-	1-1/4-2	1-2/0-2	2-0/2-1	2-0/1-5	04-01-03
Forfar v Albion	-	-	-	-	-	1-0/1-4	09-02-01
Montrose v Dumbarton	-	-	-	-	1-1/0-5	0-1/3-1	04-07-07

CONFERENCE

Altrincham v Weymouth	-	-	-	-	0-0	3-2	02-01-00
Burton v Salisbury	-	-	-	-	-	4-3	03-01-03
Crawley v Rushden & D	-	-	-	-	1-0	4-1	02-02-01
Histon v Ebbsfleet U	-	-	-	-	-	3-2	01-00-00
Lewes v Kidderminster	-	-	-	-	-	-	00-00-00
Mansfield v Forest G	-	-	-	-	-	-	00-00-00
Oxford Utd v Grays	-	-	-	-	1-1	0-0	00-02-00
Stevenage v Cambridge U	-	-	-	3-1	4-1	1-2	02-00-01
Torquay v Barrow	-	-	-	-	-	-	00-00-00
Woking v Wrexham	-	-	-	-	-	-	00-00-00
York v Kettering	-	-	-	-	-	-	00-00-00

SATURDAY 21ST MARCH 2009

PREMIER LEAGUE

Blackburn v West Ham	2-2	-	-	3-2	1-2	0-1	09-01-03
Fulham v Man Utd	1-1	1-1	1-1	2-3	1-2	0-3	00-03-04
Liverpool v Aston Villa	1-1	1-0	2-1	3-1	3-1	2-2	12-05-03
Man City v Sunderland	3-0	-	-	2-1	-	1-0	05-01-01
Newcastle v Arsenal	1-1	0-0	0-1	1-0	0-0	1-1	05-06-05
Portsmouth v Everton	-	1-2	0-1	0-1	2-0	0-0	01-01-03
Stoke v Middlesboro	-	-	-	-	-	-	01-02-01
Tottenham v Chelsea	0-0	0-1	0-2	0-2	2-1	4-4	01-07-11
WBA v Bolton	1-1	-	2-1	0-0	-	-	03-06-02
Wigan v Hull	-	-	-	-	-	-	01-00-02

CHAMPIONSHIP

Birmingham v Norwich	-	-	1-1	-	0-1	-	04-02-03
Blackpool v Southampton	-	-	-	-	-	2-2	00-01-00
Charlton v Preston	-	-	-	-	-	1-2	00-00-01
Coventry v Doncaster	-	-	-	-	-	-	00-00-00
Crystal Pal v Reading	0-1	2-2	-	1-1	-	-	01-02-02
Derby v Barnsley	-	-	-	-	2-1	-	06-01-00
Ipswich v Watford	4-2	4-1	1-2	0-1	-	1-2	06-01-04
Nottm Forest v Wolves	2-2	-	1-0	-	-	-	02-05-00
Plymouth v Burnley	-	-	1-0	1-0	0-0	3-1	04-03-01
QPR v Bristol C	1-0	1-1	-	-	-	3-0	02-03-00
Sheff Weds v Swansea	-	-	-	-	-	-	00-00-00

LEAGUE 1

Bristol R v Peterboro	-	-	-	2-3	3-2	-	04-01-02
Crewe v Leeds	-	-	2-2	1-0	-	0-1	01-01-01

Hartlepool v Millwall	-	-	-	-	-	0-1	00-00-01
Huddersfield v Cheltenham	3-3	0-0	-	-	2-0	2-3	01-02-01
Leicester v Colchester	-	-	-	-	0-0	1-1	00-02-00
Leyton O v Walsall	-	-	-	-	-	1-0	01-01-00
Northampton v Stockport	0-3	-	-	2-0	-	-	02-00-01
Oldham v Tranmere	2-0	1-1	2-2	1-0	1-0	3-1	04-04-02
Scunthorpe v Brighton	-	-	-	-	1-2	-	03-00-02
Southend v Carlisle	0-1	2-2	-	-	-	0-1	03-03-03
Swindon v Hereford	-	-	-	-	1-2	-	00-00-01
Yeovil v MK Dons	-	-	-	1-1	-	-	00-01-00

LEAGUE 2

Accrington v Exeter	-	1-2	0-0	1-2	-	-	00-01-02
Barnet v Lincoln	-	-	-	2-3	0-5	5-2	07-02-02
Bournemouth v Notts Co	-	1-0	-	-	-	-	03-01-03
Bradford v Port Vale	-	-	0-2	1-0	2-0	-	07-01-01
Bury v Chester	-	-	1-1	0-0	1-3	0-2	03-04-03
Dagenham & R v Brentford	-	-	-	-	-	1-2	00-00-01
Darlington v Aldershot	-	-	-	-	-	-	00-00-00
Grimsby v Gillingham	1-1	-	-	-	-	-	02-02-01
Luton v Macclesfield	-	-	-	-	-	-	00-01-01
Rotherham v Chesterfield	-	-	-	0-4	0-1	2-1	01-01-04
Shrewsbury v Morecambe	-	2-0	-	-	-	2-0	02-00-00
Wycombe v Rochdale	-	-	0-3	3-0	1-1	0-1	01-02-02

SCOTTISH PREMIER LEAGUE

Dundee Utd v Celtic	0-2	1-5	0-3/2-3	2-4	1-4/1-1	0-2/0-2	08-06-20
Falkirk v Inv CT	1-1/2-3	2-1/2-1	-	0-2/1-4	3-1/1-0	1-0/2-1	07-04-05
Hamilton v St Mirren	-	-	2-2/0-0	3-1/0-0	-	-	05-12-01
Hibernian v Aberdeen	1-2/2-0/3-1	1-1/0-1	2-1/1-2	1-2	1-1/0-0	3-3/3-1	13-10-14
Kilmarnock v Motherwell	0-3/1-0	2-0	2-0	4-1/2-0	1-2	0-1	11-03-12
Rangers v Hearts	2-0/1-0	2-1/0-1	3-2/2-1	1-0/2-0	2-0/0-0/2-1	2-1	31-07-02

SCOTTISH DIVISION ONE

Clyde v Dunfermline	-	-	-	-	-	2-1/1-2	01-01-03
Partick v Dundee	1-1/1-3	1-2/0-1	-	-	3-1/2-1	1-1/1-0	09-04-07
Queen of Sth v Livingston	-	-	-	-	2-0/1-1	1-0/1-0	05-04-06
Ross County v Morton	-	-	-	-	-	-	01-00-01
St Johnstone v Airdrie Utd	-	-	1-1/1-2	1-0/2-2	1-0/4-3	-	11-06-02

SCOTTISH DIVISION TWO

Arbroath v Raith	-	-	-	-	-	-	00-02-00
Ayr v Peterhead	-	-	-	1-1/1-2	1-2/0-0	1-2/0-3	00-02-04
Brechin v Alloa	-	-	4-0/2-3	-	2-0/2-3	0-0/0-0	06-02-06
East Fife v Stranraer	-	-	-	-	-	3-1/2-1	05-04-06
Queen's Park v Stirling	0-1/3-3	0-2/1-4	-	-	-	-	04-05-03

SCOTTISH DIVISION THREE

Albion v Montrose1	-1/3-0	0-1/3-0	1-2/1-2	1-1/1-1	3-1/2-2	1-3/0-3	10-09-13
Berwick v Elgin	-	-	-	3-1/1-1	3-1/0-0	-	02-02-00
Cowdenbeath v E Stirling	-	2-1/2-0	2-1/3-2	5-1/5-0	-	-	18-03-06
Dumbarton v Annan Ath	-	-	-	-	-	-	00-00-00
Stenhsmuir v Forfar	2-1/1-4	2-0/0-2	-	-	-	4-0/2-0	08-03-06

Sponsored by Stan James

Barrow v Lewes	-	-	-	-	-	-	00-00-00
Eastbourne v Burton	-	-	-	-	-	-	00-00-00
Ebbsfleet U v Altrincham	-	-	-	2-0	3-1	2-0	03-00-00
Forest G v York	-	-	1-1	1-2	0-1	1-2	00-01-03
Grays v Mansfield	-	-	-	-	-	-	00-00-00
Histon v Stevenage	-	-	-	-	-	1-4	00-00-01
Kidderminstr v Woking	-	-	-	2-1	0-1	1-1	06-02-03
Northwich v Torquay	-	-	-	-	-	1-3	00-00-01
Rushden & D v Oxford Utd	0-2	-	3-3	3-0	1-0	5-0	04-01-01
Weymouth v Kettering	-	-	-	-	-	-	02-00-00
Wrexham v Crawley	-	-	-	-	-	-	00-00-00

SUNDAY 22ND MARCH 2009
CHAMPIONSHIP

Cardiff v Sheff Utd	-	2-1	1-0	0-1	-	1-0	03-01-01

TUESDAY 24TH MARCH 2009
LEAGUE 1

Cheltenham v Oldham	1-1	-	-	-	1-2	1-1	00-02-01

CONFERENCE

Cambridge U v Northwich	-	-	-	-	0-1	2-1	01-00-01
Kettering v Eastbourne	-	-	-	-	-	-	00-00-00
Salisbury v Ebbsfleet U	-	-	-	-	-	2-1	03-00-00

FRIDAY 27TH MARCH 2009
LEAGUE 1

Southend v Hartlepool	0-1	-	-	3-0	-	2-1	05-02-01

SATURDAY 28TH MARCH 2009
LEAGUE 1

Brighton v Tranmere	-	3-0	-	-	0-1	0-0	02-01-02
Bristol R v Stockport	-	-	-	2-2	2-1	-	01-04-01
Carlisle v Northampton	-	1-1	-	0-1	1-1	2-0	06-02-04
Crewe v Millwall	-	1-2	2-1	4-2	1-0	0-0	04-02-01
Hereford v Huddersfield	-	-	-	-	-	-	00-00-00
Leeds v MK Dons	-	-	-	-	-	-	07-03-00
Leyton O v Oldham	-	-	-	-	2-2	1-0	01-01-00
Peterboro v Leicester	-	-	-	-	-	-	01-01-00
Scunthorpe v Colchester	-	-	-	0-0	-	3-3	05-04-02
Walsall v Cheltenham	-	-	-	-	-	2-0	01-00-00
Yeovil v Swindon	-	-	-	0-0	-	0-1	00-01-01

LEAGUE 2

Barnet v Darlington	-	-	-	1-0	2-1	0-0	06-04-02
Brentford v Gillingham	-	-	-	1-1	2-2	-	03-02-01
Bury v Bournemouth	2-1	-	-	-	-	-	03-01-03
Chester v Bradford	-	-	-	-	-	0-1	01-01-03
Chesterfield v Port Vale	2-1	1-0	1-0	2-0	3-0	-	05-01-01
Dagenham & R v Macclesfield	-	-	-	-	-	0-1	01-01-03
Grimsby v Aldershot	-	-	-	-	-	-	00-00-00

Lincoln v Notts Co	-	-	1-2	2-1	1-1	2-1	02-01-03
Morecambe v Luton	-	-	-	-	-	-	00-00-00
Rochdale v Exeter	3-3	-	-	-	-	-	07-02-02
Rotherham v Accrington	-	-	-	-	-	0-1	00-00-01
Wycombe v Shrewsbury	-	-	1-1	2-0	1-1	1-1	04-04-00

CONFERENCE

Altrincham v Crawley	-	-	-	1-1	1-1	2-3	00-02-01
Burton v Grays	-	-	-	1-1	3-0	2-3	01-01-01
Forest G v Lewes	-	-	-	-	-	-	00-00-00
Histon v Wrexham	-	-	-	-	-	-	00-00-00
Kettering v Ebbsfleet U	1-1	-	-	-	-	-	00-01-00
Mansfield v Torquay	-	2-1	-	3-0	5-0	-	08-03-01
Northwich v Rushden & D	-	-	-	-	4-1	1-0	04-01-02
Salisbury v Eastbourne	-	-	-	-	1-2	-	00-00-01
Stevenage v Oxford Utd	-	-	-	-	2-2	0-0	00-02-00
Weymouth v Barrow	-	-	-	-	-	-	00-00-00
Woking v Cambridge U	-	-	-	0-1	0-1	0-0	00-01-02
York v Kidderminster	0-0	1-0	-	2-2	1-0	2-2	03-03-01

SATURDAY 4TH APRIL 2009
PREMIER LEAGUE

Arsenal v Man City	2-1	2-1	1-1	1-0	3-1	1-0	11-03-00
Blackburn v Tottenham	1-2	1-0	0-1	0-0	1-1	1-1	05-04-05
Bolton v Middlesboro	2-1	2-0	0-0	1-1	0-0	0-0	05-05-00
Fulham v Liverpool	3-2	1-2	2-4	2-0	1-0	0-2	03-00-04
Hull v Portsmouth	-	-	-	-	-	-	00-01-02
Man Utd v Aston Villa	1-1	4-0	3-1	1-0	3-1	4-0	14-06-00
Newcastle v Chelsea	2-1	2-1	1-1	1-0	0-0	0-2	07-04-04
WBA v Stoke	-	1-0	-	-	1-3	1-1	02-05-05
West Ham v Sunderland	2-0	3-2	1-2	2-0	-	3-1	08-01-02

CHAMPIONSHIP

Barnsley v Nottm Forest	-	-	-	2-0	-	-	04-00-01
Birmingham v Wolves	-	2-2	-	-	1-1	-	03-04-04
Blackpool v Plymouth	1-1	0-1	-	-	-	0-0	03-05-01
Bristol C v Preston	-	-	-	-	-	3-0	04-01-01
Cardiff v Swansea	-	-	-	-	-	-	01-03-03
Coventry v Reading	2-0	1-2	3-2	1-1	-	-	02-01-01
Derby v Burnley	1-2	2-0	1-1	3-0	1-0	-	04-01-01
Doncaster v Watford	-	-	-	-	-	-	00-00-00
Norwich v Sheff Weds	3-0	-	-	0-1	1-2	0-1	06-03-03
QPR v C Palace	-	-	-	1-3	4-2	1-2	04-01-07
Sheff Utd v Ipswich	0-0	1-1	0-2	2-0	-	3-1	04-05-04
Southampton v Charlton	0-0	3-2	0-0	-	-	0-1	05-03-01

LEAGUE 1

Cheltenham v Leyton O	-	1-0	1-2	1-1	2-1	1-0	04-03-01
Colchester v Leeds	-	-	-	-	2-1	-	01-00-00
Hartlepool v Hereford	-	-	-	-	3-2	-	04-01-02
Huddersfield v Southend	-	1-0	-	0-0	-	1-2	03-02-02
Leicester v Carlisle	-	-	-	-	-	-	00-00-00
Millwall v Walsall	0-3	2-1	-	-	-	1-2	03-01-04
Milton K v Brighton	1-0	-	-	-	-	-	01-00-00
Northampton v Scunthorpe	-	1-1	1-2	-	2-1	-	05-01-04
Oldham v Peterboro	0-0	1-1	2-1	-	-	-	02-02-01

Sponsored by Stan James

Stockport v Yeovil	-	-	-	-	-	-	00-00-00
Swindon v Crewe	1-3	-	-	-	-	1-1	02-01-03

LEAGUE 2

Accrington v Lincoln	-	-	-	-	2-2	0-3	00-01-01
Aldershot v Rotherham	-	-	-	-	-	-	00-00-00
Bournemouth v Rochdale	3-3	-	-	-	-	-	00-01-00
Bradford v Brentford	-	-	4-1	3-3	1-1	1-2	04-02-03
Darlington v Morecambe	-	-	-	-	-	2-2	00-01-00
Exeter v Dagenham & R	-	1-1	1-1	3-1	3-2	-	02-02-00
Gillingham v Barnet	-	-	-	-	-	-	02-02-00
Luton v Wycombe	1-0	3-1	-	-	-	-	03-03-01
Macclesfield v Chesterfield	-	-	-	-	-	1-0	02-00-01
Notts Co v Chester	-	-	1-1	1-1	1-2	1-0	01-04-02
Port Vale v Bury	-	-	-	-	-	-	02-02-01
Shrewsbury v Grimsby	-	-	1-1	0-0	2-2	2-1	01-03-01

SCOTTISH PREMIER LEAGUE

Celtic v Hamilton	-	-	-	-	-	-	02-00-00
Dundee Utd v Hibernian	1-1/1-2	1-2/0-0	1-4	1-0	0-3/0-0	0-0/1-1/1-1	11-15-09
Falkirk v Rangers	-	-	-	1-1/1-2	1-0	1-3	01-01-10
Hearts v Kilmarnock	1-1/3-0	2-1	3-0/3-0	1-0/2-0	0-2/1-0	1-1/0-2	16-08-04
Inv CT v St Mirren	4-1/3-1	2-0/1-1	-	-	1-2/2-1	1-0/0-0	07-03-02
Motherwell v Aberdeen	1-2/0-1/2-3	1-0	0-0/0-1	3-1	0-2/0-2	3-0/2-1	10-13-16

SCOTTISH DIVISION ONE

Airdrie Utd v Dunfermline	-	-	-	-	-	-	03-04-04
Clyde v Livingston	-	-	-	-	1-1/0-1	2-1/3-2	07-04-07
Morton v Dundee	-	-	-	-	-	0-2/1-2	02-05-04
Queen of Sth v Ross County	2-0/1-0	1-0/1-1	0-1/1-0	2-3/0-0	2-0/2-0	-	06-02-04
St Johnstone v Partick	-	-	2-1/1-1	-	2-0/2-0	2-1/2-0	09-05-01

SCOTTISH DIVISION TWO

Alloa v Peterhead	-	-	-	4-1/0-2	1-1/2-4	2-0/2-0	03-01-02
Ayr v Stirling	-	-	3-2/0-3	2-5/3-0	0-0/3-2	-	08-03-05
Brechin v Queen's Park	-	-	-	-	2-1/0-1	-	12-02-02
East Fife v Arbroath	-	0-1/1-2	-	1-1/0-3	2-1/1-2	0-2/2-1	06-03-10
Stranraer v Raith	2-2/1-0	-	-	-	1-4/0-2	-	02-03-03

SCOTTISH DIVISION THREE

Annan Ath v Montrose	-	-	-	-	-	-	00-00-00
Berwick v Albion	-	-	-	0-1/2-1	1-1/3-0	-	09-07-01
Cowdenbeath v Elgin	-	3-2/2-0	3-1/1-1	5-2/2-1	-	-	07-01-00
Forfar v E Stirling	-	-	-	-	-	0-2/1-0	07-02-02
Stenhsmuir v Dumbarton	2-2/2-1	1-1/1-2	-	-	1-0/5-1	2-1/1-1	08-05-07

CONFERENCE

Barrow v Woking	-	-	-	-	-	-	00-00-01
Cambridge U v Forest G	-	-	-	2-2	1-1	2-0	01-02-00
Crawley v Burton	-	-	4-0	1-1	1-0	1-1	02-10-05
Eastbourne v Weymouth	-	2-1	4-2	0-2	-	-	02-00-01
Ebbsfleet U v Northwich	1-1	2-2	2-2	-	3-0	2-1	02-03-00
Grays v York	-	-	-	1-1	0-0	0-2	00-02-01
Kidderminstr v Stevenage	-	-	-	0-0	1-2	0-2	03-01-05
Lewes v Altrincham	-	-	-	-	-	-	00-00-00
Oxford Utd v Histon	-	-	-	-	-	3-0	01-00-00

Rushden & D v Salisbury	-	-	-	-	-	0-0	01-01-00
Torquay v Kettering	-	-	-	-	-	-	00-00-00
Wrexham v Mansfield	-	-	-	4-1	0-0	1-1	02-02-00

SUNDAY 5TH APRIL 2009
PREMIER LEAGUE

Everton v Wigan	-	-	-	0-1	2-2	2-1	01-01-01

LEAGUE 1

Tranmere v Bristol R	-	-	-	-	-	0-2	01-01-02

FRIDAY 10TH APRIL 2009
LEAGUE 1

Bristol R v Northampton	-	1-2	3-1	0-0	-	1-1	02-04-03
Carlisle v Oldham	-	-	-	-	1-1	1-0	02-01-00
Scunthorpe v Huddersfield	-	6-2	-	2-2	2-0	-	02-01-00
Southend v MK Dons	-	-	-	0-0	-	-	00-01-00
Yeovil v Millwall	-	-	-	-	0-1	0-1	00-00-02

LEAGUE 2

Bury v Shrewsbury	4-3	-	0-0	2-0	1-2	1-1	04-05-02

SATURDAY 11TH APRIL 2009
PREMIER LEAGUE

Aston Villa v Everton	3-2	0-0	1-3	4-0	1-1	2-0	12-07-01
Chelsea v Bolton	1-0	1-2	2-2	5-1	2-2	1-1	05-03-01
Liverpool v Blackburn	1-1	4-0	0-0	1-0	1-1	3-1	08-05-01
Man City v Fulham	4-1	0-0	1-1	1-2	3-1	2-3	04-02-02
Middlesboro v Hull		-	-	-	-	-	-
		02-00-00					
Portsmouth v WBA	-	-	3-2	1-0	-	-	05-03-06
Stoke v Newcastle	-	-	-	-	-	-	01-00-00
Sunderland v Man Utd	1-1	-	-	1-3	-	0-4	02-02-04
Tottenham v West Ham	3-2	-	-	1-1	1-0	4-0	09-03-03
Wigan v Arsenal	-	-	-	2-3	0-1	0-0	00-01-02

CHAMPIONSHIP

Burnley v QPR	-	-	2-0	1-0	2-0	0-2	04-00-01
Charlton v Birmingham	0-2	1-1	3-1	2-0	-	-	06-03-01
Crystal Pal v Cardiff	-	2-1	-	1-0	1-2	0-0	02-01-01
Ipswich v Doncaster	-	-	-	-	-	-	00-00-00
Nottm Forest v Bristol C	-	-	-	3-1	1-0	-	02-01-00
Plymouth v Coventry	-	-	1-1	3-1	3-2	1-0	03-01-00
Preston v Blackpool	-	-	-	-	-	0-1	04-02-02
Reading v Sheff Utd	0-2	2-1	0-0	2-1	3-1	-	05-01-04
Sheff Weds v Derby	1-3	-	-	2-1	1-2	-	02-02-05
Swansea v Norwich	-	-	-	-	-	-	00-00-00
Watford v Barnsley	-	-	-	-	-	0-3	04-04-04
Wolves v Southampton	-	1-4	-	0-0	0-6	2-2	00-02-02

LEAGUE 1

Brighton v Swindon	-	2-2	-	-	-	2-1	01-03-04
Crewe v Hartlepool	-	-	-	-	-	3-1	02-00-00
Hereford v Leicester	-	-	-	-	-	-	00-00-00
Leeds v Stockport	-	-	-	-	-	-	00-00-00

Sponsored by Stan James

Leyton O v Colchester	-	-	-	-	-	-	01-01-02
Peterboro v Cheltenham	4-1	-	-	1-0	-	-	03-00-00
Walsall v Tranmere	-	-	0-2	0-0	-	2-1	02-01-02

LEAGUE 2

Barnet v Bournemouth	-	-	-	-	-	-	00-00-01
Brentford v Exeter	-	-	-	-	-	-	04-00-00
Chester v Macclesfield	-	-	1-0	2-1	0-3	0-0	02-02-02
Chesterfield v Darlington	-	-	-	-	-	1-1	02-04-00
Dagenham & R v Aldershot	-	2-3	3-0	2-0	2-1	-	04-00-02
Grimsby v Accrington	-	-	-	-	2-0	1-2	01-00-01
Lincoln v Luton	-	-	-	-	-	-	00-01-01
Morecambe v Bradford	-	-	-	-	-	2-1	01-00-00
Rochdale v Port Vale	-	-	-	-	-	-	00-00-00
Rotherham v Notts Co	-	-	-	-	-	1-1	01-04-01
Wycombe v Gillingham	-	-	-	-	-	-	02-02-01

SCOTTISH PREMIER LEAGUE

Aberdeen v Inv CT	-	-	0-0	0-0	1-1/1-1	1-0	01-04-00
Hamilton v Dundee Utd	-	-	-	-	-	-	00-00-04
Hearts v Celtic	1-4/2-1	0-1/1-1	0-2/1-2	2-3/3-0	2-1/1-2	1-1	10-06-24
Kilmarnock v Falkirk	-	-	-	1-1/2-1	2-1	0-1/2-1	06-05-02
Rangers v Motherwell	3-0/2-0	1-0/4-0	4-1/4-1	2-0/1-0	1-1	3-1/1-0	33-02-03
St Mirren v Hibernian	-	-	-	-	1-0/1-1	2-1	06-03-05

SCOTTISH DIVISION ONE

Dundee v Airdrie Utd	-	-	-	0-2/2-3	1-0/2-1	-	07-03-05
Dunfermline v St Johnstone	-	-	-	-	-	0-0/0-1	08-08-04
Livingston v Morton	-	-	-	-	-	4-0/6-1	09-03-04
Partick v Queen of Sth	-	-	1-2/3-1	-	1-1/0-0	2-0/0-0	06-04-03
Ross County v Clyde	1-1/1-1	0-1/0-0	0-1/1-1	3-1/0-1	1-1/2-2	-	05-07-04

SCOTTISH DIVISION TWO

Arbroath v Ayr	1-1/1-2	-	0-0/2-0	-	-	-	02-02-02
Peterhead v Brechin	-	-	-	-	1-1/1-4	1-2/2-0	02-01-05
Queen's Park v East Fife	0-0/1-2	-	1-2/2-1	2-0/1-1	3-0/1-1	-	10-04-07
Raith v Alloa	-	-	-	4-2/0-1	0-0/3-0	2-1/3-2	05-02-02
Stirling v Stranraer	-	1-0/2-2	1-1/1-1	-	3-3/0-2	-	06-06-04

SCOTTISH DIVISION THREE

Albion v Cowdenbeath	-	1-2/2-4	2-3/1-4	0-3/1-3	-	-	09-02-16
Dumbarton v Berwick	1-2/2-2	1-1/4-1	3-1/1-1	-	2-0/1-2	-	08-09-07
E Stirling v Annan Ath	-	-	-	-	-	-	00-00-00
Elgin v Forfar	-	-	-	-	-	2-2/3-1	01-01-00
Montrose v Stenhsmuir	-	-	0-2/0-3	0-3/0-2	0-1/3-2	1-0/2-1	05-02-12

CONFERENCE

Altrincham v Kidderminster	-	-	-	3-0	0-1	2-1	05-04-04
Burton v Histon	-	-	-	-	-	1-3	00-00-01
Cambridge U v Eastbourne	-	-	-	-	-	-	00-00-00
Forest G v Woking	3-2	2-2	1-3	0-3	2-3	2-1	03-03-04
Grays v Salisbury	-	-	-	-	-	1-1	00-01-00
Lewes v Weymouth	-	-	0-0	2-3	-	-	00-01-01
Mansfield v Barrow	-	-	-	-	-	-	00-00-00
Oxford Utd v Wrexham	0-2	-	-	0-3	-	-	00-02-04
Rushden & D v Kettering	-	-	-	-	-	-	03-01-01

Stevenage v Ebbsfleet U	1-0	2-2	2-0	2-0	3-0	3-1	05-01-00
Torquay v Crawley	-	-	-	-	-	1-2	00-00-01
York v Northwich	-	-	0-0	-	2-1	1-1	01-02-00

MONDAY 13TH APRIL 2009
CHAMPIONSHIP

Barnsley v Swansea	-	-	-	2-2	-	-	00-01-00
Birmingham v Plymouth	-	-	-	-	3-0	-	02-00-01
Blackpool v Reading	-	-	-	-	-	-	01-01-05
Bristol C v Ipswich	-	-	-	-	-	2-0	03-00-01
Cardiff v Burnley	-	2-0	2-0	3-0	1-0	2-1	07-00-02
Coventry v Charlton	-	-	-	-	-	1-1	02-02-01
Derby v Wolves	1-4	-	3-3	0-3	0-2	-	01-03-05
Doncaster v Preston	-	-	-	-	-	-	01-02-00
Norwich v Watford	4-0	1-2	-	2-3	-	1-3	03-01-04
QPR v Sheff Weds	-	3-0	-	0-0	1-1	0-0	05-04-03
Sheff Utd v Nottm Forest	1-0	1-2	1-1	-	-	-	05-03-02
Southampton v C Palace	-	-	2-2	0-0	1-1	1-4	04-04-02

LEAGUE 1

Cheltenham v Yeovil	-	3-1	1-1	-	1-2	1-1	05-04-01
Colchester v Brighton	-	1-0	-	-	-	-	03-00-01
Hartlepool v Scunthorpe	2-2	-	-	3-3	-	-	05-02-05
Huddersfield v Carlisle	-	2-1	-	-	2-1	0-2	02-00-01
Leicester v Leeds	-	4-0	2-0	1-1	1-1	-	07-02-04
Millwall v Peterboro	-	-	-	-	-	-	02-01-01
Milton K v Bristol R	-	-	-	-	2-0	-	01-00-00
Northampton v Southend	-	2-2	1-2	-	-	0-1	02-02-02
Oldham v Crewe	1-3	-	-	-	1-0	3-2	02-00-01
Stockport v Walsall	-	-	0-1	-	1-0	-	03-01-03
Swindon v Leyton O	-	-	-	-	-	1-1	00-01-00
Tranmere v Hereford	-	-	-	-	-	-	01-00-00

LEAGUE 2

Accrington v Chester	-	0-2	-	-	0-1	3-3	00-01-02
Aldershot v Barnet	-	1-1	2-3	-	-	-	00-01-01
Bournemouth v Brentford	-	1-0	3-2	2-2	1-0	-	08-03-03
Bradford v Lincoln	-	-	-	-	-	2-1	01-00-00
Darlington v Bury	3-1	1-3	1-2	2-3	1-0	3-0	05-01-05
Exeter v Wycombe	-	-	-	-	-	-	00-00-00
Gillingham v Dagenham & R	-	-	-	-	-	-	00-00-00
Luton v Chesterfield	3-0	1-0	1-0	-	-	-	05-01-01
Macclesfield v Morecambe	-	-	-	-	-	1-2	01-01-01
Notts Co v Grimsby	-	3-1	2-2	0-1	2-0	1-1	04-02-02
Port Vale v Rotherham	-	-	-	2-0	1-3	-	03-00-02
Shrewsbury v Rochdale	3-1	-	0-2	0-1	3-0	3-4	05-01-06

CONFERENCE

Barrow v York	-	-	-	-	-	-	00-00-00
Crawley v Stevenage	-	-	1-2	1-2	3-0	2-1	02-00-02
Eastbourne v Grays	-	-	2-2	-	-	-	00-01-00
Ebbsfleet U v Lewes	-	-	-	-	-	-	00-00-00
Histon v Rushden & D	-	-	-	-	-	2-1	01-00-00
Kettering v Cambridge U	-	-	-	-	-	-	00-00-00
Kidderminstr v Burton	-	-	-	0-1	0-0	4-1	01-01-01
Northwich v Mansfield	-	-	-	-	-	-	00-00-00

Salisbury v Torquay	-	-	-	-	-	0-0	00-01-00
Weymouth v Forest G	-	-	-	-	1-0	0-6	01-00-01
Woking v Oxford Utd	-	-	-	-	1-0	1-2	01-00-01
Wrexham v Altrincham	-	-	-	-	-	-	00-00-00

SATURDAY 18TH APRIL 2009
PREMIER LEAGUE

Aston Villa v West Ham	4-1	-	-	1-2	1-0	1-0	07-05-03
Chelsea v Everton	4-1	0-0	1-0	3-0	1-1	1-1	10-07-02
Liverpool v Arsenal	2-2	1-2	2-1	1-0	4-1	1-1	11-04-05
Man City v WBA	1-2	-	1-1	0-0	-	-	03-04-01
Middlesboro v Fulham	2-2	2-1	1-1	3-2	3-1	1-0	05-02-00
Portsmouth v Bolton	-	4-0	1-1	1-1	0-1	3-1	02-05-04
Stoke v Blackburn	-	-	-	-	-	-	00-00-02
Sunderland v Hull	-	-	-	-	2-0	-	02-00-01
Tottenham v Newcastle	0-1	1-0	1-0	2-0	2-3	1-4	09-01-06
Wigan v Man Utd	-	-	-	1-2	1-3	0-2	00-00-03

CHAMPIONSHIP

Burnley v Sheff Utd	0-1	3-2	1-1	1-2	-	1-2	04-01-03
Charlton v Blackpool	-	-	-	-	-	4-1	01-00-00
Crystal Pal v Derby	0-1	1-1	-	2-0	2-0	-	04-04-01
Nottm Forest v Coventry	1-1	0-1	1-4	-	-	-	05-04-04
Plymouth v Doncaster	-	-	-	-	-	-	01-00-00
Preston v Cardiff	-	2-2	3-0	2-1	2-1	1-2	05-03-01
Reading v Barnsley	-	-	-	-	-	-	00-01-02
Sheff Weds v Southampton	-	-	-	0-1	3-3	5-0	05-06-03
Swansea v Bristol C	-	-	-	7-1	0-0	-	02-03-01
Watford v Birmingham	-	-	-	-	-	-	04-03-00
Wolves v QPR	-	-	2-1	3-1	2-0	3-3	05-03-01

LEAGUE 1

Brighton v Oldham	-	0-0	-	-	1-2	1-0	03-02-02
Bristol R v Millwall	-	-	-	-	-	2-1	08-00-01
Carlisle v Swindon	-	-	-	-	-	3-0	01-00-01
Crewe v Cheltenham	1-0	-	-	-	3-1	3-1	03-00-00
Hereford v Colchester	-	-	-	-	-	-	05-02-00
Leeds v Tranmere	-	-	-	-	-	0-2	00-00-01
Leyton O v Northampton	-	1-1	3-2	1-2	0-2	2-2	03-04-02
Peterboro v Stockport	2-0	1-2	2-1	2-0	0-3	0-1	06-01-06
Scunthorpe v MK Dons	-	-	-	2-0	-	-	01-00-00
Southend v Leicester	-	-	-	-	2-2	-	02-02-01
Walsall v Huddersfield	-	-	4-3	1-3	-	4-0	03-00-02
Yeovil v Hartlepool	-	-	-	2-0	-	3-1	02-00-00

LEAGUE 2

Barnet v Luton	-	-	-	-	-	-	00-00-00
Brentford v Accrington	-	-	-	-	-	3-1	01-00-00
Bury v Macclesfield	2-1	2-0	2-1	0-0	1-1	1-0	04-02-00
Chester v Bournemouth	-	-	-	-	-	-	01-02-01
Chesterfield v Gillingham	-	-	-	1-1	0-1	-	05-07-01
Dagenham & R v Bradford	-	-	-	-	-	1-4	00-00-01
Grimsby v Port Vale	-	1-2	-	-	-	-	03-02-02
Lincoln v Exeter	1-0	-	-	-	-	-	06-01-03
Morecambe v Notts Co	-	-	-	-	-	1-1	00-01-00
Rochdale v Darlington	1-1	4-2	1-1	0-2	0-0	3-1	07-09-02

Rotherham v Shrewsbury	-	-	-	-	-	2-0	03-02-04
Wycombe v Aldershot	-	-	-	-	-	-	00-00-00

SCOTTISH PREMIER LEAGUE

Celtic v Aberdeen	7-0	4-0/1-2	2-3/3-2/2-0	2-0/3-0	1-0/2-1	3-0/1-0	29-04-06
Dundee Utd v Kilmarnock	1-2/2-2	1-1/4-1	3-0/1-1	0-0/2-2	1-0	2-0	05-12-08
Falkirk v Hearts	-	-	-	2-2/1-2	1-1	2-1/2-1	07-02-04
Hibernian v Rangers	2-4/0-2	0-1	0-1/0-1	2-1/1-2	2-1/0-2/3-3	1-2/0-0	07-08-22
Inv CT v Hamilton	-	-	-	-	-	-	00-00-00
Motherwell v St Mirren	-	-	-	-	0-0/2-3	1-1	07-04-02

SCOTTISH DIVISION ONE

Clyde v Airdrie Utd	-	-	1-2/1-0	1-0/3-1	0-0/0-1	-	05-03-08
Morton v Partick	-	-	-	2-1/1-0	-	4-2/0-0	09-04-02
Livingston v Dundee	1-1	1-1	1-0/1-1	-	2-3/1-3	0-2/1-1	02-05-05
Ross County v Dunfermline	-	-	-	-	-	-	00-00-00
St Johnstone v Queen of Sth	2-2/0-1	4-1/2-2	1-3/0-0	4-0/2-1	5-0/3-0	2-0/2-1	09-03-02

SCOTTISH DIVISION TWO

Brechin v Ayr	-	3-1/0-3	5-0/3-0	-	0-2/2-0	2-2/5-1	05-04-05
East Fife v Alloa	-	0-1/0-1	-	-	-	-	04-04-04
Queen's Park v Arbroath	-	-	-	2-2/0-0	0-3/1-0	-	10-07-06
Stirling v Raith	-	-	-	1-0/2-2	1-1/0-1	-	03-03-04
Stranraer v Peterhead	-	0-2/1-1	-	-	2-1/1-1	-	01-02-01

SCOTTISH DIVISION THREE

Albion v Elgin	1-1/1-1	1-2/1-2	2-2/2-0	0-2/1-2	3-1/6-2	3-4/1-1	03-07-06
Berwick v Stenhsmuir	2-2/0-0	2-1/3-0	-	0-2/3-0	0-1/2-1	-	15-06-08
Cowdenbeath v Dumbarton	3-1/2-0	-	-	-	-	-	07-03-08
E Stirling v Montrose	1-1/0-3	1-1/1-4	1-1/1-2	1-1/1-0	0-3/0-2	0-3/3-1	11-06-16
Forfar v Annan Ath	-	-	-	-	-	-	00-00-00

CONFERENCE

Altrincham v Grays	-	-	-	0-2	1-0	0-1	01-00-02
Barrow v Crawley	-	-	-	-	-	-	00-00-00
Burton v Oxford Utd	-	-	-	-	1-2	1-2	00-00-02
Forest G v Rushden & D	-	-	-	-	0-2	0-1	01-01-03
Histon v Kidderminster	-	-	-	-	-	2-1	01-00-00
Kettering v Wrexham	-	-	-	-	-	-	00-00-00
Northwich v Lewes	-	-	-	-	-	-	00-00-00
Salisbury v Cambridge U	-	-	-	-	-	0-2	00-00-01
Stevenage v Torquay	-	-	-	-	-	1-3	00-00-01
Weymouth v Ebbsfleet U	-	-	-	-	2-1	2-0	03-00-01
Woking v Mansfield	-	-	-	-	-	-	00-00-00
York v Eastbourne	-	-	-	-	-	-	00-00-00

SUNDAY 19TH APRIL 2009
CHAMPIONSHIP

Ipswich v Norwich	1-1	0-2	-	0-1	3-1	2-1	07-01-05

SATURDAY 25TH APRIL 2009
PREMIER LEAGUE

Arsenal v Middlesboro	2-0	4-1	5-3	7-0	1-1	1-1	08-05-01
Blackburn v Wigan	-	-	-	1-1	2-1	3-1	02-01-00
Bolton v Aston Villa	1-0	2-2	1-2	1-1	2-2	1-1	02-04-03

250

Everton v Man City	2-2	0-0	2-1	1-0	1-1	1-0	07-05-02
Fulham v Stoke	-	-	-	-	-	-	01-02-01
Hull v Liverpool	-	-	-	-	-	-	00-00-00
Man Utd v Tottenham	1-0	3-0	0-0	1-1	1-0	1-0	15-04-01
Newcastle v Portsmouth	-	3-0	1-1	2-0	1-0	1-4	07-01-01
WBA v Sunderland	2-2	0-0	-	0-1	1-2	-	01-05-05
West Ham v Chelsea	1-0	-	-	1-3	1-4	0-4	05-03-06

CHAMPIONSHIP

Barnsley v Wolves	-	-	-	-	1-0	1-0	06-02-06
Birmingham v Preston	-	-	-	-	3-1	-	04-01-01
Blackpool v Nottm Forest	-	-	-	2-2	0-2	-	00-01-01
Bristol C v Sheff Weds	-	1-1	1-4	-	-	2-1	01-02-01
Cardiff v Ipswich	-	2-3	0-1	2-1	2-2	1-0	02-01-02
Coventry v Watford	0-1	0-0	1-0	3-1	-	0-3	03-01-03
Derby v Charlton	-	-	-	-	-	-	04-04-02
Doncaster v C Palace	-	-	-	-	-	-	00-00-00
Norwich v Reading	0-1	2-1	-	0-1	-	-	01-03-02
QPR v Plymouth	2-2	3-0	3-2	1-1	1-1	0-2	02-03-01
Sheff Utd v Swansea	-	-	-	-	-	-	01-00-00
Southampton v Burnley	-	-	-	1-1	0-0	0-1	00-02-01

LEAGUE 1

Cheltenham v Carlisle	-	2-1	-	2-3	0-1	1-0	05-00-02
Colchester v Peterboro	1-1	0-0	2-1	-	-	-	03-03-02
Hartlepool v Leeds	-	-	-	-	-	1-1	00-01-00
Huddersfield v Brighton	-	-	-	-	0-3	2-1	02-00-04
Leicester v Scunthorpe	-	-	-	-	-	1-0	01-00-00
Millwall v Leyton O	-	-	-	-	2-5	0-1	00-00-02
Milton K v Walsall	3-2	0-1	1-1	2-1	1-1	-	02-03-01
Northampton v Hereford	-	-	-	-	-	-	02-02-03
Oldham v Southend	-	-	-	0-0	-	0-1	01-02-03
Stockport v Crewe	1-4	-	-	-	-	-	04-02-04
Swindon v Bristol R	-	-	-	-	2-1	1-0	04-01-02
Tranmere v Yeovil	-	-	-	4-1	2-1	2-1	03-00-00

LEAGUE 2

Accrington v Chesterfield	-	-	-	-	-	2-1	01-00-00
Aldershot v Chester	-	1-1	-	-	-	-	00-01-00
Bournemouth v Grimsby	-	0-0	-	-	-	-	01-01-01
Bradford v Rotherham	4-2	0-2	-	1-2	1-1	3-2	06-01-04
Darlington v Brentford	-	-	-	-	-	3-1	01-01-01
Exeter v Morecambe	-	4-0	1-1	2-0	1-0	-	03-01-00
Gillingham v Bury	-	-	-	-	-	-	03-02-02
Luton v Rochdale	-	-	-	-	-	-	00-00-01
Macclesfield v Barnet	-	-	-	1-1	2-3	3-0	04-03-02
Notts Co v Dagenham & R	-	-	-	-	-	1-0	01-00-00
Port Vale v Wycombe	1-1	1-1	-	-	-	-	00-03-01
Shrewsbury v Lincoln	1-2	-	0-1	0-1	0-1	1-2	02-01-08

SCOTTISH DIVISION ONE

Airdrie Utd v Ross County	-	-	1-2/2-1	0-1/2-3	0-2/0-1	0-1/2-0	03-02-07
Dundee v St Johnstone	-	-	-	2-1/0-1	1-1/2-1	2-1/3-2	08-07-08
Dunfermline v Morton	-	-	-	-	-	0-1/2-0	07-02-03
Partick v Livingston	2-2/1-3	1-1/5-2	-	-	2-3/0-0	3-0/2-1	05-06-06
Queen of Sth v Clyde	2-1/1-1	4-1/1-2	0-1/0-1	1-2/2-1	0-2/0-0	1-1/3-1	11-06-11

SCOTTISH DIVISION TWO

Alloa v Queen's Park	-	-	-	-	-	2-0/1-2	06-06-05
Arbroath v Stranraer	-	-	0-1/0-4	-	-	2-2/0-0	07-05-05
Ayr v East Fife	-	-	-	-	-	-	01-00-01
Peterhead v Stirling	1-0/6-0	2-2/0-0	-	1-3/2-0	2-3/2-1	-	05-03-02
Raith v Brechin	3-1/1-2	2-1/1-1	-	-	1-1/1-0	1-1/1-1	04-04-02

SCOTTISH DIVISION THREE

Annan Ath v Berwick	-	-	-	-	-	-	00-00-00
Dumbarton v Forfar	1-2/1-2	2-1/1-1	0-1/1-1	2-0/0-0	-	0-0/0-0	02-07-03
Elgin v E Stirling	3-1/3-0	3-1/3-0	1-3/0-0	1-1/3-0	5-0/2-1	6-0/3-0	11-03-02
Montrose v Cowdenbeath	-	1-3/1-1	3-1/1-2	0-1/0-3	-	-	08-04-13
Stenhsmuir v Albion	-	-	3-0/1-1	1-0/4-2	3-2/0-4	0-1/2-2	09-04-05

CONFERENCE

Cambridge U v Altrincham	-	-	-	4-0	2-2	2-1	02-01-00
Crawley v Histon	-	-	-	-	-	1-0	01-00-00
Eastbourne v Barrow	-	-	-	-	-	-	00-00-00
Ebbsfleet U v Salisbury	-	-	-	-	-	2-1	02-01-00
Grays v Forest G	-	-	-	2-2	1-1	0-1	00-02-01
Kidderminstr v Kettering	-	-	-	-	-	-	05-03-04
Lewes v York	-	-	-	-	-	-	00-00-00
Mansfield v Stevenage	-	-	-	-	-	-	00-00-00
Oxford Utd v Northwich	-	-	-	-	5-1	0-1	01-00-01
Rushden & D v Woking	-	-	-	-	2-0	2-1	05-01-01
Torquay v Burton	-	-	-	-	-	1-2	00-00-01
Wrexham v Weymouth	-	-	-	-	-	-	00-00-00

SATURDAY 2ND MAY 2009
PREMIER LEAGUE

Aston Villa v Hull	-	-	-	-	-	-	00-00-00
Chelsea v Fulham	1-1	2-1	3-1	3-2	2-2	0-0	04-03-00
Liverpool v Newcastle	2-2	1-1	3-1	2-0	2-0	3-0	12-02-02
Man City v Blackburn	2-2	1-1	1-1	0-0	0-3	2-2	03-06-03
Middlesboro v Man Utd	3-1	0-1	0-2	4-1	1-2	2-2	03-03-08
Portsmouth v Arsenal	-	1-1	0-1	1-1	0-0	0-0	00-04-01
Stoke v West Ham	-	0-2	0-1	-	-	-	00-01-02
Sunderland v Everton	0-1	-	-	0-1	-	0-1	04-01-03
Tottenham v WBA	3-1	-	1-1	2-1	-	-	02-01-00
Wigan v Bolton	-	-	-	2-1	1-3	1-0	04-02-02

LEAGUE 1

Brighton v Stockport	-	0-1	-	-	-	-	02-02-01
Bristol R v Hartlepool	1-0	-	-	-	0-2	0-0	01-02-02
Carlisle v Millwall	-	-	-	-	1-2	4-0	02-00-01
Crewe v Leicester	-	-	2-2	2-2	-	-	00-02-00
Hereford v MK Dons	-	-	-	-	0-0	0-1	00-01-01
Leeds v Northampton	-	-	-	-	-	3-0	01-00-00
Leyton O v Huddersfield	-	1-1	-	-	1-0	0-1	06-01-02
Peterboro v Swindon	1-1	4-2	0-2	-	1-1	-	02-04-02
Scunthorpe v Tranmere	-	-	-	1-2	1-1	-	00-01-02
Southend v Cheltenham	-	2-0	0-2	-	-	2-2	02-01-03
Walsall v Oldham	-	-	0-1	0-2	-	0-3	02-02-03
Yeovil v Colchester	-	-	-	0-0	-	-	01-01-01

Sponsored by Stan James

LEAGUE 2

Barnet v Port Vale	-	-	-	-	-	-	00-00-01
Brentford v Luton	0-0	4-2	2-0	-	-	-	04-03-01
Bury v Accrington	-	-	-	-	2-2	2-1	01-01-00
Chester v Darlington	-	-	0-3	4-4	1-1	2-1	05-03-03
Chesterfield v Bradford	-	-	0-0	1-0	3-0	1-1	03-02-00
Dagenham & R v Shrewsbury	-	5-0	-	-	-	1-1	01-01-00
Grimsby v Macclesfield	-	-	0-0	3-1	1-1	1-1	01-03-00
Lincoln v Aldershot	-	-	-	-	-	-	00-00-00
Morecambe v Bournemouth	-	-	-	-	-	-	00-00-00
Rochdale v Gillingham	-	-	-	-	-	-	05-01-01
Rotherham v Exeter	-	-	-	-	-	-	03-02-02
Wycombe v Notts Co	3-1	1-1	1-2	2-0	0-0	3-1	07-04-01

SCOTTISH DIVISION ONE

Clyde v Dundee	-	-	-	1-1/3-3	2-1/1-1	1-2/1-1	02-04-02
Partick v Airdrie Utd	-	-	3-2/1-1	-	4-2/0-1	-	06-06-05
Queen of Sth v Dunfermline	-	-	-	-	-	0-1/1-1	00-02-02
Ross County v Livingston	-	-	-	-	0-3/0-2	-	00-02-04
St Johnstone v Morton	-	-	-	-	-	2-2/3-2	05-02-02

SCOTTISH DIVISION TWO

Arbroath v Peterhead	-	-	-	-	-	-	00-00-00
Ayr v Alloa	3-1/0-1	-	4-3/1-1	1-1/0-1	0-1/4-3	2-0/3-1	08-02-03
Brechin v Stranraer	3-1/3-1	-	4-1/2-1	2-3/0-0	3-0/1-1	-	07-07-04
East Fife v Stirling	1-1/2-1	-	-	-	-	-	06-06-05
Queen's Park v Raith	-	-	-	-	-	2-5/0-1	00-00-02

SCOTTISH DIVISION THREE

Albion v E Stirling	6-0/3-1	5-0/5-1	3-3/1-1	4-2/2-0	4-0/2-1	2-3/2-2	18-09-08
Berwick v Montrose	-	-	-	1-1/1-1	1-2/1-0	-	08-08-04
Cowdenbeath v Forfar	1-1/2-2	-	-	-	3-2/2-1	-	05-02-06
Dumbarton v Elgin	-	-	-	-	3-1/1-0	1-0/1-4	06-01-01
Stenhsmuir v Annan Ath	-	-	-	-	-	-	00-00-00

SUNDAY 3RD MAY 2009
CHAMPIONSHIP

Burnley v Bristol C	-	-	-	-	-	0-1	02-02-02
Charlton v Norwich	-	-	4-0	-	-	2-0	04-02-02
Crystal Pal v Sheff Utd	2-2	1-2	-	2-3	-	3-2	05-03-05
Ipswich v Coventry	2-1	1-1	3-2	2-2	2-1	4-1	06-03-01
Nottm Forest v Southampton	-	-	-	-	-	-	05-01-03
Plymouth v Barnsley	1-1	2-0	-	-	2-4	3-0	04-02-02
Preston v QPR	-	-	2-1	1-1	1-1	0-0	02-03-00
Reading v Birmingham	-	-	-	-	-	2-1	02-03-02
Sheff Weds v Cardiff	-	-	-	1-3	0-0	1-0	01-01-01
Swansea v Blackpool	-	-	-	3-2	3-6	-	03-02-03
Watford v Derby	2-0	2-1	2-2	2-2	-	-	03-05-02
Wolves v Doncaster	-	-	-	-	-	-	00-00-00

SATURDAY 9TH MAY 2009
PREMIER LEAGUE

Arsenal v Chelsea	3-2	2-1	2-2	0-2	1-1	1-0	12-05-02
Blackburn v Portsmouth	-	1-2	1-0	2-1	3-0	0-1	06-03-02
Bolton v Sunderland	1-1	-	-	2-0	-	2-0	03-02-02

Everton v Tottenham	2-2	3-1	0-1	0-1	1-2	0-0	05-08-07
Fulham v Aston Villa	2-1	1-2	1-1	3-3	1-1	2-1	02-04-01
Hull v Stoke	-	-	-	0-1	0-2	1-1	01-02-04
Man Utd v Man City	1-1	3-1	0-0	1-1	3-1	1-2	07-06-01
Newcastle v Middlesboro	2-0	2-1	0-0	2-2	0-0	1-1	07-07-02
WBA v Wigan	-	2-1	-	1-2	-	-	02-01-01
West Ham v Liverpool	0-3	-	-	1-2	1-2	1-0	05-04-06

SCOTTISH DIVISION ONE

Airdrie Utd v St Johnstone	-	-	1-0/0-0	3-1/2-1	2-1/1-2	-	05-06-08
Dundee v Partick	4-1	1-0/2-1	-	-	0-1/3-1	3-0/1-0	08-04-06
Dunfermline v Clyde	-	-	-	-	-	1-1/2-1	04-02-00
Morton v Ross County	-	-	-	-	-	-	00-00-02
Livingston v Queen of Sth	-	-	-	-	2-0/0-1	2-2/1-0	07-03-05

SCOTTISH DIVISION TWO

Alloa v Brechin	-	-	2-2/1-1	-	2-2/2-3	2-2/0-4	04-05-03
Peterhead v Ayr	-	-	-	3-3/1-2	3-1/2-2	3-0/4-1	03-02-01
Raith v Arbroath	-	-	-	-	-	-	01-01-00
Stirling v Queen's Park	1-0/1-0	1-0/0-0	-	-	-	-	07-03-03
Stranraer v East Fife	-	-	-	-	-	0-2/0-2	05-04-06

SCOTTISH DIVISION THREE

Annan Ath v Dumbarton	-	-	-	-	-	-	00-00-00
E Stirling v Cowdenbeath	-	1-1/0-1	0-2/2-1	0-1/1-1	-	-	09-08-11
Elgin v Berwick	-	-	-	2-2/1-3	1-2/2-1	-	01-01-02
Forfar v Stenhsmuir	1-0/3-3	2-0/1-1	-	-	-	0-1/1-2	08-05-04
Montrose v Albion	0-1/1-1	1-0/3-1	1-1/0-1	0-2/2-2	2-1/2-3	0-1/2-1	14-04-14

SATURDAY 16TH MAY 2009
PREMIER LEAGUE

Bolton v Hull	-	-	-	-	-	-	02-00-00
Chelsea v Blackburn	1-2	2-2	4-0	4-2	3-0	0-0	03-06-06
Everton v West Ham	0-0	-	-	1-2	2-0	1-1	10-03-02
Man Utd v Arsenal	2-0	0-0	2-0	2-0	0-1	2-1	10-06-04
Middlesboro v Aston Villa	2-5	1-2	3-0	0-4	1-3	0-3	03-03-08
Newcastle v Fulham	2-0	3-1	1-4	1-1	1-2	2-0	03-02-02
Portsmouth v Sunderland	-	-	-	2-1	-	1-0	05-03-03
Stoke v Wigan	-	1-1	0-1	-	-	-	05-03-01
Tottenham v Man City	0-2	1-1	2-1	2-1	2-1	2-1	09-03-02
WBA v Liverpool	0-6	-	0-5	0-2	-	-	00-00-03

SUNDAY 24TH MAY 2009
PREMIER LEAGUE

Arsenal v Stoke	-	-	-	-	-	-	00-00-00
Aston Villa v Newcastle	0-1	0-0	4-2	1-2	2-0	4-1	05-05-06
Blackburn v WBA	1-1	-	1-1	2-0	-	-	04-02-02
Fulham v Everton	2-0	2-1	2-0	1-0	1-0	1-0	07-00-00
Hull v Man Utd	-	-	-	-	-	-	00-00-00
Liverpool v Tottenham	2-1	0-0	2-2	1-0	3-0	2-2	13-06-01
Man City v Bolton	2-0	6-2	0-1	0-1	0-2	4-2	05-00-04
Sunderland v Chelsea	1-2	-	-	1-2	-	0-1	04-01-04
West Ham v Middlesboro	1-0	-	-	2-1	2-0	3-0	09-02-02
Wigan v Portsmouth	-	-	-	1-2	1-0	0-2	01-00-02

Sponsored by Stan James

odds conversion

Trad	Dec	%	Trad	Dec	%
10-1	11	9.09	6-4	2.5	40.00
9-1	10	10.00	7-5	2.4	41.67
17-2	9.5	10.53	11-8	2.375	42.11
8-1	9	11.11	13-10	2.3	43.48
15-2	8.5	11.76	5-4	2.25	44.44
7-1	8	12.50	6-5	2.2	45.45
13-2	7.5	13.33	11-10	2.1	47.62
6-1	7	14.29	21-20	2.05	48.78
11-2	6.5	15.38	Evs	2	50.00
5-1	6	16.67	20-21	1.952	51.23
9-2	5.5	18.18	10-11	1.909	52.38
4-1	5	20.00	9-10	1.9	52.63
18-5	4.6	21.74	5-6	1.833	54.56
7-2	4.5	22.22	4-5	1.8	55.56
10-3	4.333	23.08	8-11	1.727	57.90
16-5	4.2	23.81	7-10	1.7	58.82
3-1	4	25.00	4-6	1.667	59.99
14-5	3.8	26.32	5-8	1.625	61.54
11-4	3.75	26.67	8-13	1.615	61.92
13-5	3.6	27.78	3-5	1.6	62.50
5-2	3.5	28.57	4-7	1.571	63.65
12-5	3.4	29.41	8-15	1.533	65.23
95-40	3.375	29.63	1-2	1.5	66.67
23-10	3.3	30.30	40-85	1.471	67.98
9-4	3.25	30.77	9-20	1.45	68.97
11-5	3.2	31.25	4-9	1.444	69.25
85-40	3.125	32.00	2-5	1.4	71.43
21-10	3.1	32.26	4-11	1.364	73.31
2-1	3	33.33	7-20	1.35	74.07
19-10	2.9	34.48	1-3	1.333	75.02
15-8	2.875	34.78	3-10	1.3	76.92
9-5	2.8	35.71	2-7	1.286	77.76
7-4	2.75	36.36	1-4	1.25	80.00
17-10	2.7	37.04	2-9	1.222	81.83
13-8	2.625	38.10	1-5	1.2	83.33
8-5	2.6	38.46	1-10	1.1	90.91

asian handicaps

Conceding handicap		Handicap	Receiving handicap	
Bet	**Result**		**Result**	**Bet**
Win	Win	0	Win	Win
No bet	Draw		Draw	No bet
Lose	Lose		Lose	Lose
Win	Win	0.25	Win	Win
Lose half	Draw		Draw	Win half
Lose	Lose		Lose	Lose
Win	Win	0.5	Win	Win
Lose	Draw		Draw	Win
Lose	Lose		Lose	Win
Win	Win by 2+	0.75	Lose by 2+	Lose
Win half	Win by 1		Lose by 1	Lose half
Lose	Draw		Draw	Win
Lose	Lose		Lose	Win
Win	Win by 2+	1	Lose by 2+	Lose
No bet	Win by 1		Lose by 1	No bet
Lose	Draw		Draw	Win
Lose	Lose		Lose	Win
Win	Win by 2+	1.25	Lose by 2+	Lose
Lose half	Win by 1		Lose by 1	Win half
Lose	Draw		Draw	Win
Lose	Lose		Lose	Win
Win	Win by 2+	1.5	Lose by 2+	Lose
Lose	Win by 1		Lose by 1	Win
Lose	Draw		Draw	Win
Lose	Lose		Lose	Win
Win	Win by 3+	1.75	Lose by 3+	Lose
Win half	Win by 2		Lose by 2	Lose half
Lose	Win by 1		Lose by 1	Win
Lose	Draw		Draw	Win
Lose	Lose		Lose	Win
Win	Win by 3+	2	Lose by 3+	Lose
No bet	Win by 2		Lose by 2	No bet
Lose	Win by 1		Lose by 1	Win
Lose	Draw		Draw	Win
Lose	Lose		Lose	Win

scores 2007/08

	Prem	Chmp	Lg1	Lg2	Conf	SPL	Sct 1	Sct 2	Sct 3
1-0	43	56	56	55	51	21	17	12	13
2-0	34	40	50	31	35	20	14	15	13
2-1	29	55	69	49	60	20	18	13	18
3-0	11	22	24	17	15	14	9	6	7
3-1	21	17	18	21	25	10	6	8	12
3-2	6	17	12	10	15	5	4	9	4
4-0	8	5	8	7	6	5	4	5	5
4-1	9	10	10	10	10	4	2	2	1
4-2	3	2	5	6	4	7	2	2	0
4-3	0	1	3	0	6	0	1	1	0
0-0	26	48	38	32	38	15	15	4	13
1-1	52	86	77	70	61	25	26	19	16
2-2	17	31	24	23	30	3	9	10	8
3-3	2	6	1	3	11	3	2	2	3
4-4	3	0	0	1	0	0	0	0	0
0-1	31	44	56	62	39	19	11	17	14
0-2	23	18	27	34	26	6	8	7	11
1-2	21	37	32	54	42	15	9	13	3
0-3	6	10	13	12	13	8	3	4	7
1-3	8	15	11	14	19	5	6	1	5
2-3	3	13	7	11	12	1	3	6	9
0-4	4	1	2	8	4	3	2	3	1
1-4	4	3	5	5	6	2	3	7	6
2-4	0	5	1	5	0	0	1	4	1
3-4	0	0	0	2	1	1	0	0	3
Other	16	10	3	11	22	8	5	10	7

home/away/draw percentages 2007/08

	Prem	Chmp	Lg1	Lg2	Conf	SPL	Sct 1	Sct 2	Sct 3
Home	46	42	47	39	44	50	44	43	43
Draw	26	31	25	23	26	21	29	19	22
Away	27	27	28	38	31	29	27	37	35

over/under percentages 2007/08

	Prem	Chmp	Lg1	Lg2	Conf	SPL	Sct 1	Sct 2	Sct 3
<1.5 gls	26	27	27	27	23	25	24	18	22
>1.5 gls	74	73	73	73	77	75	76	82	78
<2.5 gls	55	53	55	51	45	48	51	41	44
>2.5 gls	45	47	45	49	55	52	49	59	56
<3.5 gls	73	75	80	75	69	74	72	61	64
>3.5 gls	27	25	20	25	31	26	28	39	36
<4.5 gls	88	88	91	89	84	86	87	76	81
>4.5 gls	12	12	9	11	16	14	13	24	19

top goalscorers – strikers 2007/08

	P	Goals	First	Last
S McDonald (Celtic)	35	25	10	6
E Adebayor (Arsenal)	36	24	9	7
F Torres (Liverpool)	33	24	7	8
J Beattie (Sheff Utd)	39	22	11	7
K Phillips (West Brom)	35	22	9	5
S John (Southampton)	41	19	7	10

top goalscorers – midfielders 2007/08

	P	Goals	First	Last
C Ronaldo (Man Utd)	34	31	13	9
L Lawrence (Stoke)	41	14	1	7
B Howard (Barnsley)	41	13	5	4
S Fletcher (Hibernian)	31	13	5	6
S Gerrard (Liverpool)	34	11	3	6

top goalscorers – defenders 2007/08

	P	Goals	First	Last
L Cort (Stoke)	45	8	2	3
J Lescott (Everton)	38	8	4	3
D Shittu (Watford)	39	7	2	3
R Shawcross (Stoke)	41	7	3	3
E Ward (Coventry)	36	6	3	2

☆ *Premiership, Championship and SPL matches only*